PROBABILITY TABLE
For use with Chapters 20 and 21

and

INTERPOLATION FORMULAE
For use with Table II, Ballistic Tables, enclosed.

THE GROUNDWORK OF PRACTICAL NAVAL GUNNERY

THE GROUNDWORK OF PRACTICAL NAVAL GUNNERY

A Study of the Principles and Practice of Exterior Ballistics, as Applied to Naval Gunnery

And of the

Computation and Use of Ballistic and Range Tables

BY PHILIP R. ALGER

Professor of Mathematics, U. S. Navy

Revised and Extended to Include the Formulæ and Methods of Colonel James M. Ingalls, U. S. Army

By the Officers on Duty in the Department of Ordnance and Gunnery

United States Naval Academy

1914-15

SECOND EDITION

ANNAPOLIS, MD.

THE UNITED STATES NAVAL INSTITUTE

1917

(a) An arrangement that would appear more logical and consecutive to a midshipman taking up the study of the subject for the first time.

(b) A more clear distinction between the methods and formulæ that are purely educational and those that are actually used in practice.

(c) The rendering more easily understood of quite a number of points in the older text book that seemed in the past to give great trouble to the midshipmen in their study of the subject.

(d) The modification of the problems given in the text book to make them apply to modern United States Naval Ordnance. The problems in the older text book dealt largely with foreign ordnance, and exclusively with guns, projectiles, velocities, etc., that are now obsolete, or nearly so; and, while many of the older problems have been retained as valuable examples of principles, a large number of problems dealing with present-day conditions and ordnance have been added.

(e) An effort has been made to give a complete discussion of the practical use of the range tables, a subject but lightly touched upon in the older text book. In order to accomplish this a large number of officers, in the Atlantic fleet and elsewhere, were requested to contribute such knowledge as they might have on this subject, and the matter received from them has been incorporated in the chapter on this subject. The discussion of this point should therefore include all the most up-to-date practice in the use of the range tables.

4. In preparing this revision for the purpose indicated in the preceding paragraphs, the logical treatment of the subject seemed to indicate its division under two general heads, as follows:

(A) The treatment of the trajectory as a plane curve; which, in turn, logically subdivides itself under two sub-heads, as follows:

(a) General definitions, etc.; the trajectory in vacuum; the resistance of the air and the retardation due thereto; the ballistic coefficient in its fullest form; the equation to the trajectory in air under certain specified and limited conditions; and the approximate determination of the elements of the trajectory by the use of the above special equation. In other words, the features that are of educational rather than of practical value, but which are necessary to an understanding of the practical methods that are to follow.

(b) The more exact and practical theories and formulæ; that is, the ones that are generally used in practical work. This subdivision is not a rigid one, as it will be seen that some of the approximate formulæ and methods are sufficiently accurate to permit of their use in practice, and they are so used; but the general statement of the subdivision may be accepted as logical, with this one reservation.

(B) A consideration of the variation of the actual trajectory from a plane curve, which treats of the influence upon the motion of the projectile of drift and wind, and of the effect upon the fall of the projectile relative to the target of motion of the gun and target. That is, having treated under the first division those computations that are not materially affected by the variations of the trajectory from a plane curve; in the second division we treat of the effect of such deviations upon accuracy of fire. In other words, there are here to be discussed the steps taken to overcome the inaccuracies in fire caused by the variation of the trajectory from a plane curve, in order to hit a moving target with a shot fired from a gun mounted on a moving platform, when there is a wind blowing.

5. Following these natural and logical divisions of the subject comes a full discussion of the range tables, column by column, and of the methods of computing the data contained in them, and of using this data after it has been computed and tabulated.

PART V.

CHAPTERS 18 TO 19 INCLUSIVE.

THE CALIBRATION OF SINGLE GUNS AND OF A SHIP'S BATTERY.

The determination of the error of the setting of a sight for a given range; the adjustment of the sight to make the shot fall at a given range; and the sight adjustments necessary to make all the guns of a battery or ship shoot together.

PART VI.

CHAPTERS 20 TO 21 INCLUSIVE.

THE ACCURACY AND PROBABILITY OF GUNFIRE AND THE MEAN ERRORS OF GUNS.

The errors and inaccuracies of guns. The probability of hitting under given conditions, and whether or not it would be wise to attempt to hit under these conditions. The number of shots probably necessary to give a desired number of hits under certain given conditions, and the bearing of this point upon the wisdom of attempting an attack under the given conditions, having in mind its effect upon the total amount of ammunition available. The probabilities governing the method of spotting salvos by maintaining a proper number of "shorts."

9. No claim is made to originality in any part of this revision; it is merely a compilation of what is thought to be the best and most modern practice from the works of two noted investigators of the subject, namely, Professor Philip R. Alger, U. S. Navy, and Colonel James M. Ingalls, U. S. Army. This revised work is based on Professor Alger's text book on Exterior Ballistics (edition of 1906), and the additions to it concerning the Ingalls methods are from the Handbook of Problems in Exterior Ballistics, Artillery Circular N, Series of 1893, Adjutant General's Office (edition of 1900), prepared by Colonel Ingalls. Further information has been taken from Bureau of Ordnance Pamphlet No. 500, on the Methods of Computing Range Tables. The two chapters on the calibration of guns were taken from a pamphlet on that subject written by Commander L. M. Nulton, U. S. Navy, for use in the instruction of midshipmen, and Chapter 15 was furnished by officers on duty at the Naval Proving Ground at Indian Head.

10. To summarize, it may be said that the belief is held that the only reason for teaching the science of exterior ballistics to midshipmen and the only reason for expecting officers to possess a knowledge of its principles is in order that they may intelligently and successfully use the guns committed to their care. So much as is necessary for this purpose is therefore to be taught the undergraduate and no more; and, as the information necessary for the scientific use of a gun is contained in the official range table for that gun, it may be said that this revision of the previous text book on the subject has been founded upon the question:

"What is a range table, how is the information contained in it obtained, and how is it used?"

With a very few necessary and important exceptions, such as the computations necessary in determining the marking of sights, the text of the book follows closely the question laid down above.

11. For the use of the midshipmen in connection with this revised text book, a reprint has been made of Table II for the desired initial velocities, from the Ballistic Tables computed by Major J. M. Ingalls, U. S. Army, Artillery Circular M, 1900; a reprint of the table from Bureau of Ordnance Pamphlet No. 500, for use in connection with Column 12 of the Range Tables; and a partial reprint of the Range

THE GROUNDWORK OF PRACTICAL NAVAL GUNNERY

CONTENTS.

PRELIMINARY.

PART I.

General and Approximate Deductions.

PART II.

Practical Methods.

PART III.

The Variation of the Trajectory from a Plane Curve.

PART IV.

Range Tables; Their Computation and Use.

PART V.

The Calibration of Single Guns and of a Ship's Battery.

PART VI.

The Accuracy and Probability of Gunfire and the Mean Errors of Guns

APPENDIX A.

APPENDIX B.

APPENDIX C.

PERTAINING TO ATMOSPHERIC CONDITIONS.

δ_1.... Standard density of the atmosphere, in work taken as unity.

δ.... Density of the atmosphere at the time of firing, and subsequently representing the ratio $\frac{\delta}{\delta_1} = \frac{\delta}{1}$.

f.... Altitude factor of the ballistic coefficient.

PERTAINING TO WIND AND SPEEDS.

W.... Real wind; force in feet per second.

β.... Angle between wind and line of fire.

W_x.... Component of W in line of fire in feet per second.

W_{12x}.... Wind component in feet per second of 12 knots in line of fire.

W_z.... Component of W perpendicular to line of fire in feet per second.

W_{12z}.... Wind component in feet per second of 12 knots perpendicular to the line of fire.

X.... Range in feet without considering wind.

X'.... Range in feet considering wind.

V.... Initial velocity in foot-seconds without considering wind.

V'.... Initial velocity in foot-seconds considering wind.

ϕ.... Angle of departure without considering wind.

ϕ'.... Angle of departure considering wind.

T.... Time of flight in seconds without considering wind.

T'.... Time of flight in seconds considering wind.

ΔX_W.... Variation in range in feet due to W_x.

ΔX_{12W}.... Variation in range in feet due to a wind component of 12 knots in the line of fire.

ΔR_W.... Variation in range in yards due to W_x.

ΔR_{12W}.... Variation in range in yards due to a wind component of 12 knots in the line of fire.

γ.... Angle between the trajectories relative to the air and relative to the ground.

D_W.... Deflection in yards due to W_z.

D_{12W}.... Deflection in yards due to a wind component of 12 knots perpendicular to the line of fire.

G.... Motion of gun in feet per second.

G_x.... Component of the motion of the gun in the line of fire in feet per second.

G_{12x}.... Motion of gun in line of fire in feet per second for a component of motion of gun in that line of 12 knots.

G_z.... Component of the motion of the gun perpendicular to the line of fire in feet per second.

G_{12z}.... Motion of gun perpendicular to line of fire in feet per second for a component of motion of gun of 12 knots in the same direction.

ΔX_G.... Variation in range in feet resulting from G_x.

ΔX_{12G}.... Variation in range in feet due to a motion of the gun of 12 knots in the line of fire.

ΔR_G.... Variation in range in yards resulting from G_x.

ΔR_{12G}.... Variation in range in yards due to a motion of the gun of 12 knots in the line of fire.

D_G.... Deflection in yards due to G_z.

D_{12G}.... Deflection in yards due to the motion of the gun of 12 knots perpendicular to the line of fire.

T.... Motion of target in feet per second.

T_x.... Component of the motion of the target in the line of fire in feet per second.

T_{12x}.... Motion of target in line of fire in feet per second for a component of motion of target in that line of 12 knots.

T_z.... Component of the motion of the target perpendicular to the line of fire in feet per second.

T_{12z}.... Motion of target perpendicular to line of fire in feet per second for a component of motion of target of 12 knots in the same direction.

ΔX_T.... Variation in range in feet resulting from T_s.

ΔX_{12T}.... Variation in range in feet due to a motion of the target of 12 knots in the line of fire.

ΔR_T.... Variation in range in yards resulting from T_s.

ΔR_{12T}.... Variation in range in yards due to a motion of the target of 12 knots in the line of fire.

D_T.... Deflection in yards due to T_s.

D_{12T}.... Deflection in yards due to a motion of the target of 12 knots perpendicular to the line of fire.

ϵ.... Angle of real wind with the course of the ship.

ϵ'.... Angle of apparent wind with the course of the ship.

W'.... Velocity of the real wind in knots per hour.

W''.... Velocity of the apparent wind in knots per hour.

PERTAINING TO THE THEORY OF PROBABILITY.

X.... Axis of; axis of coordinates lying along range, for points over or short of the target.

Y.... Axis of; axis of coordinates in vertical plane through target for points above or below the center of the target.

Z.... Axis of; axis of coordinates in vertical plane through target for points to right or left of the center of target.

(z_1, y_1), etc.... Coordinates of points of impact in vertical plane through target.

Σz.... Summation of z_1, z_2, etc.

Σy.... Summation of y_1, y_2, etc.

n.... Number of shot.

γ_z.... Mean deviation along axis of Z, that is, above or below.

γ_y.... Mean deviation along axis of Y, that is, to right or left.

γ_x.... Mean deviation along axis of X, that is, in range.

P.... Probability that the deviation of a single shot will be numerically less than the given quantity a.

$\frac{a}{\gamma}$ .... Argument for probability table.

PERTAINING TO VARIATIONS IN THE BALLISTIC ELEMENTS.

ΔX.... Variation in the range in feet.

ΔR.... Variation in the range in yards.

$\Delta(\sin 2\phi)$.... Variation in the sine of twice the angle of departure.

Δ_{VA}.... Quantity appearing in Table II of the Ballistic Tables in the Δ_V column pertaining to "A." With figures before the subscript V it shows the amount of variation in V for which used. (Be careful not to confuse this symbol with ΔV or δV.)

δV.... Variation in the initial velocity. (Be careful not to confuse this symbol with Δ_{VA} or ΔV.)

ΔV.... Difference between V for two successive tables in Table II. (Be careful not to confuse this symbol with Δ_{VA} or δV.)

ΔV_w.... Variation in the initial velocity in foot-seconds due to variation in the weight of the projectile in pounds. Figures before the w show the amount of variation in that quantity in pounds.

ΔX_V.... Variation in range in feet due to a variation in V in foot-seconds. Figures before the V show the amount of variation in that quantity in foot-seconds.

ΔR_V.... Variation in range in yards due to a variation in V in foot-seconds. Figures before the V show the amount of variation in that quantity in foot-seconds.

ΔC.... Variation in the ballistic coefficient in percentage.

ΔX_C.... Variation in range in feet due to a variation in C in percentage. Figures before the C show the amount of variation in that quantity in percentage.

ΔR_C.... Variation in range in yards due to a variation in C in percentage. Figures before the C show the amount of variation in that quantity in percentage.

$\Delta\delta$....Variation in δ in percentage.

ΔX_δ....Variation in range in feet due to a variation in δ in percentage. Figures before the δ show the amount of variation in that quantity in percentage.

ΔR_δ....Variation in range in yards due to a variation in δ in percentage. Figures before the δ show the amount of variation in that quantity in percentage.

Δw....Variation in w in pounds.

ΔX_w....Variation in range in feet due to a variation in w in pounds. Figures before the w show the amount of variation in that quantity in pounds.

$\Delta X'_w$....That part of ΔX_w in feet which is due to the reduction in initial velocity resulting from Δw.

$\Delta X''_w$....That part of ΔX_w in feet which is due to Δw directly.

ΔR_w....Variation in range in yards due to a variation in w in pounds. Figures before the w show the amount of variation in that quantity in pounds.

$\Delta R'_w$....That part of ΔR_w in yards which is due to the reduction in initial velocity resulting from Δw.

$\Delta R''_w$....That part of ΔR_w in yards which is due to Δw directly.

H....Change in height of point of impact on a vertical screen through the target, in feet, due to a change of ΔR in R in yards. Figures as subscripts to the H show the change in R necessary to give that particular value of H.

MATHEMATICAL AND MISCELLANEOUS.

g....Acceleration due to gravity in foot-seconds per second; $g = 32.2$.

dx....Differential increment in x.

dy....Differential increment in y.

ds....Differential increment along the curve, that is, in s.

dv....Differential increment in v.

dt....Differential increment in t.

du....Differential increment in u.

a....Mayevski's exponent.

A....Mayevski's coefficient.

R....Total air resistance in pounds.

R_f....Total air resistance in pounds under firing conditions.

R_s....Total air resistance in pounds under standard conditions.

ρ....Radius of curvature of the trajectory at any point in feet.

k....The value of $\frac{A}{C}$, in which A is Mayevski's constant and C is the ballistic coefficient.

e....The base of the Naperian system of logarithms; $e = 2.7183$.

n....The ratio between the range in vacuum and the range in air for the same angle of departure.

T_v....Value of the time integral in seconds for remaining velocity v.

T_V....Value of the time integral in seconds for initial velocity V.

S_v....Value of the space integral in feet for remaining velocity v.

S_V....Value of the space integral in feet for initial velocity V.

T_u....Value of the time function in seconds for pseudo velocity u.

T_V....Value of time function in seconds for initial velocity V.

S_u....Value of space function in feet for pseudo velocity u.

S_V....Value of space function in feet for initial velocity V.

A_u....Value of altitude function for pseudo velocity u.

A_V....Value of altitude function for initial velocity V.

I_u....Value of inclination function for pseudo velocity u.

I_V....Value of inclination function for initial velocity V.

S_{u_ω}....Value of space function in feet for pseudo velocity u_ω.

S_{u_1}....Value of space function in feet for pseudo velocity u_1.

T_{u_ω}....Value of time function in seconds for pseudo velocity u_ω.

T_{u_o}....Value of time function in seconds for pseudo velocity u_o.
A_{u_ω}....Value of altitude function for pseudo velocity u_ω.
A_{u_o}....Value of altitude function for pseudo velocity u_o.
I_{u_ω}....Value of inclination function for pseudo velocity u_ω.
I_{u_o}....Value of inclination function for pseudo velocity u_o.
ΔS....Difference between two values of the space function.
ΔT....Difference between two values of the time function.
ΔA....Difference between two values of the altitude function.
ΔI....Difference between two values of the inclination function.
z....General expression for value of argument in Column 1 of Table II of the Ballistic Tables, for any point of the trajectory; $z = \frac{x}{C}$.
Z....Special expression for value of argument in Column 1 of Table II of the Ballistic Tables, for the whole trajectory; $Z = \frac{X}{C}$.
a, b, a', t'.... General values of Ingalls' secondary functions.
A, B, A', T'...., A'' and $B' = \frac{B}{A}$ } Special value of Ingalls' secondary functions for whole trajectory.
ϕ_x....Angle of departure for a horizontal distance x.
$\mu = \frac{k^2}{R^2}$ ....A ratio used in computing the drift; in which k is the radius of gyration of the projectile about its longitudinal axis, and R is the radius of the projectile.
$\frac{\lambda}{h}$ ....A special ratio used in computing the drift.
n....The twist of the rifling, used in computing the drift.
D'....Ingalls' secondary function for drift.
D....Drift in yards.
l....Sight radius in inches.
D....Deflection in yards (used with R in yards in deflection computations).
d....Distance in inches which the sliding leaf is set over to compensate for the deflection D in yards.
i....Permanent sight-bar angle.
h....Sight bar height in inches.
E....Penetration of armor in inches.
K....Constant used in computing penetration of armor.
K'....Constant used in computing penetration of armor.
h....Height of target in feet.
S....Danger space in general.
α...., β...., γ.... } Angles for plotting fall of shot in calibration practice.
(a, a')...., (b, b')...., (c, c')...., (d, d').... } Coordinates of point of fall of shot for plotting in calibration practice.

LETTERS OF THE GREEK ALPHABET USED AS SYMBOLS.

Letter.	Pronunciation.	Letter.	Pronunciation.	Letter.	Pronunciation.
α	Alpha.	θ	Theta.	Σ or σ	Sigma.
β	Beta.	λ	Lambda.	ϕ	Phi.
γ	Gamma.	μ	Mu.	ψ	Psi.
Δ or δ	Delta.	π	Pi.	ω	Omega.
ϵ	Epsilon.	ρ	Rho.		

CHAPTER 1.

DEFINITIONS AND INTRODUCTORY EXPLANATIONS.

Symbols Introduced.

R'....Range in yards on an inclined plane.
X'....Range in feet on an inclined plane.
R....Horizontal range in yards.
X....Horizontal range in feet.
ϕ....Angle of departure.
ω....Angle of fall.
p....Angle of position.
j....Angle of jump.
ψ....Angle of elevation.
ψ'....Angle of projection.
V....Initial velocity in foot-seconds.
v....Remaining velocity at any point in the trajectory in foot-seconds.
v_o....Remaining velocity at the vertex in foot-seconds.
v_ω....Remaining velocity at the point of fall, or striking velocity, in foot-seconds.
v_h....Horizontal velocity at any point of the trajectory in foot-seconds.
v_v....Vertical velocity at any point of the trajectory in foot-seconds.
u....Pseudo velocity at any point of the trajectory in foot-seconds.
U....Pseudo velocity at the muzzle of the gun in foot-seconds; $U=V$.
u_o....Pseudo velocity at the vertex in foot-seconds.
u_ω....Pseudo velocity at the point of fall in foot-seconds.

1. **Ballistics** is the science of the motion of projectiles, and is divided into two branches; namely, interior ballistics and exterior ballistics. Definitions.

2. **Interior ballistics** is that branch of the science which treats of the motion of the projectile while in the gun and of the phenomena which cause and attend this motion.

3. **Exterior ballistics** is that branch of the science which treats of the motion of the projectile after it leaves the gun. The investigations to be conducted under exterior ballistics therefore begin at the instant when the projectile leaves the muzzle of the gun.

4. There are certain definitions connected with the travel of the projectile after it leaves the gun, and certain symbols which are used to represent the quantities covered by these definitions. These definitions and symbols will now be given.

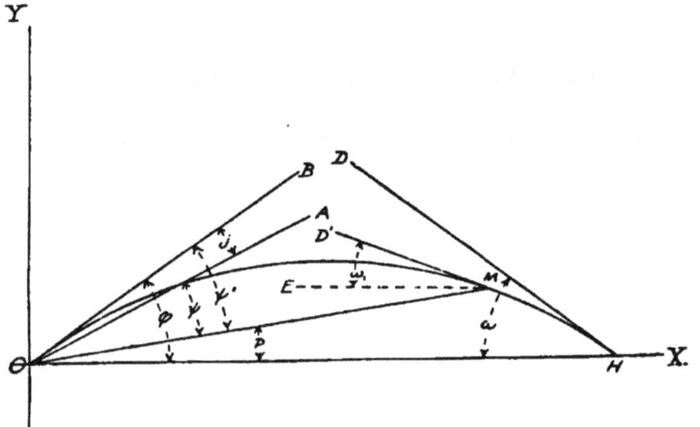

FIGURE 1.

ELEMENTS OF TRAJECTORY.

$BOH = \phi =$ Angle of Departure.
$H =$ Point of Fall, Horizontal Range.
$DHO = \omega =$ Angle of Fall.
$OH = X =$ Horizontal Range.
$OM =$ Line of Position.
$MOH = p =$ Angle of Position.
$D'ME = \omega' =$ Angle of Fall.

$OM = X' =$ Range.
$BOM = \psi' =$ Angle of Projection.
$BOA = j =$ Angle of jump.
$AOM = \psi =$ Angle of Elevation.
$\phi = \psi + j + p = \psi' + p.$
When $p = 0.$ $\phi = \psi' = \psi + j.$
When $p = j = 0,$ $\phi = \psi = \psi'.$

5. The **trajectory** is the curve traced by the projectile in its flight from the muzzle of the gun to the first point of impact, which point of impact is called the **point of fall**; in other words, it is the path of the projectile between those two points considered as a curve.

6. The **elements of the trajectory**, broadly considered, are certain quantities which are now to be defined, such as the initial velocity, range, time of flight, etc., which enter into the mathematical consideration of the trajectory.

7. The **range** is the distance in a straight line from the gun to the point of fall. It will be denoted by R' when given in yards and by X' when given in feet.

8. When the point of fall is in the same horizontal plane as the gun, the range is called the **horizontal range**. It will be denoted by R when given in yards and by X when given in feet. Unless otherwise stated, in discussions and problems, the term **range** will always mean **horizontal range**.

9. The **line of departure** is the line in which the projectile is moving when it leaves the gun. It is tangent to the trajectory at its origin, and, with modern guns, it practically coincides with the axis of the bore of the gun.

10. The **angle of departure** is the angle between the tangent to the trajectory at the origin, that is the line of departure, and the horizontal plane. It will be denoted by ϕ.

will be denoted by u. At the muzzle it becomes U, and is equal to V; at the vertex it becomes u_0; and at the point of fall it becomes u_ω.

23. The two following assumptions, which are sufficiently correct for all present practical purposes, are made throughout:

1. The force of gravity throughout the trajectory acts in parallel lines perpendicular to the horizontal plane at the gun; the value of g being 32.2 f. s. s.

2. The dimensions of the gun are negligible in comparison with the trajectory. For convenience we may therefore suppose the trajectory to begin at the axis about which the gun is being elevated or depressed, and we will take the horizontal plane through that axis to be the horizontal plane through the gun.

24. Figure 1 represents a trajectory, O indicating the position of the gun or origin, and OH the horizontal plane. Then $BOH=\phi$ is the angle of departure; H the point of fall on the horizontal plane; $DHO=\omega$ is the angle of fall; and $OH=X$ (or R) is the horizontal range. If the target be at M, then OM is the line of position; $MOH=p$ is the angle of position; $D'ME=\omega'$ is the angle of fall; and $OM=X'$ (or R') is the range. $BOM=\psi'$ is the angle of projection, which coincides with the angle of departure, ϕ, when the angle of position, p, is zero. OA represents the position of the axis of the bore at the instant before firing, and OB its position at the instant the projectile leaves the muzzle, the angle between them, $BOA=j$, being the angle of jump. The angle $AOM=\psi$ is the angle of elevation. It will be seen that $\phi=\psi+j+p=\psi'+p$; and that when $p=0$ this becomes $\phi=\psi'=\psi+j$.

25. In studying these definitions it should be noted that in them, as given for the various angles, the angle of departure (ϕ) and the angle of fall (ω) are the only ones that are measured from the horizontal plane, except that of course the position angle (p) is by its very definition the angle between the line of position and that plane. The angle of elevation (ψ) and the angle of projection (ψ') are measured from the line of position. Of course when we are working with horizontal ranges, which is generally the case, and when there is no jump, which is also generally the case (when $p=0$ and $j=0$), then the angle of elevation, angle of projection, and angle of departure all become the same, that is, $\phi=\psi=\psi'$.

26. Being now familiar with certain definitions relating to the trajectory, we may undertake its consideration in a general way. If it were possible to fire the gun and have the whole travel of the projectile take place in a non-resisting medium, as in vacuum for instance, it is apparent that, after it has acquired its initial velocity, the only force acting upon the projectile during its flight is the force of gravity. The derivation of the equation to the trajectory in vacuum and the investigation of its elements therefore becomes a very simple matter, as will be seen in the next chapter.

27. It is also apparent that, as the flight of the projectile necessarily takes place in a resisting medium, that is the atmosphere, there must really be in actual practice, in addition to the force of gravity, a force acting upon it during flight due to the atmospheric resistance. Such being the case, it is evident that the investigation of the trajectory in vacuum, while most necessary from an educational standpoint, must necessarily be of comparatively little real value in the solution of practical problems in gunnery.

28. It is proposed, in this text book, to first discuss the trajectory in vacuum, in order to derive from it such general knowledge as is of value in later work. Then an equation to the trajectory in air will be derived for certain special conditions, in order that it may be compared with the equation to the trajectory in vacuum for the same angle of departure and initial velocity. It will be shown, however, that neither of the above equations is very serviceable for the solution of practical problems in service gunnery with modern velocities, and other mathematical formulæ will be

2. For the following angles of elevation, jump and position, what are the corresponding angles of projection and departure? Draw curves showing all angles.

Problem.	DATA.			ANSWERS.	
	Angle of elevation.	Angle of jump.	Angle of position.	Angle of departure.	Angle of projection.
1...........	2° 00′	+ 5′	+ 15° 00′	+ 17° 05′	+ 2° 05′
2...........	3 00	− 3	+ 12 15	+ 15 12	+ 2 57
3...........	3 00	− 7	− 10 30	− 7 37	+ 2 53
4...........	2 00	+ 4	− 12 07	− 10 03	+ 2 04
5...........	3 00	+ 6	+ 11 15	+ 14 21	+ 3 06
6...........	5 00	− 5	+ 10 16	+ 15 11	+ 4 55
7...........	4 00	+ 6	− 9 37	− 5 31	+ 4 06
8...........	6 00	− 8	− 6 22	− 0 30	+ 5 52

3. A target is at a horizontal distance of 3000 yards from the gun, and is 750 feet higher than the gun above the water. Compute the angle of position by the use of logarithms. *Answer.* $p=4°\ 45'\ 49''$.

4. A target is at a horizontal distance of 10,000 yards from the gun, and is on the water 1500 feet below the level of the gun, the latter being in a battery on a hill. Compute the angle of position by the use of logarithms.

Answer. $p=(-)2°\ 51'\ 45''$.

5. A target is at a horizontal distance of 1924 yards from the gun, and is 1123 feet higher above the water than the gun. Find, by the use of the traverse tables, the angle of position and the distance in a straight line from the gun to the target in yards. *Answers.* $p=11°\ 00'\ 00''$. $R'=1960$ yards.

6. A target is at a horizontal distance of 1860 yards from the gun, and it is on the water 1238 feet below the level of the gun, the latter being in a battery on a hill. Find, by the use of the traverse tables, the angle of position and the distance in a straight line from the gun to the target in yards.

Answers. $p=(-)12°\ 30'\ 31''$. $R'=1905.23$ yards.

CHAPTER 2.

THE EQUATION TO THE TRAJECTORY IN A NON-RESISTING MEDIUM AND THE THEORY OF THE RIGIDITY OF THE TRAJECTORY IN VACUUM.

New Symbols Introduced.

(x, y).... Coordinates of any point of the trajectory in feet.

(x_0, y_0).... Coordinates of the highest point, or vertex, of the trajectory in feet.

θ.... Angle of inclination of the tangent to the trajectory at any point to the horizontal.

t.... Elapsed time of flight from the muzzle to any point on the trajectory in seconds.

t_0.... Elapsed time to the vertex of the trajectory in seconds.

T.... Time of flight from the muzzle to the point of fall in seconds.

g.... Acceleration due to gravity in foot-seconds per second; $g = 32.2$.

dx.... Differential increment in x.

dy.... Differential increment in y.

ds.... Differential increment along the curve, that is, in s.

32. The resistance of the air to the motion of a projectile animated with the high velocity given by a modern gun is so great that calculations which neglect it are of little practical value at the present day, except to aid in a comprehension of the underlying principles of exterior ballistics and to permit comparisons to be made between the travel of a projectile in a non-resisting and in a resisting medium. For these purposes, however, the study of the motion of a projectile in vacuum is of the utmost value, and therefore this chapter will be devoted to this subject, which, through its simplicity, furnishes a valuable groundwork for the correct understanding of the more complex problems which arise when account is taken of the atmospheric resistance.

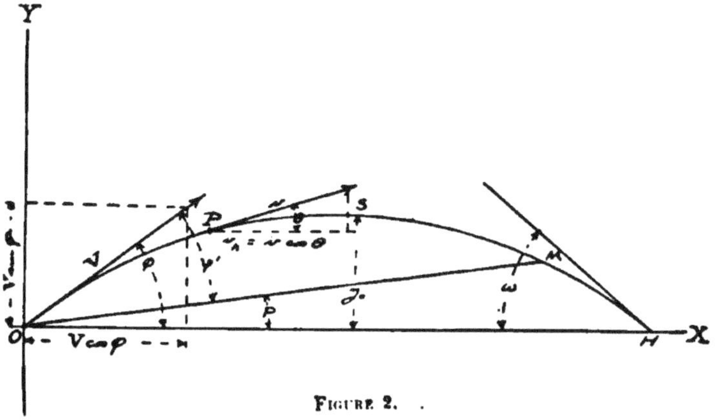

FIGURE 2.

33. Figure 2 represents the trajectory in vacuum, the origin, O, being taken at the gun, the axis of Y vertical, and the axis of X horizontal. The line marked V is the line of departure, and by its length represents the initial velocity, V; the vertical and horizontal components of which are $V \sin \phi$ and $V \cos \phi$, respectively. The remaining velocity, v, at any point of the trajectory, P, whose coordinates are (x, y), and its horizontal component, v_h, are also represented. Letting θ represent the angle at which the tangent to the trajectory at the point P is inclined to the horizontal, we have $v_h = v \cos \theta$.

34. Since the only force acting on the projectile after it leaves the gun is the vertical force of gravity, the projectile will remain throughout its travel in the vertical plane through the line of departure, and the trajectory will be a plane curve.

Primary equations. 35. Let t be the elapsed time from the origin to any point P, whose coordinates are (x, y); and then from the figure we evidently have:

$$x = tV \cos \phi \qquad y = tV \sin \phi - \tfrac{1}{2} gt^2 \tag{1}$$

as $\frac{1}{2}gt^2$ represents the vertical acceleration (in this case negative) due to the action of the force of gravity during the time t. Eliminating t between the two equations given above we have

Equation to trajectory in vacuum.

$$y = x \tan \phi - \frac{gx^2}{2V^2 \cos^2 \phi} \tag{2}$$

and (2) is the equation to the trajectory in vacuum, which trajectory, from the form of its equation, is evidently a parabola with a vertical axis.

36. From the above equation various expressions may be derived from which we can readily determine the values of the different elements of the curve.

Angle of inclination. 37. Differentiating (2) and putting $\tan \theta$ for $\frac{dy}{dx}$, we get

$$\tan \theta = \tan \phi - \frac{gx}{V^2 \cos^2 \phi} \tag{3}$$

which gives the inclination of the curve to the horizontal at any point.

Horizontal range. 38. Putting $y = 0$ in (2), we find two values of x, the first zero, and the second $\frac{V^2 \sin 2\phi}{g}$; consequently the horizontal range, OH, is given by

$$X = \frac{V^2 \sin 2\phi}{g} \tag{4}$$

This shows that, for a given initial velocity, the range increases with the angle of departure up to $\phi = 45°$, when it reaches its maximum value of $\frac{V^2}{g}$; and that the same range is given by either of two angles of departure, one as much greater than 45° as the other is less than 45°.

Variations in angle of inclination. 39. From (3) we see that, as x increases, θ decreases from its initial value of ϕ, until it becomes zero when $\tan \phi = \frac{gx}{V^2 \cos^2 \phi}$: that is, when

$$x = \frac{V^2 \cos^2 \phi \tan \phi}{g} = \frac{V^2 \cos^2 \phi \sin \phi}{g \cos \phi} = \frac{V^2 \sin \phi \cos \phi}{g}$$

$$= \frac{V^2 \sin 2\phi}{2g}\,^*, \text{ or, as } X = \frac{V^2 \sin 2\phi}{g}, \text{ when } x = \frac{X}{2}$$

We also see that after this value of x is reached, the value of θ becomes negative, as $\frac{gx}{V^2 \cos^2 \phi}$ then becomes greater than $\tan \phi$; and that for $x = X$, $\theta = -\phi$. That is to say, the highest point or vertex, S, of the curve is midway of the range, and the angle of fall, ω, is equal to the angle of departure, ϕ.

---

* $\sin 2\phi = 2 \sin \phi \cos \phi$.

Angle of departure on an incline.

44. To determine the angle of departure necessary to give a given range on an inclined plane, we have

$$y_1 = x_1 \tan\phi - \frac{g x_1^2}{2V^2 \cos^2\phi}$$

But $x_1 = X' \cos p$ and $y_1 = X' \sin p$; therefore

$$X' \sin p = X' \cos p \tan\phi - \frac{gX'^2 \cos^2 p}{2V^2 \cos^2\phi}$$

or

$$2X'V^2 \cos p \sin\phi \cos\phi - 2X'V^2 \sin p \cos^2\phi - gX'^2 \cos^2 p = 0$$

But $\sin\phi \cos\phi = \frac{1}{2}\sin 2\phi$ and $\cos^2\phi = \frac{1}{2}(1+\cos 2\phi)$, therefore

$$X'V^2(\sin 2\phi \cos p - \cos 2\phi \sin p) = gX'^2 \cos^2 p + X'V^2 \sin p$$

whence

$$\sin(2\phi - p) = \frac{gX'}{V^2}\cos^2 p + \sin p \tag{9}$$

45. If p were zero, as the angle of departure was ψ', we would have for the horizontal range from (8), $X = \frac{2V^2}{g}\sin\psi' \cos\psi'$, and so the ratio of the range on an inclined plane to the horizontal range, for the same angle of projection, would be

$$\frac{X'}{X} = \frac{\cos(\psi' + p)}{\cos\psi' \cos^2 p} = \sec p(1 - \tan\psi' \tan p) \tag{10}$$

The value of the second member of (10) is very nearly unity so long as ψ' and p are small angles, being, for example, 0.9992 for $\psi' = 3°$, $p = 5°$; and it therefore follows that, **with small angles of projection and position, we may consider the range as independent of the angle of position.**

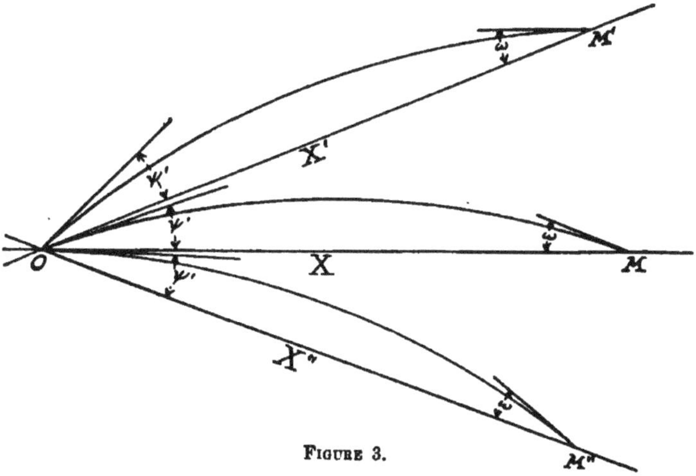

FIGURE 3.

Theory of the rigidity of the trajectory.

46. The assumption in the last line of the preceding paragraph is called the assumption of the rigidity of the trajectory, and evidently consists in supposing that the gun, trajectory, and line of position (a chord of the trajectory) may be turned through a vertical angle, as illustrated in Figure 3, without any change of form. The trajectory is assumed to be rigid in practice when the same sight graduations are used

in firing a gun at objects at different heights, or when the gun itself is at different heights relative to the target.

47. As an example of the mathematical work relative to the trajectory in vacuum, and to show the proper logarithmic forms for such work, suppose we have given, in vacuum, an angle of elevation (ψ) of 7° 50′, an angle of jump (j) of +10′, an initial velocity of 2600 f. s., and an angle of position (p) of zero; and desire to compute the horizontal range, time of flight, striking velocity, angle of fall, coordinates of vertex, and time to and remaining velocity at the vertex. (Use Table VI where convenient.)

$$\phi=\psi'=\psi+j;\quad X=\frac{V^2 \sin 2\phi}{g};\quad T=\frac{X}{V\cos\phi};\quad v_\omega=V;\quad \omega=\phi$$

$$x_0=\frac{X}{2};\quad y_0=\frac{X\tan\phi}{4};\quad t_0=\frac{T}{2};\quad v_0=V\cos\phi$$

$V=2600$ ...... 2 log 6.82994 .... colog 6.58503 − 10 .... log 3.41497

$\phi=8°\ 00'$ .... sec 0.00425 .... tan 9.14780 − 10 ... cos 9.99575 − 10

$2\phi=16°\ 00'$ .... sin 9.44034 − 10

$g=32.2$ ...... colog 8.49214 − 10

4 .... colog 9.39794 − 10

$X=57865.5'$ ... log 4.76242 .... log 4.76242 .... log 4.76242

$T=22.475$ .... log 1.35170

$y_0=2033.1$ .... log 3.30816

$v_0=2574.65$ .... log 3.41072

Results.

$R=19288.5$ yards.	$x_0=9644.25$ yards.
$T=22.475$ seconds.	$y_0=2033.1$ feet.
$\omega=8°\ 00'$.	$t_0=11.2375$ seconds.
$v_\omega=2600$ f. s.	$v_0=2574.65$ f. s.

48. And, again, suppose the angle of position (p) to be 30°, the angle of projection (ψ') to be 2° 25′ 45″, and the initial velocity 2900 f. s.; and it is desired to find the range on the incline and the time of flight, both in vacuum.

$$X'=\frac{2V^2}{g}\times\frac{\sin\psi'\cos(\psi'+p)}{\cos^2 p};\ \cos p=\frac{x}{X'};\ \text{therefore, } x=X'\cos p, \text{ and}$$

$$t=\frac{x}{V\cos\phi},\ \text{whence } T=\frac{X'\cos p}{V\cos\phi},\ \text{where } \phi=\psi'+p$$

$V=2900$ .... 2 log 6.92480 .... colog 6.53760 − 10

$p=30°\ 00'\ 00''$ ..... sec 0.06247 .... 2 sec 0.12494 .... cos 9.93753 − 10

$\psi'=\ 2°\ 25'\ 45''$ .... sin 8.62721 − 10

$\phi=32°\ 25'\ 45''$ .... cos 9.92637 − 10 .... sec 0.07363

$g=32.2$ .... log 1.50786 .... colog 8.49214 − 10

2 .... log 0.30103

$X'=24916.5$ .... log 4.39649 .... log 4.39649

$T=8.8155$ .... log 0.94525

Results. $R'=8305.5$ yards. $T=8.8155$ seconds.

EXAMPLES.

1. If the initial velocity and angle of departure are as given in the first two columns of the following table, compute the horizontal and vertical components of the velocity at the point of origin, in vacuum. Give results obtained by both the use of logarithms and by the use of the traverse tables without logarithms.

Problem.	DATA.		ANSWERS.			
	Initial velocity. f. s.	Angle of departure.	By logs.		By traverse tables.	
			v_h. f. s.	v_v. f. s.	v_h. f. s.	v_v. f. s.
1.............	1000	2° 00′ 00″	999	35	999	35
2.............	1100	3 15 42	1098	63	1098	63
3.............	1250	4 25 16	1246	96	1246	96
4.............	1400	5 10 25	1394	126	1394	126
5.............	1500	10 12 14	1476	266	1476	265
6.............	1750	7 30 00	1735	228	1735	229
7.............	2000	5 00 00	1992	174	1992	174
8.............	2400	9 21 15	2368	390	2368	390
9.............	2600	12 37 54	2537	569	2537	569
10.............	2900	17 24 24	2767	868	2767	868

NOTE.—It will be seen from the above that the traverse tables give the results correctly to the nearest foot-second, which is all that is required in ordinary work.

2. The data being as given in the first three columns of the following table, find the results, in vacuum, required by the other columns.

Problem.	DATA.			ANSWERS.				
	Initial velocity. f. s.	Angle of elevation.	Angle of jump.	Angle of departure.	Horizontal range. Yds.	Time of flight. Secs.	Angle of fall.	Striking velocity. f. s.
1	1000	5° 27′	+ 7′	5° 34′	1999	6.03	5° 34′	1000
2	1100	4 32	+ 3	4 35	1995	5.46	4 35	1100
3	1250	3 33	— 3	3 30	1971	4.74	3 30	1250
4	1400	2 15	— 5	2 10	1533	3.20	2 10	1400
5	1500	7 22	+ 6	7 28	6002	12.11	7 28	1500
6	1750	8 12	0	8 12	8951	15.50	8 12	1750
7	2000	12 37	— 7	12 30	17500	26.89	12 30	2000
8	2400	7 50	—10	7 40	15767	19.89	7 40	2400
9	2600	3 07	+ 3	3 10	7719	8.92	3 10	2600
10	2900	16 35	+ 5	16 40	47840	51.66	16 40	2900

3. Given the initial velocities and angles of departure in the table below, compute the coordinates of the vertex, and the time to and remaining velocity at the vertex, in vacuum.

Problem.	DATA.		ANSWERS.			
	Initial velocity. f. s.	Angle of departure.	x_0. Yds.	y_0. Feet.	t_0. Secs.	v_0. f. s.
1	1000	5° 34′	999	146	3.01	995
2	1100	4 35	998	120	2.73	1096
3	1250	3 30	986	90	2.37	1248
4	1400	2 10	767	44	1.64	1399
5	1500	7 28	3001	590	6.05	1487
6	1750	8 12	4475	967	7.75	1732
7	2000	12 30	8730	2910	13.44	1953
8	2400	7 40	7884	1592	9.94	2379
9	2600	3 10	3860	320	4.46	2596
10	2900	16 40	23920	10742	25.83	2778

4. A body is projected in vacuum with $V=1000$ f. s., and an angle of departure of 30°. Where is it after 3 seconds? Where after 10 seconds?

Answers. 3 seconds. $x=1500\sqrt{3}$ feet. $y=1355$ feet.
10 seconds. $x=5000\sqrt{3}$ feet. $y=3390$ feet.

5. A body is projected in vacuum from the top of a tower 200 feet high, with a velocity of 50 f. s., and an angle of departure of 60°. Find the range on the horizontal plane through the foot of the tower, and the time of flight.

Answers. Range = 128 feet. Time = 5.12 seconds.

6. What is the angle of departure in vacuum in order that the horizontal range may be: (a) Equal to the maximum ordinate of the trajectory; and (b), equal to three times the maximum ordinate?

Answers. (a) 75° 57′ 51″. (b) 53° 07′ 48″.

7. Compute the initial velocity and angle of departure in vacuum in order that the projectile may be 100 feet high at a horizontal distance from the gun of a quarter of a mile, and may have a horizontal range of one mile.

Answers. For 1 mile = 5280 feet. 5° 46′ 05″. 922 f. s.
For 1 mile = 6080 feet. 5° 00′ 07″. 1062 f. s.

8. The angle of position is 45°, the angle of projection is 1° 16′ 31″, and the initial velocity is 1500 f. s. Compute the range on the incline and the time of flight, in vacuum. *Answers.* $R'=1433$ yards. $T=2.93$ seconds.

9. What must be the angle of projection in vacuum for an initial velocity of 400 f. s. in order that the range may be 2500 yards on a plane that descends at an angle of 30°?

Answer. Angle of projection. 34° 35′ 56″ or 85° 24′ 04″.

10. A body is projected in vacuum with an angle of departure of 60°, and an initial velocity of 150 f. s. Compute the coordinates of its position and its remaining velocity after 5 seconds; also the direction of its motion.

Answers. $x=375$ feet. $y=247$ feet.
$\theta=(-)22°\ 31'\ 25''$. $v=81$ f. s.

3

11. A 12" mortar shell weighing 610 pounds, fired with an initial velocity of 591 f. s., and an angle of departure of 73°, gave an observed horizontal range in air of 1939 yards, and a time of flight of 36 seconds. What would the range and time of flight have been in vacuum? *Answers.* $R=2022$ yards. $T=35.10$ seconds.

12. The measured range in air of a 12" shell of 850 pounds weight, fired with 2800 f. s. initial velocity, and an angle of departure of 7° 32′, was 11,900 yards, and the time of flight was 19.5 seconds. What would the range and time of flight have been in vacuum? *Answers.* $R=21{,}097$ yards. $T=22.8$ seconds.

Having determined these two velocities, it is evident that the retardation of the projectile while traveling the distance, x, between the two points of measurement is v_1-v_2. Let w be the weight of the projectile, R the resistance of the air in pounds (total resistance). Then, since the work done by the resistance must equal the loss of energy of the projectile, we have

$$Rx=\frac{w}{2g}(v_1^2-v_2^2)$$

whence,

$$R=\frac{w}{2gx}(v_1^2-v_2^2) \qquad (11)$$

where R is taken to be the total resistance of the air in pounds which corresponds to the mean velocity $\frac{v_1+v_2}{2}$.

As an example of the use of the above formula, suppose we have a 12" projectile weighing 870 pounds, fired through two pairs of screens 300 feet apart, and the measured velocity at the first pair was 2819 f. s. and at the second pair was 2757 f. s. These measured velocities are the mean velocities for the spaces traversed between the two screens of each pair, that is, we may assume that each velocity is the velocity at the point midway between the two screens of its own pair. The distance given as 300 feet is the distance between the midway points of each pair of screens.

Also, for determining the value of $(v_1^2-v_2^2)$, we know that $v_1^2-v_2^2=(v_1+v_2)(v_1-v_2)$, and the work becomes:

$v_1+v_2=5576$		log 3.74632
$v_1-v_2=62$		log 1.79239
$w=870$		log 2.93952
$x=300$	log 2.47712	colog 7.52288−10
$2g=64.4$	log 1.80889	colog 8.19111−10
$R=15567.5$ pounds		log 4.19222

in which R is the resistance for the mean of the two measured velocities, that is, for $\frac{v_1+v_2}{2}=2788$ f. s.

Experimental results. **51.** As the result of many such measurements with different projectiles and different velocities, it has been shown that the resistance of the air is proportional to:

1. The cross-sectional area of the projectile; or, what is the same thing, the square of its diameter, which is the caliber.

2. The density of the air; or, what is the same thing, the weight of a cubic foot of the air.

3. A power of the velocity, of which the exponent varies with the velocity, but may be considered as a constant within certain limits of velocity.

4. A coefficient which varies with the velocity, with the form of the projectile, and with the assumed value of the exponent; but which may be considered as a constant for any given projectile between the same limits of velocity for which the exponent is considered as a constant.

Mayevski's formula. **52.** In accordance with these four experimentally determined laws, we may write a general formula expressing the retardation of a projectile caused by the atmospheric resistance to its flight; which is Mayevski's formula. It would be:

$$\text{Retardation}=\frac{dv}{dt}=-A\frac{\delta cd^2}{w}v^n \qquad (12)$$

in which n is Mayevski's exponent, A is Mayevski's constant coefficient, c is the coefficient of form of the projectile, d the diameter of the projectile, w the weight of the projectile, and v the velocity. The acceleration, which is negative in this case, is of course represented by $\frac{dv}{dt}$.

53. The quantity δ in the above equation represents the ratio of the density of half-saturated air for the temperature of the air and barometric height at the time of firing to the density of half-saturated air for 15° C. (59° F.) and 750 mm. (29.5275") barometric height. The values of δ for different readings of the barometer (in inches) and thermometer (in degrees Fahrenheit) may be found in Table III of the Ballistic Tables.

54. In the above expression, c is the coefficient of form of the projectile. It will be readily understood that if certain results are obtained with a projectile of a given shape, a change in the shape of the projectile will change the results. Therefore the factor c is introduced, and values for it for different projectiles are determined experimentally, as explained later.

55. Mayevski adopted as standard the form of projectile in most common use at the time he conducted his experiments, which was one about three calibers in length, with an ogival head the radius to the curve of which ogive was two calibers, and for that projectile called the value of c unity. He also used a temperature of 59° F. and a barometric height of 29.5275" as standard, thus reducing the value of δ to unity also. His general expression then becomes

$$\frac{dv}{dt} = -A \frac{d^2}{w} v^n \qquad (13)$$

By determining velocities experimentally as explained in paragraph 50, he proceeded, on this formula as a basis, to derive specific laws for finding the retardation at different velocities.

56. As the result of these experiments he derived the following expressions:

v between 3600 f. s. and 2600 f. s.

$$\frac{dv}{dt} = -A_1 \frac{d^2}{w} v^{1.55} \qquad \log A_1 = 7.60905 - 10$$

v between 2600 f. s. and 1800 f. s.

$$\frac{dv}{dt} = -A_2 \frac{d^2}{w} v^{1.7} \qquad \log A_2 = 7.09620 - 10$$

v between 1800 f. s. and 1370 f. s.

$$\frac{dv}{dt} = -A_3 \frac{d^2}{w} v^2 \qquad \log A_3 = 6.11926 - 10$$

v between 1370 f. s. and 1230 f. s.

$$\frac{dv}{dt} = -A_4 \frac{d^2}{w} v^3 \qquad \log A_4 = 2.98090 - 10 \qquad (14)$$

v between 1230 f. s. and 970 f. s.

$$\frac{dv}{dt} = -A_5 \frac{d^2}{w} v^5 \qquad \log A_5 = 6.80187 - 20$$

v between 970 f. s. and 790 f. s.

$$\frac{dv}{dt} = -A_6 \frac{d^2}{w} v^3 \qquad \log A_6 = 2.77344 - 10$$

v between 790 f. s. and 0 f. s.

$$\frac{dv}{dt} = -A_7 \frac{d^2}{w} v^2 \qquad \log A_7 = 5.66989 - 10$$

57. From the above expressions, by using the appropriate one, the retardation for any velocity in foot-seconds may be calculated for the standard projectile and standard condition of atmosphere as adopted by Mayevski; and thence for any other projectile or atmospheric condition by applying the proper multipliers. Of course the total resistance of the air in pounds (R) may be found by multiplying the mass of the projectile by the retardation, so we have

$$R = A\frac{d^2}{w}v^a \times \frac{w}{g} = A\frac{d^2}{g}v^a \tag{15}$$

58. For instance, given a 6" shell weighing 105 pounds, traveling with a velocity of 2500 f. s.; to find the resistance and retardation under standard atmospheric conditions, provided it be a standard shell.

$$\frac{dv}{dt} = -A\frac{d^2}{w}v^a \qquad R = A\frac{d^2}{g}v^a$$

For 2500 f. s., Mayevski's constants are $a = 1.7$ and $\log A = 7.09620 - 10$.

$v = 2500$	log 3.39794		loglog 0.53121
$a = 1.7$			log 0.23045
$v^a =$	log 5.77640		loglog 0.76166
$A =$	log 7.09620 − 10		
$d^2 = 36$	log 1.55630		
Ad^2v^a	log 4.42890	log 4.42890	
$w = 105$	log 2.02119		
$g = 32.2$		log 1.50786	
$\frac{dv}{dt} = -255.69$ f. s.	log 2.40771		
$R = 833.75$ pounds		log 2.92104	

In the case of the experimental firing, suppose the above shell gave measured velocities of 2525 f. s. and 2475 f. s. at two points 488.88 feet apart, to find the resistance:

$$R = \frac{w}{2gx}(v_1^2 - v_2^2) = \frac{w}{2gx}(v_1 + v_2)(v_1 - v_2)$$

$v_1 + v_2 = 5000$		log 3.69897
$v_1 - v_2 = 50$		log 1.69897
$w = 105$		log 2.02119
$2g = 64.4$	log 1.80889	colog 8.19111 − 10
$x = 488.88$	log 2.68920	colog 7.31080 − 10
$R = 833.75$ pounds		log 2.92104

59. These results being only for standard conditions, we must introduce another factor if we desire results for any other conditions. This factor is known as the ballistic coefficient, and is denoted by C. It is a most important quantity to which great attention must be paid and which we must strive to thoroughly understand, for it enters constantly into nearly every problem in exterior ballistics. It represents the combination of the different elements already explained as well as some other elements which will now be discussed.

60. Introducing the ballistic coefficient, equation (12) becomes:

$$\frac{dv}{dt} = -\frac{A}{C}v^a \tag{16}$$

In other words, the values resulting from the use of the specific formulæ given in (14) must be divided by C for the individual case and conditions in order to get results for any other than standard conditions.

For firing when gun and target are in approximately the same horizontal plane, correction for altitude is ordinarily a needless refinement for trajectories for which the time of flight does not exceed about 12 seconds. (This time of flight corresponds to 9700 yards for Gun "N.") In computing range table data, the correction for altitude is generally started when such correction would produce a variation in the angle of departure of about one minute in arc.

In all problems in which the vertical distance of the point aimed at above or below the horizontal plane of the gun is such that the rigidity of the trajectory cannot be

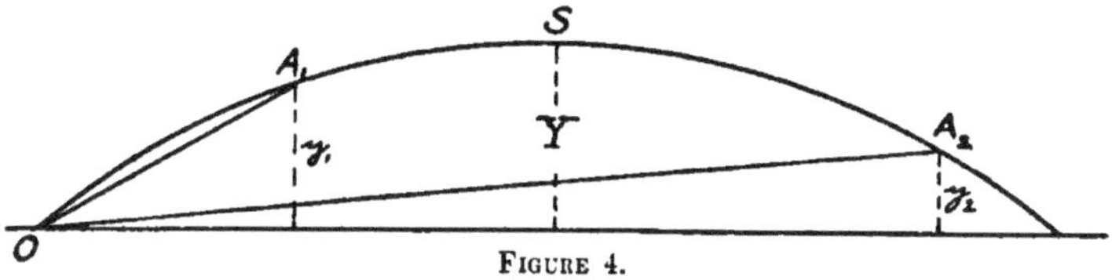

FIGURE 4.

taken for granted, the ballistic coefficient should be corrected for altitude; and an examination of Figure 4 will show that the mean height of the trajectory from gun to target is less or greater than two-thirds the height of the target above the horizontal plane of the gun according as the target is nearer to or further from the gun than the vertex of the complete trajectory. Thus, if the target be at A_1, the mean height of the arc OA_1 is less than $\frac{2}{3}y_1$, and approaches $\frac{y_1}{2}$ more and more as A_1 is nearer and nearer O; while if the target be at A_2 the mean height of the arc OA_2 is greater than $\frac{2}{3}y_2$, being about equal to y_2 when the abscissa of A_2 is $\frac{3}{4}X$. If, therefore, all possible refinements are to be introduced into the calculations, the relative positions of target and vertex must be determined before fixing the value of f. Generally speaking, however, it will be sufficiently accurate to give f the value corresponding to $Y = \frac{2}{3}y_1$.

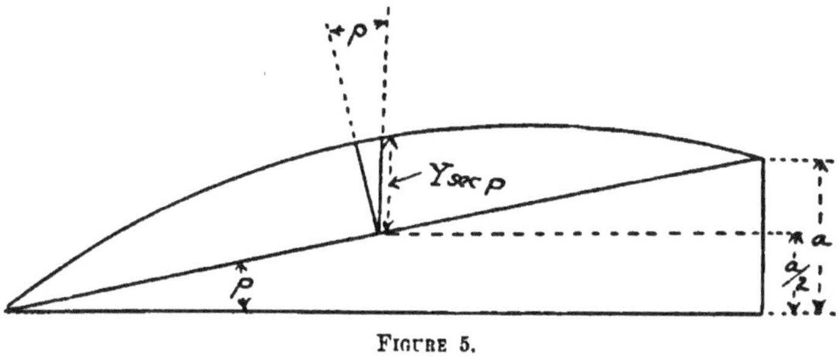

FIGURE 5.

The two preceding paragraphs explain how to determine the value of f for either: (1) A horizontal trajectory with a maximum ordinate sufficiently great to make it necessary to correct for altitude; or (2) in the case in which there is a material difference in height between the gun and the target. For the third possible case, a very likely one in naval operations, that of long-range firing at an elevated target, it is apparent that we have here both of the conditions calling for the use of the factor f as previously discussed. **In the light of what has been said, an approximate rule that would probably not lead to material error in most cases, is to take the value of f**

from the table for a height equal to two-thirds the maximum ordinate or two-thirds the height of the target, whichever of the two gives the greater height.

The rule given in the preceding subparagraph is of course only approximate, and a reference to Figure 5 will show at once that a closer approximation to the mean height of travel would really be $\frac{1}{3}a+\frac{2}{3}Y$ sec p, and that the value of f would then be taken from the table for the height determined by the above expression (not for two-thirds of it). It is believed, however, that the first rule given is sufficiently accurate for all ordinary cases; although special consideration should be given to this point in all cases involving peculiar conditions.

β is a quantity known as the integration factor, and will be explained later. (See page 83.) For the present it may be assumed to be equal to unity, and it will therefore disappear from the formula for the value of the ballistic coefficient for all our practical purposes. Integration factor.

63. C, as given in its fullest form in paragraph 61, is sometimes known as the reduced ballistic coefficient, the form used by Mayevski, $C=\frac{w}{cd^2}$, being called the ballistic coefficient. The expression for the value of this ballistic coefficient should always be remembered in its fullest form, however, and the different factors entering into it allowed to drop out by becoming unity as the conditions of actual firing approach the standard conditions.

64. Suppose we desire to find the value of the ballistic coefficient for the 12" gun, $w=870$, $c=0.61$, for 30.14" barometer and 24.5° F., when the highest point of the trajectory is 3333 feet. The formula is $C=\frac{fw}{\delta cd^2}$. We could work it out directly from this formula, but where investigations are to be carried out in regard to any one particular gun and projectile, it is convenient to work out the combined value of the constant factors for that projectile, that is, for w, c and d^2, and having once determined this, thereafter for the given gun and projectile we have only to apply δ and f to this constant to get the value of the ballistic coefficient under the given conditions. Expressed mathematically this is:

$$K=\frac{w}{cd^2} \qquad C=\frac{f}{\delta}K$$

and for the above problem the work becomes:

$w=870$		log 2.93952
$c=.61$	log 9.78533 − 10	colog 0.21467
$d^2=144$	log 2.15836	colog 7.84164 − 10
$K=9.9045$		log 0.99583

Now, from Table III, for 30.14" and 24.5°, we find $\delta=1.0947$. And, from Table V, for a height of $\frac{2\times 3333}{3}=2222$ feet, we find $f=1.059$. Hence, for our special case, we have

$K=$		log 0.99583
$f=1.059$		log 0.02490
$\delta=1.0947$	log 0.03929	colog 9.96071 − 10
$C=9.5816$		log 0.98144

65. Referring to the second part of paragraph 58, we see that we found experimentally that a certain resistance existed at the time of firing to the passage of a certain projectile through the air. Let us now suppose that the coefficient of form of the projectile used was $c=0.61$, and that the barometer stood at 30.14", and the thermometer at 24.5° F. at the time of firing. What would be, from this experimental firing, the resistance to a standard projectile under standard atmospheric conditions? The air on firing, being more dense than standard, the resistance would be less under standard conditions, that is, $R_s = \frac{1}{\delta} R_f$. The projectile used being more tapering than the standard, would pass more easily through the air, and the resistance to the standard projectile would be more than that measured, that is, $R_s = \frac{1}{c} R_f$; and combining, $R_s = \frac{1}{\delta c} R_f$

$R_f = 833.75$		log 2.92104
$\delta = 1.0947$	log 0.03929	colog 9.96071−10
$c = .61$	log 9.78533−10	colog 0.21467
$R_s = 1248.6$ pounds		log 3.09642

66. Suppose that we have given that, for a 12″ gun: $w = 870$; $c = 0.61$; two measured velocities at points 920 feet apart were 2840 f. s. and 2810 f. s.; to determine the resistance, and then discuss the difference between the results obtained by actual firing and by the use of Mayevski's formula. For simplicity in computation, consider the atmospheric conditions as standard. By Mayevski's formula

$R = A \frac{cd^2}{g} v^a$; Mean velocity = 2825 f. s.; $a = 1.55$; $\log A = 7.60905 - 10$

$v = 2825$	log 3.45102	loglog 0.53794
$a = 1.55$		log 0.19033
$v^a =$	log 5.34900	loglog 0.72827
$c = .61$	log 9.78533−10	
$A =$	log 7.60905−10	
$d^2 = 144$	log 2.15836	
$g = 32.2$ (log 1.50786)	colog 8.49214−10	
$R = 2476.7$ pounds	log 3.39388	

By actual firing: $R = \frac{w}{2gx}(v_1^2 - v_2^2) = \frac{w}{2gx}(v_1 + v_2)(v_1 - v_2)$

$v_1 + v_2 = 5650$		log 3.75205
$v_1 - v_2 = 30$		log 1.47712
$w = 870$		log 2.93952
$2g = 64.4$	log 1.80889	colog 8.19111−10
$x = 920$	log 2.96379	colog 7.03621−10
$R = 2488.9$ pounds		log 3.39601

If by our experimental firing we find as above that the resistance is 2488.9 pounds for the given projectile, when moving with a velocity of 2825 f. s., and assuming that at this velocity the resistance varies as the 1.55th power of the velocity, what would be the value of Mayevski's constant A in this case?

$$R = A \frac{cd^2}{g} v^a \quad \text{therefore} \quad A = \frac{g}{cd^2 v^a} R$$

$R = 2488.9$		log 3.39601
v^a (from preceding problem)	log 5.34900	colog 4.65100−10
$g = 32.2$		log 1.50786
$c = 0.61$	log 9.78533−10	colog 0.21467
$d^2 = 144$	log 2.15836	colog 7.84164−10
$A = .0040849$		log 7.61118−10

2. Using the values of K found in example 1 preceding, determine the values of δ, f, and log C for the conditions given in the following table. Correct for maximum ordinate or for height of target according to rule, but consider every trajectory whose time of flight is greater than five seconds as requiring correction for altitude.

	DATA.												ANSWERS.		
Problem	Gun.				R'nge. Yds.	Time of flight. Secs.	Max. ord. Feet.	Value of log K.	Diff. in ht. of gun and target. Feet.	Atmosphere.			δ.	f.	log C.
	d. In.	w. Lbs.	c.	V. f.s.						Bar. In.	Ther. °F.				
A...	3	13	1.00	1150	2600	8.25	277	0.15970	300	30.33	24.7		1.1011	1.0050	0.12004
B...	3	13	1.00	2700	4400	9.25	366	0.15970	150	30.13	17.5		1.1113	1.0063	0.11660
C...	4	33	0.67	2900	3900	5.10	105	0.48832	200	29.92	15.7		1.1080	1.0037	0.44538
D..	5	50	1.00	3150	4300	6.18	154	0.30103	225	29.83	12.4		1.1135	1.0040	0.25606
E...	5	50	0.61	3150	4300	5.19	108	0.51570	90	29.57	29.3		1.0644	1.0022	0.48956
F...	6	105	0.61	2600	14800	31.56	4215	0.67956	1200	29.45	33.8		1.0502	1.0753	0.68982
G...	6	105	1.00	2800	4000	5.56	124	0.46489	350	29.37	39.4		1.0352	1.0060	0.45247
H..	6	105	0.61	2800	3700	4.57	85	0.67956	200	29.07	43.2		1.0170	1.0037	0.67384
I...	7	165	1.00	2700	7000	11.76	563	0.52728	None	28.95	48.7		1.0009	1.0095	0.53100
J...	7	165	0.61	2700	7400	10.61	455	0.74195	175	28.83	50.3		0.9936	1.0081	0.74824
K..	8	260	0.61	2750	8300	11.49	532	0.82346	450	28.73	52.8		0.9852	1.0091	0.83387
L...	10	510	1.00	2700	10100	16.57	1116	0.70757	500	28.58	69.3		0.9475	1.0193	0.73929
M..	10	510	0.61	2700	11000	15.69	907	0.92224	1100	28.47	95.7		0.8936	1.0190	0.97927
N..	12	870	0.61	2900	23500	37.61	5758	0.99583	1500	28.36	97.4		0.8867	1.1061	1.09185
O...	13	1130	1.00	2000	10400	21.53	1889	0.82519	700	28.27	99.8		0.8790	1.0328	0.89522
P...	13	1130	0.74	2000	11300	22.28	2005	0.95596	508	28.21	74.8		0.9243	1.0351	1.00513
Q...	14	1400	0.70	2000	14100	28.36	3264	1.00877	800	28.20	71.3		0.9310	1.0583	1.06443
R...	14	1400	0.70	2600	14400	21.83	1925	1.00877	700	28.71	84.6		0.9225	1.0335	1.05811

3. Given the measured velocities of a projectile at two points, as determined by experimental firing, as given in the following table, determine the resistance of the air at the mean velocity between the two points of measurement. If the atmospheric conditions at the time of firing were as given, what would be the corresponding resistance under standard atmospheric conditions?

Problem..	DATA.					ANSWERS.	DATA.		ANSWERS.
	Projectile.		Dist. between points of measurement. Yds.	Measured velocities at.		R_f. Lbs.	Atmosphere.		R_s. Lbs.
	d. In.	w. Lbs.		First point. f. s.	Second point. f. s.		Bar. In.	Ther. °F.	
1..........	3	13	80	2650	2600	220.78	28.00	50	228.55
2..........	5	60	90	2250	2200	767.76	29.00	60	783.43
3..........	6	103	95	2550	2500	1444.5	30.00	70	1434.7
4..........	7	165	100	2680	2580	4492.2	30.50	80	4539.8
5..........	12	870	105	2870	2800	17022.0	31.00	90	17281.0
6..........	13	1130	110	1910	1880	6045.5	30.00	0	5257.0
7..........	14	1400	125	2540	2400	23188.0	29.00	25	22021.0
8..........	6	70	200	1951	1874	533.55	29.53	59	533.55

4. Under the conditions given in the following table, compute the total atmospheric resistance to the passage of the projectile, and the resultant retardation in foot-seconds.

Problem.	DATA.						ANSWERS.	
	Projectile.			Velocity. f. s.	Atmosphere.		Retardation. f. s.	Resistance. Lbs.
	d. In.	*w.* Lbs.	*c.*		Bar. In.	Ther. °F.		
1.	3	13	1.00	2300	30.00	20	493.39	199.19
2.	5	60	1.00	1300	31.00	55	130.53	243.23
3.	6	105	0.61	1300	29.00	47	44.23	144.24
4.	7	165	0.61	2700	28.50	82	141.16	723.33
5.	12	870	0.61	2850	29.45	90	86.92	2348.40
6.	13	1130	0.95	1100	30.15	95	13.74	482.27
7.	14	1400	0.70	850	28.67	64	3.43	149.27
8.	14	1400	0.70	2500	29.33	75	70.20	3052.20
9.	3	13	0.93	650	30.40	80	12.54	5.06

5. What is the resistance of the air to a baseball of 3″ diameter, weighing 8 ounces, moving at 100 f. s.; supposing the resistance of a sphere to be 1.25 times that of a standard ogival; and what would be its retardation?

Answers. Resistance, 0.16337 pound.
Retardation, 10.521 foot-seconds.

6. Given the data in the following tables, compute the value of the constant *A* in Mayevski's formula, for each individual case.

Problem.	DATA.								ANSWERS.
	Projectile.			δ.	Velocity. f. s.	Resistance. Lbs.	Retardation. f. s.	Value of *n*.	Value of *A*.
	d. In.	*w.* Lbs.	*c.*						
1	6	70	1.00	1.0000	1912.5	533.6	......	1.70	0.001259
2	6	70	1.00	1.0200	1818.0	491.8	......	1.70	0.00124023
3	6	70	1.00	1.0200	1859.5	1248.6	......	1.70	0.0030296
4	12	870	0.61	0.0354	2850.0	......	86.92	1.55	0.0040649
5	14	1400	0.70	0.9610	850.0	......	3.4328	3.00	0.0000000059353
6	14	1400	0.70	0.9000	2500.0	3052.4	......	1.70	0.001248

7. A 6″ projectile, weight 70 pounds, is fired through screens, and the velocities measured at two points 200 yards apart are 1951 f. s. and 1874 f. s. What was the mean resistance of the air? *Answer.* 533.57 pounds.

8. A 6″ ogival-headed projectile, weight 70 pounds, is fired through screens 150 yards apart, and its velocities at the first and at the second pairs of screens are 1846 f. s. and 1790 f. s., respectively. A 6″ flat-headed projectile of the same weight is fired through the same screens, and gives velocities of 1929 f. s. and 1790 f. s., respectively. What was the resistance of each projectile? If the first was a standard projectile, what was the coefficient of form of the second?

Answers. First, $R=$ 491.82 pounds.
Second, $R=$ 1248.65 pounds.
Coefficient of form of second $=2.5388$.

9. A 12″ projectile, weight 850 pounds, gave measured velocities of 1979 f. s. and 1956 f. s. at points 500 feet apart. What was the mean resistance of the air? If the density of the air at the time of firing was 1.02 times the standard density, what would be the resistance in a standard atmosphere?

Answers. $R_f=2389.0$ pounds. $R_s=2342.2$ pounds.

10. Determine the resistance of the air to and the consequent retardation of a standard 3″ projectile, weight 13 pounds, when moving: (1) at 2800 f. s.; (2) at 2000 f. s.

Answers. (1) Resistance $=250.34$ pounds. Retardation $=620.09$ f. s.
(2) Resistance $=142.67$ pounds. Retardation $=353.38$ f. s.

11. Determine the resistance of the air and the consequent retardation in the following cases. (Standard atmosphere; and $c=1.00$ in each case.)

Problem.	DATA.			ANSWERS.	
	Projectile.		Velocity. f. s.	Resistance. Lbs.	Retardation. f. s.
	d. In.	*w.* Lbs.			
1	4	33	2800	445.1	434.3
2	4	33	2000	253.6	247.5
3	6	100	2800	1001.4	322.4
4	6	100	2000	570.7	183.8
5	8	250	2800	1780.2	229.3
6	8	250	2000	1014.5	130.7
7	10	500	2800	2781.5	179.1
8	10	500	2000	1585.2	102.1
9	12	850	2800	4005.4	151.7
10	12	850	2000	2282.7	86.5
11	12.5	802.5	1400	1251.6	50.2
12	12.5	1000.0	1400	1251.6	40.3

vertical force of gravity, w, and the other the variable resistance of the air, $\frac{w}{g} \times \frac{A}{C} v^2$, acting in the tangent. Figure 6 represents the trajectory, which is, of course, a plane curve, under the foregoing suppositions, and Figure 6(a) represents the two forces acting upon the projectile at any point, the resistance of the air being denoted by $\frac{w}{g} f$, in which f is the retardation, $\frac{dv}{dt}$, which we are now taking as proportional to v^2

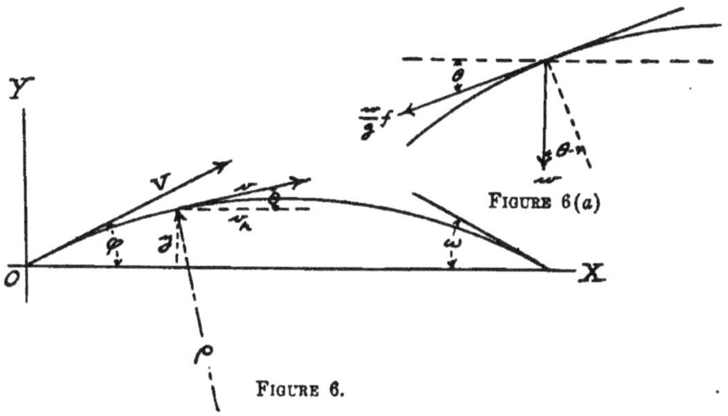

FIGURE 6(a)

FIGURE 6.

70. Taking vertical and horizontal axes at the point of departure, O, let V be the initial velocity, ϕ the angle of departure, v the velocity at any point whose coordinates are (x, y), and v_h the horizontal component of the velocity at that point. ρ is the radius of curvature of the curve at that point. Then, letting $k = \frac{A}{C}$ in equation (18), we can put $\frac{dv}{dt} = -kv^2$, and, since w has no horizontal component, the acceleration parallel to the axis of X is given by

$$\frac{d^2x}{dt^2} = -kv^2 \cos \theta \tag{19}$$

but $\frac{d^2x}{dt^2} = \frac{dv_h}{dt}$, $v \cos \theta = v_h$, and $v = \frac{ds}{dt}$; whence (19) may be written

$$\frac{dv_h}{dt} = -kv_h \frac{ds}{dt}. \tag{20}$$

$$\frac{dv_h}{v_h} = -kds \tag{21}$$

and integrating (21) between corresponding limits of v_h and s we get

$$\log_e v_h \Big]_{v_h}^{V\cos\phi} = -ks \Big]_s^0 \qquad \log_e \frac{V\cos\phi}{v_h} = ks \qquad v_h = V\cos\phi\, e^{-ks} \tag{22}$$

Next resolving along the normal, since the acceleration towards the center of curvature is given by the expression $\frac{v^2}{\rho}$, ρ being the radius of curvature at that point, we have

$$\frac{v^2}{\rho} = g \cos \theta \tag{23}$$

But $v = v_h \sec\theta$, and $\rho = -\frac{ds}{d\theta}$, whence (23) may be written

$$v_h^2 \sec^2\theta\, d\theta = -g \cos\theta\, ds = -g dx \text{ (as } dx = ds \cos\theta); \sec^2\theta\, d\theta = -\frac{g dx}{v_h^2} \quad (24)$$

Now substituting in (24) the value of v_h given in (22), we get

$$\sec^2\theta\, d\theta = -\frac{g}{V^2 \cos^2\phi} \epsilon^{2ks} dx \quad (25)$$

71. In the case of the flat trajectory, in which the angle of departure does not exceed 4° or 5°, the difference between the values of s and x is so small that it may be practically disregarded, and x may be substituted for s in (25), giving, after integration,*

$$\tan\theta\Big]_\phi^\theta = -\frac{g}{2kV^2\cos^2\phi}\epsilon^{2kx}\Big]_0^x \qquad \tan\theta = \tan\phi - \frac{g}{2kV^2\cos^2\phi}(\epsilon^{2kx} - 1) \quad (26)$$

But ϵ^{2kx}, when expanded by Maclaurin's theorem, equals †

$$1 + 2kx + 2k^2x^2 + \tfrac{4}{3}k^3x^3 + \ldots\ldots$$

so that

$$\epsilon^{2kx} - 1 = 2kx(1 + kx + \tfrac{2}{3}k^2x^2 + \ldots.)$$

whence, substituting in (26) and writing $\frac{dy}{dx}$ for $\tan\theta$, we have

$$\frac{dy}{dx} = \tan\phi - \frac{gx}{V^2\cos^2\phi}(1 + kx + \tfrac{2}{3}k^2x^2 + \ldots.)$$

or, integrating between corresponding limits of x and y,

$$y = x\tan\phi - \frac{gx^2}{2V^2\cos^2\phi}(1 + \tfrac{2}{3}kx + \tfrac{1}{3}k^2x^2 + \ldots.) \quad (27)$$

But the greatest value of kx is always a small fraction in any trajectory flat enough to justify the substitution of x for s which has already been made; hence we may neglect the terms beyond k^2x^2 in the expansion, and write for the equation to the trajectory in air when $a = 2$

Equation to trajectory in air when $a=2$.

$$y = x\tan\phi - \frac{gx^2}{2V^2\cos^2\phi}(1 + \tfrac{2}{3}kx + \tfrac{1}{3}k^2x^2) \quad (28)$$

---

* The integration in paragraph 71 is as follows: From (25)

$$\int_\phi^\theta \sec^2\theta\, d\theta = -\frac{g}{V^2\cos^2\phi}\int_0^x \epsilon^{2kx} dx$$

From calculus we know that $\int \sec^2\theta\, d\theta = \tan\theta + C_1$, C_1 being the constant of integration. From calculus we know that $\int \epsilon^y dy = \epsilon^y + C_2$, C_2 being the constant of integration. Now let $y = 2kx$ and the above becomes

$$\int \epsilon^{2kx} d(2kx) = 2k\int \epsilon^{2kx} dx = 2k\epsilon^{2kx} + C_2$$

whence

$$\int \epsilon^{2kx} dx = \frac{1}{2k}\int \epsilon^{2kx} d(2kx) = \frac{1}{2k}\epsilon^{2kx} + C_2$$

The integration between the limits given above therefore becomes

$$(\tan\theta + C_1) - (\tan\phi + C_1) = -\frac{g}{V^2\cos^2\phi}\left[\left(\frac{1}{2k}\epsilon^{2kx} + C_2\right) - \left(\frac{1}{2k}\epsilon^0 + C_2\right)\right]$$

or

$$\tan\theta = \tan\phi - \frac{g}{V^2\cos^2\phi} \times \frac{1}{2k}\left(\epsilon^{2kx} - 1\right)$$

† The expansion in paragraph 71 is: From either algebra or calculus we have that

$$\epsilon^y = 1 + y + \frac{y^2}{\lfloor 2} + \frac{y^3}{\lfloor 3} + \frac{y^4}{\lfloor 4} + \ldots.\text{etc.}$$

whence, if we let $y = 2kx$ we have

$$\epsilon^{2kx} = 1 + 2kx + \frac{4k^2x^2}{2} + \frac{8k^3x^3}{3 \times 2} + \frac{16k^4x^4}{4 \times 3 \times 2} + \ldots.\text{etc.}$$

or

$$\epsilon^{2kx} = 1 + 2kx(1 + kx + \tfrac{2}{3}k^2x^2 + \tfrac{1}{3}k^3x^3 + \ldots.\text{etc.})$$

72. Comparing this equation with (2), it will be seen that its first two terms represent the trajectory in vacuum, and that it only differs from the latter by having other terms, subtractive like the second, and containing higher powers of k and x.

73. The value of k in the equation to the trajectory in air (28) just deduced is, as already stated, $\frac{A}{C}$, where A is the experimentally determined coefficient, and $C=\frac{w}{\delta c d^2}$ is the ballistic coefficient. As a matter of general interest, it may be stated that, for the value of $A=0.0001316$, the value assigned to A by Mayevski when $a=2$, the value of k for our naval guns from the 6-pounder up to the 13″ gun, varies from about 0.00011006 to about 0.00002022, for the standard projectile and standard density of the air.

The ratio n

74. If we put $y=0$ in equation (28), we get for values of x, one equal to zero, denoting the origin, and another, the range X, given by

$$X(1+\tfrac{2}{3}kX+\tfrac{1}{3}k^2X^2)=\frac{V^2\sin 2\phi}{g} \qquad (29)$$

But the second member of (29) is the range in vacuum for the same initial velocity, V, and the same angle of departure, ϕ, so we see that the expression

$$1+\tfrac{2}{3}kX+\tfrac{1}{3}k^2X^2=\frac{X(\text{in vacuum})}{X(\text{in air})}$$

This ratio will be found to play an important part in many ballistic problems, and will hereafter be designated by the letter n. Hence we have for the range in air the expression

$$X=\frac{V^2\sin 2\phi}{gn} \qquad (30)$$

or, if it be desired to find the value of n for a given range,

$$n=\frac{V^2\sin 2\phi}{gX} \qquad (31)$$

75. Since k is a very small fraction, the value of n, which is evidently unity for $X=0$, increases slowly with X, and for moderate values of X is only slightly greater than unity. These deductions follow from the form of the equation

$$1+\tfrac{2}{3}kX+\tfrac{1}{3}k^2X^2=n$$

Assumptions made.

76. It is well to summarize here that the following suppositions have been made in deriving the equation to the trajectory in air when $a=2$, and these suppositions must be held to be correct in all consideration of this equation; and the equation is inaccurate to whatever degree results from the lack of correctness of any one or more of these assumptions:

1. That $a=2$, and that the corresponding value of A is correct.
2. That the axis of the projectile coincides with the tangent to the trajectory at every point, and that the resistance of the air will therefore act along the same tangent.
3. That the curve is so flat that we may consider $dx=ds$ without material error.
4. That kx is so small in value that any term involving powers higher than k^2x^2 may be neglected.

77. The following examples show the form for work under the formulæ derived in this chapter. It must be remembered, be it again said, that these formulæ are derived on the assumptions given in the preceding paragraph, and results obtained by their use are therefore only approximately correct for the usual present-day initial velocities.

For a 6″ gun, given that the initial velocity is 2600 f. s., and that an angle of departure of 4° 14′ 30″ gives a range of 7000 yards, to compute the value of the ratio between the ranges in vacuum and in air for that angle of departure; that is, the value of n.

$$n=\frac{V^2 \sin 2\phi}{gX}$$

$V=2600$	log 3.41497	2 log 6.82994
$2\phi=8°\ 29'\ 00''$		sin 9.16886 − 10
$g=32.2$	log 1.50786	colog 8.49214 − 10
$X=21000$	log 4.32222	colog 5.67778 − 10
$n=1.4748$		log 0.16872

78. Given that the angle of departure for the 12″ gun of 2900 f. s. initial velocity ($w=870$ pounds; $c=0.61$) for a range of 10,000 yards is 4° 13′ 12″, compute the approximate value of the ordinate at a distance of 2000 yards from the gun, and compare it with the ordinate in vacuum at the same point for the same angle of departure.

In vacuum $\quad y=x\tan\phi-\dfrac{gx^2}{2V^2\cos^2\phi}$

In air $\quad y=x\tan\phi-\dfrac{ngx^2}{2V^2\cos^2\phi}$ where $n=\dfrac{V^2\sin 2\phi}{gX}$

Work in Vacuum.

$x=6000$	log 3.77815		2 log 7.55630
$\phi=4°\ 13'\ 12''$	tan 8.86797 − 10	sec 0.00118	2 sec 0.00236
$g=32.2$			log 1.50786
2		log 0.30103	colog 9.69897 − 10
$V=2900$	log 3.46240	2 log 6.92480	2 colog 3.07520 − 10
442.710	log 2.64612		
69.294			log 1.84069
$y=373.416$			

Work in Air.

From work in vacuum; $x\tan\phi=442.71$ and $\dfrac{gx^2}{2V^2\cos^2\phi}=69.294$.

$V=2900$	log 3.46240	2 log 6.92480
$2\phi=8°\ 26'\ 24''$		sin 9.16665 − 10
$g=32.2$		colog 8.49214 − 10
$X=30000$	log 4.47712	colog 5.52288 − 10
$n=1.2778$		log 0.10647
$\dfrac{gx^2}{2V^2\cos^2\phi}=69.294$		log 1.84069
$\dfrac{ngx^2}{2V^2\cos^2\phi}=88.544$		log 1.94716
$x\tan\phi=442.710$		
$y=354.166$		

Ordinate at 2000 yards ...... { In vacuum ...... 373.416 feet. / In air .... 354.166 feet.

EXAMPLES.

1. Determine the value of the radius of curvature of the trajectory at the point of departure for a muzzle velocity of 2000 f. s., and an angle of departure (1) of 3°, and (2) of 8°.

Answers. For 3°, 124,390 feet. For 8°, 125,443 feet.

2. In the two cases given in Example 1 preceding, the striking velocities are 1600 f. s. and 1240 f. s., respectively, and the angles of fall are 3° 29′ and 11° 08′, respectively. Compute the radii of curvature at the point of fall.

Answers. For 3°, 79,648.5 feet. For 8°, 48,667.0 feet.

3. Using the equation to the trajectory in air when $a=2$, compute the value of n and the approximate angle of departure in each of the following cases:

Problem.	DATA.				ANSWERS.	
	Gun. In.	Value of k.	Initial Velocity. f. s.	Range. Yds.	n.	Angle of departure.
1............	6	0.00004738	2400	1000	1.101	0° 32′
2............	6	0.00004738	2400	2000	1.216	1 03
3............	6	0.00004738	2400	3000	1.345	1 56
4............	8	0.00003369	2400	1000	1.071	0 31
5............	8	0.00003369	2400	2000	1.148	1 06
6............	8	0.00003369	2400	3000	1.233	1 47
7............	10	0.00002632	2400	1000	1.055	0 30
8............	10	0.00002632	2400	2000	1.114	1 04
9............	10	0.00002632	2400	3000	1.177	1 42
10...........	12	0.00002229	2400	1000	1.046	0 30
11...........	12	0.00002229	2400	2000	1.095	1 03
12...........	12	0.00002229	2400	3000	1.147	1 39

4. A 6″ gun with 2900 f. s. initial velocity gave a measured range of 5394 yards for an angle of departure of 3° 03′ 51″. Compute the value of n from the firing.

Answer. $n=1.72290$.

5. A 6″ gun with 2900 f. s. initial velocity gave a measured range of 2625 yards for an angle of departure of 1° 07′ 49″. Compute the value of n from the firing.

Answer. $n=1.308$.

6. Given the data in the first six columns of the following table, compute the ordinates of the trajectory for each of the given abscissæ, in both vacuum and air, using the equation to the trajectory when $a=2$. In working in air, first determine the value of n for the given range corresponding to the given angle of departure, then determine the value of k from this by using the formula $n=1+\frac{3}{4}kX$ (neglecting the square and higher powers of kX), and the required ordinates by the use of the value of k thus found:

Problem.	DATA.						ANSWERS.	
							Ordinates in feet.	
	Gun. In.	Initial velocity. f. s.	Weight of projectile. Lbs.	Angle of departure.	Range. Yds.	Abscissa. Yds.	Vacuum.	Air.
1	12	2800	850	2° 11′	5000	1000	95.9	95.0
2	12	2800	850	2 11	5000	2000	154.7	147.7
3	12	2800	850	2 11	5000	3000	176.5	153.0
4	12	2800	850	2 11	5000	4000	161.4	105.5
5	12	2800	850	2 11	5000	5000	100.2	000.0
6	6	2900	100	1 17	3000	1000	50.0	48.2
7	6	2900	100	1 17	3000	2000	63.5	51.7
8	6	2000	100	1 17	3000	3000	46.5	00.0
9	3	2800	13	1 01	2000	500	22.0	21.5
10	3	2800	13	1 01	2000	1000	34.8	30.7
11	3	2800	13	1 01	2000	1500	38.3	24.5
12	3	2800	13	1 01	2000	2000	32.5	00.0

CHAPTER 5.

APPROXIMATE DETERMINATION OF THE VALUES OF THE ELEMENTS OF THE TRAJECTORY IN AIR WHEN MAYEVSKI'S EXPONENT IS EQUAL TO 2. THE DANGER SPACE AND THE COMPUTATION OF THE DATA CONTAINED IN COLUMN 7 OF THE RANGE TABLES.

New Symbols Introduced.

h.... Height of target in feet.

S.... Danger space in feet or yards according to work.

79. Before presenting for discussion the more exact computations of the elements of the trajectory by the use of the ballistic tables, we will in this chapter deduce formulæ by means of which the values of those elements can be determined with a sufficient degree of approximation for certain purposes; and it will be seen later that a few of these formulæ are sufficiently exact in their results to enable us to use them practically. Remember that the inaccuracies in these formulæ result from the assumptions upon which the derivation of the equation to the trajectory in air was based, as enumerated in paragraph 76 of the preceding chapter. For our present purposes we will take as the equation to the trajectory in air the one given in (28), but simplified by the omission of higher powers of kx than the first. The equation then becomes

$$y=x\tan\phi-\frac{gx^2}{2V^2\cos^2\phi}\left(1+\tfrac{2}{3}kx\right) \qquad (32)$$

In this equation k can no longer be considered as strictly constant, but its value, when found for any one value of ϕ, may be used over a considerable range of values of ϕ, since it increases slowly with increases of range, provided the trajectory be reasonably flat. We shall still denote by n the ratio of the range in vacuum to the range in air, which is now given by

$$n=1+\tfrac{2}{3}kX$$

Approximate horizontal range. **80.** To determine the approximate horizontal range, put $y=0$ in (32), and solve for x. An x factor will divide out, so one value of x is zero, for the origin, as was to be expected, and the remaining equation is

$$\frac{gX}{2V^2\cos^2\phi}\left(1+\tfrac{2}{3}kX\right)=\tan\phi \qquad (33)$$

It is at once apparent that this is an awkward equation for logarithmic work, and furthermore not very accurate for work with five place logarithmic tables owing to the decimal value of k.

Angle of fall. **81.** Differentiating (32) we get

$$\frac{dy}{dx}=\tan\theta=\tan\phi-\frac{gx}{V^2\cos^2\phi}(1+kx) \qquad (34)$$

But the angle of fall, ω, is the negative of the value of θ at the point of fall, where $x=X$, hence

$$\tan\omega=-\tan\phi+\frac{gX}{V^2\cos^2\phi}(1+kX)$$

and since $\dfrac{2V^2\sin\phi\cos\phi}{g}=nX$, this may be written

$$\tan\omega=-\tan\phi+\frac{2\tan\phi}{n}(1+kX)=\tan\phi\left(\frac{2+2kX-n}{n}\right)$$

Also from $1+\tfrac{2}{3}kX=n$ we get $2kX=3(n-1)$, whence

$$\tan\omega=\tan\phi\left(2-\frac{1}{n}\right) \qquad (35)$$

From (35) we see that the angle of fall is always greater than the angle of departure, but can never reach double the latter.*

82. Returning to equation (22) and writing $\frac{dx}{dt}$ for v_h, and x for s, we have Time of flight.

$$\frac{dx}{dt} = V\cos\phi\epsilon^{-ks}$$

Separating the variables and integrating between corresponding limits †

$$\int_0^X \epsilon^{ks}dx = V\cos\phi\int_0^T dt \qquad \frac{\epsilon^{kX}-1}{k} = TV\cos\phi$$

Expanding ϵ^{kX} and neglecting higher powers than the second ‡

$$X\left(1+\frac{kX}{2}\right) = TV\cos\phi$$

but from $1+\frac{2}{3}kX=n$ we get that $1+\frac{kX}{2}=\frac{3n+1}{4}$, therefore

$$T = \frac{3n+1}{4}\times\frac{X}{V\cos\phi} \qquad (36)$$

* This follows from the form of the expression, for from paragraph 75 we know that $n = 1 + \frac{2}{3}kX + \frac{1}{3}k^2X^2$, from which we see that n is unity when $X = 0$ and increases very slowly with X, k being a very small decimal. Therefore $\frac{1}{n}$ is always less than unity and $2 - \frac{1}{n}$ is always greater than unity; and the angle of fall must therefore always be greater than the angle of departure. Also as n must always be greater than unity for any real range, then $\frac{1}{n}$ must always be a positive real number, and therefore the value of $2-\frac{1}{n}$ must always be less than 2; therefore the angle of fall can never become twice as great as the angle of departure.

† The integration in paragraph 82 is as follows: From integral calculus

$$\int \epsilon^y dy = \epsilon^y + C$$

C being the constant of integration. Now let $y = kX$ and we have

$$\int \epsilon^{kX}dX = \frac{1}{k}\int \epsilon^{kX}d(kX) = \frac{1}{k}(\epsilon^{kX}) + C$$

Therefore $\int_0^X \epsilon^{kX}dX = V\cos\phi\int_0^T dt$

becomes $\left(\frac{\epsilon^{kX}}{k}+C\right)-\left(\frac{\epsilon^0}{k}+C\right) = (V\cos\phi\times T + C_1) - (V\cos\phi\times 0 + C_1)$

C_1 being the constant of integration in the second term. The above becomes

$$\frac{\epsilon^{kX}-1}{k} = VT\cos\phi$$

‡ The expansion of ϵ^{kX} following the integration is as follows: From either calculus or algebra we know that

$$\epsilon^y = 1 + y + \frac{y^2}{2} + \frac{y^3}{3}+\ldots.\text{etc.}$$

and substituting kX for y, and neglecting the higher powers than the square, we have

$$\epsilon^{kX} = 1 + kX + \frac{k^2X^2}{2}$$

whence $\epsilon^{kX} - 1 = kX + \frac{k^2X^2}{2}$

and $\frac{\epsilon^{kX}-1}{k} = X + \frac{kX^2}{2} = X\left(1+\frac{kX}{2}\right)$

whence $X\left(1+\frac{kX}{2}\right) = VT\cos\phi$

8. A 6″ ogival-headed projectile, weight 70 pounds, is fired through screens 150 yards apart, and its velocities at the first and at the second pairs of screens are 1846 f. s. and 1790 f. s., respectively. A 6″ flat-headed projectile of the same weight is fired through the same screens, and gives velocities of 1929 f. s. and 1790 f. s., respectively. What was the resistance of each projectile? If the first was a standard projectile, what was the coefficient of form of the second?

Answers. First, $R = 491.82$ pounds.
Second, $R = 1248.65$ pounds.
Coefficient of form of second $= 2.5388$.

9. A 12″ projectile, weight 850 pounds, gave measured velocities of 1979 f. s. and 1956 f. s. at points 500 feet apart. What was the mean resistance of the air? If the density of the air at the time of firing was 1.02 times the standard density, what would be the resistance in a standard atmosphere?

Answers. $R_f = 2389.0$ pounds. $R_s = 2342.2$ pounds.

10. Determine the resistance of the air to and the consequent retardation of a standard 3″ projectile, weight 13 pounds, when moving: (1) at 2800 f. s.; (2) at 2000 f. s.

Answers. (1) Resistance $= 250.34$ pounds. Retardation $= 620.09$ f. s.
(2) Resistance $= 142.67$ pounds. Retardation $= 353.38$ f. s.

11. Determine the resistance of the air and the consequent retardation in the following cases. (Standard atmosphere; and $c = 1.00$ in each case.)

Problem.	DATA. Projectile. *d.* In.	*w.* Lbs.	Velocity. f. s.	ANSWERS. Resistance. Lbs.	Retardation. f. s.
1	4	33	2800	445.1	434.3
2	4	33	2000	253.6	247.3
3	6	100	2800	1001.4	322.4
4	6	100	2000	570.7	183.8
5	8	250	2800	1780.2	229.3
6	8	250	2000	1014.5	130.7
7	10	500	2800	2781.5	179.1
8	10	500	2000	1585.2	102.1
9	12	850	2800	4005.4	151.7
10	12	850	2000	2282.7	86.5
11	12.5	802.5	1400	1251.6	50.2
12	12.5	1000.0	1400	1251.6	40.3

vertical force of gravity, w, and the other the variable resistance of the air, $\frac{w}{g} \times \frac{A}{C} v^2$, acting in the tangent. Figure 6 represents the trajectory, which is, of course, a plane curve, under the foregoing suppositions, and Figure 6(a) represents the two forces acting upon the projectile at any point, the resistance of the air being denoted by $\frac{w}{g} f$, in which f is the retardation, $\frac{dv}{dt}$, which we are now taking as proportional to v^2

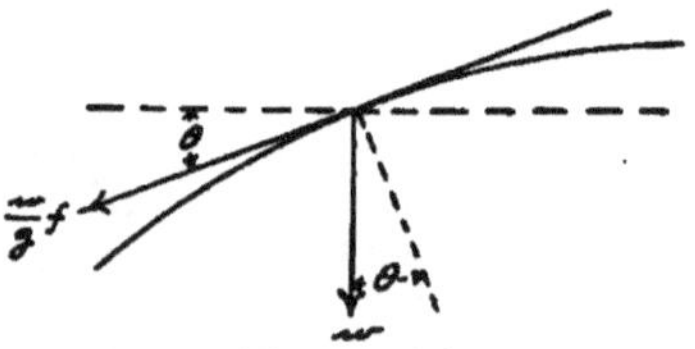

FIGURE 6(a)

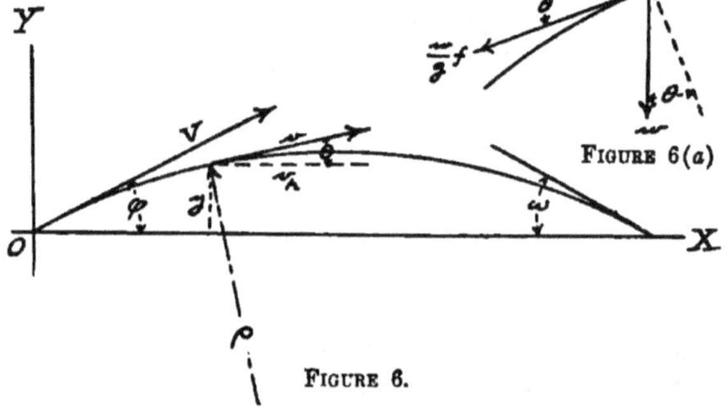

FIGURE 6.

70. Taking vertical and horizontal axes at the point of departure, O, let V be the initial velocity, ϕ the angle of departure, v the velocity at any point whose coordinates are (x, y), and v_h the horizontal component of the velocity at that point. ρ is the radius of curvature of the curve at that point. Then, letting $k = \frac{A}{C}$ in equation (18), we can put $\frac{dv}{dt} = -kv^2$, and, since w has no horizontal component, the acceleration parallel to the axis of X is given by

$$\frac{d^2x}{dt^2} = -kv^2 \cos\theta \qquad (19)$$

but $\frac{d^2x}{dt^2} = \frac{dv_h}{dt}$, $v \cos\theta = v_h$, and $v = \frac{ds}{dt}$; whence (19) may be written

$$\frac{dv_h}{dt} = -kv_h \frac{ds}{dt}. \qquad (20)$$

$$\frac{dv_h}{v_h} = -k\,ds \qquad (21)$$

and integrating (21) between corresponding limits of v_h and s we get

$$\log_e v_h \Big]_{v_h}^{V\cos\phi} = -ks\Big]_s^0 \qquad \log_e \frac{V\cos\phi}{v_h} = ks \qquad v_h = V\cos\phi\, e^{-ks} \qquad (22)$$

Next resolving along the normal, since the acceleration towards the center of curvature is given by the expression $\frac{v^2}{\rho}$, ρ being the radius of curvature at that point, we have

$$\frac{v^2}{\rho} = g\cos\theta \qquad (23)$$

87. If the value of n be known, k may be found from $n = 1 + \frac{3}{2}kX$, and then by substituting the proper value of x in the equation to the trajectory (32), the corresponding value of y, the ordinate of the trajectory at a distance x from the gun may be computed; and this was the way in which the last problems in the examples under the last chapter were worked. If, however, we know the angles of departure corresponding to various ranges (which data is contained in the range table for the gun) the approximate value of y for any value of x, for the trajectory for a given range, may be more readily found as follows. Referring to Figure 7, let (x', y') be the coordinates of the point M on the trajectory for which $\phi = \psi' + p$. Then, by the principle of the rigidity of the trajectory, if the angle of departure were ψ', the horizontal range would equal OM, or what is practically the same thing, x'. Consequently, if we take from the range table the angle of departure for a range x', and subtract it from the angle of departure for the given trajectory, the result will be the angle p. Then $y' = x' \tan p$.

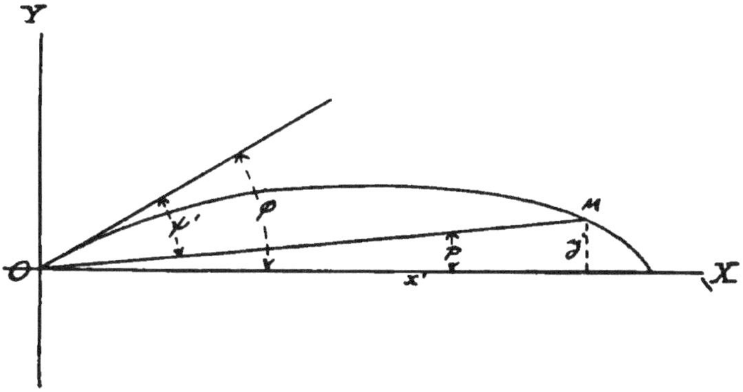

FIGURE 7.

88. By the term "danger space" is meant an interval of space, between the point of fall and the gun, such that the target will be hit if situated at any point in that space. In other words, **it is the distance from the point of fall through which a target of the given height can be moved directly towards the gun and still have the projectile pass through the target.** Therefore, within the range for which the maximum ordinate of the trajectory does not exceed the height of the target, the danger space is equal to the range, and such range is known as the "danger range." Referring to Figure 8, $AH = S$ is the danger space for a target of height $AB = h$, in the case of the trajectory OBH. It will be seen from Figure 8 that, when the value of h is very small in comparison with the range, the danger space is given with sufficient accuracy by the formula **Danger space.**

$$S = h \cot \omega \qquad (40)$$

72. Comparing this equation with (2), it will be seen that its first two terms represent the trajectory in vacuum, and that it only differs from the latter by having other terms, subtractive like the second, and containing higher powers of k and x.

73. The value of k in the equation to the trajectory in air (28) just deduced is, as already stated, $\frac{A}{C}$, where A is the experimentally determined coefficient, and $C=\frac{w}{\delta c d^2}$ is the ballistic coefficient. As a matter of general interest, it may be stated that, for the value of $A=0.0001316$, the value assigned to A by Mayevski when $a=2$, the value of k for our naval guns from the 6-pounder up to the 13" gun, varies from about 0.00011006 to about 0.00002022, for the standard projectile and standard density of the air.

The ratio n

74. If we put $y=0$ in equation (28), we get for values of x, one equal to zero, denoting the origin, and another, the range X, given by

$$X(1+\tfrac{2}{3}kX+\tfrac{1}{2}k^2X^2)=\frac{V^2 \sin 2\phi}{g} \qquad (29)$$

But the second member of (29) is the range in vacuum for the same initial velocity, V, and the same angle of departure, ϕ, so we see that the expression

$$1+\tfrac{2}{3}kX+\tfrac{1}{2}k^2X^2=\frac{X(\text{in vacuum})}{X(\text{in air})}$$

This ratio will be found to play an important part in many ballistic problems, and will hereafter be designated by the letter n. Hence we have for the range in air the expression

$$X=\frac{V^2 \sin 2\phi}{gn} \qquad (30)$$

or, if it be desired to find the value of n for a given range,

$$n=\frac{V^2 \sin 2\phi}{gX} \qquad (31)$$

75. Since k is a very small fraction, the value of n, which is evidently unity for $X=0$, increases slowly with X, and for moderate values of X is only slightly greater than unity. These deductions follow from the form of the equation

$$1+\tfrac{2}{3}kX+\tfrac{1}{2}k^2X^2=n$$

Assumptions made.

76. It is well to summarize here that the following suppositions have been made in deriving the equation to the trajectory in air when $a=2$, and these suppositions must be held to be correct in all consideration of this equation; and the equation is inaccurate to whatever degree results from the lack of correctness of any one or more of these assumptions:

1. That $a=2$, and that the corresponding value of A is correct.
2. That the axis of the projectile coincides with the tangent to the trajectory at every point, and that the resistance of the air will therefore act along the same tangent.
3. That the curve is so flat that we may consider $dx=ds$ without material error.
4. That kx is so small in value that any term involving powers higher than k^2x^2 may be neglected.

77. The following examples show the form for work under the formulæ derived in this chapter. It must be remembered, be it again said, that these formulæ are derived on the assumptions given in the preceding paragraph, and results obtained by their use are therefore only approximately correct for the usual present-day initial velocities.

$2-\frac{1}{n}=1.25785$ .... log 0.09963
$3n=4.0422$
$3n+1=5.0422$ .... log 0.70262
$3n-1=3.0422$ ..log 0.48319.................................... colog 9.51681 − 10
$\phi=3^\circ\ 02'\ 24''$ ....tan 8.72516 − 10.. sec 0.00061
4 ....log 0.60206.................. colog 9.39794 − 10
$X=16500$ .... log 4.21748
$V=2600$ ....log 3.41497.................. colog 6.58503 − 10.. log 3.41497
2 .... log 0.30103
$\omega=3^\circ\ 49'\ 19''$ ....tan 8.82479 − 10
$T=8.011$ .... log 0.90368
$v_\omega=1709.3$ .... log 3.23281

$\omega=3^\circ\ 49'\ 19''$.
$T=8.011$ seconds.
$v_\omega=1709.3$ f. s.

To find the approximate co-ordinates of the vertex for the trajectory given above.

$$x_0=\frac{\sqrt{1+3n(n-1)}-1}{3(n-1)}X;\quad y_0=\frac{gT^2}{8}$$

$n=1.3474$
$3n=4.0422$ ..log 0.60662
$n-1=0.3474$ ..log 9.54083 − 10
$3(n-1)=1.0422$ .... log 0.01795...... colog 9.98205 − 10
$3n(n-1)=1.4043$ ..log 0.14745
$1+3n(n-1)=2.4043$ ..log 0.38099
$\sqrt{1+3n(n-1)}=1.5506$. ½ log 0.19050
$\sqrt{1+3n(n-1)}-1=0.5506$ .... log 9.74084 − 10
$X=16500$ .... log 4.21748
$x_0=8716$ .... log 3.94037
$T=8.011$ ...log 0.90368......2 log 1.80736
$g=32.2$ .... log 1.50786
8 ....log 0.90309...... colog 9.09691 − 10
$y_0=258.30$ .... log 2.41213

$x_0=2905.3$ yards.
$y_0=258.30$ feet.

For the conditions given in the preceding problem, to find the danger space for a target 20 feet high. There are two formulæ possible, of which the longer is the more exact, and is the one used in computing the values of the danger space for a 20-foot target given in Column 7 of the range tables. It should be used whenever exactness is required. We will compute by both and compare the results.

$$S=h\cot\omega\qquad S=h\cot\omega\left(1+\frac{h\cot\omega}{X}\right)$$

$h=20$ ....log 1.30103

$\omega=3°\ 49'\ 19''$ .....cot 1.17519

$S=h\cot\omega=299.38$ ....log 2.47622......log 2.47622..........log 2.47622

$X=16500$..........................log 4.21748

$\dfrac{h\cot\omega}{X}=0.0181$ ....log 8.25875−10

$\dfrac{h\cot\omega}{X}+1=1.0181$ ....log 0.00779

$S=304.8$ ....log 2.48402

By approximate formula...... 99.795 yards.
By more exact formula.......101.600 yards.

The variation in the above more exact result from the value given in the range table is due to the fact that the value of the angle of fall used above is only approximate.

Standard problem. Throughout this book, in working sample problems showing the computation of the data for the range tables, the work will be done in each case for what will be known as the "standard problem" of the book. This will be for a range of 10,000 yards, for the 12″ gun for which $V=2900$ f. s., $w=870$ pounds, and $c=0.61$. This is the gun for which the range table is Bureau of Ordnance Pamphlet No. 298; which table is given in full in the edition of the Range and Ballistic Tables, printed for the use of midshipmen in connection with this text book. For this gun and range, we know, by methods that will be explained later, that the angle of fall, ω, is 5° 21′ 10″; therefore, to determine the danger space for a target 20 feet high, at the given range, the work for getting the data in Column 7 of the Range Table is as follows:

$$S=h\cot\omega\left(1+\frac{h\cot\omega}{X}\right)$$

As we desire our result in yards, however, we may reduce all units of measurement in the formula to yards, and the expression then becomes

$$S_{20}=\frac{h}{3}\cot\omega\left(1+\frac{\frac{h}{3}\cot\omega}{R}\right)$$

$\dfrac{h}{3}=6.6667$ .... log 0.82391..........log 0.82391

$\omega=5°\ 21'\ 10''$ .... cot 1.02827..........cot 1.02827

$R=10000$ ......log 4.00000......colog 6.00000−10

$\dfrac{\frac{h}{3}\cot\omega}{R}=0.0071$ .... log 7.85218−10

$1+\dfrac{\frac{h}{3}\cot\omega}{R}=1.0071$ ....log 0.00307

$S_{20}=71.655$ yards ....log 1.85525

91. We can now make a comparison between the trajectory in vacuum and that in air for the same initial velocity and angle of departure.

Figure 9 represents on the same scale the trajectories in air and in vacuum of a 12″ projectile weighing 870 pounds, $c=0.61$, fired with an initial velocity of 2900 f. s., at an angle of departure of 4° 13.2′; the range in vacuum for this angle of departure being 38315.3 feet (12771.7 yards), and in air of standard density, being 30,000 feet or 10,000 yards. In the figure the ordinates of both curves are exaggerated ten times as compared with the abscissæ, in order that the curve may be seen.

If gravity did not act, the projectile would move in the tangent to the curve OQ_1Q_2, and in traveling the horizontal distance $x = OA$, would rise to the height

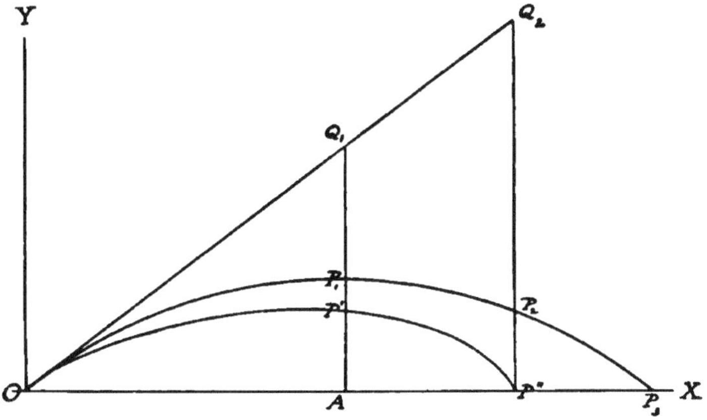

FIGURE 9.

Comparison between Trajectory in Vacuum and that in Air for same ϕ and same *I. V.*

$AQ_1 = x \tan \phi$. In this case, assuming $x = 20{,}000$ feet from the gun, we would have:

$x = 20000$ .... log 4.30103
$\phi = 4°\ 13.2'$ .... tan 8.86797 − 10

$y = 1475.7$ feet .... log 3.16900

The attraction of gravity, however, pulls the projectile down $Q_1P_1 = \frac{gX^2}{2V^2 \cos^2 \phi}$ while it moves OA horizontally, and so for the ordinate of the trajectory in vacuum we have

$$AP_1 = y_1 = x \tan \phi - \frac{gx^2}{2V^2 \cos^2 \phi}$$

We have already computed the value of $x \tan \phi$ as above and found it to be 1475.7 feet. Therefore, computing the second term of the right-hand member of the above equation, we have

$g = 32.2$ .... log 1.50786
$x = 20000$ .... log 4.30103 ...... 2 log 8.60206
2 .... log 0.30103 ...... colog 9.69897 − 10
$v = 2900$ .... 2 colog 3.07520 − 10
$\phi = 4°\ 13.2'$ .... 2 sec 0.00236

$\frac{gx^2}{2V^2 \cos^2 \phi} = 769.93$ feet .... log 2.88645
$x \tan \phi = 1475.7$ feet

$AP_1 = y_1 = x \tan \phi - \frac{gx^2}{2V^2 \cos^2 \phi} = 705.8$ feet

When the resistance of the air also acts, retarding the motion of the projectile, it takes longer for it to move OA horizontally, and so gravity has longer to act, and it has fallen the further distance

$$P_1P' = \frac{gx^2}{2V^2 \cos^2 \phi} \left(\tfrac{2}{3}kx + \tfrac{1}{2}k^2x^2\right)$$

and the ordinate of the trajectory in air is

$$AP' = y_2 = x \tan \phi - \frac{gx^2}{2V^2 \cos^2 \phi} \left(1 + \tfrac{2}{3}kx + \tfrac{1}{2}k^2x^2\right)$$

or

$$y_2 = x \tan \phi - \frac{gnx^2}{2V^2 \cos^2 \phi}$$

in which

$$n = \frac{V^2 \sin 2\phi}{gX}$$

$V = 2900$		2 log	6.92480
$2\phi = 8°\ 26.4'$		sin	9.16646−10
$g = 32.2$		colog	8.49214−10
$X = 30000$	log 4.47712	colog	5.52288−10
$n = 1.277$		log	0.10628
$\frac{gx^2}{2V^2 \cos^2 \phi} =$		log	2.88645
$\frac{gnx^2}{2V^2 \cos^2 \phi} = 983.4$		log	2.99273
$x \tan \phi = 1475.7$			
$y_2 = 492.3$			

In the particular case represented, the projectile reached the ground after having traveled, in air, the horizontal distance $X = OP'' = 30{,}000$ feet; but if it had moved in vacuum it would, at that range, have been at P_2, at a height of 481.2 feet above P''.

$$P_2P'' = x \tan \phi - \frac{gx^2}{2V^2 \cos^2 \phi} \quad \text{(in vacuum)}$$

so at $x = 30{,}000$ feet, we solve for P_2P''

$x = 30000$	log 4.47712	2 log	8.95424
$\phi = 4°\ 13.2'$	tan 8.86797	2 sec	0.00236
$g = 32.2$		log	1.50786
2		colog	9.69897−10
$V = 2900$		2 colog	3.07520−10
$x \tan \phi = 2213.5$	log 3.34509		
$\frac{gx^2}{2V^2 \cos^2 \phi} = 1732.3$		log	3.23863
$P_2P'' = 481.2$ feet			

$$n = \frac{\text{Range in vacuum}}{\text{Range in air}}, \text{ whence range in vacuum} = nX$$

$n = 1.277$	log	0.10628
$X = 30000$	log	4.47712
Range in vacuum = 38315.83	log	4.58340

The exaggeration of the ordinates in order to present a serviceable figure, as well as the arithmetical results, shows how flat is the trajectory, according to the most modern standards. It may also be noted from the figure, as we have already pointed out, that the vertex of the curve in air is reached after a shorter horizontal travel than is the case for the trajectory in vacuum.

EXAMPLES.

1. From the data given in the first four columns of the following table, compute the value of n, and thence the approximate values of the angle of fall, time of flight and striking velocity in each case.

Problem.	DATA.				ANSWERS.			
	Gun. In.	Initial velocity. f. s.	Angle of departure.	Range. Yds.	n.	Angle of fall.	Time of flight. Secs.	Striking velocity. f. s.
1........	6	2900	1° 07′ 49″	2625	1.308	1° 24′	3.34	1984
2........	6	2900	3 03 51	5394	1.723	4 21	8.62	1391
3........	4	2900	1 07 26	2600	1.313	1 24	3.32	1973
4........	4	2900	3 03 47	5166	1.798	4 25	8.56	1320
5........	4	2900	5 02 58	6599	2.313	7 53	13.60	977
6........	*	2000	1 33 00	1000	2.239	2 24	2.90	700
7........	12	2400	3 33 00	5900	1.249	4 15	8.77	1747
8........	12	2250	1 11 00	2000	1.082	1 16	2.83	2004
9........	13	2300	1 08 00	2000	1.083	1 13	2.77	2046

* Small arm.

2. A 6″ gun, with 2900 f. s. initial velocity, with an angle of departure of 1° 07′ 49″, gives a range of 2625 yards, an angle of fall of 1° 24′ 00″ and a time of flight of 3.34 seconds. Find the coordinates of the vertex and the danger space for a target 20 feet high.

Answers. $x_0 = 1382$ yards. $y_0 = 45$ feet. $S = 301$ yards.

3. A 6″ gun with 2900 f. s. initial velocity, with an angle of departure of 3° 03′ 51″, gives a range of 5394 yards, a time of flight of 8.61 seconds and an angle of fall of 4° 22′ 00″. Find the coordinates of the vertex, also the danger space for a target 20 feet high.

Answers. $x_0 = 2926$ yards. $y_0 = 298$ feet. $S = 89$ yards.

4. The range table of the 3″ gun of 2800 f. s. initial velocity gives an angle of departure of 1° 01′ 00″ for a range of 2000 yards, and shows that the range changes 100 yards for each 4′ change in the angle of departure. Find the ordinates of the trajectory for that range at points 1700, 1800 and 1900 yards from the gun.

Answers. 5.93, 4.19, 2.21 yards, respectively.

5. The angle of fall for the 2000-yard trajectory of the 3″ gun is 1° 26′ 00″. Compute the danger space for a target 20 feet high.

Answer. $S = 302$ yards.

CHAPTER 6.

THE TIME AND SPACE INTEGRALS; THE COMPUTATION OF THEIR VALUES FOR DIFFERENT VELOCITIES, AND THEIR USE IN APPROXIMATE SOLUTIONS.

New Symbols Introduced.

T_v.... Value of the time integral in seconds for remaining velocity v.
T_V.... Value of the time integral in seconds for initial velocity V.
S_v.... Value of the space integral in feet for remaining velocity v.
S_V.... Value of the space integral in feet for initial velocity V.

92. Returning now to Mayevski's equation for the retardation due to atmospheric resistance, namely, $\frac{dv}{dt} = -\frac{A}{C} v^a$, we see that it may be written, after separation of the variables **Time integral.**

$$dt = -\frac{C}{A} \times \frac{dv}{v^a} \tag{42}$$

in which A and a are Mayevski's constants and C is the reduced ballistic coefficient

$$\left(C = \frac{fw}{\delta c d^2}\right)$$

Suppose now a projectile to travel so nearly horizontally that its velocity is not affected by gravitation, but is only affected by air resistance; then the integration of (42) between corresponding limits, t_1 and t_2 of t, and v_1 and v_2 of v, will give the elapsed time $(t_2 - t_1)$ corresponding to the loss of velocity $(v_1 - v_2)$. We will assume the velocity at the origin of time (v_1) to be 3600 f. s., as that is the upper limit of initial velocities for which the values of Mayevski's constants have been experimentally determined (3600 f. s. is also well above all present-day service initial velocities, and this point of origin will therefore answer all practical purposes until initial velocities are greatly increased over any present practice), and will therefore have $t_1 = 0$ seconds, and $v_1 = 3600$ f. s.; and we will designate by T_v the elapsed time from the origin until the velocity is reduced to v. Then we have

$$\int_0^{T_v} dt = -\frac{C}{A} \int_{3600}^{v} \frac{dv}{v^a} \tag{43}$$

by integrating which we get

$$T_v = \frac{C}{A} \times \frac{1}{a-1} \left(\frac{1}{v^{a-1}} - \frac{1}{(3600)^{a-1}}\right) \tag{44}$$

Substituting in (44) the values of A and a given in the first of Mayevski's special equations (14), we get

$$T_v = C \left(\frac{[2.65059]}{v^{0.55}} - 4.9502 \right)^* \tag{45}$$

and the value of this, computed for any value of v between 3600 f. s. and 2600 f. s., is the time in seconds which it takes for the air resistance to reduce the velocity of the projectile whose ballistic coefficient is C from 3600 f. s. to v f. s., when v lies between 3600 f. s. and 2600 f. s.

---

* The number enclosed in brackets is the logarithm of the constant and not the constant itself.

Below 2600 f. s. the values of A and a change to those given in the second of Mayevski's special equations (14), and with the new values the limits of integration change also, and we have

$$\int_{T_{2600}}^{T_v} dt = -\frac{C}{A}\int_{2600}^{v}\frac{dv}{v^a}$$

whence
$$T_v = T_{2600} + \frac{C}{A} \times \frac{1}{a-1}\left(\frac{1}{v^{a-1}} - \frac{1}{(2600)^{a-1}}\right)$$

which, after substituting the values of A and a, and that of T_{2600} as computed from (45), reduces to

$$T_v = C\left(\frac{[3.05870]}{v^{0.7}} - 3.6880\right)^*$$

and the value of this, computed for any value of v between 2600 f. s. and 1800 f. s. is the time in seconds it takes for the air resistance to reduce the velocity of a projectile whose ballistic coefficient is C from 3600 f. s. to v f. s., when v lies between 2600 f. s. and 1800 f. s.

Proceeding in a similar manner with the other values of A and a, each integration being performed between the limits which correspond to the particular values of A and a used, we obtain the following expressions for T_v:

v between 3600 f. s. and 2600 f. s.
$$T_v = C\left(\frac{[2.65059]}{v^{0.55}} - 4.9502\right)$$

v between 2600 f. s. and 1800 f. s.
$$T_v = C\left(\frac{[3.05870]}{v^{0.7}} - 3.6880\right)$$

v between 1800 f. s. and 1370 f. s.
$$T_v = C\left(\frac{[3.88074]}{v} - 1.8837\right)$$

v between 1370 f. s. and 1230 f. s.
$$T_v = C\left(\frac{[6.71807]}{v^2} + 0.8790\right) \qquad (46)^*$$

v between 1230 f. s. and 970 f. s.
$$T_v = C\left(\frac{[12.59607]}{v^4} + 2.6089\right)$$

v between 970 f. s. and 790 f. s.
$$T_v = C\left(\frac{[6.92553]}{v^2} - 1.8801\right)$$

v between 790 f. s. and 0 f. s.
$$T_v = C\left(\frac{[4.33011]}{v} - 15.460\right)$$

NOTE.—The above formulæ give numerical values to five places only. In actually computing the tables, the numerical values were carried out correctly to seven or more places.

Space integral. 93. Multiplying both sides of equation (42) by v, we get $v\,dt = -\frac{C}{A} \times \frac{dv}{v^{a-1}}$, and putting ds for $v\,dt$ in this, we have

$$ds = -\frac{C}{A} \times \frac{dv}{v^{a-1}} \qquad (47)$$

* The numbers enclosed in brackets are the logarithms of the constants and not the constants themselves.

and the integration of this equation between corresponding limits, s_1 and s_2 of s, and v_1 and v_2 of v, will give the space traversed (s_2-s_1), while the velocity is reduced by the atmospheric resistance from v_1 to v_2, supposing again that the path of the projectile is so nearly horizontal that the effect of gravitation on the velocity in the trajectory may be neglected. We will assume that the origin of space, as well as the origin of time, coincides with the value of 3600 f. s. for v, or $s_1=0$ and $v_1=3600$; and we will designate by S_v the space passed over from the origin to the point where the velocity is reduced to v. Thus we have

$$\int_0^{S_v} ds = -\frac{C}{A}\int_{3600}^{v}\frac{dv}{v^{a-1}}$$

which integrates to

$$S_v=\frac{C}{A}\times\frac{1}{a-2}\left(\frac{1}{v^{a-2}}-\frac{1}{(3600)^{a-2}}\right) \tag{48}$$

Substituting in (48) the values of A and a given in the first of Mayevski's special formulæ (14), we get

$$S_v=C(21780.9-[2.73774]v^{0.45})^* \tag{49}$$

and the value of this, computed for any value of v between 3600 f. s. and 2600 f. s., is the space in feet passed over by a projectile whose ballistic coefficient is C, while the atmospheric resistance reduces its velocity from 3600 f. s. to v f. s.

Proceeding similarly for the different values of A and a between the different limits of velocity, exactly as was done in the case of the time integrals, we obtain the following expressions for S_v:

$$\left.\begin{aligned}
&v \text{ between 3600 f. s. and 2600 f. s.}\\
&\qquad S_v=C(21780.9-[2.73774]v^{0.45})\\
&v \text{ between 2600 f. s. and 1800 f. s.}\\
&\qquad S_v=C(31227.1-[3.42668]v^{0.3})\\
&v \text{ between 1800 f. s. and 1370 f. s.}\\
&\qquad S_v=C(62875.3-[4.24296]\log v)\\
&v \text{ between 1370 f. s. and 1230 f. s.}\\
&\qquad S_v=C\left(\frac{[7.01910]}{v}+365.69\right)\\
&v \text{ between 1230 f. s. and 970 f. s.}\\
&\qquad S_v=C\left(\frac{[12.72101]}{v^2}+6034.5\right)\\
&v \text{ between 970 f. s. and 790 f. s.}\\
&\qquad S_v=C\left(\frac{[7.22656]}{v}-5571.4\right)\\
&v \text{ between 790 f. s. and 0 f. s.}\\
&\qquad S_v=C(158436.8-[4.69232]\log v)
\end{aligned}\right\} \tag{50}^*$$

NOTE.—The above formulæ give numerical values to five places only. In computing the tables, the numerical values were carried out correctly to seven or more places.

---

* The numbers enclosed in brackets are the logarithms of the constants and not the constants themselves.

94. T_v and S_v are known as the "time function" and "space function," respectively, and their values have been computed for values of v from 3600 f. s. to 500 f. s., on the supposition that C is unity, and their values for the different velocities will be found in Table I of the Ballistic Tables under the headings T_u and S_u, with the velocities in the column headed u as an argument. The reason for representing the velocities in this table by the symbol u will be explained in a subsequent chapter. To apply them to any projectile for any given atmospheric conditions it is only necessary to multiply the tabular values by the particular value of C for the given projectile and atmospheric conditions.

Meaning of S and T

95. It must be clearly borne in mind just what the values of T_u and S_u tabulated in these two columns mean; that is, that they are *the time elapsed and the space covered, respectively, while the velocity of the projectile whose ballistic coefficient is unity is being reduced from 3600 f. s. to v f. s. by the atmospheric resistance.* Therefore, if we wish to find how long it takes the atmospheric resistance to reduce the velocity of a projectile whose ballistic coefficient is unity from v_1 f. s. to v_2 f. s., we would find T_{v_1} and T_{v_2} from Table I, using the values of v_1 and v_2 as arguments in the column headed u, and then we would have $T=T_{v_2}-T_{v_1}$, and similarly for the space covered we would have $S=S_{v_2}-S_{v_1}$. If the value of the ballistic coefficient be not unity, then these two equations would become

$$T=C(T_{v_2}-T_{v_1}) \tag{51}$$
$$S=C(S_{v_2}-S_{v_1}) \tag{52}$$

96. The above can perhaps be best illustrated by a reference to Figure 10, which represents the complete trajectory from the point where $V=3600$ f. s. as an origin to its end, where $v_\omega=0$. Now remembering the assumption that the trajectory is

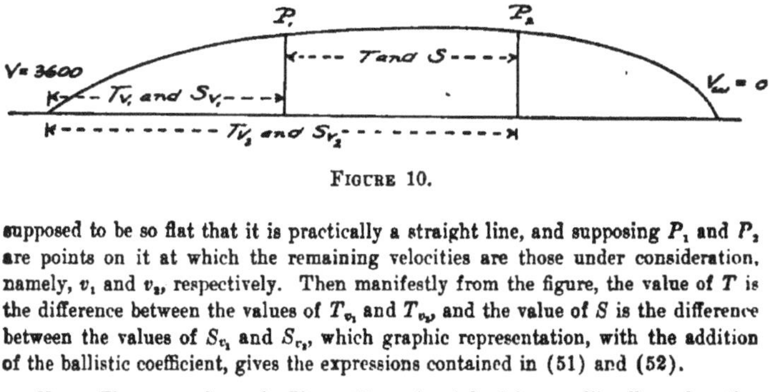

FIGURE 10.

supposed to be so flat that it is practically a straight line, and supposing P_1 and P_2 are points on it at which the remaining velocities are those under consideration, namely, v_1 and v_2, respectively. Then manifestly from the figure, the value of T is the difference between the values of T_{v_1} and T_{v_2}, and the value of S is the difference between the values of S_{v_1} and S_{v_2}, which graphic representation, with the addition of the ballistic coefficient, gives the expressions contained in (51) and (52).

NOTE.—The curve shown in Figure 10 must not be taken as literally and mathematically correct. It is simply used to illustrate the point. While the distances are marked as both T and S they do not literally represent both times and spaces.

97. Suppose we wish to find how long it will take the atmospheric resistance, under standard conditions, to reduce the velocity of a 6", 105-pound projectile from its initial velocity of 2600 f. s. to 2000 f. s., and through what space the projectile would travel while its velocity is being so reduced, the value of the ballistic coefficient being taken as unity. From Table I we see that the reduction from 3600 f. s. to 2600 f. s. would take 0.970 second, during which time the projectile would travel 2967.1 feet. That is, $T_{2600}=0.970$ second and $S_{2600}=2967.1$ feet. Similarly for the

$C=\frac{w}{\delta c d^2}$; $S=C(S_{v_2}-S_{v_1})$, whence $S_{v_1}=S_{v_2}-\frac{S}{C}$; $T=C(T_{v_2}-T_{v_1})$

$w=870$ .... log 2.93952
$\delta=0.997$ ....log 9.99870−10..colog 0.00130
$c=0.61$ ....log 9.78533−10..colog 0.21467
$d^2=144$ ....log 2.15836......colog 7.84164−10

$C=$ .... log 0.99713......colog 9.00287−10
$S=12000$ .... log 4.07918

$\frac{S}{C}=1208.0$ .... log 3.08205

$S_{v_2}=3227.5$ From Table I.

$S_{v_1}=2019.5$ hence
$v_1=2900$ f. s. From Table I.
Also $T_{v_2}=1.072$ From Table I.
$T_{v_1}=0.625$ From Table I.

$T_{v_2}-T_{v_1}=0.447$ .... log 9.65031−10
$C=$ .... log 0.99713

$T=4.4406$ .... log 0.64744

Therefore the initial velocity was 2900 f. s., and the elapsed time was 4.4406 seconds.

101. Again, suppose the projectile given in the preceding paragraph started with an initial velocity of 2900 f. s., and traveled for 3 seconds, under atmospheric conditions as given; how far did it go in that time?

$C=$as before. $T=C(T_{v_2}-T_{v_1})$, hence $T_{v_2}=\frac{T}{C}+T_{v_1}$; $S=C(S_{v_2}-S_{v_1})$

$C=$as in preceding paragraph........................colog 9.00287−10
$T=3$ .... log 0.47712

$\frac{T}{C}=0.302$ .... log 9.47999−10

$T_{v_1}=0.625$ From Table I.

$T_{v_2}=0.927$ hence
$v_2=2635$ f. s. From Table I.
Also $S_{v_2}=2853.6$ From Table I.
$S_{v_1}=2019.4$ From Table I.

$S_{v_2}-S_{v_1}=$ 834.2 ....log 2.92127
$C=$ ....log 0.99713

$S=8287$ ....log 3.91840

Therefore the space traversed was 2762.3 yards.

102. The foregoing methods are of course only strictly applicable to such parts of the trajectory as may without material error be considered as straight lines, since in deducing (51) and (52) we have entirely neglected the effect of gravitation. They will give sufficiently accurate results when applied to any arc of a trajectory if the length of the arc be not materially greater than the length of its chord, and if the latter's inclination to the horizontal be not greater than 10° to 15°; but they are principally applied to the entire trajectories of guns fired with angles of departure not exceeding 3° or 4°, giving the striking velocity and time of flight for ranges as great as 5000 yards, in the case of medium and large guns of high initial velocity, with as much accuracy as is obtainable by any other method of computation. It will

EXAMPLES.

NOTE.—The answers to these problems, being obtained by the use of formulæ and methods discussed in this chapter, all depend for their accuracy upon the correctness of the assumption that in every case the effect of gravity upon the flight of the projectile is negligible for the portion of the trajectory involved. They are, therefore, only accurate within the limits imposed by this assumption.

1. Given the data in the first five columns of the following table and two velocities; or one velocity and either S and T, compute the data in the other two of the last four columns.

Problem.	Projectile.			Atmosphere.		v_1. f. s.	v_2. f. s.	S. Feet.	T. Secs.
	d. In.	w. Lbs.	c.	Bar. In.	Ther. °F.				
A............	3	13	1.00	28.00	0	1150	935	3978.0	3.8810
B............	3	13	1.00	29.00	5	2700	2300	1763.3	0.7078
C............	4	33	0.67	30.00	10	2900	2552	3024.2	1.1110
D............	5	50	1.00	31.00	20	3150	2003	6720.9	2.6819
E............	5	50	0.61	30.00	30	3150	2561	5549.4	1.9556
F............	6	105	0.61	29.00	40	2600	2013	9779.2	4.2756
G............	6	105	1.00	28.00	50	2800	2247	5381.0	2.2253
H............	6	105	0.61	28.25	60	2800	2474	5289.8	2.0067
I............	7	165	1.00	29.50	70	2700	2313	4471.5	1.7897
J............	7	165	0.61	30.75	80	2700	2133	10799.0	4.4980
K............	8	260	0.61	31.00	90	2750	2541	4562.4	1.7241
L............	10	510	1.00	30.00	95	2700	2114	10942.0	4.5808
M............	10	510	0.61	29.00	100	2700	2316	11920.0	4.7642
N............	12	870	0.61	28.00	85	2900	2154	27530.0	11.0280
O............	13	1130	1.00	29.00	75	2000	1833	4746.7	2.4774
P............	13	1130	0.74	29.53	59	2000	1756	9042.8	4.8340
Q............	14	1400	0.70	30.00	52	2000	1900	3947.9	2.0289
R............	14	1400	0.70	29.00	45	2600	2343	8767.7	3.5527

2. Given the data contained in the first seven columns of the following table, compute the value of the coefficient of form of the projectile in each case.

Problem.	DATA.							ANSWERS.
	Projectile.		Value of δ.	Distance of pairs of screens from gun.*		Measured velocities at.		Value of c.
	d. In.	w. Lbs.		First pair. Feet.	Second pair. Yds.	First pair. f. s.	Second pair. f. s.	
A..........	3	13	1.057	75	500	1100	1017	1.00570
B..........	3	13	0.989	150	1000	2650	2000	1.00120
C..........	4	33	1.111	150	1500	2875	2390	0.67250
D..........	5	50	1.062	200	1500	3130	2399	1.01260
E..........	5	50	0.899	200	1200	3130	2830	0.59322
F..........	6	105	0.950	200	1200	2550	2348	0.62045
G..........	6	105	1.107	250	900	2750	2461	1.01390
H..........	6	105	1.009	250	800	2760	2020	0.60165
I..........	7	165	0.937	250	900	2650	2448	0.97983

* The distance given in these columns is in each case the distance from the muzzle of the gun to a point midway between the two screens composing the pair.

CHAPTER 7.

THE DIFFERENTIAL EQUATIONS GIVING THE RELATIONS BETWEEN THE SEVERAL ELEMENTS OF THE GENERAL TRAJECTORY IN AIR. SIACCI'S METHOD. THE FUNDAMENTAL BALLISTIC FORMULÆ. THE COMPUTATION OF THE DATA GIVEN IN THE BALLISTIC TABLES, AND THE USE OF THE BALLISTIC TABLES.

New Symbols Introduced.

u.... Pseudo velocity at any point of the trajectory in foot-seconds.
du.... Differential increment in u.
S_u.... Value of space function in feet for pseudo velocity u.
S_V.... Value of space function in feet for initial velocity V.
T_u.... Value of time function in seconds for pseudo velocity u.
T_V.... Value of time function in seconds for initial velocity V.
A_u.... Value of altitude function for pseudo velocity u.
A_V.... Value of altitude function for initial velocity V.
I_u.... Value of inclination function for pseudo velocity u.
I_V.... Value of inclination function for initial velocity V.

109. From the hypothesis already made in paragraph 69 that the resultant atmospheric resistance acts in the line of the projectile's axis, which itself coincides with the tangent to the trajectory at every point, it follows that the trajectory is a plane curve. For, if a vertical plane be passed through the gun and through any point of the trajectory, that plane will contain the only two forces acting upon the projectile while it is at that point, namely, gravity and the resistance of the air; and so their resultant will lie in that plane also, and there will be no force tending to draw the projectile from that plane, and so the next consecutive point of the curve must lie in the same plane also; and so on to the end.

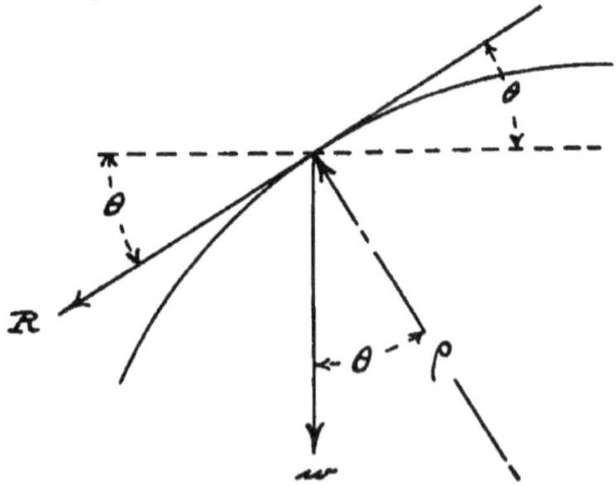

FIGURE 11.

Derivation of the differential equations.

110. Figure 11 represents a portion of the trajectory with the two forces acting upon the projectile, namely, its weight, w, acting vertically downward, and the resistance of the air, $R = \frac{w}{g} \times \frac{A}{C} v^n$, acting along the tangent to the curve in a direction opposite to that in which the projectile is moving. Kinetic equilibrium results from the balancing of these two forces by the inertia forces $\frac{w}{g} \times \frac{dv}{dt}$ acting in the tangent, and $\frac{w}{g} \times \frac{v^2}{\rho}$ acting in the normal, ρ being the radius of curvature of the curve at the point under consideration.* Resolving forces along the normal to the trajectory, the inertia force $\frac{w}{g} \times \frac{v^2}{\rho}$, commonly called the centrifugal force, must balance the resolved part of w along the same line, whence we have $\frac{w}{g} \times \frac{v^2}{\rho} = w \cos\theta$,

or
$$\frac{v^2}{\rho} = g\cos\theta \qquad (54)$$

In other words, the acceleration towards the center of curvature is the resolved part of g in that direction. But the radius of curvature $\rho = -\frac{ds^*}{d\theta}$, whence

$$v^2 d\theta = -g\cos\theta\, ds = -g dx, \text{ or } g dx = -v^2 d\theta \qquad (55)$$

111. Dividing each side of (55) by dt and putting v_h for $\frac{dx}{dt}$, we have

$$g v_h = -v^2 \frac{d\theta}{dt}, \text{ whence } g dt = -\frac{v^2 d\theta}{v_h} = -\frac{v^2 d\theta}{v\cos\theta},$$

whence
$$g dt = -v \sec\theta\, d\theta \qquad (56)$$

112. By putting $\cot\theta\, dy$ for dx in (55) we get

$$g\cot\theta\, dy = -v^2 d\theta \text{ or } g dy = -v^2 \tan\theta\, d\theta \qquad (57)$$

113. By putting $\cos\theta\, ds = dx$ in (55) we get

$$g\cos\theta\, ds = -v^2 d\theta \text{ or } g ds = -v^2 \sec\theta\, d\theta \qquad (58)$$

114. Now resolving horizontally, since the horizontal component of the atmospheric resistance, $\frac{w}{g} \times \frac{A}{C} v^n \cos\theta$, is the only force which acts to produce horizontal acceleration, $\frac{d^2x}{dt^2} = \frac{dv_h}{dt}$, which in this case is negative acceleration, we have

$$\frac{dv_h}{dt} = \frac{d(v\cos\theta)}{dt} = -\frac{A}{C} v^n \cos\theta$$

but from (56) we know that $g dt = -v\sec\theta\, d\theta$, therefore the above expression becomes

$$g d(v\cos\theta) = \frac{A}{C} v^{(n+1)} d\theta \qquad (59)$$

115. Grouping the expressions derived above together, we have *The differential equations.*

$$g d(v\cos\theta) = \frac{A}{C} v^{(n+1)} d\theta \qquad (60)$$
$$g dx = -v^2 d\theta \qquad (61)$$
$$g dt = -v\sec\theta\, d\theta \qquad (62)$$
$$g dy = -v^2 \tan\theta\, d\theta \qquad (63)$$
$$g ds = -v^2 \sec\theta\, d\theta \qquad (64)$$

and these equations, (60) to (64) inclusive, are the differential equations giving the relations between the several elements of the trajectory; and, could (60) be integrated, thus giving a finite relation between v and θ, one of those variables could

---

* See any standard work on the subject for the derivation of this expression.

be eliminated from equations (61) to (64) inclusive, and then values of x, y, t and s could all be obtained.

116. Since we cannot integrate (60), it is necessary to resort to methods of approximation, and a method devised by Major F. Siacci (Sē-ā-chē), of the Italian Army, has been generally adopted by artillerists because of its comparative simplicity and readiness of application. It is to be noted that in all the preceding chapters discussing the trajectory in air and deriving mathematical expressions in regard to it, we have dealt with approximate methods only, and we now see that we are again, and for our final and most approved methods, driven to fall back upon another approximate system. However, this one, Siacci's method, has been found to be accurate within all necessary limits for ordinary ballistic problems, and for our purposes we may consider it as exact, in contradistinction to the more approximate methods that we have hitherto considered. It should not be forgotten, however, that the method is not literally exact, and that it might be possible, under unusual and peculiar conditions, that results might vary appreciably from those actually existent in practice. It is not ordinarily necessary to consider this point, but should some unusual and peculiar problem present itself, it would be necessary to consider whether the conditions were such as to introduce material inaccuracies into results obtained by the ordinary methods.

117. Taking rectangular axes in the plane of fire; origin at the gun; X, as always, horizontal, and positive in the direction of projection; Y, as always, vertical, and positive upward; let V, in Figure 12, be the initial velocity, and ϕ the angle of departure, and let v be the remaining velocity at any point, P, of the trajectory. Revolving v horizontally, we have $v \cos \theta$, and, parallel to the line of departure

$$u = v \cos \theta \sec \phi \tag{65}$$

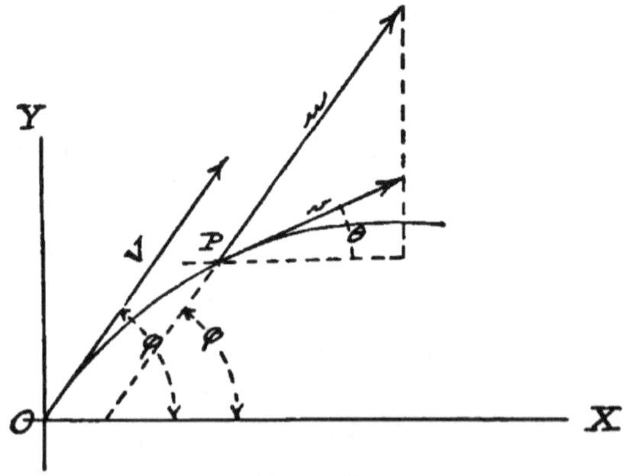

FIGURE 12.

Pseudo velocity. **118.** The quantity u, which is represented in Figure 12, is known as the "pseudo velocity" (see definition in paragraph 22), and its use in the solution of practical ballistic problems is due to Major Siacci, and is the essence of his method. It will readily be seen that $u = V$ at the origin, where $\theta = \phi$, and also at another point in the descending branch of the trajectory where $\theta = -\phi$. At the vertex, where $\theta = 0$, the pseudo velocity differs most from the true velocity, its value there being $u = v \sec \phi$, whence $$x=C(S_u-S_V) \tag{70}$$

in which S_u stands for $-\frac{1}{A}\int\frac{du}{u^{(a-1)}}$

121. Proceeding in exactly the same way with (62), we get

$$gdt=-u\cos\phi\sec^2\theta\,d\theta=-\frac{C}{\cos\phi}\times\frac{g}{A}\times\frac{du}{u^a}$$

or
$$\int_0^t dt=-\frac{C}{\cos\phi}\int_V^u\frac{1}{A}\times\frac{du}{u^a}$$

or
$$t=\frac{C}{\cos\phi}(T_u-T_V) \tag{71}$$

in which T_u stands for $-\frac{1}{A}\int\frac{du}{u^a}$

122. Now, multiplying (68) by the differential of (70), and putting dy for $\tan\theta\,dx$, we have

$$dy-\tan\phi\,dx=\frac{C^2}{2\cos^2\phi}(I_u-I_V)\times\frac{1}{A}\times\frac{du}{u^{(a-1)}}$$

and by putting $-\frac{1}{A}\int I_u\times\frac{du}{u^{(a-1)}}=A_u$, this becomes, after integrating,

$$y-x\tan\phi=-\frac{C}{2\cos^2\phi}[A_u-A_V-I_V(S_u-S_V)]$$

and, finally, dividing by (70), we get

$$\frac{y}{x}=\tan\phi-\frac{C}{2\cos^2\phi}\left(\frac{A_u-A_V}{S_u-S_V}-I_V\right) \tag{72}$$

Note that in this substitution that A_u means the A function of u, otherwise known as the altitude function, this A having of course nothing in common with the constant A on the other side of the equation.

The ballistic formulæ. 123. The formulæ given in equations (65), (68), (70), (71) and (72) are known as the ballistic equations, and are the ones on which are based all the principal problems in exterior ballistics. They are here repeated, grouped, for convenience, as follows:

$$x=C(S_u-S_V) \tag{73}$$

$$\frac{y}{x}=\tan\phi-\frac{C}{2\cos^2\phi}\left(\frac{A_u-A_V}{S_u-S_V}-I_V\right) \tag{74}$$

$$\tan\theta=\tan\phi-\frac{C}{2\cos^2\phi}(I_u-I_V) \tag{75}$$

$$t=\frac{C}{\cos\phi}(T_u-T_V) \tag{76}$$

$$v=u\cos\phi\sec\theta \tag{77}$$

124. These ballistic formulæ express the values of

(a) The two coordinates of any point of the trajectory;

(b) The tangent of the angle of inclination of the curve to the horizontal at any point of the trajectory:

(c) The time of flight to any point of the trajectory; and

(d) The remaining velocity at any point in the trajectory directly as functions of

1. A new variable, u, known as the pseudo velocity, and already defined;
2. The ballistic coefficient;
3. The angle of departure; and
4. The initial velocity.

well to have tabulated the values of $-\frac{2g}{A}\int_{3600}^{u}\frac{du}{u^{(a+1)}}$, making $I_{3600}=0$ instead of $I_{3600}=.03138$, as is the case with the integration performed as indicated for a lower limit of infinity. This would have made the series of values of the inclination function, like those of the space, time and altitude functions, begin at the imagined origin where $u=3600$ f. s., but as we deal entirely with differences, the point of origin is immaterial.

128. The equations from which I_u are computed are obtained by substituting successive values of A and a in

$$I_u=-\frac{2g}{A}\int\frac{du}{u^{(a+1)}}$$

and integrating, the first integration being between infinity and u (u from 3600 f. s. to 2600 f. s.); the second between 2600 and u (u from 2600 to 1800); the third between 1800 and u (u between 1800 and 1370); and so on; the results being as follows:

u between 3600 f. s. and 2600 f. s.

$$I_u=\frac{[4.00897]}{u^{1.55}}$$

u between 2600 f. s. and 1800 f. s.

$$I_u=\frac{[4.48170]}{u^{1.7}}+0.00452$$

u between 1800 f. s. and 1370 f. s.

$$I_u=\frac{[5.38806]}{u^{2}}+0.01776$$

u between 1370 f. s. and 1230 f. s.

$$I_u=\frac{[8.35032]}{u^{3}}+0.06083$$

u between 1230 f. s. and 970 f. s.

$$I_u=\frac{[14.30751]}{u^{5}}+0.10912$$

u between 970 f. s. and 790 f. s.

$$I_u=\frac{[8.55778]}{u^{3}}-0.05028$$

u between 790 f. s. and 0 f. s.

$$I_u=\frac{[5.83743]}{u^{2}}-0.41960$$

(78) The numbers enclosed in brackets are the logarithms of the constants and not the constants themselves.

NOTE.—The above formulæ give numerical values correct to five places only. In computing the tables the numerical values were carried out correctly to seven or more places.

The altitude function.

129. As explained in paragraph 122, A_u-A_V stands for the value of the definite integral $-\frac{1}{A}\int_V^u I_u\frac{du}{u^{(a-1)}}$, or, substituting for I_u its value of $-\frac{2g}{A}\int\frac{du}{u^{(a+1)}}$, we have

$$A_u-A_V=-\frac{2g}{A^2a}\int_V^u\frac{du}{u^{(2a-1)}}$$

and in order that the value of this integral may be found for any given values of V and u, the values of $-\frac{2g}{A^2 a}\int_{3600}^{u}\frac{du}{u^{(2n-1)}}$ have been computed for values of u from 3600 f. s. to 500 f. s., and will be found in Table I under the heading A_u, with values of u as arguments in the left-hand column. Then, as in the case of the space, time and inclination functions, we have always $A_{u_2}-A_{u_1}=A_{v_2}-A_{v_1}$, and the tabulated values of the altitude function may be used for either real or pseudo velocities indiscriminately, provided the proper argument be used.

130. The equations from which the values of A_u are computed are obtained by substituting the successive values of A and a in the expression

$$A_u=-\frac{2g}{A^2 a}\int\frac{du}{u^{(2n-1)}}$$

and integrating, exactly as was done in Chapter 6 in finding the values of T_v, except that the values of I_u to be substituted in the integral expression for the value of A_u-A_V must include the constants of integration whose values are given in (78). The results are:

u between 3600 f. s. and 2600 f. s.

$$A_u=\frac{[6.35853]}{u^{1.1}}-279.64$$

u between 2600 f. s. and 1800 f. s.

$$A_u=\frac{[7.23937]}{u^{1.4}}-[1.08179]u^{0.3}-39.264$$

u between 1800 f. s. and 1370 f. s.

$$A_u=\frac{[8.96777]}{u^2}-[2.49233]\log u+1052.0$$

u between 1370 f. s. and 1230 f. s.

$$A_u=\frac{[14.76736]}{u^4}+\frac{[5.80321]}{u}-57.984$$

u between 1230 f. s. and 970 f. s.

$$A_u=\frac{[26.60254]}{u^6}+\frac{[11.75890]}{u^3}+329.62$$

u between 970 f. s. and 790 f. s.

$$A_u=\frac{[15.18228]}{u^4}-\frac{[5.92791]}{u}+624.05$$

u between 790 f. s. and 0 f. s.

$$A_u=\frac{[9.86650]}{u^2}+[4.31515]\log u-68192.0$$

The numbers enclosed in brackets are the logarithms of the constants and not the constants themselves. (79)

NOTE.—The above formulæ give numerical values correct to five places only. In computing the tables the numerical values were carried out correctly to seven or more places.

131. In the preceding work in this chapter we have followed the methods given by Professor Alger in his most excellent book on Exterior Ballistics, which are the generally accepted methods, and have derived certain ballistic formulæ as given in equations (73) to (77) inclusive. We have also shown how the values of the space (S_u), time (T_u), inclination (I_u) and altitude (A_u) functions for varying values of the real or pseudo velocities have been computed and made readily available in Table I of the Ballistic Tables. Professor Alger accepts the results already obtained as being sufficient for all practical purposes, and uses these equations in the form in which we already have them (rearranged to suit each special problem) in the solution of ballistic problems. Colonel Ingalls, however, proceeded still further with the reduction of these formulæ, and by most noteworthy mathematical work succeeded in getting resulting expressions that vastly reduce the labor of the computer below that involved in the use of the formulæ as they stand above. These reductions are somewhat involved, but, when once carried through, so simplify the solutions of problems and reduce the labor connected therewith, that Ingalls' methods have become generally accepted for work of this nature. Their acceptance and use involved the computation of another extensive table, Table II of the Ballistic Tables, but with this table and Ingalls' formulæ, the work of the computer is reduced to a minimum. Ingalls' methods and formulæ may be more appropriately considered in the solution of certain special problems, and the study of them is therefore deferred to the next chapter.

Use of Table I. **132.** As an example of the use of Table I, let us suppose that it is desired to take from it the values of the four functions corresponding to a velocity, either real or pseudo, of 2727 f. s.

For determining the value of S_u, we have: For $u=2720$, $S_u=2581.1$, and the difference between that value and the value for the next tabulated value of u, namely, $u=2740$, is, by subtraction or as given in the difference column headed Δ_S, 63.4; that is, a change of 20 f. s. (at this part of the table; note the reduction in the tabulated intervals as the velocity decreases) in the velocity changes the value of the space function 63.4. (Note that the difference given in the Δ columns is in each case that between the value of the function on the same line and the one on the line next below it.) Therefore, for $u=2727$ f. s., we have

$$S_u=2581.1-\frac{63.4\times7}{20}=2581.1-22.2=2558.9$$

or

$$S_u=2517.7+\frac{63.4\times13}{20}=2517.7+41.2=2558.9$$

and similarly

$$A_u=97.94+\frac{3.05\times13}{20}=97.94+1.98=99.92$$

$$I_u=.04791+\frac{.00055\times13}{20}=.04791+.00036=.04827$$

$$T_u=.802+\frac{.023\times13}{20}=.802+.015=.817$$

133. And, similarly, suppose that we want to find the value of the real or pseudo velocity (which one it is depends upon the formula in use) corresponding to a value of $I_u=.05767$.

The nearest tabular value to this is $I_u=.05775$, corresponding to $u=2430$ f. s., from which, by interpolation,

$$u(\text{or } v)=2430+\frac{8\times10}{37}=2430+2.2=2432.2 \text{ f. s.}$$

134. If we had desired to find the value of A_u corresponding to the value of $I_u=.05767$ given above, we could find u as just described, and then find the value of A_u thus

$$A_u=151.46-\frac{1.97\times2.2}{10}=151.46-0.43=151.03$$

5. The 4000-yard trajectory of a 3" gun ($V=2800$ f. s., $w=13$ pounds) has $\phi=3°\ 10'$. What is the pseudo velocity at a point horizontally distant from the gun 2000 yards, and what is the time of flight to that point?

Answers. 1671 f. s.; 2.791 seconds.

6. The 4000-yard trajectory of a 6" gun ($V=2400$ f. s., $w=100$ pounds) has $\phi=2°\ 52'$. What is the pseudo velocity at a point horizontally distant from the gun 2000 yards, and what is the time of flight to that point?

Answers. 1829 f. s.; 2.856 seconds.

7. In the 4000-yard trajectory of a 5" gun ($V=2550$ f. s., $w=50$ pounds), $\phi=3°\ 01'$. What is the pseudo velocity at a point horizontally distant from the gun 2200 yards, and what is the inclination of the curve at that point?

Answers. 1683 f. s.; 0° 07' 12".

8. In the 6000-yard trajectory of a 6" gun ($V=2300$ f. s., $w=100$ pounds), $\phi=5°\ 53'$. What is the pseudo velocity after 1000 and after 2000 yards horizontal travel, and what are the ordinates of the trajectory at those distances?

Answers. 2010 and 1747 f. s.; 279 and 485 feet.

9. In the 3000-yard trajectory of a 3" gun ($V=2800$ f. s., $w=13$ pounds), $\phi=1°\ 53'$. What are the pseudo velocities and what the horizontal distances traveled after 1, 2 and 3 seconds flight?

Answers. 2276, 1898 and 1619 f. s.; 840, 1529 and 2117 yards.

10. Determine the reduced ballistic coefficient for a 10", 500-pound projectile of standard form, if the temperature and barometric height at the gun be 84° F. and 29.12", and the time of flight be 16 seconds. If the initial velocity be 2000 f. s., given the above time of flight, find the range and the pseudo velocity at the point of fall.

Answers. $C=5.432$; $R=7927$ yards; $u_\omega=1151$ f. s.

11. Determine the reduced ballistic coefficient for an 8", 250-pound projectile of standard form, the temperature being 46° F., and the barometer 30.11", the time of flight being 22 seconds. If the initial velocity be 2300 f. s. and the angle of departure be 11° 00', find u_ω from the given value of the time of flight, and then find the range. *Answers.* $C=3.8581$; $u_\omega=974.3$ f. s.; $R=9947$ yards.

CHAPTER 8.

THE DERIVATION AND USE OF SPECIAL FORMULÆ FOR FINDING THE ANGLE OF DEPARTURE, ANGLE OF FALL, TIME OF FLIGHT AND STRIKING VELOCITY FOR A GIVEN HORIZONTAL RANGE AND INITIAL VELOCITY; THAT IS, THE DATA CONTAINED IN COLUMNS 2, 3, 4 AND 5 OF THE RANGE TABLES. INGALLS' METHODS.

New Symbols Introduced.

u_ω.... Pseudo velocity at the point of fall.
v_ω.... Remaining velocity at point of fall, or striking velocity.
S_{u_ω}.... Value of the space function for pseudo velocity u_ω.
T_{u_ω}.... Value of the time function for pseudo velocity u_ω.
A_{u_ω}.... Value of the altitude function for pseudo velocity u_ω.
I_{u_ω}.... Value of the inclination function for pseudo velocity u_ω.
S_{u_0}.... Value of the space function for pseudo velocity u_0.
T_{u_0}.... Value of the time function for pseudo velocity u_0.
A_{u_0}.... Value of the altitude function for pseudo velocity u_0.
I_{u_0}.... Value of the inclination function for pseudo velocity u_0.
ΔS.... Difference between two values of the space function.
ΔT.... Difference between two values of the time function.
ΔA.... Difference between two values of the altitude function.
ΔI.... Difference between two values of the inclination function.

$z = \frac{x}{C}$ .... General expression for value of argument for Column 1 of Table II.

$Z = \frac{X}{C}$ .... Special expression for value of argument for Column 1 of Table II.

a...
b...
a'...
t'...
} General values of Ingalls' secondary functions.

A...
B...
A'...
T'...
$B' = \frac{B}{A}$...
A''...
} Special values of Ingalls' secondary functions for whole trajectory.

C_1, C_2, C_3, etc... Successive values of C. The same system of notation by subscripts also applies for successive approximate values of other quantities where such use of them is necessary.

136. As already deduced, the six fundamental ballistic formulæ are:

$$C=\frac{fw}{\delta c d^2} \tag{80}$$

$$x=C(S_u-S_V) \tag{81}$$

$$\frac{y}{x}=\tan\phi-\frac{C}{2\cos^2\phi}\left(\frac{A_u-A_V}{S_u-S_V}-I_V\right) \tag{82}$$

$$\tan\theta=\tan\phi-\frac{C}{2\cos^2\phi}\,(I_u-I_V) \tag{83}$$

$$t=C\sec\phi(T_u-T_V) \tag{84}$$

$$v=u\cos\phi\sec\theta \tag{85}$$

137. It will be seen from the above that special formulæ may be derived to fit all particular cases, which special formulæ will contain only the quantities contained in the above fundamental equations; that is, quantities that are either known or contained in the Ballistic Tables, or the values of which are to be found.

Transformation of ballistic formulæ. **138.** Let us apply these formulæ to the special case under consideration, that is, to the derivation of special formulæ for computing the values shown in Columns 2, 3, 4 and 5 of the range tables. For the complete horizontal trajectory we may substitute in the fundamental equations as given above, as follows: $x=X$, $y=0$, $t=T$, $v=v_\omega$ and $\theta=-\omega$. If we make these substitutions we get:

From (80)
$$C=\frac{fw}{\delta c d^2} \tag{86}$$

From (81)
$$S_{u_\omega}=S_V+\frac{X}{C} \tag{87}$$

From (82)
$$\tan\phi=\frac{C}{2\cos^2\phi}\left(\frac{A_{u_\omega}-A_V}{S_{u_\omega}-S_V}-I_V\right)$$

$$\frac{2\sin\phi\cos^2\phi}{\cos\phi}=\sin 2\phi=C\left(\frac{A_{u_\omega}-A_V}{S_{u_\omega}-S_V}-I_V\right) \tag{88}$$

From (83)
$$\tan(-\omega)=\tan\phi-\frac{C}{2\cos^2\phi}\,(I_{u_\omega}-I_V)$$

and substituting in this the value of tan ϕ given above we get

$$\tan\omega=\frac{C}{2\cos^2\phi}\left(I_{u_\omega}-\frac{A_{u_\omega}-A_V}{S_{u_\omega}-S_V}\right) \tag{89}$$

From (84)
$$T=C\sec\phi(T_{u_\omega}-T_V) \tag{90}$$

From (85)
$$v_\omega=u_\omega\cos\phi\sec\omega \tag{91}$$

139. Considering the above expressions, we may note that, with the exception of the quantities that we desire to find, all the quantities contained in them are either known or else may be found in the Ballistic Tables (exclusive of Table II). Professor Alger uses them in this form, in his text book, for computing the values of the unknown quantities in those expressions. As an example of his methods we will now solve a problem by the use of the above formulæ as they stand, and without using Table II of the Ballistic Tables.

Alger's method. **140.** For the 12″ gun, $V=2900$ f. s., $w=870$ pounds, $c=0.61$, atmosphere at standard density, to compute the values of the angle of departure, angle of fall, time of flight, and striking velocity, for a horizontal range of 10,000 yards (without using Table II) by Alger's method.

$$C = \frac{fw}{cd^2}\ ;\ S_{u_\omega} = S_V + \frac{X}{C}\ ;\ \sin 2\phi = C\left(\frac{A_{u_\omega} - A_V}{S_{u_\omega} - S_V} - I_V\right)$$

$$\tan \omega = \frac{C}{2\cos^2\phi}\left(I_{u_\omega} - \frac{A_{u_\omega} - A_V}{S_{u_\omega} - S_V}\right);\ T = C \sec\phi (T_{u_\omega} - T_V)\ ;\ v_\omega = u_\omega \cos\phi \sec\omega$$

We cannot get a correct result without determining the value of f; but let us disregard that for the moment nevertheless, and proceed for the present as though $f=1$. The value of C for standard conditions could be taken from Table VI, and this will usually be done to save labor, but for this first problem we will compute it.

$w = 870$ .... log 2.93952
$c = 0.61$ ....log 9.78533−10..colog 0.21467
$d^2 = 144$ ....log 2.15836......colog 7.84164−10

$C =$ .... log 0.99583......colog 9.00417−10
$X = 30000$ .... log 4.47712

$\frac{X}{C} = \Delta S = 3029.0$ .... log 3.48129

$S_V = 2019.4$	From Table I.		
$S_{u_\omega} = 5048.4$	$A_{u_\omega} = 253.05$	$T_{u_\omega} = 1.880$	
$u_\omega = 2014.8$	$A_V = 75.09$	$T_V = 0.625$	$I_V = 0.4388$
	$\Delta A = 177.96$	$\Delta T = 1.255$	

$\Delta A = 177.96$ ....log 2.25032
$\Delta S = 3029$ ....log 3.48129

$\frac{\Delta A}{\Delta S} = .05875$ ....log 8.76903−10
$I_V = .04388$

$\frac{\Delta A}{\Delta S} - I_V = .01487$ ....log 8.17231−10

$\Delta T = 1.255$ .... log 0.09864
$C =$ ....log 0.99583...... log 0.99583

$2\phi = 8°\ 28'\ 09''$......................sin 9.16814−10
$\phi = 4°\ 14'\ 05''$.................................... sec 0.00119

$T = 12.464$ .... log 1.09566

Let us now determine the approximate maximum ordinate for the above trajectory. To do this we have

$$Y = \frac{gT^2}{8}$$

$T = 12.464$ ....log 1.09566................2 log 2.19132
$g = 32.2$ .... log 1.50786
8 ....log 0.90309................colog 9.09691−10

$Y = 625.3$ .... log 2.79541
$\frac{2}{3}Y = 416.87$ feet, whence, from Table V, $f = 1.0105$.

We will now repeat the preceding process, using the found value of f to correct the original value of C, in which f was considered as unity, and introducing consecutive subscripts to the several symbols to represent successive approximate found values.

$C_1 =$ ....log 0.99583
$f_1 = 1.0105$ ....log 0.00454

$C_2 =$ ....log 1.00037............colog 8.99963 − 10
$X = 30000$ .... log 4.47712

$\Delta S = 2997.4$ .... log 3.47675
$S_V = 2019.4$ From Table I.

$S_{u_\omega} = 5016.8$	$A_{u_\omega} = 250.60$	$T_{u_\omega} = 1.864$	$I_{u_\omega} = .07722$
$u_\omega = 2022.9$	$A_V = 75.09$	$T_V = 0.625$	$I_V = .04388$
	$\Delta A = 175.51$	$\Delta T = 1.239$	

$\Delta A = 175.51$ ....log 2.24430
$\Delta S = 2997.4$ ....log 3.47675
$\dfrac{\Delta A}{\Delta S} = .05855$ ....log 8.76755 − 10
$I_V = .04388$
$\dfrac{\Delta A}{\Delta S} - I_V = .01467$ .....log 8.16643 − 10

$I_{u_\omega} = .07722$
$\dfrac{\Delta A}{\Delta S} = .05855$
$I_{u_\omega} - \dfrac{\Delta A}{\Delta S} = .01867$

$I_{u_\omega} - \dfrac{\Delta A}{\Delta S} = .01867$ .... log 8.27114 − 10
$\Delta T = 1.239$ ....log 0.09307
$C_2 =$ ....log 1.00037....... log 1.00037.......log 1.00037
2 ....colog 9.69897 − 10
$u_\omega = 2022.9$ ....log 3.30[illegible]
$2\phi = 8°\ 26'\ 35''$ ..sin 9.16680 − 10
$\phi = 4°\ 13'\ 18''$ ....2 sec 0.00236.......sec 0.00118..cos 9.99[illegible]
$\omega = 5°\ 22'\ 00''$ .... tan 8.97284 − 10..............sec 0.001[illegible]
$T = 12.434$ ....log 1.09462
$v_\omega = 2026.3$..log 3.30671

Results. $\phi = 4°\ 13'\ 18''$
$\omega = 5°\ 22'\ 00''$
$T = 12.434$ seconds.
$v_\omega = 2026.3$ foot-seconds.

It will be noted that the two values of T found above, first by using f as unity, and second by using the first found value of f, differ so very slightly that a value of f found from the second value of T would not be sufficiently different from the first to materially affect the value of the ballistic coefficient. Therefore we concluded that the limit of accuracy of the method had been reached, and proceeded to use the values already derived to find the values of the other unknown elements. For a longer range it would probably be necessary to repeat the work again, and get a second, and perhaps even a third value of f.

141. The above is the method employed by Professor Alger, and it will be noted that considerable mathematical work is required. Colonel Ingalls further reduced the formulæ in such a way that, while the original work of reduction of formulæ is much greater and is somewhat involved, nevertheless the work to be done by the computer in practical cases is very much reduced, thereby reducing the amount of labor involved and time expended in computing a range table, as well as reducing the probability of error in doing the work. He computed an additional table, Table II of the Ballistic Tables, to assist in this. We will now follow through his method.

142. From equation (83) we have

$$\tan\phi=\tan\theta+\frac{C}{2\cos^2\phi}(I_u-I_V)$$

and if we substitute this value in (82) we get

$$\frac{y}{x}=\tan\theta+\frac{C}{2\cos^2\phi}\left(I_u-\frac{A_u-A_V}{S_u-S_V}\right) \qquad (92)$$

143. Let us now introduce into the fundamental equations (80) to (85) inclusive, and into (92) four so-called "secondary functions," as follows: **Ingalls' secondary functions in general.**

$$a=\frac{A_u-A_V}{S_u-S_V}-I_V \qquad (93)$$

$$b=I_u-\frac{A_u-A_V}{S_u-S_V} \qquad (94)$$

$$a'=a+b=I_u-I_V \qquad (95)$$

$$t'=T_u-T_V \qquad (96)$$

The fundamental equations then become

From (80) $$C=\frac{fw}{\delta cd^2} \qquad (97)$$

From (81) $$x=C(S_u-S_V) \qquad (98)$$

From (82) and (92)

$$\frac{y}{x}=\tan\phi-\frac{aC}{2\cos^2\phi}=\tan\theta+\frac{bC}{2\cos^2\phi} \qquad (99)$$

From (83) $$\tan\theta=\tan\phi-\frac{a'C}{2\cos^2\phi} \qquad (100)$$

From (84) $$t=Ct'\sec\phi \qquad (101)$$

From (85) $$v=u\cos\phi\sec\theta \qquad (102)$$

144. Now Ingalls' Ballistic Tables, Table II, give values for a, b, a' and t' for different values of V and of $z=\frac{x}{C}$, so that, in any given problem, knowing V and x, we can compute the value of z from the proper formula, and then take the corresponding values of the secondary functions from Table II.

145. For a complete horizontal trajectory, however, certain other simplifications become possible, if we have Table II available for use. The relations between ϕ, ω, T and r_ω, and the other elements of the trajectory involve the complete curve from the gun to the point of fall in the same horizontal plane with the gun. Under these conditions we have that **Secondary functions for entire trajectory.**

$$y=0;\quad \frac{y}{x}=0;\quad \text{and } \theta=-\omega$$

When this is the case our equations become:

$$C=\frac{fw}{\delta cd^2} \qquad (103)$$

$$X=C(S_{u_\omega}-S_V) \qquad (104)$$

$$\tan\phi=\frac{C}{2\cos^2\phi}\left(\frac{A_{u_\omega}-A_V}{S_{u_\omega}-S_V}-I_V\right)$$

or, as $2\tan\phi\cos^2\phi=2\sin\phi\cos\phi=\sin 2\phi$

$$\sin 2\phi=C\left(\frac{A_{u_\omega}-A_V}{S_{u_\omega}-S_V}-I_V\right) \qquad (105)$$

$$\tan\omega=-\tan\phi+\frac{C}{2\cos^2\phi}(I_{u_\omega}-I_V)$$

Substituting in this the value of $\tan\phi$ from the first expression used in deducing equation (105) we get

$$\tan\omega=\frac{C}{2\cos^2\phi}\left(I_{v_\omega}-\frac{A_{v_\omega}-A_V}{S_{v_\omega}-S_V}\right) \tag{106}$$

$$T=C\sec\phi(T_{v_\omega}-T_V) \tag{107}$$

$$v_\omega=u_\omega\cos\phi\sec\omega \tag{108}$$

146. Now let us take another set of secondary functions, or rather a set of special values of the regular secondary functions, as follows:

$$A=\frac{A_{v_\omega}-A_V}{S_{v_\omega}-S_V}-I_V \tag{109}$$

$$B=I_{v_\omega}-\frac{A_{v_\omega}-A_V}{S_{v_\omega}-S_V} \tag{110}$$

$$A'=A+B=I_{v_\omega}-I_V \tag{111}$$

$$T'=T_{v_\omega}-T_V \tag{112}$$

Ingalls' ballistic formulæ.

147. Now by combining these special values of the secondary functions given in equations (109) to (112) inclusive with the formulæ in (103) to (108) inclusive, we get

$$C=\frac{fw}{\delta c d^2} \tag{113}$$

$$X=C(S_{v_\omega}-S_V) \tag{114}$$

$$\sin 2\phi=AC \tag{115}$$

From (115) we have that $C=\dfrac{\sin 2\phi}{A}$, and we also have that

$$\tan\omega=\frac{BC}{2\cos^2\phi}\text{ or } C=\frac{2\cos^2\phi\tan\omega}{B}$$

therefore $$\frac{\sin 2\phi}{A}=\frac{2\cos^2\phi\tan\omega}{B}$$

whence we have $$\tan\omega=B'\tan\phi \tag{116}$$

in which $B'=\dfrac{B}{A}$, and tabulated values of $\log B'$ will be found in Table II.

$$T=CT'\sec\phi \tag{117}$$

$$v_\omega=u_\omega\cos\phi\sec\omega \tag{118}$$

148. It will readily be seen, as already stated, that, as A, B, A' and T' are only special values of a, b, a' and t', the values of both sets of secondary functions, the general and the special, may be taken from Table II, provided we enter the table with the proper argument in each case, that is, with the corresponding values of V and of $z=\dfrac{x}{C}$ or $Z=\dfrac{X}{C}$, z being of course for any point in the trajectory whose abscissa is x, and Z being for the entire horizontal trajectory, where the abscissa is the range X. And, as stated above, values of $\log B$ may also be taken from Table II as required, with the same arguments.

149. We therefore see that, by certain somewhat involved mathematical processes, Colonel Ingalls put the ballistic formulæ into such form that their use involves the least possible amount of logarithmic work. By the use of equations (113) to (118) inclusive, we can find the value of ϕ, ω, T and v_ω, by Ingalls' methods, provided we have Table II from which to take the values of the secondary functions, and provided the several columns of the Ballistic Tables, under the several symbols which we used to represent these integral expressions.

Let us consider the trajectory *ONPQ* in Figure 13. The ballistic formulæ represent certain relations existing between the elements of the trajectory at any point. For the point *P*, for instance, the equations would contain certain integral expressions which we have called the "secondary functions," and have represented by a, a', b, b' (of which the logarithm is always used), and t', and also the pseudo velocity u. Now for this particular point, *P*, the integral expressions in each of the formulæ must be integrated between the proper limits for that particular point and their numerical values for this special case determined; a space integral being given the limits x and 0 for instance. Instead of having to actually perform this integration in each case, however, Colonel Ingalls has already done the work for us; and we simply compute the value of the argument $z=\frac{x}{C}$, and, knowing V, we can take from Table II each of the numerical results of integration between the proper limits that we desire. So for each point of the curve there is a special numerical value of each of the integrals represented by the symbols a, a', etc.

In a subsequent chapter we will use values so found for different points of the curve, but for the present we are dealing with the entire trajectory, and want to find the values of the functions for the point of fall, *Q*. Therefore, x becomes X, the range, and our integral expressions are represented by A, A', B, B' and T', and u becomes u_ω. Knowing V, we therefore compute the value of $Z=\frac{X}{C}$, and thence from Table II we

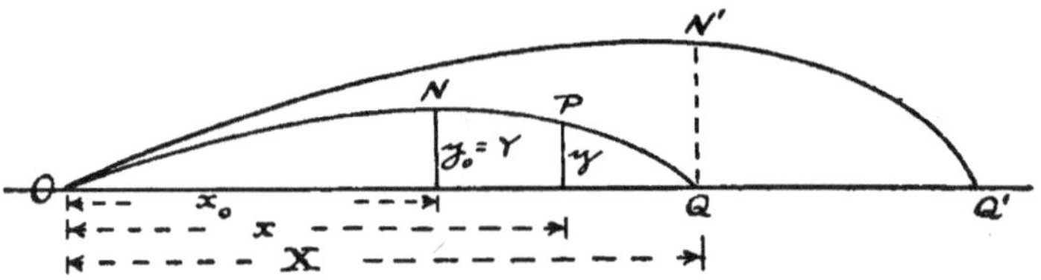

FIGURE 13.

may find the correct values of each of the integral expressions represented by the symbols A, A', etc., and also of the pseudo velocity at the point of fall, u_ω. Keep it firmly in mind that these particular symbols and values, A, A', etc., are only special symbols and values of the general symbols a, a', etc., at one particular point of the trajectory, that is, at the point of fall, or, expressed in another way, that they *pertain to the entire trajectory* and not to any part thereof or to any other point of the curve than the point of fall.

Similarly, for the vertex, where $x=x_0$, we have another set of special values, but here another symbol (which also represents an integral expression) A'' has been introduced. So we would have as our special symbols for the vertex a_0, a_0', A'', b_0, b_0' and t_0', and the pseudo velocity u_0. Remember that A'' pertains exclusively to the vertex, and to no other point of the curve. If we only knew the value of x_0, we could find the numerical values of each of the symbols for the vertex (each an integral expression integrated for the proper limits for the vertex) by computing the value of $z_0=\frac{x_0}{C}$, and thence with that value and the value of V as arguments taking them from Table II just as for any other case. *But we do not know the value of x_0.* Fortunately, however, it happens to be a fact (susceptible of mathematical proof, as will be shown in a later chapter) that the value of A for the point of fall is always numerically equal to the value of a_0' for the vertex. Now we have already a method of finding the value of A for the point of fall when we know the [illegible] the initial velocity, and having

are the next lower tabular values of Z and V below the given values; ΔV is the difference between successive tabular values of V (that is, 50 f. s. for the table $V=1150$ to 1200 f. s., and 100 f. s. for all other tables given in the tables to be used with this book). ΔZ is always 100 for all tables, and it is therefore allowed to remain in numerical form in the above algebraic expression. Δ_{ZA} and Δ_{VA} are the differences given in the proper line of the Δ columns pertaining to A. Care must be taken to use the proper signs for all the quantities given in the above expression. It will also be seen at once that any other one of the secondary functions may be substituted for A in the above expression provided we exercise due care in regard to the signs. It must also be noted that the formula applies for the *next lower* tabular values only. If we work from the *nearest* tabular values, there would be a change of signs in the expression if the *nearest* tabular value happens to be the *next higher* tabular value in any case.

Interpolation formulæ.

Repeating the expression just derived, and also solving it for Z and V, we get

$$A=A_t+\frac{Z-Z_t}{100}\Delta_{ZA}+\frac{V-V_t}{\Delta V}\Delta_{VA} \qquad (126)^*$$

$$V=V_t+\frac{\Delta V}{\Delta_{VA}}\left[(A-A_t)-\frac{Z-Z_t}{100}\Delta_{ZA}\right] \qquad (127)^*$$

$$Z=Z_t+\frac{100}{\Delta_{ZA}}\left[(A-A_t)-\frac{V-V_t}{\Delta V}\Delta_{VA}\right] \qquad (128)^*$$

From the first of these we find the value of A, given Z and V (or of any other of the secondary functions in place of A). From (127) we can find V, and from (128) we can find Z, given Z or V respectively, and A or any other secondary function in its place. The expressions of course simplify greatly when working with a tabular value of either Z or V, in which case $Z-Z_t$ or $V-V_t$ becomes zero.

Cross interpolation formulæ from A' to A''

154. In practice it is often necessary to find the value of A'' corresponding to a found value of A, knowing V, in finding the value of the maximum ordinate, as will be shown later, under circumstances when we do not care to know the value of Z or of any other of the secondary functions. To do this, that is, to find the double interpolation formula for crossing direct from A' to A'' without finding Z, knowing V, substitute in (126) expressed for A'', the value of Z found from (128) expressed for A'. The resultant expression is

$$A''=A_t''-\frac{V-V_t}{\Delta V}\times\frac{\Delta_{VA'}\Delta_{ZA''}}{\Delta_{ZA'}}+\frac{V-V_t}{\Delta V}\Delta_{VA''}+(A'-A_t')\frac{\Delta_{ZA''}}{\Delta_{ZA'}} \qquad (129)^*$$

If we are working with a tabular value of V, which is fortunately generally the case, then $V-V_t=0$, and the above formula simplifies greatly, becoming

$$A''=A_t''+(A'-A_t')\frac{\Delta_{ZA''}}{\Delta_{ZA'}} \qquad (130)^*$$

As examples, suppose we have $V=1175$ and $Z=2760$, and desire to find the corresponding values of the secondary functions. Then $V-V_t=25$ and $Z-Z_t=60$, and we have

$$A=.07643+\frac{.00322\times 60}{100}+\frac{(-.00496)\times 25}{50}=.07643+.00193-.00248=.07588$$

$$A'=.1631+\frac{.0072\times 60}{100}+\frac{(-.0096)\times 25}{50}=.1631+.00432-.0048=.16262$$

* It must be noted that the interpolation formulæ here derived for use with Table II of the Ballistic Tables, neglect second and higher differences. They therefore give results that are accurate only within certain limits, which limits are sufficiently narrow to permit the formulæ to be used for the purposes for which employed in this text book. A caution must be given, however, against using them for other purposes without ascertaining whether or not they will give sufficiently accurate results for the purpose in view. A case where they cannot be successfully used is given in Chapter 14. (See foot-note to paragraph 239, Chapter 14.)

matical process which it is unnecessary to follow through, derives an equation for determining the value of f as follows:

$$\log\log f = \log Y + 5.01765 - 10 \qquad (131)$$

Ingalls' solution by successive approximations.

157. With the aid of the formulæ of Colonel Ingalls already given, we may now proceed to the solution of the original problem already solved by Alger's method, as given in paragraph 140, by the methods used in preparing the range tables by the expert computers of the Bureau of Ordnance. The data is the same as before.

$$C_1 = \frac{w}{cd^2}\text{ ; argument for Table II, } Z = \frac{X}{C}\text{ ; } \sin 2\phi = AC$$

$w=870$		log 2.93952		
$c=0.61$	log 9.78533−10	colog 0.21467		
$d^2=144$	log 2.15836	colog 7.84164−10		
$C_1=$		log 0.99583	colog 9.00417−10	
$X=30000$			log 4.47712	
$Z_1=3029$			log 3.48129	

For $V=2900$ (table for $V=2900$ to 3000), for $Z=3029$, we have $A_1=.014882$

$A=.014882$	log 8.17266−10
$C_1=$	log 0.99583
$2\phi_1=8°\ 28'\ 34''$	sin 9.16849−10

$\phi_1=4°\ 14'\ 17''$.... First approximation, disregarding f.

Having obtained the preceding approximation to the value of ϕ, we may now proceed to determine a second approximation to the value of the same quantity, and this time we can correct for a value of f, using equations (125) and (131).

$$Y = A''C \tan\phi \qquad \log\log f = \log Y + 5.01765 - 10$$

For finding A'' from Table II we use $a_{o_1}' = \frac{\sin 2\phi}{C} = .014882$, as already determined, as an argument, in its proper column. For this the table gives for

$$A' = .0148 \quad \Delta_{ZA'} = .0012 \quad A'' = 849 \quad \Delta_{ZA''} = 57$$

therefore $$A_1'' = 849 + \frac{.000082 \times 57}{.0012} = 852.9$$

$A_1''=852.9$			log 2.93090
$C_1=$			log 0.99583
$\phi_1=4°\ 14'\ 17''$			tan 8.86983−10
$Y_1=$			log 2.79656
Constant			log 5.01765−10
$f_1=$	log 0.00652		loglog 7.81465−10
$C_1=$	log 0.99583		
$C_2=$	log 1.00235		colog 8.99765−10
$X=30000$			log 4.47712
$Z_2=2983.8$			log 3.47477

From Table II, $A_2 = .014599$

$A_2 = .014599$ .... log 8.16432 − 10

$C_2 =$ .... log 1.00235

$2\phi_2 = 8°\ 26'\ 26''$ .... sin 9.16667 − 10

$\phi_2 = 4°\ 13'\ 13''$.... Second approximation.

Having obtained the above second approximation to the value of ϕ, we see that it differs from the first approximation by over one minute of arc, and we therefore cannot assume that the second value is sufficiently accurate. We therefore repeat the above process to get a third approximation.

From above work $Z_2 = 2983.8$ and $A_2 = a_{0_2}' = .014559$, which gives, from Table II,

$$A_2'' = 793 + \frac{.000859 \times 56}{.0011} = 836.73$$

$A_2'' = 836.7$ .... log 2.92257

$C_2 =$ .... log 1.00235

$\phi_2 = 4°\ 13'\ 13''$ .... tan 8.86800 − 10

$Y_2 =$ .... log 2.79292

Constant .... log 5.01765 − 10

$f_2 =$ .... log 0.00646 .... loglog 7.81057 − 10

$C_1 =$ .... log 0.99583

$C_3 =$ .... log 1.00229 .... colog 8.99771 − 10

$X = 30000$ .... log 4.47712

$Z_2 = 2984.1$ .... log 3.47483

Hence from Table II, as before,

$$A_3 = .014602$$

$A_3 = .014602$ .... log 8.16438 − 10

$C_3 =$ .... log 1.00231

$2\phi_3 = 8°\ 26'\ 28''$ .... sin 9.16669 − 10

$\phi_3 = 4°\ 13'\ 14''$.... Third approximation.

This value is only one second in value different from the second approximation, and is therefore practically correct; but we see that there is still a small difference between the last two successive values of C, and as we desire to determine accurately and definitely a correct value of C for use in further work, we will proceed with another approximation.

$$A_3 = .014602$$

$$A_3'' = 793 + \frac{.000901 \times 56}{.0011} = 838.9$$

$A_3'' = 838.9$ .... log 2.92371

$C_3 =$ .... log 1.00231

$\phi_3 = 4°\ 13'\ 14''$ .... tan 8.86803 − 10

$Y_3 =$ .... log 2.79405

Constant .... log 5.01765 − 10

$f_3 =$ .... log 0.00648 .... loglog 7.81170 − 10

$C_1 =$ .... log 0.99583

$C_4 =$ .... log 1.00231

Now we see that $C_4=C_3$, and that we have therefore reached the limit of accuracy possible by the method of successive approximations and have verified the value of C, and no further work in this connection is therefore necessary. We therefore have for further work in connection with this trajectory:

$$\phi=4° \ 13' \ 14'' \qquad Z=2984.1 \qquad \log C=1.00231$$

To determine the angle of fall, time of flight and striking velocity, we have, from (116), (117) and (118)

$$\tan \omega=B' \tan \phi \qquad T=CT' \sec \phi \qquad v_\omega=u_\omega \cos \phi \sec \omega$$

From Table II

$$\log B'=.10371 \qquad T'=1.2332 \qquad u_\omega=2026.1$$

$B'=$	log 0.10371			
$C=$		log 1.00231		
$\phi=4° \ 13' \ 14''$	tan 8.86803−10	sec 0.00118	cos 9.99882−10	
$T'=1.2332$		log 0.09103		
$u_\omega=2026.1$			log 3.30666	
$\omega=5° \ 21' \ 11''$	tan 8.97174−10		sec 0.00190	
$T=12.43$		log 1.09452		
$v_\omega=2029$			log 3.30738	

Hence we have as the solutions to this problem

$$\phi=4° \ 13' \ 14''.$$
$$\omega=5° \ 21' \ 11''.$$
$$T=12.43 \text{ seconds.}$$
$$v_\omega=2029 \text{ f. s.}$$

These are the correct and final results, and it will be observed that they are the values which appear in Columns 2, 3, 4 and 5 of the range table for this gun, for a range of 10,000 yards. We have therefore learned how to compute the values for these columns in the range tables. In a later chapter will be given the forms used by the computers in actually computing the data for the range tables.

NOTE.—The mathematical processes carried through in the preceding chapters may be briefly and generally described as follows:

1. Considering the forces acting on the projectile in flight, that is, the force of gravity and the atmospheric resistance, and dealing with differential increments at any point of the trajectory, certain equations are derived (from the laws of physics governing motion) which show the relations existing between these differential increments in the different elements of the trajectory at the given point. These are not equations to the curve itself as a whole, but simply express the relations between the differential increments referred to above. Could they be integrated in general form, they could be generally used for solutions, but such integration is impossible owing to fractional exponents, and some other method must be adopted. The accepted method is known as Siacci's method, from its deviser, its essential point being the introduction into the computations of a new quantity known as the "pseudo velocity," which was defined in paragraph 22, page 23. By the introduction of this quantity, it becomes possible to reduce the differential equations to certain others that are known as the "ballistic formulæ," which are used in the practical solutions of ballistic problems. Each of these formulæ contains certain integral expressions, which are represented in the formulæ by the symbols A, I, S and T (the altitude, inclination, space and time functions), and the values of these functions for any given velocity, whether real or pseudo, may be found in Table I of the Ballistic Tables. That is, the tabulated values of

EXAMPLES.

1. Given the values of V and Z contained in the first two columns of the following table, take from Table II of the Ballistic Tables the corresponding values of $A, A', B, \log B', u, T'$ and D'.

Problem.	DATA.		ANSWERS.						
	$Z=\frac{X}{C}$.	V.	A.	A'.	B.	$\log B'$.	u.	T'.	D'.
1	3370	1150	.09855	.21279	.11431	.06440	914.07	3.3323	192.10
2	1763	1150	.04755	.09963	.05214	.03935	1002.5	1.6510	46.780
3	6982	1150	.23947	.54902	.30961	.11151	763.85	7.6714	1055.3
4	1326	2000	.01200	.02550	.01354	.04989	1683.3	0.72534	9.2600
5	4173	2000	.04992	.12123	.07132	.15484	1175.2	2.7711	136.57
6	7652	2000	.12736	.33625	.20885	.21477	919.40	6.1727	786.12
7	1943	2600	.01087	.02365	.01274	.06869	2050.8	0.84207	11.860
8	3756	2600	.02489	.05904	.03414	.13693	1619.7	1.8427	59.240
9	9743	2600	.12187	.35927	.23739	.28950	921.85	7.0604	1139.1
10	10742	2600	.14759	.43913	.29149	.29561	873.90	8.1739	1599.4
11	1818	2700	.00931	.02005	.01074	.06345	2169.1	0.75228	9.1800
12	4747	2700	.03210	.07981	.04774	.17323	1484.6	2.3925	101.82
13	5561	2700	.04095	.10630	.06536	.20376	1332.6	2.9718	162.49
14	7937	2700	.07613	.21928	.14322	.27450	1050.0	5.0092	514.14
15	9541	2700	.10868	.32365	.21501	.29617	948.95	6.6211	988.58
16	1856	2900	.00823	.01777	.00959	.06326	2331.8	0.71408	8.5600
17	2942	2900	.01434	.03253	.01818	.10215	2037.1	1.2126	24.840
18	3839	2900	.02034	.04814	.02787	.13558	1813.6	1.6795	50.170
19	4815	2000	.02809	.06988	.04176	.17277	1595.8	2.2535	90.730
20	8634	2900	.07677	.22861	.15189	.29651	1044.3	5.3016	592.50
21	3231	3100	.01404	.03213	.01808	.10982	2119.6	1.2026	27.620
22	5742	3100	.03182	.08283	.05106	.20430	1530.2	2.6633	129.36
23	8841	3100	.06943	.21036	.14094	.30760	1076.3	5.1291	553.84
24	10305	3100	.09566	.30074	.20504	.33126	974.70	6.5632	998.90

NOTE FOR INSTRUCTOR.—In exercising class in these interpolations, give to each midshipman one problem from each of the tables given in this and in the following five examples.

2. Given the values of V and Z contained in the two first columns of the following table, take from Table II of the Ballistic Tables the corresponding values of $A, A', B, \log B', u, T'$ and D'.

Problem.	DATA.		ANSWERS.						
	$Z=\frac{X}{C}$.	V.	A.	A'.	B.	$\log B'$.	u.	T'.	D'.
1	2200	1162	.05974	.12640	.06666	.04798	981.92	2.0769	73.800
2	5500	1173	.17257	.38758	.21499	.09544	826.98	5.7299	581.98
3	8100	1187	.28010	.65643	.37621	.12808	735.41	9.0164	1492.5
4	1800	2030	.01654	.03592	.01936	.06810	1606.6	0.99900	17.400
5	4200	2057	.04764	.11600	.00828	.15644	1200.5	2.7176	131.02
6	7700	2082	.12004	.32104	.20103	.22389	932.58	6.0389	753.90
7	3100	2618	.01002	.04359	.02456	.11167	1779.7	1.4399	35.460
8	7300	2643	.06832	.19222	.12389	.25853	1087.5	4.5167	403.81
9	9400	2663	.10854	.32104	.21254	.29194	950.71	6.5537	961.42
10	5100	2730	.03494	.08853	.05304	.18625	1433.0	2.6048	122.00
11	6100	2750	.04581	.12240	.07660	.22305	1271.0	3.3235	205.50
12	8700	2779	.08543	.25263	.10723	.29158	1012.8	5.5986	668.13
13	5500	2913	.03410	.08787	.05378	.19836	1465.8	2.6889	131.57
14	8200	2954	.06667	.19629	.12959	.28890	1093.6	4.7975	471.02
15	9700	2982	.09156	.28154	.19002	.31698	989.76	6.1909	860.34
16	4600	3140	.02210	.05408	.03198	.16032	1804.6	1.9410	66.000
17	7000	3150	.04201	.11930	.07645	.25060	1322.5	3.4925	232.00
18	9900	3160	.08423	.26308	.17978	.32934	1009.4	6.0338	819.60

3. Given the values of V and Z contained in the first two columns of the following table, take from Table II of the Ballistic Tables the corresponding values of A, A', B, $\log B'$, u, T' and D'.

Problem.	DATA.		ANSWERS.						
	$Z=\frac{X}{C}$.	V.	A.	A'.	B.	log B'.	u.	T'.	D'.
1	2730	1157	.07670	.16392	.08716	.05583	950.07	2.6336	119.16
2	5980	1169	.19258	.43558	.24299	.10109	806.72	6.3303	713.94
3	8730	1182	.31173	.73709	.42530	.13503	712.68	9.9097	1814.7
4	1936	2028	.01807	.03947	.02138	.07330	1576.1	1.0858	20.160
5	4757	2048	.05773	.14308	.08599	.17296	1131.5	3.2098	187.20
6	7915	2063	.12780	.34164	.21386	.22372	918.22	6.3151	833.56
7	3342	2628	.02082	.04836	.02753	.12076	1731.1	1.5724	42.840
8	7539	2644	.07243	.20534	.13292	.26385	1067.8	4.7373	450.35
9	9526	2684	.10970	.32588	.21624	.29471	946.98	6.6413	994.18
10	5433	2733	.03848	.09921	.06078	.19856	1373.2	2.8391	147.01
11	6214	2748	.04734	.12721	.07993	.22720	1253.1	3.4172	218.04
12	8848	2763	.08944	.26494	.17552	.29272	1000.7	5.7785	719.75
13	5584	2925	.03464	.08970	.05506	.20142	1457.0	2.7347	136.13
14	8282	2944	.06853	.20229	.13369	.29045	1084.3	4.8913	492.76
15	9748	2962	.09391	.28840	.19452	.31627	983.28	6.2813	890.22
16	4632	3148	.02221	.05445	.03224	.16136	1802.8	1.9536	67.200
17	7148	3155	.04439	.12447	.08010	.25606	1300.2	3.5098	248.31
18	9923	3163	.06449	.26497	.18052	.32979	1008.6	6.0511	825.65

4. Given the values of V contained in the first column and of the secondary functions contained in the second column of the following table, take from Table II of the Ballistic Tables the corresponding values of Z.

Problem.	DATA.		ANSWERS.
	V.	Secondary function.	Z.
1	1157	$A=0.06256$	2278.0
2	1172	$A'=0.12163$	2150.4
3	2030	$B=0.03845$	2911.0
4	2053	$T'=1.0956$	1971.0
5	2075	$A=0.04133$	3833.7
6	2615	$A'=0.03115$	2428.3
7	2691	$B=0.14932$	8061.7
8	2743	$T'=1.0756$	2522.7
9	2772	$A=0.01793$	3241.8
10	2784	$A'=0.23795$	8468.7
11	2947	$B=0.01932$	3123.1
12	2962	$T'=5.2227$	8669.3
13	3121	$A=0.00985$	2457.2
14	3178	$A'=0.19555$	8761.7
15	3191	$T'=5.1563$	9040.5

5. Given the value of Z contained in the first column, the value of the secondary function contained in the second column, and the limits near which the value of V lies contained in the third column of the following table, take from Table II of the Ballistic Tables the corresponding value of V.

Problem.	DATA.			ANSWERS.
	$Z=\frac{X}{C}$.	Secondary function.	Limits of V.*	V.
1	1732	$A=$ 0.04632	1150–1200	1154.9
2	4140	$A'=$ 0.27837	1150–1200	1137.0
3	1232	$B=$ 0.01273	2000–2100	1962.4
4	4381	$u=$ 1154.7	2000–2100	2007.4
5	8175	$T'=$ 6.7324	2000–2100	2007.5
6	2222	$A=$ 0.01278	2600–2700	2595.9
7	4444	$A'=$ 0.07735	2600–2700	2602.0
8	2551	$B=$ 0.01693	2700–2800	2715.0
9	5743	$u=$ 1298.4	2700–2800	2693.0
10	9107	$T'=$ 6.2333	2700–2800	2668.9
11	3232	$A=$ 0.01607	2900–3000	2909.6
12	6474	$A'=$ 0.12067	2900–3000	2916.8
13	1334	$B=$ 0.00555	3100–3200	3080.0
14	4321	$u=$ 1835.2	3100–3200	3089.0
15	8448	$T'=$ 4.7867	3100–3200	3090.1

* These limits determine the table to be used; in some cases it will be found that the interpolation gives a value of V lying outside of the limits indicated.

6. Given the values of V and of A contained in the first two columns of the following table, take from Table II of the Ballistic Tables the corresponding values of A'', without determining the corresponding value of Z.

Problem.	DATA.		ANSWERS.
	V.	A.	A''.
1	1150	0.19787	1690.6
2	1179	0.32995	2692.0
3	1192	0.40843	3234.5
4	2000	0.04932	1236.5
5	2053	0.15563	3009.1
6	2086	0.37543	5293.2
7	2600	0.05837	2154.4
8	2677	0.12647	3752.0
9	2689	0.27563	5805.7
10	2700	0.02343	1194.3
11	2750	0.10023	3376.6
12	2772	0.00995	547.19
13	2900	0.03613	1786.5
14	2932	0.13333	4357.5
15	2988	0.30057	6760.3
16	3118	0.20475	5880.7
17	3150	0.27777	6877.5
18	3173	0.02975	1774.1

7. Compute by Ingalls' method for standard atmospheric conditions, using successive approximations, the values of the angle of departure, angle of fall, time of flight and striking velocity in the following cases.

Problem.	DATA.					ANSWERS.			
	Projectile.			Velocity. f. s.	Range. Yds.	ϕ.	ω.	*T*. Secs.	v_ω. f. s.
	d. In.	*w*. Lbs.	*c*.						
A........	3	13	1.00	1150	2130	5° 39.1′	6° 46′	6.56	867
B........	3	13	1.00	2700	3720	2 59.3	5 33	6.94	1074
C........	4	33	0.67	2900	3825	1 43.4	2 20	4.98	1843
D........	5	50	1.00	3150	4370	2 11.4	3 44	6.33	1408
E........	5	50	0.61	3150	4465	1 44.8	2 25	5.44	1941
F........	6	105	0.61	2600	12690	11 03.4	19 38	24.70	1104
G........	6	105	1.00	2800	3875	1 55.7	2 41	5.34	1712
H........	6	105	0.61	2800	3022	1 32.3	1 51	4.46	2134
I........	7	163	1.00	2700	7230	5 00.7	8 31	12.32	1221
J........	7	165	0.61	2700	7357	3 57.4	5 30	10.54	1650
K........	8	260	0.61	2750	8390	4 15.3	5 49	11.62	1735
L........	10	510	1.00	2700	10310	6 49.8	11 09	17.05	1293
M........	10	510	0.61	2700	11333	6 07.6	8 30	16.30	1653
N........	12	870	0.61	2900	21650	12 30.9	19 55	33.59	1441
O........	13	1130	1.00	2000	10370	11 15.2	16 09	21.45	1108
P........	13	1130	0.74	2000	11111	10 58.0	14 44	21.57	1281
Q........	14	1400	0.70	2000	14220	14 48.8	20 15	28.68	1251
R........	14	1400	0.70	2600	14370	8 32.4	11 55	21.76	1577

8. Given the data contained in the first eight columns of the following table, compute in each case the values of ϕ, ω, T and v_ω, by Ingalls' method, using Table II, and using in each case the value of f from Table V corresponding to the maximum ordinate given in the table below.

Problem.	DATA.								ANSWERS.			
	Projectile.			Atmosphere.		*V*. f. s.	*R*. Yds.	Max. ord. Feet.	ϕ.	ω.	*T*. Secs.	v_ω. f. s.
	d. In.	*w*. Lbs.	*c*.	Bar. In.	Ther. °F.							
A........	3	13	1.00	Standard	..	1150	2350	265	7° 03.4′	8° 40′	8.07	832
B........	3	13	1.00	Standard	..	2700	3450	138	2 36.4	4 42	6.20	1122
C........	4	33	0.67	Standard	..	2900	4000	112	1 49.8	2 31	5.27	1802
D........	5	50	1.00	29.00	20	3150	3870	108	1 52.1	3 06	5.46	1475
E........	5	50	0.61	29.50	22	3150	3850	80	1 28.0	1 58	4.61	2011
F........	6	105	0.61	30.00	25	2600	14530	3798	15 42.4	28 31	32.04	1036
G........	6	105	1.00	30.15	27	2800	4570	169	2 33.0	3 55	6.82	1476
H........	6	105	0.61	30.25	30	2800	4030	101	1 47.2	2 14	5.11	2010
I........	7	165	1.00	30.33	33	2700	6030	363	3 55.2	6 22	9.85	1301
J........	7	165	0.61	30.50	35	2700	6540	328	3 28.3	4 46	9.29	1676
K........	8	260	0.61	30.67	40	2750	8080	485	4 10.0	5 45	11.32	1698
L........	10	510	1.00	31.00	45	2700	9090	807	5 52.9	9 28	14.80	1320
M........	10	510	0.61	30.75	50	2700	10070	784	5 20.3	7 17	14.28	1691
N........	12	870	0.61	30.33	60	2900	22030	4801	13 23.2	21 56	35.37	1377
O........	13	1130	1.00	30.25	70	2000	10560	1937	11 39.1	16 51	22.08	1154
P........	13	1130	0.74	29.50	80	2000	11050	1830	10 45.6	14 19	21.24	1299
Q........	14	1400	0.70	29.00	90	2000	14020	3204	14 09.7	19 00	27.67	1284
R........	14	1400	0.70	28.75	100	2600	14590	1960	8 23.2	11 23	21.63	1645

9. Compute by Alger's method, without using Table II, the values of ϕ, ω, T and v_ω, from the data contained in the following table, correcting for altitude in each case by successive approximations.

Problem.	DATA.									ANSWERS.			
	Projectile.			Atmosphere.			V. f. s.	R'nge. Yds.	Wind* compon't. f. s.	ϕ.	ω.	T. Secs.	v_ω. f. s.
	d. In.	w. Lbs.	c.	Bar. In.	Ther. °F.	Value of δ.							
1......	3	13	1	Standard	..	......	2800	2000	None	1° 00.9′	1° 25′	2.79	1671
2......	5	50	1	Standard	..	......	2550	3000	None	1 54.4	2 49	4.76	1439
3......	6	100	1	Standard	..	......	2300	4000	None	3 07.5	4 31	6.97	1321
4......	8	250	1	Standard	..	......	2300	4000	None	2 45.1	3 36	6.38	1552
5......	12	850	1	Standard	..	......	2250	5000	None	3 26.0	4 15	7.88	1626
6......	11.024	760.4	1	.....	..	1.0306	1733	2260	+ 19	2 21.5	2 36	4.27	1480
7......	11.024	760.4	1	.....	..	1.0058	1733	6788	— 14	8 25.7	11 01	14.64	1173
8......	6	100	1	30.05	70	......	2900	9700	None	8 53.3	17 58	19.80	987
9......	12	850	1	30.19	59	......	2827	11566	None	6 55.0	11 14	18.16	1364
10.....	11.024	760.4	1	.....	..	1.0174	1733	11207	— 12	17 32.7	24 33	28.06	1046
11.....	15.75	2028	1	Standard	..	......	1805	1004	None	0 57.8	1 00	1.86	1712
12.....	15.75	2028	1	Standard	..	......	1805	3281	None	3 06.2	3 27	5.91	1542
13.....	15.75	2028	1	Standard	..	......	1805	5468	None	5 36.4	6 42	10.43	1391
14.....	3	13	1	Standard	..	......	2800	2000	None	1 00.7	1 26	2.79	1672
15.....	3	15	1	Standard	..	......	2628	1883	None	1 00.0	1 21	2.66	1720
16.....	5	60	1	Standard	..	......	2900	3000	None	1 21.2	1 50	3.91	1837
17.....	5	55	1	Standard	..	......	2097	3095	None	1 21.7	1 55	4.02	1796

* The sign + means a wind with the flight of the projectile, and a — sign a wind against it. Therefore, in problem 6, say, in order to get the desired range we would have to proceed as though the initial velocity were really 1733 — 19 = 1714 f. s. and there were no wind, and compute results accordingly.

NOTE.—The above problems in Example 9 are taken from Alger's text book, and cover guns of older date, both U. S. Navy and foreign. Note the difference between this data and modern weights and velocities; and observe care to use correct data as given in the table.

CHAPTER 9.

THE DERIVATION AND USE OF SPECIAL FORMULÆ FOR FINDING THE COORDINATES OF THE VERTEX AND THE TIME OF FLIGHT TO AND THE REMAINING VELOCITY AT THE VERTEX, FOR A GIVEN ANGLE OF DEPARTURE AND INITIAL VELOCITY, WHICH INCLUDES THE DATA GIVEN IN COLUMN 8 OF THE RANGE TABLES.

158. Equations (74) and (75) are **Ballistic formulæ.**

$$\frac{y}{x}=\tan\phi-\frac{C}{2\cos^2\phi}\left(\frac{A_u-A_V}{S_u-S_V}-I_V\right) \tag{132}$$

$$\tan\theta=\tan\phi-\frac{C}{2\cos^2\phi}\,(I_u-I_V) \tag{133}$$

and by eliminating I_V from the above we get

$$\frac{y}{x}=\tan\theta+\frac{C}{2\cos^2\phi}\left(I_u-\frac{A_u-A_V}{S_u-S_V}\right) \tag{134}$$

159. Equation (76) is

$$t=C\sec\phi(T_u-T_V) \tag{135}$$

160. Equations (132), (133), (134) and (135) may be written

$$\frac{y}{x}=\tan\phi-\frac{aC}{2\cos^2\phi}=\tan\theta+\frac{bC}{2\cos^2\phi} \tag{136}$$

$$\tan\theta=\tan\phi-\frac{a'C}{2\cos^2\phi} \tag{137}$$

$$t=Ct'\sec\phi \tag{138}$$

by the introduction of the general forms, a, a', b and t' of Ingalls' secondary functions, as explained in the last chapter.

161. Equations (136) and (137) may be written **Transformation of equations.**

$$\frac{y}{x}=\tan\phi\left(1-\frac{aC}{\sin 2\phi}\right) \tag{139}$$

$$\tan\theta=\tan\phi\left(1-\frac{a'C}{\sin 2\phi}\right) \tag{140}$$

Substituting in these the value of $\sin 2\phi=AC$ from (115), we get

$$\frac{y}{x}=\frac{\tan\phi}{A}(A-a)=\frac{C}{2\cos^2\phi}(A-a) \tag{141}$$

$$\tan\theta=\frac{\tan\phi}{A}(A-a')=\frac{C}{2\cos^2\phi}(A-a') \tag{142}$$

162. Now by taking the first two members of each of the above equations, that is, **Equations for ordinate and inclination.**

$$y=\frac{\tan\phi}{A}(A-a)x \tag{143}$$

$$\tan\theta=\frac{\tan\phi}{A}(A-a') \tag{144}$$

we can readily find the values of y and θ corresponding to any given value of x for any given trajectory; that is, by computing the ordinates and angles of inclination corresponding to any necessary number of abscissæ, we are in a position to actually plot the trajectory to scale, provided we have determined or know the values of ϕ,

V, X and C for that trajectory; for a knowledge of the values of V and of $Z=\frac{X}{C}$ is necessary to enable us to use Table II.

163. The quantity a varies with x, and must be taken from the "A" column of Table II with V and $z=\frac{x}{C}$ as arguments. Similarly, a' must be taken from the "A'" column with the same arguments.

164. For the vertex, we know that $\theta=0$, and (144) therefore becomes, for that particular point,

$$\frac{\tan\phi}{A}(A-a_0')=0$$

and, as $\frac{\tan\phi}{A}$ cannot be equal to zero, then we must have

$$A-a_0'=0 \quad\text{or}\quad A=a_0' \tag{145}$$

165. Also, if we suppose $\theta=-\phi$ at some point in the descending branch of the trajectory, which point manifestly exists, as in that branch the value of θ varies from zero at the vertex to $-\omega$ at the point of fall, and we have seen that ω is always numerically greater than ϕ, equation (142) will become for that point

$$\tan(-\phi)=\frac{\tan\phi}{A}(A-a'_{-\phi})$$

or

$$A-a'_{-\phi}=-A$$

or

$$a'_{-\phi}=2A \tag{146}$$

whence, from (145) and (146)

$$a_0'=A=\tfrac{1}{2}a'_{-\phi}$$

166. Substituting a_0' for A in (141) and designating symbols relating to the vertex by the subscript zero, we get

$$\frac{y_0}{x_0}=\frac{a_0'-a_0}{a_0'}\tan\phi=\frac{b_0}{a_0'}\tan\phi$$

whence

$$y_0=\frac{b_0x_0}{a_0'}\tan\phi=C\frac{b_0x_0}{a_0'C}\tan\phi$$

The secondary function A''

167. Now if we let $A''=\frac{b_0x_0}{a_0'C}=\frac{b_0z_0}{a_0'}$, in which A'' may be taken from Table II, using V and $a_0'=A=\frac{\sin 2\phi}{C}$, we will have the expression for the summit ordinate, or ordinate of the vertex

$$y_0=Y=A''C\tan\phi \tag{147}$$

It will be observed that a_0' is a special value of A', this latter symbol referring to the entire trajectory. This value of the ordinate at the vertex, y_0, is ordinarily denoted by Y in work.

168. We have already shown that, for the whole trajectory, $A=\frac{\sin 2\phi}{C}$, and also that, *for the vertex of the curve*, $a_0'=A$, and from this we see that, *for that particular point* $a_0'=\frac{\sin 2\phi}{C}$; and we also know that a_0' is merely the special value of A' for that particular point in the trajectory, namely, the vertex. Hence if we know the values of ϕ, V and C, we can compute this particular value of A', namely, a_0', from the expression $a_0'=\frac{\sin 2\phi}{C}$; and then, as this is a special value of A', we may look for it in the A' column of Table II, and by interpolation in the usual manner we may take

from that table the corresponding value of A''; and, in fact, the corresponding values of any other of the secondary functions for the vertex. This explains the reasons for the method of determining the value of A'' described and used in the last chapter.*

169. We also find, in the Z column corresponding to the above interpolation, the value of $z_0 = \frac{x_0}{C}$, and we therefore have

$$x_0 = Cz_0 \tag{148}$$

170. Assembling the equations already derived, we see that our formulæ for finding the elements at the vertex are *Equations for vertex.*

$$y_0 = Y = A''C \tan \phi \tag{149}$$
$$x_0 = Cz_0 \tag{150}$$
$$t_0 = Ct_0' \sec \phi \tag{151}$$
$$v_0 = u_0 \cos \phi \tag{152}$$

171. Let us now proceed with our standard problem, the 12" gun, for which $V = 2900$ f. s., $w = 870$ pounds and $c = 0.61$, for which, at 10,000 yards range, we have already determined in the last chapter that $\log C = 1.00231$, $Z = 2984.1$ and $\phi = 4° \ 13' \ 14''$.

$$Y = A''C \tan \phi \qquad x_0 = Cz_0 \qquad t_0 = Ct' \sec \phi \qquad v_0 = u_0 \cos \phi$$

From Table II

$$A = .01408 + \frac{.00063 \times 84.1}{100} = .014601$$

for the entire trajectory, which equals a_0' for the vertex. This could also be determined by solving $A = \frac{\sin 2\phi}{C}$ for the above values instead of taking it from the table.

$$A'' = 793 + \frac{9 \times 56}{11} = 838.87$$

by using the value of A given above as an argument in the A' column, and working, as should always be done, from the *next lower tabular value.*

$$z_0 = 1500 + \frac{100 \times .0009}{.0011} = 1581.8$$

$$t_0' = .565 + \frac{.041 \times 81.9}{100} = .59858$$

$$u_0 = 2435 - \frac{30 \times 81.9}{100} = 2410.4$$

$C =$	log 1.00231	log 1.00231	log 1.00231	
$A'' = 838.87$	log 2.92370			
$\phi = 4° 13' 14''$	tan 8.86803−10		sec 0.00116	cos 9.99882−10
$z_0 = 1581.9$		log 3.19918		
$t_0' = .59858$			log 9.77712−10	
$u_0 = 2410.4$				log 3.38209
$Y = 622.36$	log 2.79404			
$x_0 = 15903.3$		log 4.20149		
$t_0 = 6.034$			log 0.78061	
$v_0 = 2403.9$				log 3.38091

$x_0 = 5301.1$ yards. $\qquad t_0 = 6.034$ seconds.
$Y = 622.36$ feet. $\qquad v_0 = 2403.9$ foot-seconds.

---

* See paragraph 152.

172. Had we not known the correct value of C, as corrected for altitude, but had only known ϕ and V, the work would then have been by successive approximations, as follows:

$V=2900$ f. s. $\quad \phi=4°\ 13'\ 14'' \quad w=870$ pounds $\quad c=0.61$

$Y=A''C\tan\phi \quad \log\log f=\log Y+5.01765-10 \quad x_0=Cz_0$

$t_0=Ct_0'\sec\phi \quad v_0=u_0\cos\phi$

$w=870$ .... log 2.93952

$c=0.61$ ....log 9.78533−10..colog 0.21467

$d^2=144$ ....log 2.15836......colog 7.84164−10

$C_1=$ .... log 0.99583......colog 9.00417−10

$2\phi=8°\ 26'\ 28''$ .... sin 9.16670−10

$a_{0_1}'=.01482$ .... log 8.17087−10

From Table II, with .01482 in the A' column as an argument,

$$A_1''=849+\frac{.2\times 100}{12}\times\frac{57}{100}=849+1=850$$

$A_1''=850$ .... log 2.92942

$C_1=$ .... log 0.99503

$\phi=4°\ 13'\ 14''$ .... tan 8.86803−10

$Y_1=$ .... log 2.79328

Constant .... log 5.01765−10

$f_1=$ ....log 0.00647..........loglog 7.81093−10

$C_1=$ ....log 0.99583

$C_2=$ ....log 1.00230.......... colog 8.99770−10

$2\phi=8°\ 26'\ 28''$ .... sin 9.16670−10

$a_{0_2}'=.0146$ .... log 8.16440−10

From Table II as above

$$A_2''=793+\frac{9\times 56}{11}=793+46=839$$

$A_2''=839$ .... log 2.92376

$C_2=$ .... log 1.00230

$\phi=4°\ 13'\ 14''$ .... tan 8.86803−10

$Y_2=622.43$ .... log 2.79409

Constant .... log 5.01765−10

$f_2=$ ....log 0.00648..........loglog 7.81174−10

$C_1=$ ....log 0.99583

$C_3=$ ....log 1.00231.......... colog 8.99769−10

$2\phi=8°\ 26'\ 28''$ .... sin 9.16670−10

$a_{0_3}'=.0146$ .... log 8.16439−10

As these last two successive values of a_0' are equal, we have evidently reached the limit of accuracy in our approximations, and we have for the remainder of the problem

$$a_0'=.0146 \quad\text{and}\quad \log C=1.00231$$

Also, from log Y_s as found above, we have that $Y=622.43$ feet, and from Table II

$$s_o=1581.8 \qquad t_o'=.59854 \qquad u_o=2410.5$$

$C=$	log 1.00231	log 1.00231	
$\phi=4°\ 13'\ 14''$		sec 0.00118	cos 9.99882−10
$s_o=1581.8$	log 3.19915		
$t_o'=.59854$		log 9.77709−10	
$u_o=2410.5$			log 3.38093
$x_o=15902.3$	log 4.20146		
$t_o=6.0336$		log 0.78058	
$v_o=2404.0$			log 3.38093

$x_o=5300.7$ yards.
$Y=622.43$ feet.
$t_o=6.0366$ seconds.
$v_o=2404.0$ foot-seconds.

173. If we desire to plot any particular trajectory to scale, we can determine the ordinate corresponding to any given abscissa, and also the angle of inclination of the curve at the given point as follows:

We have from (143) and (144)

$$y=\frac{\tan\phi}{A}(A-a)x \tag{153}$$

and

$$\tan\theta=\frac{\tan\phi}{A}(A-a') \tag{154}$$

Suppose we wish to plot the 10,000-yard trajectory for our standard problem, for which we now know that $\phi=4°\ 13'\ 14''$ and $\log C=1.00231$.

$2\phi=8°\ 26'\ 28''$	sin 9.16670−10
$C=$	colog 8.99769−10
$A=.014601$	log 8.16439−10

$a_o'=A=.014601$

$$A''=793+\frac{.00901\times 56}{.0011}=838.87 \qquad s_o=1500+\frac{100\times .000901}{.0011}=1581.9$$

$A''=838.87$	log 2.92370	
$C=$	log 1.00231	log 1.00231
$\phi=4°\ 13'\ 14''$	tan 8.86803−10	
$s_o=1581.9$		log 3.19918
$y_o=Y=622.35$	log 2.79404	
$x_o=15903$		log 4.20149

The coordinates of the vertex are therefore 5301 yards in range and 622.35 feet in altitude.

174. In the equations given we now find the value of $\frac{\tan\phi}{A}$ for the given trajectory, having the value of A as above.

$\phi=4°\ 13'\ 14''$		log 8.86803−10
$A=.014601$	log 8.16439−10	colog 1.83561
$\frac{\tan\phi}{A}=5.054$		log 0.70364

and our equations become

$$y=5.054(.014601-a)x \qquad \tan\theta=5.054(.014601-a')$$

175. The following table gives the results of work with these equations for abscissæ varying by 1000 yards for this trajectory, some of the cases being worked out below:

Abscissæ. Yards.	Ordinates. Feet.	θ.	Remarks.
0	0	4° 13′ 14″	Origin.
1000	203.58	3 31 57	
2000	370.06	2 48 55	
3000	497.25	2 02 20	
4000	581.62	1 10 37	
5000	620.81	0 17 11	
5301	622.35	0 00 00	Vertex.
6000	610.34	(—)0 41 35	
7000	547.66	(—)1 43 08	
8000	427.21	(—)2 50 43	
9000	246.44	(—)4 04 16	
10000	0	(—)5 21 34	Point of fall; $\theta = -\omega$.

Work for 3000 yards:

$C =$ ....colog 3.99769 − 10

$x = 9000$ .... log 3.95424

$z = 895.21$ .... log 2.95193

$a = .00326 + \dfrac{.00043 \times 95.21}{100} = .003669 \qquad a' = .0067 + \dfrac{.0009 \times 95.21}{100} = .007557$

$A = .014601 \qquad A = .014601$

$a = .003669 \qquad a' = .007557$

$A - a = .010932$ ....log 8.03870 − 10

$A - a' = .007044$ ....log 7.84782 − 10

$\dfrac{\tan\phi}{A} = 5.054$ ....log 0.70364..........log 0.70364

$x = 9000$ ....log 3.95424

$y = 497.25$ ....log 2.69658

$\theta = 2°\ 02'\ 20''$ ....tan 8.55146 − 10

Work for 8000 yards:

$C =$ ....colog 8.99769 − 10

$x = 24000$ .... log 4.38021

$z = 2387.3$ .... log 3.37790

$a = .01059 + \dfrac{.00056 \times 87.3}{100} = .011079 \qquad a' = .0233 + \dfrac{.0013 \times 87.3}{100} = .024435$

$A = .014601 \qquad A = .014601$

$a = .011079 \qquad a' = .024435$

$A - a = .003522$ ....log 7.54679 − 10

$A - a' = (-).009834$ ....(−)log 7.99273 − 10

$\dfrac{\tan\phi}{A} = 5.054$ ....log 0.70364...... log 0.70364

$x = 24000$ ....log 4.38021

$y = 427.21$ ....log 2.63064

$\theta = (-)2°\ 50'\ 43''$ ....(−)tan 8.69637 − 10

The work for the point of fall, that is, for an abscissa of $x=10{,}000$ yards, becomes:

$C=$ .... colog $8.99769-10$

$x=30000$ .... log 4.47712

$s=2984.1$ .... log 3.47481

$a=.01408+\dfrac{.00062\times 84.1}{100}=.014601 \qquad a'=.0319+\dfrac{.0015\times 84.1}{100}=.033162$

$A=.014601 \qquad A=\ \ .014601$

$a=.014601 \qquad a'=\ \ .033162$

$A-a=0$

$A-a'=(-).018561$ .... $(-)$log $8.26860-10$

$\dfrac{\tan\phi}{A}=5.054$ .... log 0.70364

$\theta=(-)5°\ 21'\ 34''$ .... $(-)$tan $8.97224-10$

$y=0$

176. A reversal of the original formulæ would enable us to find the abscissa corresponding to any given ordinate; but there are some practical difficulties in the way of a simple use of the formulæ for this purpose, and as it is not a usual case it is not considered necessary to go into the matter here. Reverse formulæ.

EXAMPLES.

1. Given the data contained in the following table, compute the values of x_ω, $y_\omega(Y)$, t_ω and v_ω by Ingalls' method, using Table II, and correcting for altitude in each case by computing successive approximations to the value of C.

Problem.	DATA.							ANSWERS.			
	Projectile.			Atmosphere.		ϕ.	Velocity. f. s.	x_ω. Yds.	$y_\omega=Y$. Feet.	t_ω. Secs.	v_ω. f. s.
	d. In.	w. Lbs.	c.	Bar. In.	Ther. °F.						
A...........	3	13	1.00	28.00	100	6° 52′ 54″	1150	1340	257	3.88	958
B...........	3	13	1.00	28.40	95	2 40 24	2700	2106	171	3.00	1659
C...........	4	33	0.67	29.15	93	1 50 00	2900	2196	113	2.55	2300
D...........	5	50	1.00	29.90	87	1 53 12	3150	2272	127	2.62	2154
E...........	5	50	0.61	30.00	84	1 45 48	3150	2453	123	2.65	2460
F...........	6	105	0.61	30.10	79	14 01 06	2600	8529	3827	13.88	1373
G...........	6	105	1.00	30.70	75	2 18 48	2800	2407	160	3.00	2075
H...........	6	105	0.61	30.90	73	1 44 06	2800	2091	100	2.43	2392
I...........	7	165	1.00	31.00	67	5 20 18	2700	4227	686	6.01	1667
J...........	7	165	0.61	30.75	58	3 41 36	2700	3747	393	4.75	2088
K...........	8	260	0.61	30.50	49	4 03 06	2750	4292	493	5.31	2154
L...........	10	510	1.00	30.17	35	6 30 06	2700	5483	1067	7.58	1766
M...........	10	510	0.61	30.00	29	5 52 42	2700	5849	984	7.49	2064
N...........	12	870	0.61	29.75	23	13 49 48	2900	12661	5365	16.90	1808
O...........	13	1130	1.00	29.33	18	10 40 18	2000	5353	1676	9.65	1418
P...........	13	1130	0.74	29.00	15	10 08 42	2000	5642	1610	9.58	1535
Q...........	14	1400	0.70	28.50	10	13 54 00	2000	7245	2938	12.89	1471
R...........	14	1400	0.70	28.25	5	8 14 06	2600	7466	1770	10.01	1960

2. Given the data contained in the following table, compute the values of x_0, y_0 (Y), t_0 and v_0 by Ingalls' method, using Table II, and correcting for f for the mean altitude during flight given in Column 8 of the table. (Note that this is not the maximum ordinate.)

Problem.	DATA.									ANSWERS.			
	Projectile.			Atmosphere.		ϕ.	Velocity. f. s.	Mean height of flight. Feet.				
	d. In.	w. Lbs.	c.	Bar. In.	Ther. °F.				x_0. Yds.	$y_0=Y$. Feet.	t_0. Secs.	v_0. f. s.
A....	3	13	1.00	28.15	0	5° 14′ 18″	1150	100	1032	150	2.97	966
B....	3	13	1.00	28.75	5	2 48 54	2700	120	2011	176	3.00	1524
C....	4	33	0.67	29.00	10	1 18 42	2900	40	1619	59	1.85	2371
D....	5	50	1.00	29.30	20	1 44 12	3150	72	2070	106	2.44	2131
E....	5	50	0.61	29.70	25	1 39 24	3150	72	2278	107	2.47	2436
F....	6	105	0.61	29.90	30	9 18 54	2600	1257	6378	1841	9.77	1514
G....	6	105	1.00	30.00	40	1 48 36	2800	68	1971	101	2.41	2167
H....	6	105	0.61	30.15	50	1 37 54	2800	60	1976	89	2.29	2416
I....	7	165	1.00	30.33	60	4 38 00	2700	360	3856	536	5.34	1744
J....	7	165	0.61	30.50	70	3 37 18	2700	254	3709	381	4.67	2110
K....	8	260	0.61	30.67	75	4 07 12	2750	344	4391	512	5.42	2165
L....	10	510	1.00	30.90	80	6 36 24	2700	744	5649	1113	7.76	1789
M....	10	510	0.61	31.00	85	5 57 06	2700	680	6009	1019	7.64	2081
N....	12	870	0.61	30.75	90	9 04 36	2000	1706	9655	2564	11.92	2065
O....	13	1130	1.00	30.00	95	10 21 36	2000	1076	5408	1626	9.56	1471
P....	13	1130	0.74	29.50	100	10 48 54	2000	1220	5998	1851	10.30	1560
Q....	14	1400	0.70	29.00	80	14 02 42	2000	2018	7472	3043	13.16	1502
R....	14	1400	0.70	28.00	60	8 23 54	2600	1238	7783	1869	10.33	1989

3. Knowing that $y=\frac{\tan\phi}{A}(A-a)x$ and that $\tan\theta=\frac{\tan\phi}{A}(A-a')$, derive expressions for the values of y and $\tan\theta$ in terms of a, a', x and of the numerical coefficients, for any point in each of the trajectories given below, atmospheric conditions being standard.

Problem.	DATA.							ANSWERS.	
	Projectile.			V. f. s.	R. Yds	Value of log C.	ϕ.	$y=$	$\tan\theta=$
	d. In.	w. Lbs.	c.						
A...	3	13	1.00	1150	2130	0.16152	5° 39′ 06″	$0.73236(.135125-a)x$	$0.73236(.135125-a')$
B...	3	13	1.00	2700	3720	0.16179	2 59 18	$0.72758(.071750-a)x$	$0.72758(.071750-a')$
C...	4	33	0.67	2900	3825	0.48936	1 43 24	$1.54425(.019483-a)x$	$1.54425(.019483-a')$
D...	5	50	1.00	3150	4370	0.30272	2 11 24	$1.00530(.038037-a)x$	$1.00530(.038037-a')$
E...	5	50	0.61	3150	4465	0.51695	1 44 48	$1.64560(.018531-a)x$	$1.64560(.018531-a')$
F...	6	105	0.61	2600	12690	0.70596	11 03 24	$2.63750(.074085-a)x$	$2.63750(.074085-a')$
G...	6	105	1.00	2800	3875	0.46608	1 55 48	$1.46400(.023017-a)x$	$1.46400(.023017-a')$
H...	6	105	0.61	2800	3622	0.68039	1 32 18	$2.39700(.011203-a)x$	$2.39700(.011203-a')$
I...	7	165	1.00	2700	7230	0.53374	5 00 42	$1.72170(.050924-a)x$	$1.72170(.050924-a')$
J...	7	165	0.61	2700	7357	0.74663	3 57 24	$2.80300(.024675-a)x$	$2.80300(.024675-a')$
K...	8	260	0.61	2750	8390	0.82912	4 15 18	$3.39220(.021932-a)x$	$3.39220(.021932-a')$
L...	10	510	1.00	2700	10310	0.71990	6 49 48	$2.66130(.045010-a)x$	$2.66130(.045010-a')$
M...	10	510	0.61	2700	11333	0.93343	6 07 36	$4.33860(.024739-a)x$	$4.33860(.024739-a')$
N...	12	870	0.61	2900	21650	1.04355	12 30 54	$5.79990(.038272-a)x$	$5.79990(.038272-a')$
O...	13	1130	1.00	2000	10370	0.84469	11 15 12	$3.63520(.054735-a)x$	$3.63520(.054735-a')$
P...	13	1130	0.74	2000	11111	0.97554	10 58 00	$4.90370(.039516-a)x$	$4.90370(.039516-a')$
Q...	14	1400	0.70	2000	14220	1.04355	14 48 48	$5.91410(.044718-a)x$	$5.91410(.044718-a')$
R...	14	1400	0.70	2600	14370	1.02872	8 32 24	$5.46220(.027492-a)x$	$5.46220(.027492-a')$

NOTE.—Values of R and log C are taken from the results of work in Example 7, Chapter 8.

4. For the trajectories given in the preceding example (Example 3) compute the abscissa and ordinate of the vertex; and the ordinate and inclination of the curve at each of the points whose abscissæ are given below, and also at the point of fall.

Problem.	ANSWERS.									
	Vertex.		Point of fall.		For different abscissæ.					
	x_0. Yds.	$y_0=Y$. Feet.	y_ω. Feet.	$\theta=-\omega$.	x_1. Yds.	y_1. Feet.	θ_1.	x_2. Yds.	y_2. Feet.	θ_2.
A...	1112	175	0.	(—) 6° 45.0′	750	154.5	2° 02.9′	1800	96.7	(—) 4° 24.8′
B...	2160	200	0.08	(—) 5 32.4	1000	133.0	2 00.5	3000	149.2	(—) 2 29.4
C...	2056	100	0.	(—) 2 19.9	1000	71.7	0 59.2	3000	73.7	(—) 1 07.2
D...	2476	163	0.05	(—) 3 44.4	1000	98.3	1 31.9	3000	152.7	(—) 0 46.5
E...	2414	120	0.64	(—) 2 24.7	1000	75.8	1 07.8	3000	111.2	(—) 0 34.8
F...	7329	2534	(—) 1.61	(—) 19 38.2	4000	1910.7	6 34.8	9000	2332.6	(—) 4 50.6
G...	2097	115	0.49	(—) 2 40.6	1000	81.1	1 08.1	3000	87.9	(—) 1 11.9
H...	1888	80	0.03	(—) 1 50.8	1000	61.1	0 47.3	3000	48.1	(—) 1 07.7
I...	4102	620	0.37	(—) 8 30.6	2000	433.7	3 11.3	4000	618.9	(+) 0 11.2
J...	3990	450	0.19	(—) 5 29.1	2000	328.0	2 14.3	4000	448.6	0 00.0
K...	4511	544	0.43	(—) 5 46.7	2000	388.1	2 37.3	4000	535.9	(+) 0 35.7
L...	5799	1184	0.17	(—) 11 08.4	3000	869.7	4 00.3	9000	629.4	(—) 7 08.8
M...	6146	1075	(—) 0.30	(—) 8 29.0	3000	769.4	3 33.0	9000	770.2	(—) 4 12.5
N...	12154	4581	0.38	(—) 19 55.7	9000	4209.5	4 20.3	19000	2360.4	(—) 13 14.0
O...	5675	1873	(—) 1.47	(—) 16 10.0	3000	1411.2	6 15.0	9000	980.3	(—) 10 47.5
P...	5976	1879	0.33	(—) 14 44.2	3000	1376.5	6 11.5	9000	1272.3	(—) 8 02.4
Q...	7714	3339	(—) 0.25	(—) 20 15.0	3000	2006.0	10 06.3	9000	3220.6	(—) 3 28.2
R...	7810	1916	0.47	(—) 11 54.7	3000	1141.0	5 47.7	9000	1857.2	(—) 1 48.8

NOTE.—Of course, the found values of the ordinate and of the angle of inclination at the point of fall should be numerically equal to zero and to the angle of fall, respectively. The actual results obtained by the above work show the degree of accuracy of the method.

CHAPTER 10.

THE DERIVATION AND USE OF SPECIAL FORMULÆ FOR FINDING THE HORIZONTAL RANGE, TIME OF FLIGHT, ANGLE OF FALL, AND STRIKING VELOCITY FOR A GIVEN ANGLE OF DEPARTURE AND INITIAL VELOCITY.

Ballistic formulæ transformed.

177. For this problem we use expressions that have already been derived, namely, equations (113), (115), (116), (117) and (118); in some cases somewhat transposed, as follows (neglecting the altitude factor):

$$C=\frac{w}{\delta c d^2} \qquad (155)$$

$$A=\frac{\sin 2\phi}{C} \qquad (156)$$

$$X=CZ \qquad (157)$$

$$\tan \omega = B' \tan \phi \qquad (158)$$

$$T=CT' \sec \phi \qquad (159)$$

$$v_\omega = u_\omega \cos \phi \sec \omega \qquad (160)$$

178. As no account is taken of the altitude factor in the above expression, we cannot use our standard problem at present, so we will take a different case for our first solution, and one at such a short range that the altitude factor may be neglected without material error. Let us therefore compute the values of X, ω, T and v_ω for an angle of departure of 1° 02′ 24″, for the 5″ gun for which $V=3150$ f. s., $w=50$ pounds and $c=0.61$, for a barometer reading of 30.00″ and a thermometer reading of 50° F.

From Table VI.

$K=$	log 0.51570		
$\delta=1.035$	log 0.01494		
$C=$	log 0.50076	.... colog	9.49924 − 10
$2\phi=2°$ 04′ 48″		sin	8.55984 − 10
$A=.01146$		log	8.05908 − 10

From which, from Table II, we get

$$Z=2700+\frac{100}{.00052}\left(\frac{50\times .00072}{100}+.01146-.01119\right)=2700+121.1=2821.1$$

$$\log B'=.0945+\frac{.0035\times 21.1}{100}-\frac{.0015\times 50}{100}=.09449$$

$$u_\omega=2235-\frac{27\times 21.1}{100}+\frac{83\times 50}{100}=2270.8$$

$$T'=1.064+\frac{.045\times 21.1}{100}-\frac{.035\times 50}{100}=1.0560$$

$C=$ ....log 0.50076..................log 0.50076
$Z=2821.1$ log.3.45042
$\phi=1°\ 02'\ 24''$ ....tan 8.25894−10..sec 0.00007..cos 9.99993−10
$B'=$ ....log 0.09449
$u_\omega=2270.8$ ....log 3.35618
$T'=1.056$ ....log 0.02366

$X=8936.7$ .....log 3.95118

$\omega=1°\ 17'\ 34''$ ....tan 8.35343−10..............sec 0.00011

$T=3.3457$ ....log 0.52449

$v_\omega=2271$ ....log 3.35622

$X=2978.9$ yards. $T=3.3457$ seconds.
$\omega=1°\ 17'\ 34''$. $v_\omega=2271$ f. s.

179. Or, with perhaps no more labor, we may avoid the double interpolation necessary in the above solution by working the problem for $V=3100$ f. s. and then again for $V=3200$ f. s., and then get our final results by interpolation between those obtained for the two velocities. In this case, as $V=3150$, our final results should be half way between the results obtained for the two values of V with which we work. The value of C and that of A are of course the same as in the preceding problem, so starting from that point, with $A=.01146$ and $\log C=0.50076$, we have

For $V=3100$ f. s.

$Z=2751.9$ $\log B'=.09282$ $u_\omega=2248.5$ $T'=1.0428$

$C=$ ....log 0.50076..................log 0.50076
$Z=2751.9$ .....log 3.43963
$\phi=1°\ 02'\ 24''$ ....tan 8.25894−10..sec 0.00007..cos 9.99993−10
$B'=$ ....log 0.09282
$u_\omega=2248.5$ ....log 3.35190
$T'=1.0428$ ....log 0.01820

$X=8717.4$ .....log 3.94039

$\omega=1°\ 17'\ 16''$ ....tan 8.35176−10..............sec 0.00011

$T=3.3039$ ....log 0.51903

$v_\omega=2248.75$ ....log 3.35194

For $V=3200$ f. s.

$Z=2904$ $\log B'=.09674$ $u_\omega=2288.9$ $T'=1.0738$

$C=$ ....log 0.50076..................log 0.50076
$Z=2904$ ....log 3.46300
$\phi=1°\ 02'\ 24''$ ....tan 8.25894−10..sec 0.00007..cos 9.99993−10
$B'=$ ....log 0.09674
$u_\omega=2288.9$ ....log 3.35963
$T'=1.0738$ ....log 0.03092

$X=9199.4$ .....log 3.96376

$\omega=1°\ 17'\ 58''$ ....tan 8.35568−10..............sec 0.00011

$T=3.4021$ ....log 0.53175

$v_\omega=2289.1$ ....log 3.35967

Our results then are

	For $V=3100$ f. s.	For $V=3200$ f. s.	For $V=3150$ f. s. (By interpolation between the results obtained for 3100 and 3200 f. s.)
X	2905.8 yards.	3066.5 yards.	2986.1 yards.
ω	1° 17′ 16″.	1° 17′ 57″.	1° 17′ 37″.
T	3.3039 seconds.	3.4022 seconds.	3.3531 seconds.
v_ω	2248.75 f. s.	2289.1 f. s.	2268.9 f. s.

130. We will now take our standard problem, introduce the altitude factor, and solve. This for the 12″ gun, for which $V=2900$ f. s., $w=870$ pounds and $c=0.61$. For this problem we will take the angle of departure as 4° 13′ 14″, which we already know corresponds to a range of 10,000 yards, and will consider the atmospheric conditions as standard. Proceeding in a manner similar to that employed in originally computing the angle of departure, that is, by performing the work first without considering f until we have gone far enough to enable us to determine the value of f by a series of approximations, and then introducing it, we have, by the use of the formulæ employed in the preceding problem, and in addition of

$$Y=A''C\tan\phi \quad \text{and} \quad \text{loglog}\, f=\log Y+5.01765-10$$

$C_1=K=$ (from Table VI)		colog 9.00417−10
$2\phi=8°\ 26'\ 28''$		sin 9.16670−10
$a_{\omega_1}'=.014821$		log 8.17087−10

$$A_1''=849+\frac{.000021\times 57}{.0012}=850$$

$A_1''=850$		log 2.92942
$C_1=$		log 0.99583
$\phi=4°\ 13'\ 14''$		tan 8.86803−10
$Y_1=$		log 2.79328
Constant		log 5.01765−10
$f_1=$	log 0.00647	loglog 7.81093−10
$C_1=$	log 0.99583	
$C_2=$	log 1.00230	colog 8.99770−10
$2\phi=8°\ 26'\ 28''$		sin 9.16670−10
$a_{\omega_2}'=.014602$		log 8.16440−10

$$A_2''=793+\frac{.000902\times 56}{.0011}=838.92$$

$A_2''=838.92$		log 2.92372
$C_2=$		log 1.00230
$\phi=4°\ 13'\ 14''$		tan 8.86803−10
$Y_2=$		log 2.79405
Constant		log 5.01765−10
$f_2=$	log 0.00648	loglog 7.81170−10
$C_1=$	log 0.99583	
$C_3=$	log 1.00231	colog 8.99769−10
$2\phi=8°\ 26'\ 28''$		sin 9.16670−10
$a_{\omega_3}'=.014601$		log 8.16439−10

$$A_3'' = 793 + \frac{.000901 \times 56}{.0011} = 838.87$$

$A_3''=838.87$		log 2.92370
$C_3=$		log 1.00231
$\phi=4°\ 13'\ 14''$		tan 8.86803−10
$Y_3=$		log 2.79404
Constant		log 5.01765−10
$f_3=$	log 0.00648	loglog 7.81169−10
$C_1=$	log 0.99583	
$C_4=$	log 1.00231	

and as $C_4 = C_3$, we see that we have reached the limit of accuracy in determining the value of C, and we therefore proceed with the work with $\log C = 1.00231$, $A = a_\omega'$ $= .014601$, $V = 2900$, and from Table II $Z = 2984$, $\log B' = .10371$, $T' = 1.2332$ and $u_\omega = 2026.2$. The further work then becomes

$C=$	log 1.00231	log 1.00231		
$Z=2984$	log 3.47480			
$\phi=4°\ 13'\ 14''$	tan 8.86803−10	sec 0.00118	cos 9.99882−10	
$B'=$	log 0.10371			
$T'=1.2332$		log 0.09103		
$u_\omega=2026.2$			log 3.30668	
$X=29999$	log 4.47711			
$\omega=5°\ 21'\ 11''$	tan 8.97174−10		sec 0.00190	
$T=12.431$		log 1.09452		
$v_\omega=2029.55$			log 3.30740	

A comparison between these results and those obtained in Chapter 8, where we computed the values of the same elements with V and X as the data, gives an interesting measure of the accuracy of the methods employed. Tabulating these results for comparison, we have:

Element.	Value by work under Chapter 8.	This Chapter.
R	10,000 yards.	10,000 yards.
ω	5° 21′ 11″.	5° 21′ 11″.
T	12.43 seconds.	12.431 seconds.
v_ω	2029.0 foot-seconds.	2029.6 foot-seconds.

EXAMPLES.

1. Given the data contained in the following table, compute the values of R, ω, T and v_ω by Ingalls' methods, using Table II, and determining the value of f by successive approximations, and applying it to get the correct value of the ballistic coefficient.

Problem.	DATA. Projectile. d. In.	w. Lbs.	c.	Atmosphere. Bar. In.	Ther. °F.	Velocity. f. s.	ϕ.			ANSWERS. Range. Yds.	ω.		T. Secs.	v_ω. f. s.
A	3	13	1.00	28.00	0	1150	7°	13′	36″	2564	8°	59′	8.22	816
B	3	13	1.00	28.10	5	2700	3	45	36	4072	7	18	8.22	968
C	4	33	0.67	28.50	10	2900	1	35	36	3547	2	09	4.61	1850
D	5	50	1.00	28.67	15	3150	2	02	42	4088	3	29	5.90	1412
E	5	50	0.61	29.00	20	3150	1	30	12	3934	2	02	4.71	2004
F	6	105	0.61	29.33	25	2600	12	30	06	13201	22	36	26.98	1067
G	6	105	1.00	29.75	35	2800	1	48	36	3646	2	30	5.01	1716
H	6	105	0.61	30.00	43	2800	1	00	00	2486	1	08	2.94	2306
I	7	165	1.00	30.20	47	2700	3	59	54	6189	6	28	10.06	1311
J	7	165	0.61	30.50	51	2700	3	00	24	5929	3	58	8.15	1781
K	8	260	0.61	30.75	58	2750	3	31	54	7214	4	39	9.73	1773
L	10	510	1.00	31.00	65	2700	6	17	48	9665	10	10	15.81	1313
M	10	510	0.61	30.45	75	2700	5	43	54	10806	7	50	15.34	1602
N	12	870	0.61	30.20	80	2900	10	45	00	19751	16	32	29.40	1516
O	13	1130	1.00	30.00	85	2000	10	12	24	9810	14	20	19.73	1205
P	13	1130	0.74	29.50	90	2000	10	40	48	11086	14	06	21.16	1315
Q	14	1400	0.70	29.00	95	2000	13	45	18	13838	18	17	27.01	1302
R	14	1400	0.70	28.67	100	2600	8	19	00	14653	11	14	21.44	1657

2. Given the data contained in the following table, compute the values of R, ω, T and v_ω by Ingalls' methods, using Table II, and correcting for f by the use of the maximum ordinate given in the table.

Problem.	DATA. Projectile. d. In.	w. Lbs.	c.	Atmosphere. Bar. In.	Ther. °F.	Velocity. f. s.	ϕ.			Maximum ordinate. Feet.	ANSWERS. Range. Yds.	ω.		T. Secs.	v_ω. f. s.
A	3	13	1.00	28.10	100	1150	5°	14′	18″	150	2042	6°	08′	6.14	900
B	3	13	1.00	28.40	95	2700	2	00	24	115	3245	3	35	5.38	1263
C	4	33	0.67	28.25	90	2900	1	06	06	43	2757	1	20	3.29	2179
D	5	50	1.00	29.00	87	3150	1	27	42	79	3479	2	09	4.46	1759
E	5	50	0.61	29.20	85	3150	1	02	24	45	3035	1	16	3.36	2333
F	6	105	0.61	29.50	80	2600	10	55	18	2481	12755	19	16	24.58	1115
G	6	105	1.00	29.75	77	2800	2	18	48	159	4447	3	20	6.32	1616
H	6	105	0.61	30.00	73	2800	1	41	00	96	3912	2	03	4.86	2094
I	7	165	1.00	30.10	70	2700	5	05	48	638	7298	8	42	12.50	1213
J	7	165	0.61	30.20	60	2700	4	03	48	471	7449	5	43	10.79	1619
K	8	260	0.61	31.00	50	2750	4	11	18	532	8132	5	46	11.38	1708
L	10	510	1.00	30.50	40	2700	6	55	36	1214	10073	11	37	17.08	1245
M	10	510	0.61	30.30	35	2700	5	18	24	824	9991	7	16	14.19	1685
N	12	870	0.61	30.00	31	2900	13	44	18	5363	21969	22	52	35.96	1345
O	13	1130	1.00	29.75	20	2000	9	54	12	1488	9220	14	13	18.94	1167
P	13	1130	0.74	29.50	22	2000	9	45	12	1511	9978	13	05	19.34	1284
Q	14	1400	0.70	29.00	20	2000	15	05	00	3450	14043	21	01	23.22	1219
R	14	1400	0.70	28.50	10	2600	7	40	18	1569	13017	10	40	19.60	1585

185. Now for any given point (x, y) we may compute the value of z from $z=\frac{x}{C}$, and then, with z and V as arguments, we may take the value of a from the A column of Table II.

186. We may then compute the value of $\sin 2\phi_\omega$ from $\sin 2\phi_\omega=aC$ and thence of ϕ from (167). Also, with the same arguments, we may take from Table II the values of a', u and t' for the point (x, y).

187. Assembling the formulæ deduced in this chapter, and also the other necessary formulæ previously deduced as given in (85), (113), (138) and (144), we have, for the solution of this problem,

$$C=\frac{fw}{\delta cd^2} \tag{168}$$

$$\tan p=\frac{y}{x} \tag{169}$$

$$z=\frac{x}{C} \tag{170}$$

$$\sin 2\phi_\omega=aC \tag{171}$$

$$\sin(2\phi-p)=\sin p(1+\cot p\sin 2\phi_\omega) \tag{172}$$

$$\psi=\phi-p \tag{173}$$

$$A=\frac{\sin 2\phi}{C} \tag{174}$$

$$\tan\theta=\frac{\tan\phi}{A}(A-a') \tag{175}$$

$$t=Ct'\sec\phi \tag{176}$$

$$v=u\cos\phi\sec\theta \tag{177}$$

Elevated target.

188. Let us now compute these several elements for our standard problem 12″ gun, $V=2900$ f. s., $w=870$ pounds, $c=0.61$, for a target at a horizontal distance of 10,000 yards from the gun, and 1500 feet above the level of the gun, the barometer being at 29.00″ and the thermometer at 90° F. Also, instead of computing the altitude factor, we will take it from Table V as being sufficiently accurate for this purpose.

Taking the mean altitude as two-thirds of 1500 feet, that is, 1000 feet, Table V gives us that $f=1.026$. Taking K from Table VI.

$K=$		log 0.99583		
$f=1.026$		log 0.01115		
$\delta=.921$	log 9.96426−10	colog 0.03574		
$C=$		log 1.04272	colog 8.95728−10	
$y=1500$	log 3.17609			
$x=30000$	log 4.47712			log 4.47712
$p=2°\ 51'\ 45''$	tan 8.69897−10			
$z=2719.0$				log 3.43440

From Table II

$a=.01299$ $a'=.0292$ $u=2095.1$ $t'=1.104$

$C=$ .... log 1.04272

$a=.01299$ .... log 8.11361−10

$2\phi_\omega=$ .... sin 9.15633−10

$p=2°\ 51'\ 45''$ .... cot 1.30103

$\cot p \sin 2\phi_\omega=2.8665$ .... log 0.45736

$1+\cot p \sin 2\phi_\omega=3.8665$ .... log 0.58732

$p=2°\ 51'\ 45''$ .... sin 8.69844−10

$2\phi-p=11°\ 07'\ 59''$ ..... sin 9.28576−10

$p=\ 2°\ 51'\ 45''$ $\phi=6°\ 59'\ 52''$

$2\phi=13°\ 59'\ 44''$ $p=2°\ 51'\ 45''$

$\phi=\ 6°\ 59'\ 52''$ $\psi=4°\ 08'\ 07''$

$2\phi=13°\ 59'\ 44''$ .... sin 9.38356−10

$C=$ .... colog 8.95728−10

$A=\ .02192$ .... log 8.34084−10

$a'=\ .02920$

$A-a'=(-).00728$ ..... (−)log 7.86213−10

$\phi=6°\ 59'\ 52''$ .... tan 9.08908−10 .. sec 0.00324 ... cos 9.99676−10

$A=.02192$ .... colog 1.65916

$t'=1.104$ .... log 0.04297

$u=2095.1$ .... log 3.32120

$C=$ .... log 1.04272

$\theta=(-)2°\ 20'\ 05''$ .. (−)tan 8.61037−10 .... sec 0.00036

$t=12.273$ .... log 1.08893

$v=2081.2$ .... log 3.31832

169. Now suppose that, instead of the conditions worked out above, the gun had been in a battery on the hill and the ship had been the target, all other conditions being the same. The work would have been the same down to and including the determination of the values of a, a', u and t', except that y is negative, and therefore $p=(-)2°\ 51'\ 45''$. We then proceed as before, but with this negative value of p instead of the positive one employed before, and the subsequent work becomes: **Depressed target.**

$\cot p \sin 2\phi_\omega=(-)2.8665$

$1+\cot p \sin 2\phi_\omega=(-)1.8665$ .... (−)log 0.27103

$p=(-)2°\ 51'\ 45''$ .... (−)sin 8.69844−10

$2\phi-p=5°\ 19'\ 32''$ .... (+)sin 8.96947−10

$p=(-)2°\ 51'\ 45''$ $\phi=\ 1°\ 13'\ 54''$

$2\phi=\ 2°\ 27'\ 47''$ $p=(-)2°\ 51'\ 45''$

$\phi=\ 1°\ 13'\ 54''$ $\psi=\ 4°\ 05'\ 39''$

$2\phi = 2°\ 27'\ 47''$			sin 8.63321−10
$C =$			colog 8.95728−10
$A =$ .00390			log 7.59049−10
$\alpha' =$ .02920			
$A-\alpha' = (-).02530$	(−)log 8.40312−10		
$\phi = 1°\ 13'\ 54''$	tan 8.33243−10	sec 0.00010	cos 9.99990−10
$A = .0039$	colog 2.40951		
$t' = 1.104$	log 0.04297		
$u = 2095.1$			log 3.32120
$C =$	log 1.04272		
$\theta = (-)7°\ 57'\ 01''$	(−)tan 9.14506−10		sec 0.00419
$t = 12.184$	log 1.08579		
$v = 2114.9$			log 3.32529

190. Assembling the results of these last two problems for comparison, we have:

	Value for Ship attacking battery.	Value for Battery attacking ship.
ψ	4° 08′ 07″.	4° 05′ 39″.
θ	(−)2° 20′ 05″.	(−)7° 57′ 01″.
t	12.273 seconds.	12.184 seconds.
v	2081.2 f. s.	2114.9 f. s.

In working problems similar to the above, great care must be taken to carry through consistently the signs of the several quantities and logarithms.

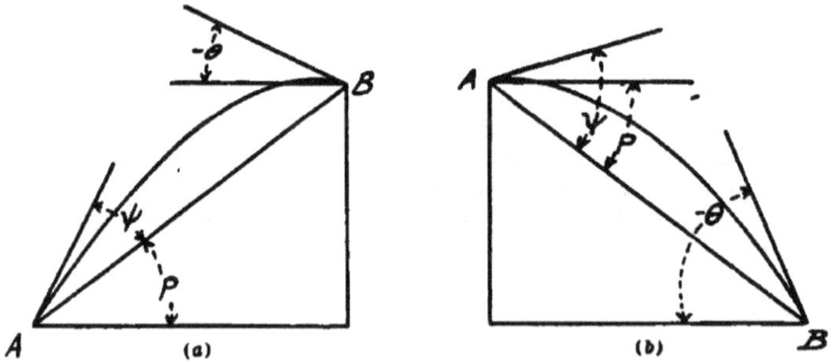

FIGURE 14.

191. From Figure 14, in which (*a*) represents the first case and (*b*) the second, we plainly see that in (*a*) the force of gravity acts to reduce the velocity of the projectile, and in (*b*) to increase it from what it would be in the horizontal trajectory. Therefore we would expect to find it necessary to give the gun a greater elevation relative to the line of sight in order to hit in (*a*) than in (*b*), and the results of the work show that such is the case.

192. Also, from the figures we can see that the angle of inclination of the curve to the horizontal at the point of impact would be greater in (*b*) than in (*a*), which is again shown by the work.

193. Also, as gravity in (*a*) reduces and in (*b*) increases the velocity, we would expect to have the remaining velocity less and the time of flight greater in (*a*) than in (*b*), and again the work shows this to be the case.

194. The angle of elevation resulting from the work is of course the angle at which the gun must be pointed above the target in either case, that is, above the line of sight *AB*. The sight drums are marked in yards, however, and not in degrees of elevation; so to practically set the sights we look in the range table of the gun and find in Column 2 an angle of departure equal to our found angle of elevation, and find in Column 1 the range in yards corresponding to that angle of departure. We then set our sights in range to that number of yards, and point the gun at the target, that is, bring the line of sight to coincide with the line *AB* of the figure. The gun is then elevated at the proper angle above the line *AB*, ψ from the work, and at an angle of departure above the horizontal of $\phi=\psi+p$.

195. In the problem shown in Figure 14(*a*), we have by a simple interpolation between Columns 1 and 2, that the range corresponding to an angle of departure of 4° 08′ 07″ is 9841 yards, which is the range at which the sight should be set.

196. Similarly, in Figure 14(*b*), the sight should be set for an angle of departure of 4° 05′ 39″, that is, at 9764 yards.

197. In Chapters 8, 9 and 10, and in this chapter, we have shown the methods and formulæ to be employed in solving certain of the more common and more important ballistic problems. Those selected for the purposes of this book are the ones most likely to be encountered in naval practice, but there are a large number of others that may arise under special circumstances, which may be solved by similar methods. Some of the more important of these are enumerated below, to show the scope of the methods that have been taught, for they are all solved in similar ways. In each case the solution consists of a preliminary transformation of the fundamental ballistic formulæ, in a manner similar to those shown in the preceding pages of this book, in order to fit them for use in the particular problem under consideration; and then the necessary computations may be made from the resultant equations. It should also be borne in mind that all our work has so far applied only to direct fire, as do also the problems enumerated below, and that when problems incident to mortar fire and other special classes of work are added, the number of problems that may present themselves becomes very large. Beside the problems already explained in these pages, some of the simpler direct fire problems that may be readily solved by similar methods are:

(a) Knowing X, C and v_ω; to compute V.
(b) Knowing V, C and v_ω; to compute X.
(c) Knowing V, X and C; to compute T.
(d) Knowing V, T and C; to compute v_ω.
(e) Knowing V, C and v_ω; to compute X, ϕ, ω and T.
(f) Knowing V, C and ω; to compute X, ϕ, T and v_ω.
(g) Knowing X, ϕ and C; to compute V.
(h) Knowing T, ϕ and C; to compute V.

$\Delta R_w''$.... That part of ΔR_w in yards which is due to Δw directly.

H.... Change in height of point of impact on vertical screen in feet, due to a change of ΔR in R. Figures as subscripts to the H show the change in range necessary to give that value of H.

Range tables.

198. The range tables are computed for standard conditions, but there are certain elements that are not always standard; for instance, the density of the atmosphere, which rarely is standard. The principal elements that may vary from standard are the initial velocity, variation in which may result from a variation of the temperature of the powder charge from standard or other causes; the density of the atmosphere and the weight of the projectile. In order that a satisfactory use may be made of the range tables, it is therefore necessary to include in them data showing the effect upon the trajectory of small variations from standard in the elements enumerated above. Columns 10, 11 and 12 of the range table therefore contain data showing the effect upon the range of small variations from standard in the initial velocity, in the weight of the projectile and in the density of the atmosphere, respectively. It is the province of this chapter to show how the data in these columns is derived, and also that in Column 19, which shows the effect upon the position of the point of impact in the vertical plane through the target of a small variation of the setting of the sight in range, or, as it was formerly called, the sight bar height.

199. Let us take the two principal equations of exterior ballistics, namely:

$$X = C(S_u - S_V) \tag{178}$$

$$\sin 2\phi = C\left(\frac{A_u - A_V}{S_u - S_V} - I_V\right) \tag{179}$$

These involve the range, X; the angle of departure, ϕ; the ballistic coefficient, C; and the initial velocity, V; either directly or through their functions as given in Table I. These four are the elements in which variations from standard may be expected, as indicated in the preceding paragraph; as a change in the density of the atmosphere involves a corresponding change in the value of C, and as a change in the weight of the projectile involves a corresponding change in both the initial velocity and ballistic coefficient, as will be explained later.

Formula for variations.

200. For our present purpose, therefore, we wish, if practicable, to derive from (178) and (179) a single differential equation in which all four of the quantities enumerated shall appear as variables. By a noteworthy series of mathematical combinations and differentiations, which need not be followed here, Colonel Ingalls has derived such an equation, his result being

$$\Delta(\sin 2\phi) = -C\Delta_{VA} - (B-A)\Delta C + BC\,\frac{\Delta X}{X} \tag{180}$$

In this equation the symbol Δ indicates a comparatively small difference in value or differential increment (either positive or negative) in the value of the quantity to which prefixed. C is the ballistic coefficient; ϕ is the angle of departure; A and B are Ingalls' secondary functions as they appear in Table II; and Δ_{VA} is the quantity contained in Table II in the Δ_V column pertaining to A, where Δ_{VA} is for ± 50 or ± 100 f. s. according to the table used. For 100 f. s. difference in velocity between successive tables, the solution of the above equation would give the proper result as it stands; but for 50 f. s. difference in velocity, fifty one-hundredths, or one-half, of the variation should be taken, as shown later. Great care must be exercised not to confuse the three quantities represented by the symbols Δ_{VA} as given above, δV, which represents a differential increment of the initial velocity and ΔV, which represents the difference in velocity between two successive tables in Table II. (Ingalls' tables

CHAPTER 12.

THE EFFECT UPON THE RANGE OF VARIATIONS IN THE OTHER BALLISTIC ELEMENTS, WHICH INCLUDES THE DATA GIVEN IN COLUMNS 10, 11, 12 AND 19 OF THE RANGE TABLES.

New Symbols Introduced.

ΔX.... Variation in the range in feet.

ΔR.... Variation in the range in yards.

$\Delta(\sin 2\phi)$.... Variation in the sine of twice the angle of departure.

Δ_{VA}.... Quantity appearing in Table II, in the Δ_V column pertaining to A. With figures before the V it shows the amount of variation in V for which used. (Be careful not to confuse this symbol with ΔV or δV.)

δV.... Variation in the initial velocity. (Be careful not to confuse this symbol with Δ_{VA} or ΔV.)

ΔV.... Difference between V for two successive tables in Table II (Ingalls' table as originally computed; not the abridged tables reproduced for use with this text book) being either 50 f. s. or 100 f. s. (Be careful not to confuse this symbol with Δ_{VA} or δV.)

ΔV_w.... Variation in the initial velocity due to a variation in weight of projectile. Figures before the w show amount of variation in w in pounds.

ΔX_V.... Variation in the range in feet due to a variation in V. Figures before the V show the amount of variation in V in foot-seconds.

ΔR_V.... Variation in the range in yards due to a variation in V. Figures before the V show the amount of variation in V in foot-seconds.

ΔC.... Variation in the ballistic coefficient.

ΔX_C.... Variation in the range in feet due to a variation in C. Figures before the C show the percentage variation in that quantity.

ΔR_C.... Variation in the range in yards due to a variation in C. Figures before the C show the percentage variation in that quantity.

$\Delta\delta$.... Variation in the value of δ.

ΔX_δ.... Variation in the range in feet due to a variation in δ. Figures before the δ show the percentage variation in that quantity.

ΔR_δ.... Variation in the range in yards due to a variation in δ. Figures before the δ show the percentage variation in that quantity.

Δw.... Variation in w in pounds.

ΔX_w.... Variation in the range in feet due to a variation in w. Figures before the w show the amount of variation in that quantity in pounds.

$\Delta X_w'$.... That part of ΔX_w in feet which is due to the variation in initial velocity resulting from Δw.

$\Delta X_w''$.... That part of ΔX_w in feet which is due to Δw directly.

ΔR_w.... Variation in the range in yards due to a variation in w. Figures before the w show the amount of variation in that quantity in pounds.

$\Delta R_w'$.... That part of ΔR_w in yards which is due to the variation in initial velocity resulting from Δw.

$\Delta R_w''$.... That part of ΔR_w in yards which is due to Δw directly.

H.... Change in height of point of impact on vertical screen in feet, due to a change of ΔR in R. Figures as subscripts to the H show the change in range necessary to give that value of H.

Range tables.

198. The range tables are computed for standard conditions, but there are certain elements that are not always standard; for instance, the density of the atmosphere, which rarely is standard. The principal elements that may vary from standard are the initial velocity, variation in which may result from a variation of the temperature of the powder charge from standard or other causes; the density of the atmosphere and the weight of the projectile. In order that a satisfactory use may be made of the range tables, it is therefore necessary to include in them data showing the effect upon the trajectory of small variations from standard in the elements enumerated above. Columns 10, 11 and 12 of the range table therefore contain data showing the effect upon the range of small variations from standard in the initial velocity, in the weight of the projectile and in the density of the atmosphere, respectively. It is the province of this chapter to show how the data in these columns is derived, and also that in Column 19, which shows the effect upon the position of the point of impact in the vertical plane through the target of a small variation of the setting of the sight in range, or, as it was formerly called, the sight bar height.

199. Let us take the two principal equations of exterior ballistics, namely:

$$X=C(S_\omega-S_V) \qquad (178)$$

$$\sin 2\phi=C\left(\frac{A_\omega-A_V}{S_\omega-S_V}-I_V\right) \qquad (179)$$

These involve the range, X; the angle of departure, ϕ; the ballistic coefficient, C; and the initial velocity, V; either directly or through their functions as given in Table I. These four are the elements in which variations from standard may be expected, as indicated in the preceding paragraph; as a change in the density of the atmosphere involves a corresponding change in the value of C, and as a change in the weight of the projectile involves a corresponding change in both the initial velocity and ballistic coefficient, as will be explained later.

Formula for variations.

200. For our present purpose, therefore, we wish, if practicable, to derive from (178) and (179) a single differential equation in which all four of the quantities enumerated shall appear as variables. By a noteworthy series of mathematical combinations and differentiations, which need not be followed here, Colonel Ingalls has derived such an equation, his result being

$$\Delta(\sin 2\phi)=-C\Delta_{VA}-(B-A)\Delta C+BC\,\frac{\Delta X}{X} \qquad (180)$$

In this equation the symbol Δ indicates a comparatively small difference in value or differential increment (either positive or negative) in the value of the quantity to which prefixed. C is the ballistic coefficient; ϕ is the angle of departure; A and B are Ingalls' secondary functions as they appear in Table II; and Δ_{VA} is the quantity contained in Table II in the Δ_V column pertaining to A, where Δ_{VA} is for ± 50 or ± 100 f. s. according to the table used. For 100 f. s. difference in velocity between successive tables, the solution of the above equation would give the proper result as it stands; but for 50 f. s. difference in velocity, fifty one-hundredths, or one-half, of the variation should be taken, as shown later. Great care must be exercised not to confuse the three quantities represented by the symbols Δ_{VA} as given above, δV, which represents a differential increment of the initial velocity and ΔV, which represents the difference in velocity between two successive tables in Table II. (Ingalls' tables

feet, we may use the range in yards, which will give a result also in yards. Also the difference Δ_{VA} at this point in the table is for a difference ΔV in velocity between two successive tables ($\Delta V = 100$ f. s., between tables 2900 to 3000 f. s., and 3000 to 3100 f. s.), therefore we apply a factor of $\frac{\delta V}{\Delta V}\left(\frac{50}{100}\text{ in this case}\right)$. Therefore if we let ΔR_V represent the change in range in yards for a variation of $\delta V = 50$ f. s. in the initial velocity, the expression becomes

$$\Delta R_V = \frac{\Delta_{VA}}{B} \times \frac{\delta V}{\Delta V} \times R$$

The work then becomes, from Table II:

$$\Delta_{VA} = .00099 + \frac{.00004 \times 84.1}{100} = .001024$$

$$B = .0178 + \frac{.0009 \times 84.1}{100} = .01856$$

$\Delta_{VA} = .001024$		log 7.01030 − 10
$\delta V = \pm 50$		±log 1.69897
$R = 10000$		log 4.00000
$B = .01856$	log 8.26857 − 10	colog 1.73142
$\Delta V = 100$	log 2.00000	colog 8.00000 − 10
$\Delta R_V = \pm 276$ yards		±log 2.44069

and the signs show that an increase in initial velocity will give an increase in range, and the reverse, which was of course to be expected.

For variation in density of atmosphere.

203. Again, suppose that the density of the air varies from standard, as it generally does, and we wish to determine the resultant effect upon the range. We know that $C = \frac{fw}{\delta c d^2}$, and in this case the only variables are X and δ, as ϕ, V and w are supposed to be constant. A change in the value of δ therefore causes a change of the same amount in the value of C, but as δ appears in the denominator of C, an increase of a certain per cent in the value of δ will cause a decrease of the same per cent in the value of C, that is, a $\pm\Delta\delta$ gives a $\mp\Delta C$. Equation (180) therefore becomes

$$BC\frac{\Delta X_C}{X} = -(B-A)\Delta C$$

or

$$\Delta X_C = -\frac{(B-A)X}{B} \times \frac{\Delta C}{C} \qquad (182)$$

204. As an example of the use of this formula, let us take the same data as in paragraph 202, and compute the change of range resulting from a variation from standard of ±10 per cent in the density of the atmosphere, letting $\Delta R_{10\delta}$ represent the desired result in yards, and again substituting R for X to get the result in yards. Equation (182) then becomes

$$\Delta R_\delta = -\frac{(B-A)R}{B} \times \frac{\Delta C}{C} = -\frac{(B-A)R}{B} \times \frac{\Delta\delta}{\delta}$$

$B = .018560$
$A = .014601$

$B - A = .003959$		log 7.59759 − 10
$R = 10000$		log 4.00000
$B = .01856$	log 8.26857 − 10	colog 1.73143 − 10
$\frac{\Delta\delta}{\delta} = \pm .1$		±log 9.00000 − 10
$\Delta R_{10\delta} = \mp 213$ yards		±log 2.32902

and substituting R for X to get the result in yards

$$\Delta R_w'' = \frac{(B-A)R}{B} \times \frac{\Delta w}{w} \tag{187}$$

To combine the two results to get the total change in range resulting from both causes in yards, we would have

$$\Delta R_w = \mp \Delta R_w' + \Delta R_w'' = \frac{\Delta_{VA}}{B} \times \frac{\delta V}{\Delta V} \times R + \frac{(B-A)R}{B} \times \frac{\Delta w}{w} \tag{188}$$

the sign of the first term of the second member being inverted to make the last two terms of opposite sign and the final result of the proper sign.

208. As an illustration of the use of this formula, let us revert once more to our standard problem as given in paragraph 202, and compute the change in range in that case resulting from a variation from standard of ± 10 pounds in the weight of the projectile. Using the formulæ given in paragraphs 206 and 207 we have

$\Delta_{VA} = .001024 \qquad A = .014601 \qquad B = .018560$

$\Delta w = \pm 10$		$\pm$log 1.00000
$w = 870$	log 2.93952	colog 7.06048 − 10
$V = 2900$		log 3.46240
$M = .36$		log 9.55630 − 10
$\delta V = \mp 12$ f. s.		$\pm$log 1.07918
$\Delta_{VA} = .001024$		log 7.01030 − 10
$\delta V = \mp 12$		$\mp$log 1.07918
$R = 10000$		log 4.00000
$B = .01856$	log 8.26857 − 10	colog 1.73143
$\Delta V = 100$	log 2.00000	colog 8.00000 − 10
$\Delta R_w' = \mp 66.21$		$\mp$log 1.82091
$B = .018560$		
$A = .014601$		
$B - A = .003959$		log 7.59759 − 10
$R = 10000$		log 4.00000
$B = .01856$	log 8.26857 − 10	colog 1.73143
$\Delta w = \pm 10$		$\pm$log 1.00000
$w = 870$	log 2.93952	colog 7.06048 − 10
$\Delta R_w'' = \pm 24.52$		$\pm$log 1.38950

$\Delta R_w = \mp 41.69$ yards

which shows that for this gun, at this range, an increase of 10 pounds above standard in the weight of the projectile decreases the range 41.6 yards, and the reverse. Note also that here a positive value of Δw gives a negative value of ΔR_w, but that in the range table there is no negative sign attached to the figures in the appropriate column. The above is of course the correct mathematical convention, but after the work is all done, as a decrease in range is the normal and general result of an increase in weight, in making up the range tables such a decrease is considered as positive and the signs in the tables are given accordingly.

Short method for variation in weight of projectile.

209. The above is the general method, but in actually computing the data for the range tables there is a short cut that may advantageously be used to reduce the amount of labor involved in the computations for Column 11. If we first compute the data for Columns 10 and 12, as is actually done in such computations and as we have already done here; that is, if we have already found, for the given range, the change in range resulting from a variation in the initial velocity of $\pm\delta V$, and also that resulting from a variation of $\pm\Delta C$ in the value of the ballistic coefficient which is the same as that due to a variation of $\mp\Delta\delta$ in the density of the air, we readily derive the following formulæ:

$$\Delta R_w' = \Delta R_v \times \frac{\delta V}{\delta V'} \tag{189}$$

$$\Delta R_w'' = \Delta R_\delta \times \frac{\Delta w}{w} \times \frac{\delta}{\Delta\delta} \tag{190}$$

$$\Delta R_w = \Delta R_w' + \Delta R_w'' = \Delta R_V \times \frac{\delta V}{\delta V'} + \Delta R_\delta \times \frac{\Delta w}{w} \times \frac{\delta}{\Delta\delta} \tag{191}$$

the two terms being combined with the proper signs.

For our given problem the work then becomes, after finding that $V = 12$ f. s. in the same way that we did before

	$\Delta R_V = 276$		log 2.44070
	$\delta V = \mp 12$		$\mp$log 1.07918
	$\delta V' = 50$	log 1.69897	colog 8.30103 − 10
$\Delta R_w' = \mp 66.21$			$\mp$log 1.82091
	$\Delta R_\delta = 213$		log 2.32901
	$\Delta w = \pm 10$		$\pm$log 1.00000
	$w = 870$	log 2.93952	colog 7.06048 − 10
	$\Delta\delta = 10$		log 1.00000
$\Delta R_w'' = \pm 24.52$			$\pm$log 1.38949
$\Delta R_w = \mp 41.62$ yards			

Note that the logarithms used above for 276 and 213 are not taken from the log table, but are the exact logarithms resulting from the previous work, as given in paragraphs 202 and 204.

The $\Delta\delta = 10$ in the last part of the above work comes in because the $\Delta R_\delta = 213$ is for 10 per cent variation in density; therefore for 100 per cent variation it would be $\Delta\delta \times \Delta R_\delta = 213 \times 10$, of which we take $\frac{\Delta w}{w} = \frac{10}{870}$.

210. We will now investigate the method of computing the data contained in Column 19 of the range tables; that is, of determining how much vertical displacement in the vertical plane through the target at the given range will result from an increase or decrease of a few yards in the setting of the sight in range; or, as it was formerly called, in the sight bar height. **Change of point of impact in vertical plane.**

211. Assuming that, for flat trajectories, when the point of fall is not far from the target as compared to the range, the portion of the trajectory between the target and the point of fall is practically a straight line, we see from Figure 15, in which $AB=\Delta X$, $AC=H$ and $ABC=\omega$, that, if we let H represent the vertical change of

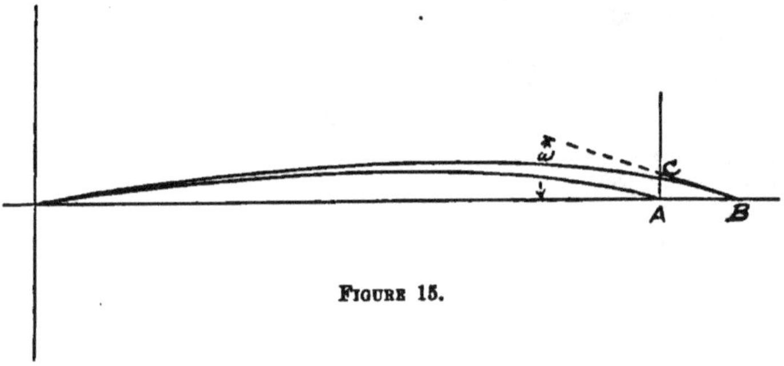

FIGURE 15.

point of impact in feet, and ΔX the change in range that will correspond, also in feet, we will have

$$\tan\omega=\frac{H}{\Delta X}, \text{ or } H=\Delta X\tan\omega \qquad (192)$$

212. As an example, we will take our standard problem, for a range of 10,000 yards, and will find the change in the point of impact in the vertical plane through the target resulting from a change in sight setting of ±100 yards. By equation (192) the work becomes

$\Delta X=\pm300$	$\pm\log$ 2.47712
$\omega=5^\circ\ 21'\ 11''$	tan 8.97174−10
$H_{100}=\pm28$ feet	$\pm\log$ 1.44886

The value of ω employed above is taken from paragraph 157 of Chapter 8, where we explained the opening work of computation relative to this particular trajectory.

EXAMPLES.

1. Require to be taken from the range tables the amount of change of range resulting from any reasonable:

(a) Variation from standard in the initial velocity.

(b) Variation from standard in the weight of the projectile.

(c) Variation from standard in the density of the atmosphere. The readings of barometer and thermometer should be given, and determination of change of range made by use of Table IV. Also exercise in the same problem, using Table III instead of Table IV.

(d) In addition to the above, call for the taking from the tables of the effect upon the range of two or more of the above variations combined.

(e) Also call for the determination from the tables of the change of the point of impact in the vertical plane resulting from a change in the setting of the sight in range, and *vice versa*.

2. Compute the change in range resulting from the variation from standard in the initial velocity given below, all other conditions being standard.

Problem.	DATA.							ANSWERS.
	Projectile.			Velocity. f. s.	Range. Yds.	Maxi-mum. ordinate. Feet.	Variation in initial velocity. f. s.	Change in range. Yds.
	d. In.	w. Lbs.	c.					
A	3	13	1.00	1150	2000	150	+25	+ 49.8
B	3	13	1.00	2700	3600	180	—30	— 44.7
C	4	33	0.67	2900	3000	55	+50	+ 83.4
D	5	50	1.00	3150	4000	125	—60	— 98.4
E	5	50	0.61	3150	4000	90	+75	+144.8
F	6	105	0.61	2600	11500	1887	—45	—220.8
G	6	105	1.00	2900	4500	169	+50	+110.5
H	6	105	0.61	2800	3500	75	—40	— 82.9
I	7	165	1.00	2700	7000	563	+40	+127.4
J	7	165	0.61	2700	7000	395	—60	—227.0
K	8	260	0.61	2750	8000	485	+60	+260.7
L	10	510	1.00	2700	10000	1085	—45	—211.2
M	10	510	0.61	2700	11000	997	+45	+266.9
N	12	870	0.61	2900	21000	4218	—70	—647.2
O	13	1130	1.00	2000	10000	1701	+70	+460.7
P	13	1130	0.74	2000	11000	1830	—60	—467.3
Q	14	1400	0.70	2000	14000	3204	+45	+431.8
R	14	1400	0.70	2600	14000	1790	—45	—347.6

NOTE.—The above results vary slightly from those taken from the range tables. The reason for this is that the range table results are more accurately determined by using the corrected value of *C*, found by the methods of Chapter 8, Example 7; whereas in the above the value of *C* is determined by the use of a value of *f* determined by the use of the maximum ordinate given above and of Table V. The same variation from range table results will be found in all problems in which this latter process is employed.

3. Compute the change in range resulting from the variation from standard in the density of the atmosphere given below, other conditions being standard.

Problem.	DATA.							ANSWERS.
	Projectile.			Velocity. f. s.	Range. Yds.	Maxi mum ordinate. Feet.	Varia-tion in density %.	Change in range. Yds.
	d. In.	w. Lbs.	c.					
A	3	13	1.00	1150	1600	79	+ 5	— 10.9
B	3	13	1.00	2700	3000	104	— 7	+ 85.7
C	4	33	0.67	2900	3500	80	+10	— 83.7
D	5	50	1.00	3150	3000	57	—10	+ 90.9
E	5	50	0.61	3150	3000	45	+ 7	— 40.5
F	6	105	0.61	2600	13000	2725	— 5	+298.3
G	6	105	1.00	2800	3000	61	+ 6	— 39.7
H	6	105	0.61	2800	2500	35	— 6	+ 18.2
I	7	165	1.00	2700	6000	363	+ 8	—173.1
J	7	165	0.61	2700	6000	260	— 8	+113.3
K	8	260	0.61	2750	7000	350	+12	—190.3
L	10	510	1.00	2700	9000	807	—12	+384.3
M	10	510	0.61	2700	10000	784	+ 7	—177.8
N	12	870	0.61	2900	22000	4801	— 7	+617.5
O	13	1130	1.00	2000	9000	1292	+ 6	—155.7
P	13	1130	0.74	2000	10000	1438	— 6	+147.2
Q	14	1400	0.70	2000	13000	2637	+ 5	—176.1
R	14	1400	0.70	2000	13000	1480	— 5	+175.1

4. Compute the change in range resulting from the variation from standard in the weight of the projectile given below, other conditions being standard. Use the direct method, without the use of Columns 10 and 12 of the range tables.

Problem.	DATA.							ANSWERS.
	Projectile.			Velocity. f. s.	Range. Yds.	Maximum ordinate. Feet.	Variation in weight. Lbs.	Change in range. Yds.
	d. In.	*ır.* Lbs.	*c.*					
C................	4	33	0.67	2900	3000	55	+ 1	—33.7
F................	6	105	0.61	2600	13600	3123	— 2	—22.2
H................	6	105	0.61	2800	2600	38	— 5	+62.0
J................	7	165	0.61	2700	6100	280	— 3	+34.1
K................	8	260	0.61	2750	7100	362	+ 4	—35.4
M................	10	510	0.61	2700	10100	804	+ 5	—27.7
N................	12	870	0.61	2900	21000	4218	— 5	+ 8.3
P................	13	1130	0.74	2000	10100	1474	—15	+36.7
Q................	14	1400	0.70	2000	13100	2690	+12	—26.0
R................	14	1400	0.70	2600	13100	1509	—12	+28.4

NOTE.—The signs in the above results are mathematically correct; that is, a positive result means an increase in range. But remember the convention reversing these signs in the range tables, whereby a positive sign (or no sign) means a decrease in range, the normal and most common result of an increase in weight of projectile.

5. Compute the change in range resulting from the variation from standard in the weight of the projectile given below, other conditions being standard; using the data from Columns 10 and 12 of the range tables.

Problem.	DATA.								ANSWERS.
	Projectile.			*V.* f. s.	Range. Yds.	Variation in weight. Lbs.	Col. 10. Change in range for var. of ±50 f. s. in *I. V.* Yds.	Col. 12 Change in range for var. of ±10% in density. Yds.	Change in Range. Yds.
	d. In.	*w.* Lbs.	*c.*						
C.......	4	33	0.67	2900	4000	+ 1	103	109	—32.1
F.......	6	105	0.61	2600	12000	— 2	260	531	— 8.4
H.......	6	105	0.61	2800	3500	— 5	103	57	+71.7
J.......	7	165	0.61	2700	7000	— 5	190	188	+33.0
K.......	8	260	0.61	2750	8000	+ 7	217	204	—60.8
M.......	10	510	0.61	2700	11000	+ 8	296	300	—23.2
N.......	12	870	0.61	2900	18500	— 8	432	648	+24.4
P.......	13	1130	0.74	2000	11000	—12	391	286	+29.4
Q.......	14	1400	0.70	2000	14000	+12	484	392	—26.1
R.......	14	1400	0.70	2600	14000	—13	388	395	+30.8

NOTE.—See note to Example 4 about signs, which applies to this example also.

6. Compute the change in the position of the point of impact in the vertical plane through the target for the following variations in the setting of the sight in range, taking the values of the angle of fall from the range tables. Conditions standard.

Problem.	DATA.						ANSWERS.
	Projectile.			Velocity. f. s.	Range. Yds.	Variation in setting of sight in range. Yds. + = incr'se. — = decr'se.	Change in point of impact. Ft. + = raise. — = lower.
	d. In.	*W.* Lbs.	*c.*				
A	3	13	1.00	1150	2100	+ 50	+17.4
B	3	13	1.00	2700	3600	— 50	—13.5
C	4	33	0.67	2000	4000	+100	+13.2
D	5	50	1.00	3150	3900	—100	—12.9
E	5	50	0.61	3150	3000	+ 75	+ 6.6
F	6	105	0.61	2600	14000	— 75	—98.4
G	6	105	1.00	2800	3600	+ 60	+ 7.4
H	6	105	0.61	2800	3100	— 60	— 4.7
I	7	165	1.00	2700	6000	+ 80	+29.5
J	7	165	0.61	2700	6000	— 80	—19.2
K	8	260	0.61	2750	7000	+ 90	+23.2
L	10	510	1.00	2700	9600	— 90	—45.9
M	10	510	0.61	2700	10000	+110	+44.0
N	12	870	0.61	2900	17000	—110	—75.5
O	13	1130	1.00	2000	9600	+ 70	+53.1
P	13	1130	0.74	2000	10600	— 70	—51.0
Q	14	1400	0.70	2000	13600	+ 60	+61.4
R	14	1400	0.70	2600	13600	— 60	—34.6

PART III.

THE VARIATION OF THE TRAJECTORY FROM A PLANE CURVE.

INTRODUCTION TO PART III.

Having completed the consideration of the general trajectory in air for all velocities when considered as a plane curve, by means of the differential equations connected therewith, and having seen that for the purposes discussed in Parts I and II no material error is introduced into the results by such assumption that the trajectory is a plane curve, we now come to the question of how to hit a given spot with the projectile from a given gun, under given conditions, so far as the deflection of the projectile from the original plane of fire is concerned. Although such variation will not materially affect the results of computations of the values of the ranges, angles, velocities, times, etc., as already shown, it will at once be apparent that a variation of a very few yards from the original plane of fire will cause a miss, unless compensated for in the sighting of the gun. In Part III we therefore take up the study of the forces acting to deflect the projectile from the original plane of fire, thereby causing a miss unless compensated. These are drift, wind and motion of the gun or target; and expressions will be derived to determine the extent of the deflections arising from each cause, and methods will be devised for applying the necessary corrections in aiming to overcome these errors.

was first deflected. (The imprints of projectiles at their points of fall upon the ground at long ranges show this to be the case.) Therefore, with right-handed rifling, the projectile during its flight always points very slightly to the right of the direction of motion; and, as a result, the resistance of the air has a component normal to that direction, which carries the projectile bodily to the right with increasing velocity. (This applies only to direct fire. When the angle of departure exceeds 70°, as it sometimes does in mortar fire, the drift is reversed in direction. The reason for this appears to be that, at the vertex of the trajectory, the direction of the tangent changes so suddenly that the slow movement of precession is insufficient to cause the axis of the projectile to keep pace with it. The angle between the tangent and the axis of the projectile therefore becomes greater than 90°; the projectile moves approximately base first; the resistance of the air acts upon the opposite side of the projectile from that upon which it acted in the ascending branch of the curve; and the lateral movement to the right is speedily checked and reversed. With these very high angle trajectories the projectile always strikes base first.)

Computation of drift.

216. The precise experimental determination of the amount of drift is a matter of great difficulty, as its value is materially affected by lateral wind pressure and by unavoidable differences between different projectiles. For computing its value, Mayevski derived an approximate formula, which has been reduced by Ingalls to the form

$$D=\frac{\mu}{n}\times\frac{\lambda}{h}\times\frac{C^2D'}{\cos^2\phi} \tag{193}$$

In which

$\mu=\frac{k^2}{R^2}$, where k is the radius of gyration of the projectile and R is its radius.

$\frac{\lambda}{h}$ = a quantity which depends upon the length of the projectile, the shape of the head, the angle which the resultant resistance makes with the axis and the distance of the center of pressure from the center of gravity.

n = the twist of the rifling in calibers at the muzzle, that is, the distance in calibers that the projectile advances along the trajectory at the muzzle while making one revolution.

C = the ballistic coefficient.

ϕ = the angle of departure.

D' = Ingalls' secondary function for drift, to be found in Table II, with V and Z as arguments.

D = drift in yards for the given range and angle of departure.

217. It has also been found necessary in some cases to multiply the results obtained by the use of the above formula by a certain empirical multiplier in order to get correct results. The data required for the drift computation is therefore:

Problem.	DATA.							
	Gun and projectile.			Velocity. f. s.	μ.	$\frac{\lambda}{h}$.	n.	Multiplier.
	d. In.	w. Lbs.	c.					
A	3	13	1.00	1150	0.53	0.32	25	1.0
B	3	13	1.00	2700	0.53	0.32	25	1.0
C	4	33	0.67	2900	0.53	0.32	25	1.0
D	5	50	1.00	3150	0.53	0.32	25	1.5
E	5	50	0.61	3150	0.53	0.32	25	1.5
F	6	105	0.61	2600	0.53	0.32	25	1.5
G	6	105	1.00	2800	0.53	0.32	25	1.0
H	6	105	0.61	2800	0.53	0.32	25	1.5
I	7	165	1.00	2700	0.53	0.32	25	1.0
J	7	165	0.61	2700	0.53	0.32	25	1.5
K	8	260	0.61	2750	0.53	0.32	25	1.5
L	10	510	1.00	2700	0.53	0.32	25	1.0
M	10	510	0.61	2700	0.53	0.32	25	1.5
N	12	870	0.61	2900	0.53	0.32	25	1.5
O	13	1130	1.00	2000	0.53	0.32	25	1.0
P	13	1130	0.74	2000	0.53	0.32	25	1.5
Q	14	1400	0.70	2000	0.53	0.32	25	1.5
R	14	1400	0.70	2600	0.53	0.32	25	1.5

218. Returning to our standard problem, we will compute the drift for the 12″ gun ($V=2900$ f. s., $w=870$ pounds, $c=0.61$) for a range of 10,000 yards, for which conditions we found in Chapter 8 that the angle of departure was 4° 13′ 14″, $Z=2984.1$ and $\log C=1.00231$. The computation then becomes

1.5		log 0.17609
$\mu=0.53$		log 9.72428 – 10
$\frac{\lambda}{h}=0.32$		log 9.50515 – 10
$n=25$	log 1.39794	colog 8.60206 – 10
$C=$	log 1.00231	2 log 2.00462
$D'=25.7$		log 1.40824
$\phi=4°\ 13'\ 14''$	sec 0.00118	3 sec 0.00354
$D=26.5$ yards		log 1.42398

219. Guns are usually, and naval guns always, pointed by directing what is called the "line of sight" at the target. Originally the upper surface of the gun itself was used as the line of sight; this was called "sighting by the line of metal," and resulted in giving to the gun an angular elevation corresponding to the difference in thickness of metal at the breech and at the muzzle. Later on, a piece of wood, called a "dispart," was secured to the muzzle, so as to give a line from breech to muzzle parallel to the axis of the gun. Such a line of sight had to be directed more or less above the target according to the range. Early in the last century came into use the method of having one fixed and one movable sight, so that the line between them, which is the line of sight, could be adjusted at any desired angle with the axis of the gun. The rear sight was usually the movable one. At the present time the most approved form of sight, and practically the only one in use in the navy, is that Sights.

in which a telescope has been substituted for the old pair of sights, front and rear. This telescope is so mounted that it is capable of being set at any desired angle with the axis of the gun, within necessary limits. The principles involved in the telescopic sight are the same as in the old bar sights, but in the former they are not so clearly apparent or so easily studied as in the latter. For this reason we will take up the theory of sights from the point of view of the old system of bar sights, rear sight adjustable, and the application of these theories to the telescopic sight will be plainly apparent.

Theory of bar sights.

220. The rear sight being movable, it is customary to graduate its bar in yards of range (and sometimes with the elevation in degrees corresponding to the range in yards), and sometimes there is added the time of flight in seconds corresponding to each range, this last information being for use in setting time fuses when using shrapnel, etc. This information is ordinarily not placed on the range scale of a telescopic sight, which shows only the range in yards; and if such information be wanted it must be taken from the range table for the gun which is now furnished to ships.

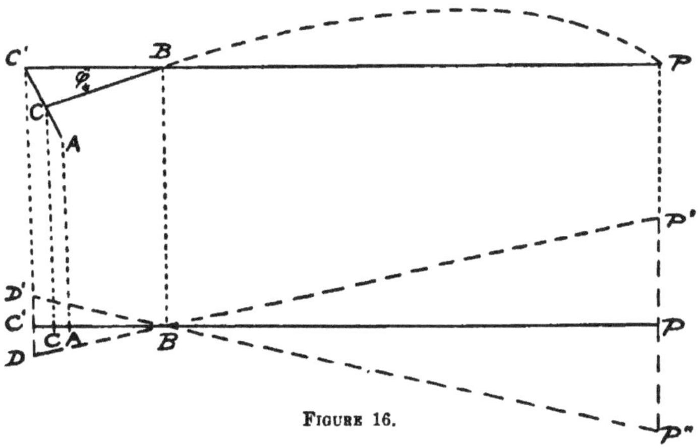

FIGURE 16.

Sight bar height.

221. Figure 16 represents the usual arrangement of bar sights, AC' being the movable graduated rear sight bar, at right angles to the axis of the gun, and B the fixed front sight. $C'B$ is the line of sight, being a line from the notch in the rear sight C' to the top of the front sight B, and CB is the position of the line of sight when it is parallel to the axis of the gun, the rear sight notch being then lowered to C, usually its lowest position. The distance $CB=l$ is called the "sight radius" of the gun, and the line CB is sometimes called the "natural line of sight." It will be seen that when the rear sight notch is raised to C', and the line of sight $C'B$ is directed at the target P, the axis of the gun, which is parallel to CB, is elevated at the angle $CBC'=\psi$, or the angle of elevation above the target. As we will deal only with horizontal trajectories, and disregard jump, the angle of departure will be equal to the angle of elevation, so $CBC'=\psi=\phi$. The distance $CC'=h$ is the "sight bar height" for the angle of departure ϕ, and it is evidently given by the equation

$$h=l\tan\phi \qquad (194)$$

Permanent angle.

225. It was common practice with naval guns and bar sights to correct for the greater part of the drift automatically by inclining the bar sight in a plane perpendicular to the axis of the bore of the gun, so as to make with the vertical an angle i called the "permanent angle." Referring to Figure 17, we see that the three points D, C and C' are in the same plane, which is perpendicular to the line CB, the angles $CC'D$ and $BC'D$ being right angles; the points B, C and C' are all three in the same plane, which is at right angles to DCC'; B, C' and D are in the same plane, which is at right angles to BCC'; and, similarly, for P, P' and Q. Then we have that

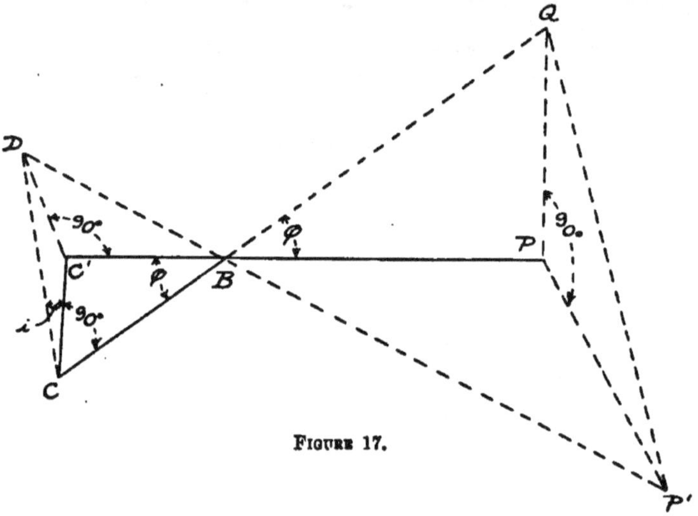

FIGURE 17.

$CB=l$, being the natural line of sight, and $CD=h$ is the sight bar height for the angle of departure ϕ, and is now given by

$$h=l\tan\phi\sec i \tag{197}$$

Then if PP' be the drift in yards, at the range R, from the similar triangles we have $\frac{DC'}{C'B}=\frac{D}{R}$; but $DC'=h\sin i=l\tan\phi\tan i$, and $C'B=l\sec\phi$. Therefore $\frac{\tan\phi\tan i}{\sec\phi}=\sin\phi\tan i=\frac{D}{R}$, whence we have

$$\tan i=\frac{D}{R\sin\phi}\text{*} \tag{198}$$

226. If D were proportional to $X\sin\phi$, which it is not far from being, setting the sight bar at the permanent angle i given by (198) would exactly compensate for drift at all ranges. Actually, however, D increases a little more rapidly in proportion than $X\sin\phi$, and so the sight should be more inclined for long than for short ranges. In practice, when bar sights are used, it is customary to compute the value

* D and R must be in the same units. In the above equation they are both expressed in yards.

EXAMPLES.

1. Compute the drift in yards for the following conditions, taking the angle of departure and the maximum ordinate from the range tables. Conditions standard.

Problem.	DATA.					ANSWERS.
	Projectile.			Velocity. f. s.	Range. Yds.	Drift. Yds.
	d. In.	*w.* Lbs.	*c.*			
A	3	13	1.00	1150	2500	7.5
B	3	13	1.00	2700	4000	8.5
C	4	33	0.67	2900	3500	2.4
D	5	50	1.00	3150	4000	5.8
E	5	50	0.61	3150	3700	3.3
F	6	105	0.61	2600	10500	69.4
G	6	105	1.00	2800	3800	3.2
H	6	105	0.61	2800	3200	2.6
I	7	165	1.00	2700	7000	17.6
J	7	165	0.61	2700	6700	15.7
K	8	260	0.61	2750	8000	21.5
L	10	510	1.00	2700	10000	33.9
M	10	510	0.61	2700	11000	44.3
N	12	870	0.61	2900	22000	233.8
O	13	1130	1.00	2000	10000	52.1
P	13	1130	0.74	2000	11000	82.9
Q	14	1400	0.70	2000	14000	148.1
R	14	1400	0.70	2600	14500	89.3

2. Compute the sight bar heights in inches, and the distance in inches that the sliding leaf must be set over for the data given in the following table, conditions being standard.

Problem.	DATA.						ANSWERS.		
	Gun.		Range. Yds.	ϕ.	Sight radius or radius of curvature of sword arm. In.	Deflection to be compensated. Yds.	Sight bar height. In.	Set of sliding leaf.	
	Cal. In.	*I.V.* f. s.						Inches.	Right or left.
A	3	1150	1700	4° 19′ 06″	24.750	25 R.	1.869	0.365	Left
B	3	2700	3600	2 48 54	28.625	20 L.	1.408	0.159	Right
C	4	2900	3100	1 18 42	45.900	40 L.	1.031	0.502	Right
D	5	3150	4000	1 53 12	58.500	50 R.	1.927	0.732	Left
E	5	3150	4500	1 45 48	42.625	30 R.	1.312	0.284	Left
F	6	2600	13500	12 20 18	42.625	75 L.	9.324	0.242	Right
G	6	2800	4100	2 05 18	42.625	50 R.	1.554	0.520	Left
H	6	2800	3400	1 23 42	42.625	30 L.	1.063	0.376	Right
I	7	2700	7000	4 44 48	55.850	100 R.	4.637	0.801	Left
J	7	2700	6700	3 28 48	62.500	75 L.	3.801	0.701	Right
K	8	2750	7800	3 51 12	41.125	50 R.	2.770	0.264	Left
L	10	2700	9700	6 11 42	44.675	60 L.	4.849	0.278	Right
M	10	2700	10900	5 48 18	44.675	50 R.	4.542	0.206	Left
N	12	2900	23500	14 12 12	47.469	150 L.	12.014	0.313	Right
O	13	2000	9600	10 03 18	61.094	70 R.	10.833	0.452	Left
P	13	2000	10800	10 32 42	61.094	60 R.	11.373	0.345	Left
Q	14	2000	13600	13 54 00	36.219	50 L.	8.963	0.137	Right
R	14	2600	14000	8 14 06	36.219	75 L.	5.242	0.196	Right

NOTE.—The data given in the sight radius column is approximate only, and must not be accepted as reliable. The computed sight bar heights and the set of the sliding leaf are for the old bar sight. To use them for the telescopic sight they must be transformed as necessary into the proper distances for marking on sword arm scales or range or deflection scales, as the case may be. These supplementary computations have to do with the mechanical features of the sight only, and not with the principles of exterior ballistics, and are therefore not considered here.

CHAPTER 14.

THE EFFECT OF WIND UPON THE MOTION OF THE PROJECTILE. THE EFFECT OF MOTION OF THE GUN UPON THE MOTION OF THE PROJECTILE. THE EFFECT OF MOTION OF THE TARGET UPON THE MOTION OF THE PROJECTILE RELATIVE TO THE TARGET. THE EFFECT UPON THE MOTION OF THE PROJECTILE RELATIVE TO THE TARGET OF ALL THREE MOTIONS COMBINED. THE COMPUTATION OF THE DATA CONTAINED IN COLUMNS 13, 14, 15, 16, 17 AND 18 OF THE RANGE TABLES.

New Symbols Introduced.

W.... Real wind, velocity in feet per second.
β.... Angle between wind and line of fire.
W_x.... Component of W in line of fire in feet per second.
W_{12x}.... Wind component of 12 knots in line of fire in feet per second.
W_z.... Component of W perpendicular to line of fire in feet per second.
W_{12z}.... Wind component of 12 knots perpendicular to line of fire in feet per second.
X.... Range in feet without considering wind.
X'.... Range in feet considering wind.
V.... Initial velocity in foot-seconds without considering wind.
V'.... Initial velocity in foot-seconds considering wind.
ϕ.... Angle of departure without considering wind.
ϕ'.... Angle of departure considering wind.
T.... Time of flight in seconds without considering wind.
T'.... Time of flight in seconds considering wind.
ΔX_W.... Variation in range in feet due to W_x.
ΔX_{12W}.... Variation in range in feet due to a wind component of 12 knots in line of fire.
ΔR_W.... Variation in range in yards due to W_x.
ΔR_{12W}.... Variation in range in yards due to a wind component of 12 knots in line of fire.
γ.... Angle between trajectories relative to air and relative to ground.
D_W.... Deflection in yards due to wind component W_z perpendicular to line of fire.
D_{12W}.... Deflection in yards due to wind component of 12 knots perpendicular to line of fire.
G.... Motion of gun in feet per second.
G_x.... Component of G in line of fire in feet per second.
G_{12x}.... Motion of gun of 12 knots in line of fire in feet per second.
G_z.... Component of G perpendicular to line of fire in feet per second.
G_{12z}.... Motion of gun of 12 knots perpendicular to line of fire in feet per second.
ΔX_G.... Variation in range in feet due to G_x.
ΔX_{12G}.... Variation in range in feet due to a motion of gun in line of fire of 12 knots.
ΔR_G.... Variation in range in yards due to G_x.
ΔR_{12G}.... Variation in range in yards due to a motion of gun in line of fire of 12 knots.

D_G.... Deflection in yards due to a motion of gun of G_z perpendicular to line of fire.

D_{12G}.... Deflection in yards due to a motion of gun of 12 knots perpendicular to line of fire.

T.... Motion of target in feet per second.

T_x.... Motion of target in line of fire in feet per second.

T_{12x}.... Motion of target of 12 knots in line of fire in feet per second.

T_z.... Motion of target perpendicular to line of fire in feet per second.

T_{12z}.... Motion of target of 12 knots perpendicular to line of fire in feet per second.

ΔX_T.... Variation in range in feet due to T.

ΔX_{12T}.... Variation in range in feet due to a motion of target of 12 knots in line of fire.

ΔR_T.... Variation in range in yards due to T.

ΔR_{12T}.... Variation in range in yards due to a motion of target of 12 knots in line of fire.

D_T.... Deflection in yards due to a motion of target T_z perpendicular to line of fire.

D_{12T}.... Deflection in yards due to a motion of target of 12 knots perpendicular to line of fire.

α.... Angle of real wind with course of ship.

α'.... Angle of apparent wind with course of ship.

W_1.... Velocity of real wind in knots per hour.

W_2.... Velocity of apparent wind in knots per hour.

Section 1.—The Effect of Wind Upon the Motion of the Projectile.

229. In considering the effect of wind upon the flight of the projectile, we are obliged, for want of a better knowledge, to assume that the air moves horizontally only, and that its direction and velocity are the same throughout the trajectory as we observe them to be at the gun. Actually the wind is never steady, either in force or in direction; its velocity usually increases with the height above the gun, and its motion is not always confined to the horizontal plane. Moreover, lateral wind pressure alters the drift due to rotation.

230. It is for these reasons that the deviations caused by the wind can only be roughly approximated; and, consequently, that experiments for determining any of the ballistic constants, to be of value, must be made when it is calm or very nearly so.

Primary planes.

231. Let us denote by W the velocity of the wind in feet per second, and by W_x and W_z, respectively, the components of that velocity in and at right angles to the plane of fire. Also let us call W_x positive when it is with the flight of the projectile, and negative when it is against it. Let us also call W_z positive when it tends to carry the projectile from right to left of an observer looking from gun to target, and negative in the opposite case. In Figure 18 let us denote by β the angle between the direction from gun to target and the direction towards which the wind is blowing, measuring the angle to the left from the first direction around to the second.

Then in Figure 18(a), β is in the first quadrant, and W_x is blowing with the projectile and is positive, and W_z causes lateral motion to the left and is also positive. In Figure 18(b), β is in the second quadrant, and W_x is negative and W_z is positive. In Figure 18(c), β is in the third quadrant, and both W_x and W_z are negative. In Figure 18(d), β is in the fourth quadrant, and W_x is positive and W_z is negative. Note especially that, in the system of notation adopted, β is the angle between the plane of fire and the direction *towards* and not that *from* which the wind is blowing.

Force diagrams.

236. In order to use the above equation it is necessary to determine the values of X' and T', and we can do this by methods previously explained if we can determine the corresponding values of V' and ϕ'. This we can do if we can find the values of dV and $d\phi$. To do this let us draw the triangle of forces acting in this case (and also for a negative wind). We would have the results as shown in Figure 19.

Figure 19(a) is for a positive wind, for which W_x is positive (being drawn in the proper direction for constructing a triangle of forces with all parts of proper relation to one another), and from the diagram it will be seen that $OA=V$ combined with

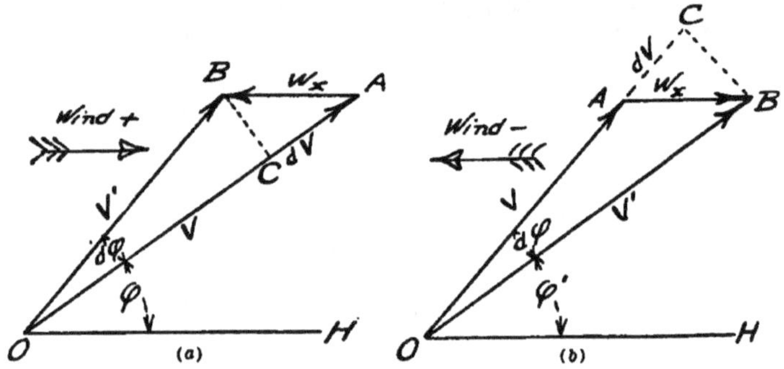

Figure 19.

$AB=W_x$ gives $OB=V'$, which is *less* than $OA=V$ by the amount $dV=AC=W_x\cos\phi$. Also the angle, $BOH=\phi'$ is *greater* than the angle $AOH=\phi$ by the angle

$$d\phi=AOB=\frac{BC}{OB}=\frac{W_x\sin\phi}{V'}$$

(assuming that for this small angle the sine and the circular measure of the angle are equal). In other words, the forces acting would produce a trajectory *relative to the moving air* for which the initial velocity is $V'=V-dV$ and the angle of departure is $\phi'=\phi+d\phi$. Similarly, from Figure 19(b), where W_x is negative or against the flight of the projectile, we would have V' *greater* than V by the amount $dV=W_x\cos\phi$, and ϕ' *less* than ϕ by the amount $d\phi=\frac{BC}{OB}=\frac{W_x\sin\phi}{V'}$. Thus, in both cases we can obtain the values of the changes in V and ϕ with their proper signs from the expressions

$$dV=-W_x\cos\phi \tag{202}$$

$$d\phi=\frac{W_x\sin\phi}{V'} \tag{203}$$

The negative sign is arbitrarily introduced into the second term of (202) to ensure that a positive value of W_x shall always produce a negative value of dV, and that a negative value of W_x shall always produce a positive value of dV, as is seen from the triangles of forces must always be the case.

237. To determine the effect of a wind W_x, therefore, we compute dV by (202) and $d\phi$ by (203); compute the range X given by V and ϕ by methods heretofore explained; compute the range X' and the time of flight T' given by $V'=V+dV$ and $\phi'=\phi+d\phi$ by methods heretofore explained, and then by (201) we can compute the change in range due to the wind.

238. An examination of Figure 20(a) and Figure 20(b) will help to reach a clear understanding of the foregoing method of determining the effect of wind upon the range. Let O represent the stationary gun and M the stationary target, which would be hit on a calm day at a range X by a projectile fired from O with an initial velocity of V and an angle of departure ϕ (Figure 20(a)).

If this same projectile were fired with the same V and the same ϕ on a day when a wind was blowing from the gun towards the target we know that the projectile will land at same point H', a distance ΔX, beyond M (Figure 20(a)).

Now $1+\frac{2}{3}kX=n$; whence $1+\frac{4}{3}kX=2n-1$, and so (205) becomes

$$\frac{2d\phi}{\tan 2\phi}=\frac{2n-1}{n}\times\frac{dX}{X}$$

whence

$$\frac{dX}{X}=\frac{2n}{2n-1}\times\frac{d\phi}{\tan 2\phi} \tag{206}$$

240. In this and in similar expressions the value of $d\phi$ must of course be expressed in circular measure ($1'=.0002909$), but when the form is the ratio $\frac{d\phi}{\phi}$, the value is the same whether $d\phi$ and ϕ are expressed in minutes of arc or in circular measure. Now returning to (204) and writing it in the form

$$V^2 \sin 2\phi = gX(1+\tfrac{2}{3}kX)$$

and taking logarithmic differentials with regard to V and X as variables, we get

$$\frac{2dV}{V}=\frac{1+\frac{4}{3}kX}{1+\frac{2}{3}kX}\times\frac{dX}{X} \tag{207}$$

which, substituting n for $1+\frac{2}{3}kX$ and $2n-1$ for $1+\frac{4}{3}kX$, becomes

$$\frac{dX}{X}=\frac{2n}{2n-1}\times\frac{dV}{V} \tag{208}$$

241. We have found in (208) an expression for the variation in range due to a variation in initial velocity, and in (206) an expression for the variation in range due to a variation in the angle of departure; and we have already seen that the effect upon the range of a wind component in the plane of fire is to give, so far as results are concerned, an apparent variation in both V and ϕ. Therefore $X'-X$ is nothing but the change in range which would result from increasing V by dV and ϕ by $d\phi$, dV being determined by (202) and $d\phi$ by (203). Then by employing (208) and (206) we see that the change in X due to simultaneous changes $dV=-W_s\cos\phi$ and $d\phi=\frac{W_s\sin\phi}{V'}$ is given by the expression

$$\frac{X'-X}{X}=\frac{2n}{2n-1}\left(\frac{W_s\sin\phi}{V'\tan 2\phi}-\frac{W_s\cos\phi}{V}\right) \tag{209}$$

Now we may put V for V' in the preceding expression without material error, because dV is always very small compared with V, and the expression then reduces to

$$\frac{X'-X}{X}=\frac{2n}{2n-1}\times\frac{W_s}{V}\left(\frac{\sin\phi}{\tan 2\phi}-\cos\phi\right)$$

Now

$$\frac{\sin\phi}{\tan 2\phi}-\cos\phi=\cos\phi\left(\frac{\tan\phi}{\tan 2\phi}-1\right)$$

and

$$\tan 2\phi=\frac{\sin 2\phi}{\cos 2\phi}=\frac{2\sin\phi\cos\phi}{\cos^2\phi-\sin^2\phi}$$

whence

$$\cos\phi\left(\frac{\tan\phi}{\tan 2\phi}-1\right)=\cos\phi\left(\frac{\sin\phi}{\cos\phi}\times\frac{\cos^2\phi-\sin^2\phi}{2\sin\phi\cos\phi}-1\right)$$

$$=\cos\phi\left(\frac{\cos^2\phi-\sin^2\phi}{2\cos^2\phi}-1\right)$$

$$=\frac{\cos\phi}{2}(1-\tan^2\phi-2)$$

whence

$$\frac{\sin\phi}{\tan 2\phi}-\cos\phi=\frac{\cos\phi}{2}(-\tan^2\phi-1) \tag{210}$$

Therefore, from the above, we get

$$\frac{X'-X}{X}=\frac{n}{2n-1}\times\frac{W_s\cos\phi}{V}(-\tan^2\phi-1)$$

whence, neglecting $\tan^2\phi$ in comparison with unity,

$$X'-X=-\frac{n}{2n-1}\times\frac{X\cos\phi}{V}W_s$$

and substituting this in (201) we finally get for the change in range due to the wind component W_s

$$\Delta X=W_s\left\{T-\left(\frac{n}{2n-1}\times\frac{X\cos\phi}{V}\right)\right\}^* \qquad (211)$$

In the above equation, T, although actually the time of flight for V' and ϕ', may be taken as the time of flight for the actual firing data, V and ϕ, without introducing any material errors. This formula is the one employed in computing the data in Column 13 of the range tables, giving the change in range resulting from a wind component of 12 knots in the plane of fire.

242. Now let us compute the data for that column for our standard problem, the 12" gun, $V=2900$ f. s., $w=870$ pounds, $c=0.61$, $R=10{,}000$, $T=12.43$, and $\phi=4°\ 13'\ 14''$. We have the formula given in the preceding paragraph and

$$n=\frac{V^2\sin 2\phi}{gX} \text{ and } W_{12w}=\frac{12\times 6080}{60\times 60\times 3} \text{ yards per second}$$

$V=2900$	log 3.46239	2 log	6.92480
$2\phi=8°\ 26'\ 28''$		sin	9.16669−10
$g=32.2$	log 1.50786	colog	8.49214−10
$X=30000$	log 4.47712	colog	5.52288−10
$n=1.278$		log	0.10651
$2n=2.556$			
$2n-1=1.556$	log 0.19200	colog	9.80800−10
$n=1.278$		log	0.10651
$X=30000$		log	4.47712
$\phi=4°\ 13'\ 14''$		cos	9.99882−10
$V=2900$	log 3.46239	colog	6.53761−10
8.47		log	0.92806
$T=12.43$			
3.96		log	0.59770
12		log	1.07918
6080		log	3.78390
$60\times 60\times 3=10800$	log 4.03342	colog	5.96658−10
$\Delta R_{12W}=26.7$ yards		log	1.42736

* The above is the formula actually employed. There seems to be no good reason, however, for neglecting $\tan^2\phi$, for $\tan^2\phi+1=\sec^2\phi$, and if we substitute this value, instead of dropping the $\tan^2\phi$, we would get as a final result

$$X=W_s\left(T-\frac{n}{2n-1}\times\frac{X}{V\cos\phi}\right)$$

which is equally easy for work, and is more in keeping with the form of the expression for determining the deflection due to wind given in equation (212). The difference in results is not material however.

Lateral deviation due to wind.

243. To determine the lateral deviation due to wind, let W_z be the lateral wind component in foot-seconds, positive when it blows from right to left across the line of fire, and negative when it blows in the reverse direction; let V and ϕ be the initial velocity and angle of departure *relative to still air or to the ground,* and X be the corresponding range, that is, the range *when there is no wind.* Then if we draw the triangle of forces for this case, we may obtain the initial velocity and direction of flight *relative to the moving air.* Thus referring to Figure 21 (a), which represents the case of a negative wind, the resultant of $OA = V$ with $OC = -W_z$ is $OB = V'$, which is very slightly greater than V; the angle $BOD = \phi'$, which V' makes with the horizontal, is very slightly less than $AOE = \phi$; and V' is inclined to the left so as to make with V the small angle BOA.

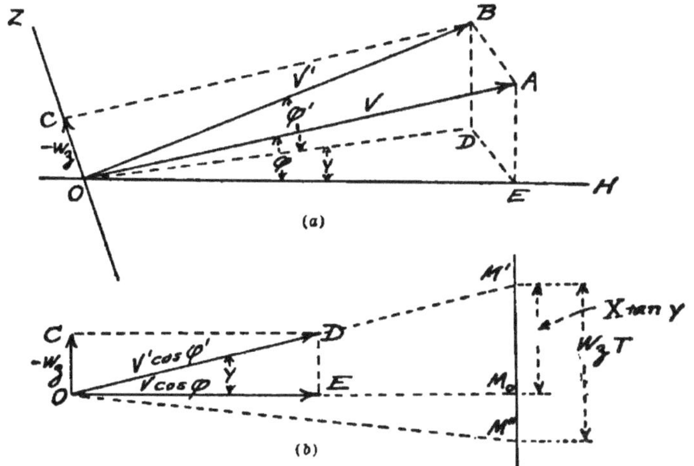

FIGURE 21.

244. Now since V' and ϕ' differ so little from V and ϕ, and since the effect of the increase in V is offset by that of the decrease in ϕ, we may take the range X' corresponding to V', ϕ', to be practically the same as the range X corresponding to V, ϕ. Therefore the only essential difference between the trajectory *relative to the moving air* and that *relative to the ground or still air* is that the plane of the former makes the angle $DOE = \gamma$ with the plane of the latter. Referring now to Figure 21 (b), in which O represents the gun and M_0 the target at the range $OM_0 = X$, we see that $\tan \gamma = \frac{W_z}{V \cos \phi}$; and OM' is the horizontal trace of the trajectory *relative to the moving air.* But while the projectile moves through the air from O to M', the air itself has moved $W_z T$ to the right, and so the projectile really strikes to the right of the target by the distance

$$M_0 M'' = W_z T - X \tan \gamma = W_z \left(T - \frac{X}{V \cos \phi} \right)$$

Thus the lateral deviation caused by the wind component W_z normal to the line of fire is given by the expression

$$D_W = W_z \left(T - \frac{X}{V \cos \phi} \right) \tag{212}$$

in which T, though really the time of flight corresponding to V', ϕ', may without appreciable error be taken as the time of flight for the actual firing data.

245. Now let us return to our standard problem and find the data for Column 16 in the range table; deviation for lateral wind component of 12 knots; for our 12" gun at 10,000 yards. We have the above formula, and also $W_{12z} = \frac{6080 \times 12}{60 \times 60 \times 3}$ yards per second.

$X = 30000$		log 4.47712
$V = 2900$	log 3.46240	colog 6.53760−10
$\phi = 4°\ 13'\ 14''$		sec 0.00118
10.37		log 1.01590
$T = 12.43$		
2.06		log 0.31387
12		log 1.07918
6080		log 3.78390
$60 \times 60 \times 3 = 10800$	log 4.03342	colog 5.96658−10
$D_{12W} = 13.9$ yards		log 1.14353

Section 2.—The Effect of Motion of the Gun Upon the Motion of the Projectile.

246. As in the case of the wind, we resolve the horizontal velocity of the gun due to the ship's motion into two components, G_x in the plane of fire, and G_z at right angles to that plane; and determine their effects separately, the first affecting the range only and the second the lateral deflection only.

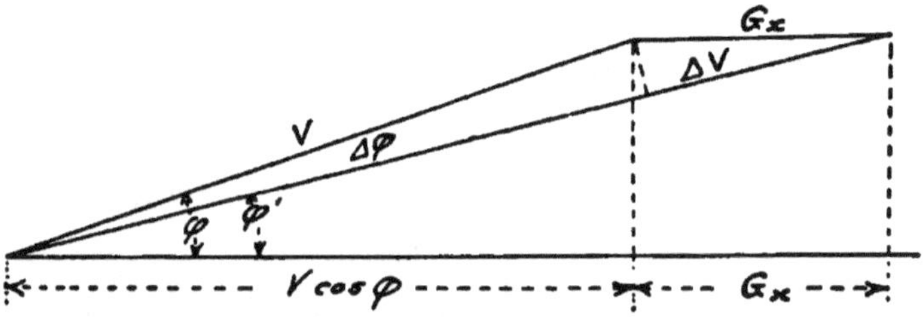

FIGURE 22.

247. Let G_x be the resolved part of the speed in the line of fire in foot-seconds, positive when with and negative when contrary to the flight of the projectile. Then evidently the true initial velocity of the projectile is the resultant of G_x and V, and, as shown in Figure 22, V receives the increment $\Delta V = G_x \cos\phi$, while ϕ is decreased by $\Delta\phi = \frac{G_x \sin\phi}{V}$. But by equations (208) and (206), these two changes in V and ϕ, respectively, will cause a change in range given by **Change in range due to motion of gun.**

$$\frac{\Delta X_G}{X} = \frac{2n}{2n-1}\left(\frac{G_x \cos\phi}{V} - \frac{G_x \sin\phi}{V \tan 2\phi}\right)$$

$$\frac{\Delta X_G}{X} = \frac{n}{2n-1} \times \frac{G_x \cos\phi}{V}\left(2 - \frac{2\tan\phi}{\tan 2\phi}\right)$$

Now as
$$\tan 2\phi = \frac{2\tan\phi}{1-\tan^2\phi}$$
the above expression becomes
$$\frac{\Delta X_G}{X} = \frac{n}{2n-1} \times \frac{G_s \cos\phi}{V} (1+\tan^2\phi)$$
which, when ϕ is small enough to make $\tan^2\phi$ negligible in comparison to unity, reduces to
$$\frac{\Delta X_G}{X} = \frac{n}{2n-1} \times \frac{G_s \cos\phi}{V}$$
or
$$\Delta X_G = \frac{n}{2n-1} \times \frac{X\cos\phi}{V} G_s\text{*} \tag{213}$$

248. As an illustration, let us return to our standard problem 12" gun, and compute for a range of 10,000 yards the data contained in Column 14 of the range table; change of range for motion of gun in plane of fire of 12 knots. We have the above formula and
$$n = \frac{V^2 \sin 2\phi}{gX} \qquad G_s = \frac{12\times 6080}{60\times 60\times 3} \text{ yards per second}$$

$V=2900$	log 3.46239	2 log 6.92478
$2\phi=8°\ 26'\ 28''$		sin 9.16669−10
$g=32.2$	log 1.50785	colog 8.49214−10
$X=30000$	log 4.47712	colog 5.52288−10
$n=1.278$		log 0.10649
$2n=2.556$		
$2n-1=1.556$	log 0.19200	colog 9.80800−10
$n=1.278$		log 0.10649
$X=30000$		log 4.47712
$\phi=4°\ 13'\ 14''$		cos 9.99882−10
$V=2900$	log 3.46239	colog 6.53761−10
12		log 1.07918
6080		log 3.78390
$60\times 60\times 3=10800$	log 4.03342	colog 5.96658−10
$\Delta R_{12G}=57$ yards		log 1.75770

Lateral deviation due to motion of gun.

249. Now let G_s be the resolved part of the motion of the gun at right angles to the line of fire in foot-seconds. Then, in addition to the initial velocity V in the line of the axis of the gun, the projectile on leaving the gun has a lateral velocity G_s, and so, as may be seen from Figure 21(*b*), the real plane of departure makes an angle with the vertical plane of the gun's axis given by $\tan\gamma = \frac{G_s}{V\cos\phi}$, and the resultant deviation at range X is given by
$$D_G = X\tan\gamma \quad \text{or} \quad D_G = \frac{X}{V\cos\phi} G_s \tag{214}$$

* The above is the formula actually employed. There seems to be no good reason, however, for neglecting the $\tan^2\phi$, for $\tan^2\phi + 1 = \sec^2\phi$, and if we substitute this value, instead of dropping the $\tan^2\phi$, we would get as the final result
$$X_G = \frac{n}{2n-1} \times \frac{X}{V\cos\phi} \times G_s$$
which is equally easy for work, and more in keeping with the form of the expression for determining the deflection due to motion of the gun given in equation (214). The difference is not material however.

250. Taking our standard problem again, we have the above formula and $G_s = \frac{12 \times 6080}{60 \times 60 \times 3}$ yards per second.

$X = 30000$		log 4.47712
$V = 2900$	log 3.46240	colog 6.53760−10
$\phi = 4°\ 13'\ 14''$		sec 0.00118
12		log 1.07918
6080		log 3.78390
$60 \times 60 \times 3 = 10800$	log 4.03342	colog 5.96658−10
$D_{12G} = 70.1$ yards		log 1.84556

Section 3.—The Effect of the Motion of the Target Upon the Motion of the Projectile Relative to the Target.

251. Motion of the target evidently has no effect upon the actual flight of the projectile, but it is equally clear that it will affect the relative positions of the target and of the point of fall of the projectile, as the target has been in motion during the time of flight of the projectile.

252. Evidently, if the target be moving in the line of fire with the velocity T_s, in order to hit it the sight must be set for a range greater or less than the true range at the instant of firing by the distance which the target will traverse in the time of flight, or T_sT. So, also, if the speed of the target at right angles to the plane of fire be T_s, the shot will fall T_sT to one side of the target unless that much deviation is allowed for in pointing. Once more we consider the motion as resolved into two components, one in and the other normal to the plane of fire, and consider the two as producing results entirely independent of each other. And it is readily seen that, for the effect of the motion of the target we must correct the range and deviation by the quantities given by the expressions **Effect of motion of target.**

$$\Delta X_T = T_sT \qquad (215)$$

$$D_T = T_sT \qquad (216)$$

253. For our standard 12″ gun, again, for 10,000 yards, to compute the data in Columns 15 and 18 of the range tables, for 12 knots speed of target, the work would be

$$T_s = T_s = \frac{12 \times 6080}{60 \times 60 \times 3} \qquad X_{12T} = D_{12T} = T_{12s} \times T = T_{12s} \times T$$

$T = 12.43$		log 1.09452
12		log 1.07918
6080		log 3.78390
$60 \times 60 \times 3 = 10800$	log 4.03342	colog 5.96658−10
$R_{12T} = D_{12T} = 84$ yards		log 1.92418

Section 4.—The Effect Upon the Motion of the Projectile of All Three Motions Combined.

254. In the preceding sections we have discussed the effects upon the motion of the projectile of the wind and of the motions of the firing and target ships. The resultant combined effect of all three of these causes of error would of course be obtained by computing them separately and then performing the necessary algebraic additions, first for all range effects to get the total effect upon the range, and then of all deflection effects to get the total effect in deflection.

NOTE.—Professor Alger appends to this chapter the following foot-note:

The method herein adopted for the treatment of the problem of wind effect was first set forth, so far as I am aware, in General Didion's Traité de Ballistique though it has been generally accepted since. It is mathematically correct only for spherical projectiles, to the motion of which the air offers a resistance which is independent of the direction of motion. With elongated projectiles it will be seen that the initial motion *relative to the air* is not exactly in the line of the projectile's axis, so that we have no right to assume, as we do, that the flight *relative to the air* is the same when the air is moving as when it is still. It has been supposed by some writers that the lateral wind component produces the same pressure on the side of the moving projectile as it would if the projectile were stationary, and that the deviation can be computed upon that basis. If this were true, the deviation would be proportional to the square of the lateral wind component, whereas it is really much more nearly proportional to its first power. Actually the pressure is much greater when the projectile is moving at right angles to the wind current than when it is stationary, on account of the increased number of air particles which strike it.

EXAMPLES.

1. Compute the errors in range and in deflection caused by the wind components as given below.

	DATA.									ANSWERS.			
	Projectile.					Wind component in knots per hour.				In line of fire.		Perpendicular to line of fire.	
				V. f.s.	Range. Yds.	In line of fire.		Perpendicular to line of fire.					
Problem.	d. In.	w. Lbs.	c.			Knots.	With or against.	Knots.	To the right or left	Yards.	Short or over.	Yards.	To the right or left.
A..	3	13	1.00	1150	3000	8	With	6	Right	16.5	Over	6.3	Right
B..	3	13	1.00	2700	4500	10	Against	8	Left	34.5	Short	19.1	Left
C..	4	33	0.67	2900	4000	11	With	9	Right	12.7	Over	5.7	Right
D.	5	50	1.00	3150	4500	13	Against	11	Left	26.8	Short	14.4	Left
E..	5	50	0.61	3150	4500	14	With	13	Right	17.1	Over	8.8	Right
F..	6	105	0.61	2600	13600	15	Against	14	Left	146.0	Short	88.8	Left
G..	6	105	1.00	2800	4500	16	With	15	Right	25.9	Over	14.0	Right
H.	6	105	0.61	2800	4000	17	Against	16	Left	13.3	Short	6.4	Left
I..	7	165	1.00	2700	7500	18	With	17	Right	74.2	Over	44.3	Right
J..	7	165	0.61	2700	7500	19	Against	18	Left	47.0	Short	24.8	Left
K.	8	260	0.61	2750	8500	20	With	19	Right	51.5	Over	26.9	Right
L..	10	510	1.00	2700	10500	19	Against	20	Left	100.4	Short	64.7	Left
M.	10	510	0.61	2700	11500	18	With	19	Right	69.0	Over	40.2	Right
N.	12	870	0.61	2900	19500	17	With	18	Left	141.5	Over	87.0	Left
O..	13	1130	1.00	2000	10500	16	Against	17	Right	93.3	Short	54.8	Right
P..	13	1130	0.74	2000	11500	15	With	16	Left	79.6	Over	44.4	Left
Q..	14	1400	0.70	2000	14500	14	Against	15	Right	105.6	Short	58.1	Right
R..	14	1400	0.70	2600	14000	13	With	14	Left	63.7	Over	37.3	Left

2. Compute the errors in range and in deflection caused by the motion of the gun as given below. Conditions standard.

Problem.	DATA. Projectile. d. In.	w. Lbs.	c.	V. f.s.	Range. Yds.	Speed component in knots per hour. In line of fire. Knots.	With or against.	Perpendicular to line of fire. Knots.	To the right or left.	ANSWERS. In line of fire. Yards.	Short or over.	Perpendicular to line of fire. Yards.	To the right or left.
A..	3	13	1.00	1150	2000	6	Against	8	Left	14.7	Short	23.6	Left
B..	3	13	1.00	2700	3500	7	With	8	Right	10.2	Over	17.5	Right
C..	4	33	0.67	2900	3000	8	Against	9	Left	11.5	Short	15.7	Left
D.	5	50	1.00	3150	3500	9	With	10	Right	12.4	Over	18.8	Right
E..	5	50	0.61	3150	3900	10	Against	11	Left	16.4	Short	22.4	Left
F..	6	105	0.61	2600	12600	11	With	13	Left	58.3	Over	108.4	Left
G..	6	105	1.00	2800	4000	13	Against	14	Right	24.1	Short	33.8	Right
H.	6	105	0.61	2800	3000	14	With	15	Left	22.2	Over	27.1	Left
I..	7	165	1.00	2700	6500	15	Against	16	Right	43.1	Short	65.2	Right
J..	7	165	0.61	2700	6700	16	With	17	Left	52.8	Over	71.4	Left
K.	8	260	0.61	2750	7500	17	With	18	Right	62.6	Over	83.1	Right
L..	10	510	1.00	2700	9500	18	Against	19	Left	76.3	Short	113.5	Left
M.	10	510	0.61	2700	10500	19	With	20	Right	97.6	Over	132.0	Right
N.	12	870	0.61	2900	23000	20	Against	19	Left	182.3	Short	262.0	Left
O..	13	1130	1.00	2000	10000	19	With	18	Right	118.0	Over	154.7	Right
P..	13	1130	0.74	2000	11000	18	Against	17	Left	128.4	Short	160.8	Left
Q..	14	1400	0.70	2000	14000	17	With	16	Right	149.5	Over	195.4	Right
R..	14	1400	0.70	2600	13700	16	Against	15	Left	109.4	Short	134.8	Left

3. Compute the errors in range and in deflection caused by the motion of the target as given below. Conditions standard.

Problem.	DATA. Projectile. d. In.	w. Lbs.	c.	V. f.s.	Range. Yds.	Speed component in knots per hour. In line of fire. Knots.	With or against.	Perpendicular to line of fire. Knots.	To the right or left.	ANSWERS. In line of fire. Yards.	Short or over.	Perpendicular to line of fire. Yards.	To the right or left.
A..	3	13	1.00	1150	1800	7	With	8	Right	21.4	Short	24.4	Left
B..	3	13	1.00	2700	3300	8	Against	9	Left	26.2	Over	29.4	Right
C..	4	33	0.67	2900	2800	9	With	10	Right	17.3	Short	19.2	Left
D.	5	50	1.00	3150	3300	10	Against	11	Left	24.0	Over	26.4	Right
E..	5	50	0.61	3150	3400	11	With	13	Right	24.1	Short	28.5	Left
F..	6	105	0.61	2000	13800	13	With	14	Left	204.3	Short	220.1	Right
G..	6	105	1.00	2800	3800	14	Against	15	Right	41.1	Over	44.0	Left
H.	6	105	0.61	2800	2800	15	With	16	Left	28.1	Short	30.0	Right
I..	7	165	1.00	2700	6300	16	Against	17	Right	91.1	Over	96.9	Left
J..	7	165	0.61	2700	6700	17	With	18	Left	89.5	Short	94.7	Right
K.	8	260	0.61	2750	7300	18	Against	19	Left	99.2	Over	104.6	Right
L..	10	510	1.00	2700	9300	19	With	20	Right	157.9	Short	166.2	Left
M.	10	510	0.61	2700	10300	20	Against	19	Left	162.7	Over	154.6	Right
N.	12	870	0.61	2900	20200	19	With	20	Right	326.7	Short	343.9	Left
O..	13	1130	1.00	2000	9300	18	Against	19	Left	188.6	Over	199.1	Right
P..	13	1130	0.74	2000	10300	17	With	18	Right	187.6	Short	198.6	Left
Q..	14	1400	0.70	2000	13300	16	Against	17	Left	236.8	Over	251.6	Right
R..	14	1400	0.70	2600	13700	15	With	16	Right	172.4	Short	184.5	Left

CHAPTER 15.

DETERMINATION OF JUMP. EXPERIMENTAL RANGING AND THE REDUCTION OF OBSERVED RANGES.

Jump. **255.** Primarily and in its narrowest sense, jump is the increase (algebraic, and generally positive) in the angle of elevation resulting from the angular motion of the gun in the vertical plane caused by the shock of discharge, as a result of which the projectile strikes above (for positive jump; below for negative) the point at which it theoretically should for the given angle of elevation. A definition which thus confines jump to the result of such angular motion is a narrow and restricted one, however, and other elements may enter to give similar results, all of which may be and are properly included in that resultant variation generally called jump. For instance, in the old gravity return mounts, the gun did not recoil directly in the line of its own axis, as it does in the most modern mounts, but rose up an inclined plane as it recoiled. As the projectile did not clear the muzzle until the gun had recoiled an appreciable distance, this upward motion of the gun imparted a similar upward motion to the projectile, which resulted in making the projectile strike slightly higher than it would otherwise have done. This small discrepancy, unimportant at battle ranges, but necessarily considered in such work as firing test shots at armor plate at close range, was properly included in the jump. Also most modern guns of any considerable length have what is known as "droop," that is, the muzzle of the gun sags a little, due to the length and weight of the gun, the axis of the gun being no longer a theoretical straight line; and this causes the projectile to strike slightly lower than it otherwise would, and introduces another slight error which may properly be included in the jump. Also it is probable that this droop causes the muzzle of the gun to move slightly in firing as the gun tends to straighten out under internal pressure, and perhaps this motion tends to produce another variation, "whip," in the motion of the projectile, which would modify the result of the droop. All these may therefore be properly included in the jump.

256. This matter has a direct bearing, under our present system of considering such matters, upon the factor of the ballistic coefficient which we have designated as the coefficient of form of the projectile, and which is supposed, under our previous definition, to be the ratio of the resistance the projectile meets in flight to the resistance that would be encountered in the same air, at the same velocity, by the standard projectile; that is, by a projectile about three calibers long and similar in all respects except in possessing a standard head, namely, one whose ogival has a two-caliber radius. Imagine that the gun jumps a little and increases the range in so doing. It gives the same range as a similar gun firing without jump a projectile exactly similar in all respects except in possessing a slightly lower coefficient of form. Suppose a gun droops and shoots lower. The coefficient of form calculated back from the range obtained by actual firing would work out a little large. And in practice we would probably have both jump and droop affecting the range, but by our method of determining the coefficient of form from actual firing, by comparing actual with computed ranges, all such effects are hidden in the found value of the coefficient of form.

Broader definition of coefficient of form. **257.** As a matter of fact, as intimated above, the value of the coefficient of form is determined by firing ranging shots, and then computing its value from the results.

Lateral deviation due to wind. **243.** To determine the lateral deviation due to wind, let W_z be the lateral wind component in foot-seconds, positive when it blows from right to left across the line of fire, and negative when it blows in the reverse direction; let V and ϕ be the initial velocity and angle of departure *relative to still air or to the ground,* and X be the corresponding range, that is, the range *when there is no wind.* Then if we draw the triangle of forces for this case, we may obtain the initial velocity and direction of flight *relative to the moving air.* Thus referring to Figure 21(a), which represents the case of a negative wind, the resultant of $OA=V$ with $OC=-W_z$ is $OB=V'$, which is very slightly greater than V; the angle $BOD=\phi'$, which V' makes with the horizontal, is very slightly less than $AOE=\phi$; and V' is inclined to the left so as to make with V the small angle BOA.

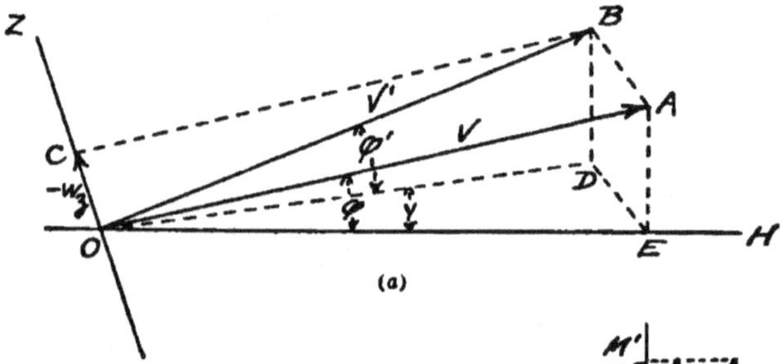

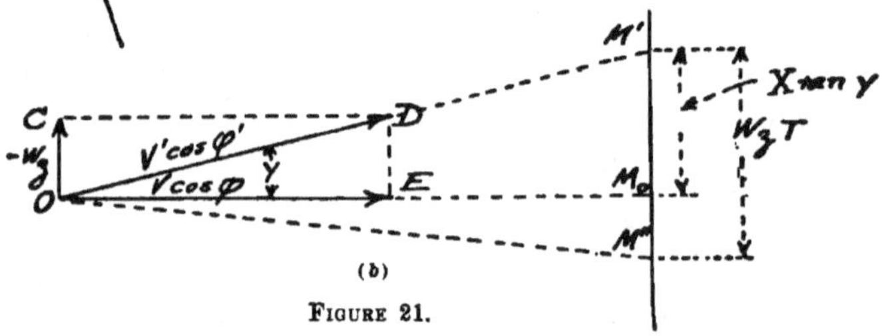

FIGURE 21.

244. Now since V' and ϕ' differ so little from V and ϕ, and since the effect of the increase in V is offset by that of the decrease in ϕ, we may take the range X' corresponding to V', ϕ', to be practically the same as the range X corresponding to V, ϕ. Therefore the only essential difference between the trajectory *relative to the moving air* and that *relative to the ground or still air* is that the plane of the former makes the angle $DOE=\gamma$ with the plane of the latter. Referring now to Figure 21(b), in which O represents the gun and M_0 the target at the range $OM_0=X$, we see that $\tan\gamma=\frac{W_z}{V\cos\phi}$; and OM' is the horizontal trace of the trajectory *relative to the moving air.* But while the projectile moves through the air from O to M', the air itself has moved W_zT to the right, and so the projectile really strikes to the right of the target by the distance

$$M_0M''=W_zT-X\tan\gamma=W_z\left(T-\frac{X}{V\cos\phi}\right)$$

Thus the lateral deviation caused by the wind component W_z normal to the line of fire is given by the expression

$$D_w=W_z\left(T-\frac{X}{V\cos\phi}\right) \tag{212}$$

PART IV.

RANGE TABLES; THEIR COMPUTATION AND USE.

INTRODUCTION TO PART IV.

Having completed the study of all computations connected with the trajectory in air, both as a plane curve and allowing for existing variations from that plane, we are now in a position to make use of our knowledge in a practical way. The practical and useful expression of the knowledge thus acquired takes the form of: first, the preparation of the range tables; and after that, second, their use. Part IV will be devoted to a consideration of the range tables from these two points of view: first, as to their preparation; and, second, as to their actual practical use in service. Each column in the tables will be considered separately, the method and computations by which the data contained in it is obtained will be indicated, and then consideration will be given to the practical use of this data by officers aboard ship in service.

Now as $$\tan 2\phi = \frac{2\tan\phi}{1-\tan^2\phi}$$

the above expression becomes

$$\frac{\Delta X_G}{X} = \frac{n}{2n-1} \times \frac{G_s \cos\phi}{V}(1+\tan^2\phi)$$

which, when ϕ is small enough to make $\tan^2\phi$ negligible in comparison to unity, reduces to

$$\frac{\Delta X_G}{X} = \frac{n}{2n-1} \times \frac{G_s \cos\phi}{V}$$

or

$$\Delta X_G = \frac{n}{2n-1} \times \frac{X\cos\phi}{V} G_s\text{*} \qquad (213)$$

248. As an illustration, let us return to our standard problem 12" gun, and compute for a range of 10,000 yards the data contained in Column 14 of the range table; change of range for motion of gun in plane of fire of 12 knots. We have the above formula and

$$n = \frac{V^2 \sin 2\phi}{gX} \qquad G_s = \frac{12\times 6080}{60\times 60\times 3} \text{ yards per second}$$

$V=2900$	log 3.46239	2 log	6.92478
$2\phi=8°\ 26'\ 28''$		sin	9.16669−10
$g=32.2$	log 1.50785	colog	8.49214−10
$X=30000$	log 4.47712	colog	5.52288−10
$n=1.278$		log	0.10649
$2n=2.556$			
$2n-1=1.556$	log 0.19200	colog	9.80800−10
$n=1.278$		log	0.10649
$X=30000$		log	4.47712
$\phi=4°\ 13'\ 14''$		cos	9.99882−10
$V=2900$	log 3.46239	colog	6.53761−10
12		log	1.07918
6080		log	3.78390
$60\times 60\times 3=10800$	log 4.03342	colog	5.96658−10
$\Delta R_{12G}=57$ yards		log	1.75770

Lateral deviation due to motion of gun.

249. Now let G_s be the resolved part of the motion of the gun at right angles to the line of fire in foot-seconds. Then, in addition to the initial velocity V in the line of the axis of the gun, the projectile on leaving the gun has a lateral velocity G_s, and so, as may be seen from Figure 21(*b*), the real plane of departure makes an angle with the vertical plane of the gun's axis given by $\tan\gamma = \frac{G_s}{V\cos\phi}$, and the resultant deviation at range X is given by

$$D_G = X\tan\gamma \quad \text{or} \quad D_G = \frac{X}{V\cos\phi} G_s \qquad (214)$$

* The above is the formula actually employed. There seems to be no good reason, however, for neglecting the $\tan^2\phi$, for $\tan^2\phi + 1 = \sec^2\phi$, and if we substitute this value, instead of dropping the $\tan^2\phi$, we would get as the final result

$$X_G = \frac{n}{2n-1} \times \frac{X}{V\cos\phi} \times G_s$$

which is equally easy for work, and more in keeping with the form of the expression for determining the deflection due to motion of the gun given in equation (214). The difference is not material however.

250. Taking our standard problem again, we have the above formula and $G_s = \frac{12 \times 6080}{60 \times 60 \times 3}$ yards per second.

$X = 30000$		log 4.47712
$V = 2900$	log 3.46240	colog 6.53760 − 10
$\phi = 4° \; 13' \; 14''$		sec 0.00118
12		log 1.07918
6080		log 3.78390
$60 \times 60 \times 3 = 10800$	log 4.03342	colog 5.96658 − 10
$D_{1sG} = 70.1$ yards		log 1.84556

Section 3.—The Effect of the Motion of the Target Upon the Motion of the Projectile Relative to the Target.

251. Motion of the target evidently has no effect upon the actual flight of the projectile, but it is equally clear that it will affect the relative positions of the target and of the point of fall of the projectile, as the target has been in motion during the time of flight of the projectile.

252. Evidently, if the target be moving in the line of fire with the velocity T_s, in order to hit it the sight must be set for a range greater or less than the true range at the instant of firing by the distance which the target will traverse in the time of flight, or T_sT. So, also, if the speed of the target at right angles to the plane of fire be T_s, the shot will fall T_sT to one side of the target unless that much deviation is allowed for in pointing. Once more we consider the motion as resolved into two components, one in and the other normal to the plane of fire, and consider the two as producing results entirely independent of each other. And it is readily seen that, for the effect of the motion of the target we must correct the range and deviation by the quantities given by the expressions

Effect of motion of target.

$$\Delta X_T = T_sT \tag{215}$$

$$D_T = T_sT \tag{216}$$

253. For our standard 12" gun, again, for 10,000 yards, to compute the data in Columns 15 and 18 of the range tables, for 12 knots speed of target, the work would be

$$T_s = T_s = \frac{12 \times 6080}{60 \times 60 \times 3} \qquad X_{12T} = D_{12T} = T_{12s} \times T = T_{12s} \times T$$

$T = 12.43$		log 1.09452
12		log 1.07918
6080		log 3.78390
$60 \times 60 \times 3 = 10800$	log 4.03342	colog 5.96658 − 10
$R_{12T} = D_{12T} = 84$ yards		log 1.92418

Section 4.—The Effect Upon the Motion of the Projectile of All Three Motions Combined.

254. In the preceding sections we have discussed the effects upon the motion of the projectile of the wind and of the motions of the firing and target ships. The resultant combined effect of all three of these causes of error would of course be obtained by computing them separately and then performing the necessary algebraic additions, first for all range effects to get the total effect upon the range, and then of all deflection effects to get the total effect in deflection.

NOTE.—Professor Alger appends to this chapter the following foot-note:

The method herein adopted for the treatment of the problem of wind effect was first set forth, so far as I am aware, in General Didion's Traité de Ballistique though it has been generally accepted since. It is mathematically correct only for spherical projectiles, to the motion of which the air offers a resistance which is independent of the direction of motion. With elongated projectiles it will be seen that the initial motion *relative to the air* is not exactly in the line of the projectile's axis, so that we have no right to assume, as we do, that the flight *relative to the air* is the same when the air is moving as when it is still. It has been supposed by some writers that the lateral wind component produces the same pressure on the side of the moving projectile as it would if the projectile were stationary, and that the deviation can be computed upon that basis. If this were true, the deviation would be proportional to the square of the lateral wind component, whereas it is really much more nearly proportional to its first power. Actually the pressure is much greater when the projectile is moving at right angles to the wind current than when it is stationary, on account of the increased number of air particles which strike it.

EXAMPLES.

1. Compute the errors in range and in deflection caused by the wind components as given below.

Problem.	DATA.									ANSWERS.			
	Projectile.			V. f.s.	Range. Yds.	Wind component in knots per hour.				In line of fire.		Perpendicular to line of fire.	
						In line of fire.		Perpendicular to line of fire.					
	d. In.	w. Lbs.	c.			Knots.	With or against.	Knots.	To the right or left	Yards.	Short or over.	Yards.	To the right or left.
A..	3	13	1.00	1150	3000	8	With	6	Right	16.5	Over	6.3	Right
B..	3	13	1.00	2700	4500	10	Against	8	Left	34.3	Short	19.1	Left
C..	4	33	0.67	2900	4000	11	With	9	Right	12.7	Over	5.7	Right
D .	5	50	1.00	3150	4500	13	Against	11	Left	26.8	Short	14.4	Left
E..	5	50	0.61	3150	4500	14	With	13	Right	17.1	Over	8.8	Right
F..	6	105	0.61	2600	13600	15	Against	14	Left	146.9	Short	88.8	Left
G..	6	105	1.00	2800	4500	16	With	15	Right	23.9	Over	14.0	Right
H .	6	105	0.61	2800	4000	17	Against	16	Left	13.3	Short	6.4	Left
I . .	7	165	1.00	2700	7500	18	With	17	Right	74.2	Over	44.3	Right
J..	7	165	0.61	2700	7500	19	Against	18	Left	47.0	Short	24.8	Left
K .	8	260	0.61	2750	8500	20	With	19	Right	51.5	Over	26.9	Right
L..	10	510	1.00	2700	10500	19	Against	20	Left	100.4	Short	64.7	Left
M .	10	510	0.61	2700	11500	18	With	19	Right	60.0	Over	40.2	Right
N .	12	870	0.61	2900	10500	17	With	18	Left	141.5	Over	87.0	Left
O..	13	1130	1.00	2000	10500	16	Against	17	Right	93.3	Short	54.8	Right
P..	13	1130	0.74	2000	11500	15	With	16	Left	79.6	Over	44.4	Left
Q..	14	1400	0.70	2000	14500	14	Against	15	Right	105.6	Short	58.1	Right
R..	14	1400	0.70	2600	14000	13	With	14	Left	63.7	Over	37.3	Left

2. Compute the errors in range and in deflection caused by the motion of the gun as given below. Conditions standard.

Problem.	DATA.									ANSWERS.			
	Projectile.			V. f.s.	Range. Yds.	Speed component in knots per hour.				In line of fire.		Perpendicular to line of fire.	
						In line of fire.		Perpendicular to line of fire.					
	d. In.	w. Lbs.	c.			Knots.	With or against.	Knots.	To the right or left.	Yards.	Short or over.	Yards.	To the right or left.
A..	3	13	1.00	1150	2000	6	Against	8	Left	14.7	Short	23.6	Left
B..	3	13	1.00	2700	3500	7	With	8	Right	10.2	Over	17.5	Right
C..	4	33	0.67	2900	3000	8	Against	9	Left	11.5	Short	15.7	Left
D.	5	50	1.00	3150	3500	9	With	10	Right	12.4	Over	18.8	Right
E..	5	50	0.61	3150	3900	10	Against	11	Left	16.4	Short	22.4	Left
F..	6	105	0.61	2600	12600	11	With	13	Left	58.3	Over	108.4	Left
G..	6	105	1.00	2800	4000	13	Against	14	Right	24.1	Short	33.8	Right
H.	6	105	0.61	2800	3000	14	With	15	Left	22.2	Over	27.1	Left
I..	7	165	1.00	2700	6500	15	Against	16	Right	43.1	Short	65.2	Right
J..	7	165	0.61	2700	6700	16	With	17	Left	52.8	Over	71.4	Left
K.	8	260	0.61	2750	7500	17	With	18	Right	62.6	Over	83.1	Right
L..	10	510	1.00	2700	9500	18	Against	19	Left	76.3	Short	113.5	Left
M.	10	510	0.61	2700	10500	19	With	20	Right	97.6	Over	132.0	Right
N.	12	870	0.61	2900	23000	20	Against	19	Left	182.3	Short	262.0	Left
O..	13	1130	1.00	2000	10000	19	With	18	Right	118.0	Over	154.7	Right
P..	13	1130	0.74	2000	11000	18	Against	17	Left	128.4	Short	160.8	Left
Q..	14	1400	0.70	2000	14000	17	With	16	Right	149.5	Over	195.4	Right
R..	14	1400	0.70	2600	13700	16	Against	15	Left	109.4	Short	134.8	Left

3. Compute the errors in range and in deflection caused by the motion of the target as given below. Conditions standard.

Problem.	DATA.									ANSWERS.			
	Projectile.			V. f.s.	Range. Yds.	Speed component in knots per hour.				In line of fire.		Perpendicular to line of fire.	
						In line of fire.		Perpendicular to line of fire.					
	d. In.	w. Lbs.	c.			Knots.	With or against.	Knots.	To the right or left.	Yards.	Short or over.	Yards.	To the right or left.
A..	3	13	1.00	1150	1800	7	With	8	Right	21.4	Short	24.4	Left
B..	3	13	1.00	2700	3300	8	Against	9	Left	26.2	Over	29.4	Right
C..	4	33	0.67	2900	2800	9	With	10	Right	17.3	Short	19.2	Left
D.	5	50	1.00	3150	3300	10	Against	11	Left	24.0	Over	26.4	Right
E..	5	50	0.61	3150	3400	11	With	13	Right	24.1	Short	28.5	Left
F..	6	105	0.61	2800	13800	13	With	14	Left	204.3	Short	220.1	Right
G..	6	105	1.00	2800	3800	14	Against	15	Right	41.1	Over	44.0	Left
H.	6	105	0.61	2800	2800	15	With	16	Left	28.1	Short	30.0	Right
I..	7	165	1.00	2700	6300	16	Against	17	Right	91.1	Over	96.0	Left
J..	7	165	0.61	2700	6700	17	With	18	Left	89.5	Short	94.7	Right
K.	8	260	0.61	2750	7300	18	Against	19	Left	99.2	Over	104.6	Right
L..	10	510	1.00	2700	9300	19	With	20	Right	157.9	Short	166.2	Left
M.	10	510	0.61	2700	10300	20	Against	19	Left	162.7	Over	154.6	Right
N.	12	870	0.61	2800	20200	19	With	20	Right	326.7	Short	343.9	Left
O..	13	1130	1.00	2000	9300	18	Against	19	Left	188.6	Over	190.1	Right
P..	13	1130	0.74	2000	10300	17	With	18	Right	187.6	Short	198.6	Left
Q..	14	1400	0.70	2000	13300	16	Against	17	Left	236.8	Over	251.6	Right
R..	14	1400	0.70	2000	13700	15	With	16	Right	172.4	Short	184.5	Left

CHAPTER 15.

DETERMINATION OF JUMP. EXPERIMENTAL RANGING AND THE REDUCTION OF OBSERVED RANGES.

Jump.

255. Primarily and in its narrowest sense, jump is the increase (algebraic, and generally positive) in the angle of elevation resulting from the angular motion of the gun in the vertical plane caused by the shock of discharge, as a result of which the projectile strikes above (for positive jump; below for negative) the point at which it theoretically should for the given angle of elevation. A definition which thus confines jump to the result of such angular motion is a narrow and restricted one, however, and other elements may enter to give similar results, all of which may be and are properly included in that resultant variation generally called jump. For instance, in the old gravity return mounts, the gun did not recoil directly in the line of its own axis, as it does in the most modern mounts, but rose up an inclined plane as it recoiled. As the projectile did not clear the muzzle until the gun had recoiled an appreciable distance, this upward motion of the gun imparted a similar upward motion to the projectile, which resulted in making the projectile strike slightly higher than it would otherwise have done. This small discrepancy, unimportant at battle ranges, but necessarily considered in such work as firing test shots at armor plate at close range, was properly included in the jump. Also most modern guns of any considerable length have what is known as "droop," that is. the muzzle of the gun sags a little, due to the length and weight of the gun, the axis of the gun being no longer a theoretical straight line; and this causes the projectile to strike slightly lower than it otherwise would, and introduces another slight error which may properly be included in the jump. Also it is probable that this droop causes the muzzle of the gun to move slightly in firing as the gun tends to straighten out under internal pressure, and perhaps this motion tends to produce another variation, "whip," in the motion of the projectile, which would modify the result of the droop. All these may therefore be properly included in the jump.

256. This matter has a direct bearing, under our present system of considering such matters, upon the factor of the ballistic coefficient which we have designated as the coefficient of form of the projectile, and which is supposed, under our previous definition, to be the ratio of the resistance the projectile meets in flight to the resistance that would be encountered in the same air, at the same velocity, by the standard projectile; that is, by a projectile about three calibers long and similar in all respects except in possessing a standard head, namely, one whose ogival has a two-caliber radius. Imagine that the gun jumps a little and increases the range in so doing. It gives the same range as a similar gun firing without jump a projectile exactly similar in all respects except in possessing a slightly lower coefficient of form. Suppose a gun droops and shoots lower. The coefficient of form calculated back from the range obtained by actual firing would work out a little large. And in practice we would probably have both jump and droop affecting the range, but by our method of determining the coefficient of form from actual firing, by comparing actual with computed ranges, all such effects are hidden in the found value of the coefficient of form.

Broader definition of coefficient of form.

257. As a matter of fact, as intimated above, the value of the coefficient of form is determined by firing ranging shots, and then computing its value from the results.

and a running record is kept, so that a great number of results will be available as a cumulative check on the range table. For a new caliber, a curve of "corrected range" and "coefficient of form" is kept until enough data has been collected with which to start a range table. For rough work, the formula for change of range resulting from a variation in the value of the ballistic coefficient may be used in the absence of curves.

Computation of range tables.

261. Prior to the appearance of the present range tables, guns were ranged by firing experimental shots at a number of different angles of elevation, and a curve of angles and ranges was plotted. From these faired curves the angles corresponding to all ranges were taken and a range table was made up from the results. As more confidence in the mathematical process was acquired, through the accumulation of considerable data, we began to get our range tables by computation, gradually abandoning the old system of ranging by experimental firing; and the use of the value of the coefficient of form as unity, with the projectiles then in use, was found to give range tables that agreed with the results of experimental ranging. When different lots of projectiles are presented for acceptance, a few have to be tested for flight from each lot; and these are ranged at the Proving Ground at 8° elevation in all cases, in order to make comparisons possible. At this angle there are no dangerous ricochets, and variations in the coefficient of form and differences between different projectiles will show up best at these long ranges. With a coefficient of form accurately determined by firing at the longest practicable ranges, we can compute an extremely accurate range table extending down through the medium and short ranges. The method of ranging only at a single elevation was therefore adopted, an occasional check by firing at short ranges being made.

262. The process of experimental ranging, as formerly carried out, was to fire a number of shots at different angles of elevation. The results for these shots were reduced to standard conditions, and the reduced observed ranges were plotted as abscissæ, with the corresponding angles of elevation as ordinates. A fair curve was then drawn through these points, and from this curve the angle of elevation corresponding to any range could be obtained.

Reduction of observed ranges.

263. The process of reducing observed ranges to standard conditions was carried out in accordance with the principles and formulæ already explained in this book, and this still has to be done for every ranging shot fired; but as this process is one that pertains purely to Proving Ground work and has no bearing on the service use of the gun, it is not considered necessary to go into it at length here; nor is it considered necessary to further discuss the details of the methods used for determining the actual magnitude of the jump, etc.

PART IV.

RANGE TABLES; THEIR COMPUTATION AND USE.

INTRODUCTION TO PART IV.

Having completed the study of all computations connected with the trajectory in air, both as a plane curve and allowing for existing variations from that plane, we are now in a position to make use of our knowledge in a practical way. The practical and useful expression of the knowledge thus acquired takes the form of: first, the preparation of the range tables; and after that, second, their use. Part IV will be devoted to a consideration of the range tables from these two points of view: first, as to their preparation; and, second, as to their actual practical use in service. Each column in the tables will be considered separately, the method and computations by which the data contained in it is obtained will be indicated, and then consideration will be given to the practical use of this data by officers aboard ship in service.

For projectiles without caps.

$$v=\frac{d^{0.5}E_1^{0.75}}{w^{0.5}}K \quad \text{or} \quad E_1^{0.75}=\frac{vw^{0.5}}{Kd^{0.5}} \tag{217}$$

in which E_1 = the penetration of Harveyized armor in inches.
v = the striking velocity in foot-seconds.
w = the weight of the projectile in pounds.
d = the diameter of the projectile in inches.
$\log K=3.34512$.

For capped projectiles.

$$v=\frac{d^{0.5}E_1^{0.8}}{w^{0.5}}K' \quad \text{or} \quad E_1^{0.8}=\frac{vw^{0.5}}{K'd^{0.5}} \tag{218}$$

in which $\log K'=3.25312$, and the other quantities are as before.

De Marre's formula for face-hardened armor is based on the following equation:

$$v=\frac{d^{0.75}E^{0.7}}{w^{0.5}}K \quad \text{or} \quad E^{0.7}=\frac{vw^{0.5}}{Kd^{0.75}} \tag{219}$$

in which $\log K=3.00945$, E = the penetration of oil tempered and annealed armor that has not been face hardened. For face-hardened armor (for the range tables accompanying this book and marked as *C, F, H, K, M, N, P, Q* and *R*), the results obtained by the use of the above formula must be divided by De Marre's coefficient, which has been found to be 1.5 for such purpose. (For the other range tables accompanying this book, the value of this coefficient was taken as unity.)

267. As an example of the work under Davis's formula, let us compute the penetration by a capped projectile of Harveyized armor by the 5″ gun; $V=3150$ f. s., $w=50$ pounds; for a range of 4000 yards, first for a projectile for which $c=1$, and next for a projectile whose coefficient of form is 0.61. For these two projectiles, the range tables give the remaining velocities at the given range as $v_1=1510$ f. s. for $c=1.00$ and $v_2=2048$ f. s. for $c=0.61$.

$w=50$	log 1.69897		0.5 log 0.84948
$K'=$	log 3.25312		colog 6.74688−10
$d=5$	log 0.69897	0.5 log 0.34948	0.5 colog 9.65052−10
		log 7.24688−10	log 7.24688−10
$v_1=1510$		log 3.17898	
$v_2=2048$			log 3.31133
$E^{0.8}$		log 0.42586	log 0.55821
		10	10
		8)4.25860	8)5.58210
$E_{1(c=1)}=3.4067''$		log 0.53233	
$E_{1(c=.61)}=4.9861''$			log 0.69776

Comparison of long and short pointed projectiles.

268. As the coefficient of form does not enter into the above equation, we see that the only thing that gives a long pointed projectile a greater penetration than a blunt pointed one at the same range is the fact that, at that range, the long pointed projectile will have a greater striking velocity than the blunt one. As a matter of fact, as far as their effect upon armor plate is concerned, the two projectiles are the same; for the main body of the projectile is the same in each case, the only difference between them being in the shape of the wind shield. In other words, that part of the projectile which really acts to penetrate armor is the same for both the standard and for the long pointed shell, but one has no wind shield and the other a sharply pointed one, the actual points of the two shells being equally efficient in their effect upon the penetration. No difference in penetration could therefore be expected for equal striking velocities.

STANDARD FORMS FOR COMPUTATION OF RANGE TABLE DATA.

Specific Problem.

Compute the data for all columns of the range table for a range of 10,000 yards for a 12" gun for which $V = 2900$ f. s., $w = 870$ pounds, and $c = 0.61$.

FORM No. 1.

For Computation of Angle of Departure.

Column 2.

Uncorrected value of C

$$C_1 = \frac{w}{cd^2} = 9.9045$$

log w	2	9	3	9	5	2	
colog c	0	2	1	4	6	7	
colog d^2	7	8	4	1	6	4	
log C_1	0	9	9	5	8	3	

$$Z_1 = \frac{X}{C_1} = 3029$$

log X	4	4	7	7	1	2	
colog C_1	9	0	0	4	1	7	—10
log Z_1	3	4	8	1	2	9	

$A_1 = .01470 + .00063 \times 20 = .014882$

$\sin 2\phi_1 = A_1 C_1$

log A_1	8	1	7	2	6	6	—10
log C_1	0	9	9	5	8	3	
log sin $2\phi_1$	9	1	6	8	4	9	—10

$2\phi_1 = 8°\ 28'\ 34''$

$\phi_1 = 4°\ 14'\ 17''$ first approximation

$A_1'' = 849 + \frac{.82 \times 57}{12} = 852.9$

$Z_2 = 2983.8$

$A_2 = .01408 + .838 \times .00062 = .014599$

log A_2	8	1	6	4	3	2	—10
log C_2	1	0	0	2	3	5	
log sin $2\phi_2$	9	1	6	6	6	7	—10

$2\phi_2 = 8°\ 26'\ 26''$

$\phi_2 = 4°\ 13'\ 13''$ second approximation

$A_2'' = 793 + \frac{8.99 \times 56}{11} = 838.7$

$Z_3 = 2984.1$

$A_3 = .01408 + .00062 \times .841 = .014601$

log A_3	8	1	6	4	3	8	—10
log C_3	1	0	0	2	3	1	
log sin $2\phi_3$	9	1	6	6	6	9	—10

$2\phi_3 = 8°\ 26'\ 28''$

$\phi_3 = 4°\ 13'\ 14''$ third approximation

$R = 10{,}000$ yards $X = 30{,}000$ feet.

loglog $f = \log Y + 5.01765$

$Y = A''C \tan \phi$

log A''_1	2	9	3	0	9	0	
log C_1	0	9	9	5	8	3	
log tan ϕ_1	8	8	6	9	8	3	—10
log constant	5	0	1	7	6	5	—10
loglog f_1	7	8	1	4	2	1	—10
log f_1	0	0	0	6	5	2	
log C_1	0	9	9	5	8	3	
log C_2	1	0	0	2	3	5	
log X	4	4	7	7	1	2	
log Z_2	3	4	7	4	7	7	

$Z_2 = 2983.8$

log A_2''	2	9	2	3	6	1	
log C_2	1	0	0	2	3	5	
log tan ϕ_2	8	8	6	8	0	0	—10
log constant	5	0	1	7	6	5	—10
loglog f_2	7	8	1	1	6	1	—10
log f_2	0	0	0	6	4	8	
log C_1	0	9	9	5	8	3	
log C_3	1	0	0	2	3	1	
log X	4	4	7	7	1	2	
log Z_3	3	4	7	4	8	1	

$Z_3 = 2984.1$

From the above work, we have for our final values:

$$\phi = 4°\ 13'\ 14''$$
$$Z = 2984.1$$
$$\log C = 1.00231$$

Form No. 2.

For Computation of

Column 2. Angle of Departure (if C be already correctly known, and work on Form No. 1 is therefore unnecessary, except for Z).

Column 3. Angle of Fall. Column 4. Time of flight. Column 5. Striking velocity.
Column 6. Drift. Column 8. Maximum ordinate. Column 9. Penetration.

DATA.

$R = 10{,}000$ yards $\quad X = 30{,}000$ feet $\quad \log C = 1.00231 \quad Z = 2084.1$

$A = .01408 + .00062 \times .841 = .014601 \quad \log B' = .1006 + .0037 \times .841 = .10371$

$u = 2048 - 26 \times .841 = 2026.1 \quad T' = 1.192 + .049 \times .841 = 1.2332 \quad D' = 24 + 2 \times .841 = 25.9$

$B = .0178 + .0009 \times .841 = .01856$

$A'' = 793 + \dfrac{8.99 \times 56}{11} = 838.8 \quad \Delta_{v_A} = .00099 + .0004 \times .841 = .001024$

---

2. Angle of departure, $\phi = 4° \ 13' \ 14''$
$\sin 2\phi = AC$

log C.......	1	0	0	2	3	1	
log A.......	8	1	6	4	3	8	—10
log sin 2ϕ...	9	1	6	6	6	9	—10

$2\phi = 8° \ 26' \ 28''$

3. Angle of fall, $\omega = 5° \ 21' \ 11''$
$\tan \omega = B' \tan \phi$

log B'.......	0	1	0	3	7	1	
log tan ϕ....	8	8	6	8	0	3	—10
log tan ω....	8	9	7	1	7	4	—10

4. Time of flight, $T = 12.43$ seconds
$T = CT' \sec \phi$

log C.......	1	0	0	2	3	1
log T'.......	0	0	9	1	0	3
log sec ϕ....	0	0	0	1	1	8
log T.......	1	0	9	4	5	2

5. Striking velocity, $v_\omega = 2029$ f. s.
$v_\omega = u \cos \phi \sec \omega$

log u.......	3	3	0	6	6	6	
log cos ϕ ...	9	9	9	8	8	2	—10
log sec ω. ..	0	0	0	1	9	0	
log v_ω.....	3	3	0	7	3	8	

6. Drift, $D = 26.5$ yards

$D = \text{constant} \times \dfrac{C^2 D'}{\cos^2 \phi}$, where constant $= \dfrac{\mu\lambda}{n\lambda}$

(See page 147)

log constant.	7	8	3	1	4	9	—10
log C^2.......	2	0	0	4	6	2	
log D'.......	1	4	0	8	2	4	
log sec² ϕ ...	0	0	0	3	5	4	
	1	2	4	7	8	9	
log 1.5	0	1	7	6	0	9	
log D......	1	4	2	3	9	8	

As the value of $\frac{\mu\lambda}{n\lambda}$ is constant for the same gun for all ranges, its value is computed first and then carried on as a constant through all the drift computations for the range table for the particular gun in question.

8. Maximum ordinate, $Y = 622$ feet
$Y = A''C \tan \phi$

log A''.....	2	9	2	3	6	6	
log C	1	0	0	2	3	1	
log tan ϕ	8	8	6	8	0	3	—10
log Y	2	7	9	4	0	0	

9. Penetration of armor, $E = 15.59''$

$E^{0.7} = \dfrac{v w^{0.5}}{K d^{0.75}} = \text{constant} \times v$, where

$\text{constant} = \dfrac{w^{0.5}}{K d^{0.75}}$

log constant.	7	6	5	0	9	3	—10
log v........	3	3	0	7	3	8	
log $E^{0.7}$.....	0	9	5	8	3	1	
					1	0	
7)	9	5	8	3	1	0	
log ($E_1 \times 1.5$)	1	3	6	9	0	1	
colog 1.5....	9	8	2	3	9	1	—10
log E_1......	1	1	9	2	9	2	

1.5 is De Marre's coefficient for face-hardened armor as compared to simple oil tempered and annealed armor.

As the value of $\frac{w^{0.5}}{K d^{0.75}}$ is constant for the same gun for all ranges, its value is computed first and then carried through all the penetration computations for the entire range table for the particular gun in question.

Note—In forms Nos. 3 and 4, whenever it becomes necessary to use the logarithms of T, v_ω, etc., take the exact values of those logarithms correct to five decimal places from the work on this sheet, and do not use the approximate logarithms taken from the log tables for the values of the elements given here and correct only to two places as required for the range table.

FORM No. 3.

For Computation of

Column 7. Danger space for target 20 feet high.
Column 10. Change in range for variation of ± 50 f. s. in initial velocity.
Column 11. Change in range for variation of ± 10 pounds in weight of projectile.
Column 12. Change in range for variation of ± 10 per cent in density of air.

7. Danger space, $S_\omega = 72$ yards

$$S = \frac{h}{3}\cot\omega\left(1 + \frac{\frac{h}{3}\cot\omega}{R}\right)$$

$\log \frac{h}{3}$	0	8	2	3	0	1	
log cot ω	1	0	2	8	2	6	
$\log\left(\frac{h}{3}\cot\omega\right)$	1	8	5	2	1	7	
colog R	6	0	0	0	0	0	−10
$\frac{h}{3} \times \frac{\cot\omega}{R}$ = .0071 log	7	8	5	2	1	7	−10

$1 + .0071 = 1.0071$

log (h cot ω)	1	8	5	2	1	7
log 1.0071	0	0	0	3	0	7
log S_ω	1	8	5	5	2	4

10. $\Delta R_{50V} = 276$ yards

$$\Delta R_{50V} = \frac{\Delta v_A R}{2B}$$

log Δv_A	7	0	1	0	3	0	−10
log R	4	0	0	0	0	0	
colog 2	9	6	9	8	9	7	−10
colog B	1	7	3	1	4	2	
log ΔR_{50V}	2	4	4	0	6	9	

12. $\Delta R_{10C} = 213$ yards

$$\Delta R_{10C} = \frac{B - A}{10B} R \qquad B - A = .003959 \qquad 10B = .1856$$

log $(B - A)$	7	5	9	7	5	9	−10
log R	4	0	0	0	0	0	
colog $10B$	0	7	3	1	4	2	
log ΔR_{10C}	2	3	2	9	0	1	

11. ΔR_w for ± 10 pounds in w, $\Delta R_w = \pm 42$ yards

a. $\delta V = 0.36 \frac{\Delta w}{w} V$; $\Delta R' = \Delta R_{50V} \times \frac{12}{50}$ — For change in initial velocity.
b. $\Delta R'' = \Delta R_{10C} \times \frac{10}{87}$
c. $\Delta R_w = \Delta R' + \Delta R''$ — For change in weight.

(See page 136.)

log 0.36	9	5	5	6	3	0	−10
log Δw	1	0	0	0	0	0	
colog w	7	0	6	0	4	8	−10
log V	3	4	6	2	4	0	
log δV	1	0	7	9	1	8	

$\delta V = 12$ f. s., $\Delta v_A = .001024$

log ΔR_{50V}	2	4	4	0	7	0	
log 12	1	0	7	9	1	8	
colog 50	8	3	0	1	0	3	−10
log $\Delta R'$	1	8	2	0	9	1	

$\Delta R' = 66.21$

log ΔR_{10C}	2	3	2	9	0	1	
log 10	1	0	0	0	0	0	
colog 87	8	0	6	0	4	8	−10
log $\Delta R''$	1	3	8	9	4	9	

$\Delta R'' = 24.52$

$\Delta R' = 66.21$
$\Delta R'' = 24.52$

$\Delta R_{10w} = 41.62$

Determination of n, $n = \frac{V^2 \sin 2\phi}{gX}$

log V^2	6	9	2	4	8	0	
log sin 2φ	9	1	6	6	6	9	−10
colog g	8	4	9	2	1	4	−10
colog X	5	5	2	2	8	8	−10
log n	0	1	0	6	5	1	

$n = 1.278$
$2n = 2.556$
$2n - 1 = 1.556$ log $(2n - 1) = 0.19201$
$R = 10000$ log $R = 4.00000$
$X = 30000$ log $X = 4.47712$

Form No. 4.

For Computation of

Column 13. Wind effect in range.
Column 14. Gun motion in range.
Columns 15 and 18. Target motion effect in range and deflection.
Column 16. Wind effect in deflection.
Column 17. Gun motion effect in deflection.
Column 19. Change in height of impact for variation of ± 100 yards in sight bar.

13. Wind effect in range,
$\Delta R_w = 26.7$ yards.

$$\Delta X_W = W_{128}\left(T - \frac{n}{2n-1} \times \frac{X \cos\phi}{V}\right)$$

$$W_{128} = W_{128} = G_{128} = G_{128} = T_{128} = T_{128}$$

$$= \frac{12 \times 6080}{60 \times 60 \times 3} = 6.7556$$

log n	0	1	0	6	5	1	
log X	4	4	7	7	1	2	
log cos ϕ	9	9	9	8	8	2	−10
colog $(2n-1)$	9	8	0	7	9	9	−10
colog V	6	5	3	7	6	0	−10
log $\frac{nX \cos\phi}{(2n-1)V}$	0	9	2	8	0	4	

$$\frac{nX \cos\phi}{(2n-1)V} = 8.47$$

$$T = 12.43$$

$$3.96$$

log W_{128}	0	8	2	9	6	7
log 3.96	0	5	9	7	7	0
log ΔR_w	1	4	2	7	3	7

14. Gun motion effect in range,
$\Delta R_G = 57$ yards

$$\Delta X_G = \frac{nX \cos\phi}{(2n-1)V} G_{128}$$

log $\frac{nX \cos\phi}{(2n-1)V}$	0	9	2	8	0	4
log G_{128}	0	8	2	9	6	7
log ΔR_G	1	7	5	7	7	1

15 and 18. Target motion effect in range and deflection.
$\Delta R_T = D_T = T_{128} T = T_{128} T = 94$ yards

log T_{128} = log T_{128}	0	8	2	9	6	7
log T	1	0	9	4	5	2
log ΔR_T = log D_T	1	9	2	4	1	9

16. Wind effect in deflection,
$D_W = 13.9$ yards

$$D_W = W_{128}\left(T - \frac{X}{V \cos\phi}\right)$$

log X	4	4	7	7	1	2	
colog V	6	5	3	7	6	0	−10
log sec ϕ	0	0	0	1	1	8	
log $\frac{X}{V \cos\phi}$	1	0	1	5	9	0	

$$\frac{X}{V \cos\phi} = 10.37$$

$$T = 12.43$$

$$2.06$$

log W_{128}	0	8	2	9	6	7
log 2.06	0	3	1	3	8	7
log D_W	1	1	4	3	5	4

17. Gun motion effect in deflection,
$D_G = 70.1$ yards

$$D_G = \frac{X}{V \cos\phi} G_{128}$$

log G_{128}	0	8	2	9	6	7
log $\frac{X}{V \cos\phi}$	1	0	1	5	9	0
log D_G	1	8	4	5	5	7

19. Change in height of impact for variation of ± 100 yards in sight bar, $H = 28$ feet

$H = \Delta X \tan\omega$ $\Delta X = 300$ feet

log ΔX	2	4	7	7	1	2	
log tan ω	8	9	7	1	7	4	−10
log H_{100}	1	4	4	8	8	6	

EXAMPLES.

1. For examples in determining the angle of departure corresponding to any given range, the data in the range tables may be used, computing for standard atmospheric condition, and proceeding to determine the true value of the ballistic coefficient by successive approximations. (See also Examples in Chapter 8.)

2. As the process of successive approximations is somewhat long for section room work, the following are given. Given the data contained in the following table, compute the corresponding values of ϕ, ω, T and v_ω of the drift, of the maximum ordinate, and of the penetration of armor by capped projectiles (Harveyized armor, by Davis's formula for guns *A, B, D, E, G, I, J, L* and *O*; face-hardened armor, by De Marre's formula for guns *C, F, H, K, M, N, P, Q* and *R*. De Marre's coefficient =1.5). Atmosphere standard.

Problem.	DATA. Projectile. d. In.	w. Lbs.	c.	Value of f.	V. f.s.	Range. Yds.	Multiplier for drift.	ANSWERS. ϕ.	ω.	T. Secs.	v_ω. f.s.	Drift. Yds.	Maximum ordinate. Ft.	Penetration. Harv. In.	F.H. In.
A...	3	13	1.00	1.0044	1150	2500	1.0	6° 53.1′	8° 26′	7.89	837	7.5	253	0.96	....
B...	3	13	1.00	1.0034	2700	3600	1.0	2 48.9	5 10	6.61	1094	5.9	181	1.30	....
C...	4	33	0.67	1.0011	2900	3000	1.0	1 15.3	1 35	3.71	2043	1.6	55	....	4.9
D...	5	50	1.00	1.0025	3150	4000	1.5	1 53.4	3 05	5.57	1511	5.8	126	3.40	....
E...	5	50	0.61	1.0024	3150	4500	1.5	1 45.7	2 26	5.49	1032	5.4	122	4.6	....
F...	6	105	0.61	1.0605	2600	14000	1.5	13 27.3	24 17	28.88	1070	183.0	3513	....	2.9
G...	6	105	1.00	1.0022	2800	3800	1.0	1 52.6	2 35	5.21	1729	3.2	109	5.7	....
H..	6	105	0.61	1.0015	2800	3500	1.5	1 28.6	1 46	4.29	2153	3.0	74	....	7.9
I...	7	165	1.00	1.0095	2700	7000	1.0	4 45.6	7 59	11.78	1243	17.6	566	4.6	....
J...	7	165	0.61	1.0083	2700	7500	1.5	4 04.1	5 42	10.82	1631	20.9	473	6.4	....
K..	8	260	0.61	1.0085	2750	8000	1.5	3 59.8	5 21	10.96	1771	21.5	484	....	8.4
L...	10	510	1.00	1.0141	2700	9000	1.0	5 31.6	8 33	14.14	1401	24.6	811	8.6	....
M..	10	510	0.61	1.0137	2700	10000	1.5	5 10.5	6 55	13.95	1744	34.5	785	....	10.4
N..	12	870	0.61	1.1130	2900	24000	1.5	15 07.7	25 01	39.51	1359	309.9	6358	....	8.8
O...	13	1130	1.00	1.0337	2000	10500	1.0	11 32.4	16 40	21.90	1157	59.9	1955	9.4	....
P...	13	1130	0.74	1.0316	2000	11000	1.5	10 52.1	14 37	21.36	1279	82.9	1845	....	8.9
Q...	14	1400	0.70	1.0571	2000	14000	1.5	14 37.1	20 02	28.28	1246	148.4	3246	....	9.3
R...	14	1400	0.70	1.0342	2600	14500	1.5	8 41.7	12 13	22.10	1560	89.3	1975	....	12.8

3. Given the data and results contained in Example 2, compute the corresponding values of:

1. Danger space for a target 20 feet high.
2. Change in range resulting from a variation from standard of ±50 f. s. in the initial velocity.
3. Change in range resulting from a variation from standard of ±10 per cent in the density of the atmosphere.
4. Change in range resulting from a variation from standard as given below in the weight of the projectile:

Gun *C* .... ± 1 pound.
Guns *F* and *H* .... ± 3 pounds.
Gun *J* .... ± 4 pounds.
Gun *K* .... ± 5 pounds.
Guns *M, N, P, Q* and *R* .... ±10 pounds.

ANSWERS.

Problem.	Danger space. Yds.	Change in range for variation in V. Yds.	Change in range for variation in density. Yds.	Change in range for variation in w. Yds.
A	45.8	± 114.5	∓ 46.3	......
B	75.2	± 74.4	∓ 163.9	......
C	260.6	± 83.2	∓ 63.0	∓ 33.6
D	127.3	± 82.3	∓ 154.7	......
E	162.4	± 104.4	∓ 125.6	......
F	14.8	± 279.8	∓ 656.4	± 37.0
G	153.5	± 99.0	∓ 104.7	......
H	229.5	± 103.2	∓ 56.8	∓ 43.2
I	47.9	± 159.1	∓ 284.4	......
J	67.4	± 199.9	∓ 214.7	∓ 42.2
K	71.8	± 217.4	∓ 204.3	∓ 41.6
L	44.6	± 220.4	∓ 319.9	......
M	55.3	± 275.9	∓ 253.9	∓ 55.4
N	14.3	± 522.0	∓ 1010.3	∓ 9.2
O	22.3	± 339.9	∓ 333.7	......
P	25.6	± 389.5	∓ 290.0	∓ 24.0
Q	18.3	± 479.8	∓ 399.0	∓ 20.9
R	30.9	± 395.4	∓ 425.2	∓ 22.5

4. Given the data and results contained in Example 2, compute the corresponding values of (atmospheric conditions being standard):

1. n.
2. Effect in range and deflection of wind components of 12 knots.
3. Effect in range and deflection of a speed of gun of 12 knots.
4. Effect in range and deflection of a speed of target of 12 knots.
5. Change in position of point of impact in the vertical plane through the target for a variation of ±100 yards in the setting of the sight in range.

ANSWERS.

Problem.	Value of n.	Wind. Range. Yds.	Wind. Deflection. Yds.	Speed of gun. Range. Yds.	Speed of gun. Deflection. Yds.	Speed of target. Range and deflection. Yds.	Change of point of impact in vertical plane. Ft.
A	1.3032	17.8	8.9	35.5	44.4	53.3	± 44.5
B	2.0577	26.8	17.6	17.8	27.1	44.7	± 27.1
C	1.2709	7.8	4.1	17.3	21.0	25.1	± 8.3
D	1.6029	19.4	11.9	18.3	25.7	37.6	± 16.2
E	1.4028	14.6	8.1	22.5	29.0	87.1	± 12.7
F	2.2622	126.9	82.9	68.1	112.1	195.1	± 135.4
G	1.3981	13.8	7.7	21.4	27.5	35.2	± 13.5
H	1.1047	7.2	3.6	21.8	25.3	29.0	± 9.3
I	1.7830	43.2	26.9	36.4	52.7	79.6	± 42.1
J	1.4241	29.8	16.7	43.3	56.4	73.1	± 29.9
K	1.5009	27.6	14.0	46.5	59.1	74.0	± 28.1
L	1.6075	46.7	27.7	48.8	67.9	95.5	± 45.1
M	1.3558	35.0	18.9	59.2	75.4	94.2	± 30.4
N	1.8278	155.4	94.2	111.5	173.7	266.9	± 140.0
O	1.5459	70.9	39.4	77.0	108.6	147.9	± 89.8
P	1.3941	59.0	30.8	85.3	113.5	144.0	± 78.2
Q	1.4446	86.1	44.4	105.0	146.6	191.1	± 109.4
R	1.4424	63.8	35.0	85.5	114.3	149.3	± 65.0

Col. 13, wind in range.

317. Column 13. Change of Range for Wind Component in Plane of Fire of 12 Knots.—This column is constantly used. For our standard problem 12" gun, at 10,000 yards, a wind blowing directly from the target to the gun with a velocity of 12 knots would decrease the actual range 27 yards, and would increase it the same

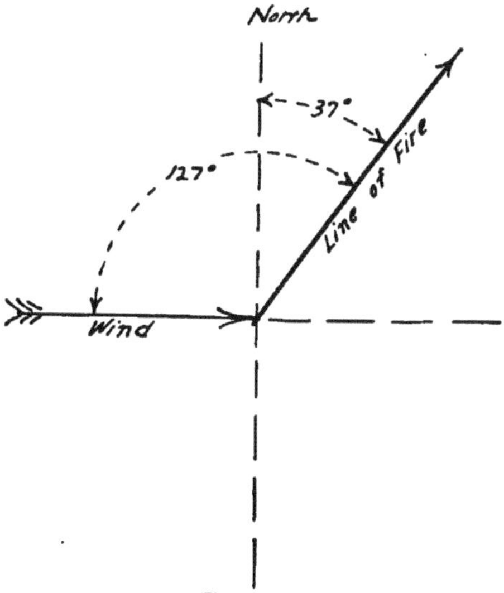

FIGURE 23.

amount if blowing the other way. Suppose the line of fire were 37° true, and the wind were blowing from 270° true with a velocity of 25 knots. Then the wind component in the line of fire would be 25 cos 53°, or (by use of the traverse tables) 15 knots, and the range would be increased $\frac{27 \times 15}{12} = 34$ yards by this component.

318. Column 14. Change of Range for Motion of Gun in Plane of Fire of 12 Knots.—This column is also constantly used. For our standard problem 12" gun, at 10,000 yards, if the gun be moving at 12 knots directly towards the target, it will overshoot 57 yards unless the motion of the gun be allowed for in pointing; and if Col. 14. gun motion in range.

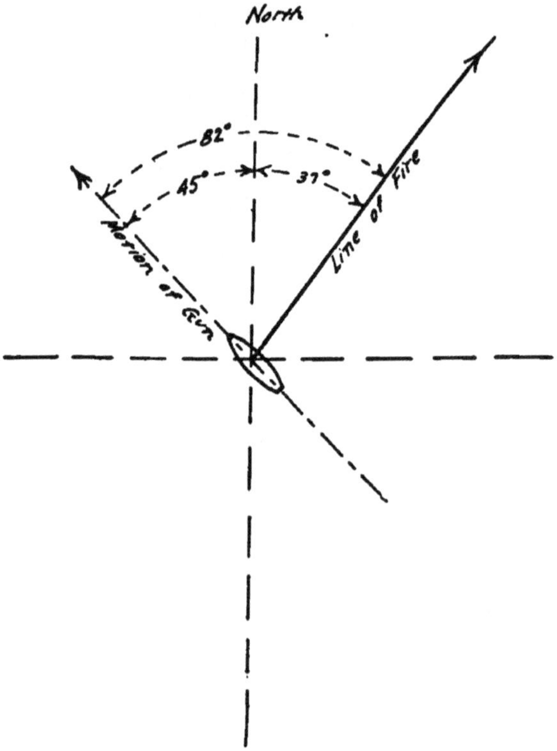

FIGURE 24.

moving in the opposite direction it would undershoot by the same amount. If the line of fire be 37° true, and the firing ship be steaming 315° true at 20 knots, the component speed in the line of fire would be 20 cos 82°, or (by the use of the traverse tables) 2.8 knots towards the target, and the gun would over-shoot $\frac{57 \times 2.8}{12} = 13.3$ yards.

seconds instead of ± 35 foot-seconds. For instance, with our standard problem 12″ gun, we see that the variation in initial velocity for a variation of $\pm 10°$ from standard is ± 35 foot-seconds. Therefore, if the temperature of the charge were 80° F., our initial velocity would be 2865 foot-seconds and not 2900 foot-seconds. If the temperature of the charge were 100° F., the initial velocity would be 2935 foot-seconds. A variation of $\pm 5°$ in the temperature of the charge gives a proportionate change in the initial velocity, that is, $\pm \frac{35}{10} \times 5 = \pm 17.5$ foot-seconds; and if the temperature of the charge were 77° F., we would have a resultant initial velocity of

$$2900 - \frac{35 \times 13}{10} = 2854.5 \text{ foot-seconds}$$

and similarly for other variations. (See note after paragraph 303.)

Col. 1, range. **281. Column 1. Range.**—As already explained, this is the argument column of the table. The data in the other columns is obtained by computation for ranges beginning at one thousand yards and increasing by five-hundred yard increments, and that for intermediate ranges by interpolation from the computed results (using second or higher differences where such use would affect the results). Therefore, to obtain the value of any element corresponding to a range lying between the tabulated ranges as given in Column 1, proceed by interpolation by the ordinary rules of proportion.

Col. 2, ϕ. **282. Column 2. Angle of Departure = Angle of Elevation + Jump.**—As has been said, although jump must be watched for and considered in any special case where it may be suspected or found to exist, still it is normally practically nonexistent in service, and the angle of departure and angle of elevation coincide for horizontal trajectories.

To lay gun at given angle of elevation. **283.** To lay the gun at any desired angle of elevation, the sights being marked in yards and not in degrees; find the angle of elevation in Column 2, and the corresponding range from Column 1. Set the sight at this range, point at the target, and the gun will then be elevated at the desired angle. An example of this kind is given in paragraphs 188, 189, 190 and 191 of Chapter 11. As there seen, this process is necessary when shooting at an object that is materially elevated or depressed relative to the horizontal plane through the gun.

Let us now see how correctly the range tables may be used to determine the proper angle of elevation to be used to hit an elevated target; assuming the theory of the rigidity of the trajectory as true within the angular limits probable with naval gun mounts. For this purpose we will consider the problem solved in paragraph 188 of Chapter 11, which was for the 12″ gun; $V = 2900$ f. s.; $w = 870$ pounds; $c = 0.61$; horizontal distance = 10,000 yards; elevation of the target = 1500 feet above the gun; barometer = 29.00″; thermometer = 90° F. In paragraph 188 we computed that the correct angle of elevation for this case is 4° 08.1′.

Now let us use Column 12 and correct for atmospheric conditions, for which, from Table IV, the multiplier is $+0.79$; from which we have that for a sight setting of 10,000 yards the shell would range $10000 + (215 \times .79) = 10169.85$ yards. Therefore in order to make the shell travel 10,000 yards we must set the sight in range for 9830.15 yards. From the range table, by interpolation, the proper angle of departure for this range is 4° 07.9′. If we use this for the angle of elevation desired (instead of the computed value of 4° 08.1′) we will have an error of 2′, that is, of about 7 yards short.

Now if we solve the triangle to determine the actual distance from the gun to the target in a straight line, we will find it to be 9857.8 yards (by use of traverse tables), using the horizontal distance corrected for atmospheric conditions as the base. From

320. Column 16. Deviation for Lateral Wind Component of 12 Knots.—This column is also constantly used. For our standard problem 12″ gun at 10,000 yards, if the wind were blowing perpendicular to the line of fire and across it from right to left, with a velocity of 12 knots, the shot would fall 14 yards to the left of the target Col. 16. wind in deflection.

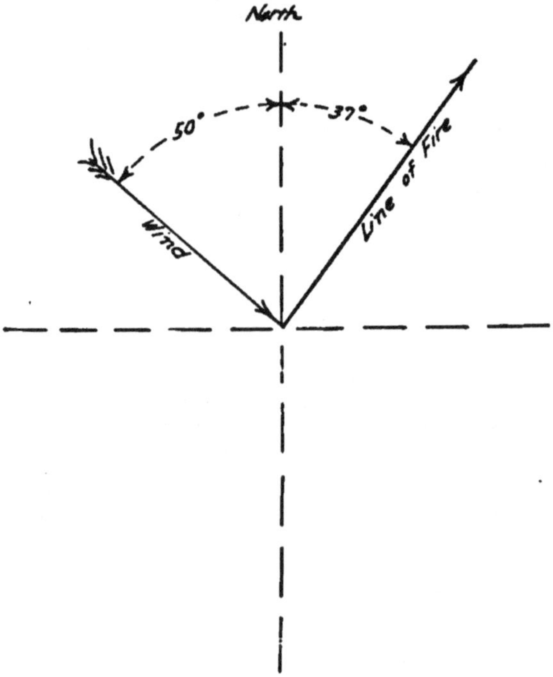

FIGURE 26.

unless the effect of the wind were allowed for in pointing. If the line of fire be 37° true, and the wind be blowing from 310° true at 23 knots, the wind component perpendicular to the line of fire would be 23 sin 87°, or (by the use of the traverse tables) 23 knots, and the shot would fall $\frac{14 \times 23}{12} = 27$ yards to the right of the target.

Col. 17, gun motion in deflection.

321. Column 17. Deviation for Lateral Motion of Gun Perpendicular to Line of Fire, Speed 12 Knots.—This column is also constantly used. For our standard problem 12" gun, at 10,000 yards, if the gun be moving at 12 knots perpendicular to the line of fire, and from right to left, the shot would fall 70 yards to the left of the

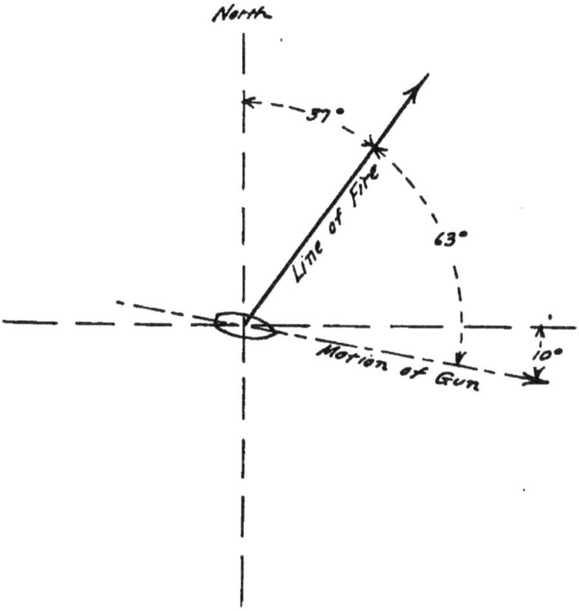

FIGURE 27.

target unless the motion were allowed for in pointing. If the line of fire be 37° true, and the firing ship be steaming 100° true at 21 knots, the component of this motion perpendicular to the line of fire would be 21 sin 63°, or (by use of the traverse tables) 18.7 knots to the right, and the shot would fall $\frac{18.7 \times 70}{12} = 109$ yards to the right.

Col. 18, target motion in deflection.

322. Column 18. Deviation for Lateral Motion of Target Perpendicular to Line of Fire, Speed 12 Knots.—This column is also constantly used. Note that the change of range in yards for the given speed when the target is moving in the line of fire is always the same numerically as the deviation in yards for the same speed when the motion is perpendicular to the line of fire. This is manifestly correct, as the motion of the target, unlike any of the other motions considered, has no effect upon the actual motion of the projectile relative to the ground. This motion of the target simply removes the target from the point aimed at by an amount equal to the dis-

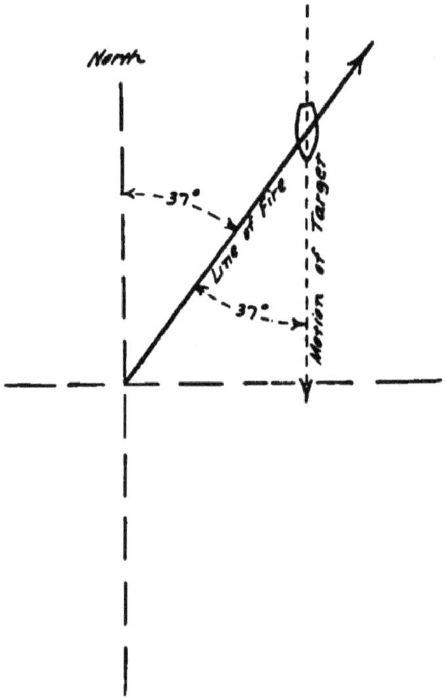

FIGURE 28.

tance traveled by it during the time of flight. For our standard problem 12" gun at 10,000 yards, if the target be moving at 12 knots perpendicular to the line of fire, from right to left, the shot would fall 84 yards astern of, that is, to the right of the target unless allowance were made for this motion in pointing. If the line of fire be 37° true, and the target be steaming 180° true at 20 knots, then the component of motion perpendicular to the line of fire would be 20 sin 37°, or (by the use of the traverse tables), 12 knots to the left, and the shot would fall $\frac{84 \times 12}{12} = 84$ yards to the left.

small as compared to penetration proper. This subject is not particularly well understood up to the present time.

299. The tables which give the penetration in Harveyized armor were computed before the present form of face-hardened armor came into general use. A rough approximation to the penetration of face-hardened armor may be obtained from those tables by multiplying the penetration in Harveyized armor by 0.8.

300. For our standard problem 12″ gun, at 10,000 yards range, the angle of fall, as given by the range table, is 5° 21′. The angle of impact against a vertical side armor plate would therefore be 84° 39′. The angle of impact against a protective deck plate inclined to the horizontal at an angle of 15° would be 20° 21′, which is probably very near or less than the biting angle, and little if any penetrative effect could be expected; in other words, the protective deck would probably deflect the projectile, thus fulfilling the purpose for which it was designed. If, however, the ships being on parallel courses, the target ship were rolled 10° towards the gun at the moment of impact, the angle of impact against the vertical side armor would be 74° 39′; and that against the protective deck plate would be 30° 21′.

301. For an elevated target, a vertical armor plate, taking the problem given in paragraph 188 of Chapter 11, the angle of inclination to the horizontal at the target is $\theta = 2°\ 20.1'$, and the angle of impact would therefore be 87° 39.9′. For the problem given in paragraph 189 of Chapter 11, the angle of impact against the vertical plate would similarly be 82° 03′, as we have $\theta = (-)7°\ 57'$ in this case.

Col. 10. ΔR_{50v}. **302. Column 10. Change of Range for a Variation of ± 50 Foot-Seconds Initial Velocity.**—A number of causes tend to produce variations in initial velocity, one being a variation in the temperature of the charge, which has already been discussed. The volatiles in the powder may dry out, giving a resultant quicker burning powder, with an increase in both pressure and initial velocity. A damp powder will burn more slowly and give a reduced initial velocity. Slight deterioration in the powder not sufficient in amount or of a character to cause danger may reduce the initial velocity (any deterioration that causes an increase in the initial velocity will cause increased pressure, and should be looked upon as dangerous). There is no means of determining the amount of variation of initial velocity due to these last two causes except experimental firing. Firing at a given range under known conditions, with all known causes of variation eliminated, as will hereafter be explained in the discussion of calibration practice, and a comparison of the resulting actual range with that given in the range tables for the given angle of elevation, would give an approximate idea of any such change in initial velocity, by working backwards in this column.

303. For our standard problem 12″ gun, suppose we know that our charge was at a temperature of 100° F.; that the solvent had dried out enough to cause an increase in initial velocity of 15 f. s., and that deterioration of the non-dangerous kind had reduced the initial velocity by 20 f. s. Our final initial velocity would then be:

Standard initial velocity..........................		2900 f. s.
Variation due to temperature of charge....	+35 f. s.	
Variation due to drying out of volatiles....	+15 f. s.	
Variation due to deterioration of powder...	−20 f. s.	
Total variation	+30 f. s...	30 f. s.
Actual initial velocity..........................		2930 f. s.

And at 10,000 yards range, this variation in initial velocity would give us, from Column 10, a resulting actual range of $10000 + \frac{277}{50} \times 30 = 10166$ yards, or the gun

310. The physical reason why, under some conditions, an increase in weight of projectile gives a decrease in range at one range and an increase at another may be readily understood if we remember that the effect upon the range of an increase in the weight of the projectile is the result of two entirely independent causes. The first acts entirely before the projectile leaves the gun, and an increase of weight thus acting always causes a decrease in the initial velocity, and hence, so far as this part of the effect alone is concerned, an increase in weight would always cause a decrease in range. The second part of the effect, however, which acts entirely outside the gun, is that due to the momentum stored in the moving projectile; that is, it depends upon the weight. As the weight is a factor in Mayevski's expression for retardation, we see that an increase in weight increases the power of the projectile to overcome the atmospheric resistance, and hence increases the range. Therefore of two similar projectiles, differing somewhat in weight but leaving the gun with the same initial velocity, the heavier would travel the further; and, so far as this part of the effect alone is concerned, an increase in weight of the projectile would always give an increase in the range. We do not have equal initial velocities in the case under consideration, however, and the increase in the weight of the projectile acts first to decrease the initial velocity, and then, after leaving the gun, to make the projectile travel further than would one of standard weight if fired with the same reduced initial velocity. It can readily be conceived from this line of reasoning that, under some conditions, this second effect might more than balance that due to loss of initial velocity, and in all such cases an increase in the weight of the shell will increase the range. The proper sign for the data in Column 11 is determined by a careful consideration of the relative values of the two parts in the formulæ from which the data is derived.

311. An inspection of the range table for the 6″ gun referred to in paragraph 309 above will show that for ranges from 1000 yards to 10,800 yards an increase in the weight of the projectile will cause a decrease in the range; at 10,900 yards it will cause no change in the range; and from 11,000 yards up an increase in range will result.

312. For the standard problem 12″ gun, through the entire table, from 1000 to 24,000 yards, it will be seen that increase in weight of projectile causes decrease in range. It is of interest to note, however, that from 1000 yards to about 12,000 yards this decrease in range increases with the range from a minimum of 8 yards at 1000 yards to a maximum of 42 yards at about 12,000 yards; and that from about 12,000 yards up the variation decreases until, at the highest point of the table, 24,000 yards, the decrease in range, due to an overweight of 10 pounds in the projectile, is only 12 yards. Apparently there is some theoretical point beyond the upper limit of the range table at which this quantity would change sign, and beyond which an increase of 10 pounds in the weight of the projectile would cause an increase in range, in a manner similar to that discussed above in regard to the 6″ gun. This point is of course of no practical value in connection with the 12″ gun, whereas it must necessarily be taken into account in dealing with the 6″ gun.

Col. 12, ΔR_{10c}. **313. Column 12. Change of Range for a Variation of Density of Air of ±10 Per Cent.**—As has been stated, the range tables have been computed for a standard atmosphere of half-saturated air, for 59° F. (15° C.) and 29.53″ (750 mm.) barometric height. Of course this exact atmospheric condition will rarely exist in actual firing, and the data in this column has been computed to enable allowance to be made for variations from standard density. It is of course easier for a projectile to travel through a less dense than through a more dense medium; and if the air be below the standard density the range will therefore be greater than the standard range, etc.

Col. 13, wind in range.

317. Column 13. Change of Range for Wind Component in Plane of Fire of 12 Knots.—This column is constantly used. For our standard problem 12" gun, at 10,000 yards, a wind blowing directly from the target to the gun with a velocity of 12 knots would decrease the actual range 27 yards, and would increase it the same

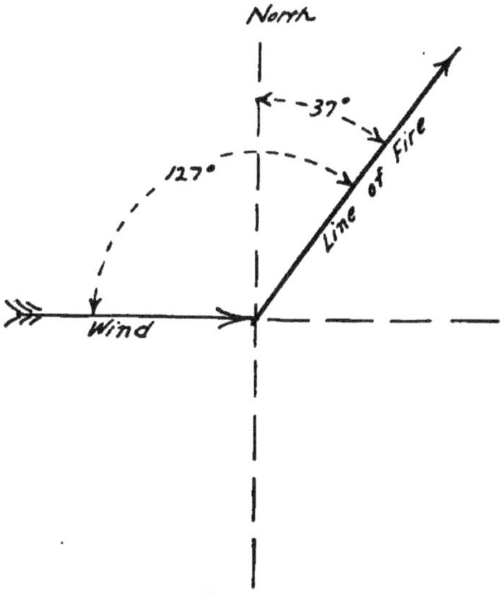

FIGURE 23.

amount if blowing the other way. Suppose the line of fire were 37° true, and the wind were blowing from 270° true with a velocity of 25 knots. Then the wind component in the line of fire would be 25 cos 53°, or (by use of the traverse tables) 15 knots, and the range would be increased $\frac{27\times 15}{12}=34$ yards by this component.

318. Column 14. Change of Range for Motion of Gun in Plane of Fire of 12 Knots.—This column is also constantly used. For our standard problem 12″ gun, at 10,000 yards, if the gun be moving at 12 knots directly towards the target, it will overshoot 57 yards unless the motion of the gun be allowed for in pointing; and if **Col. 14, gun motion in range.**

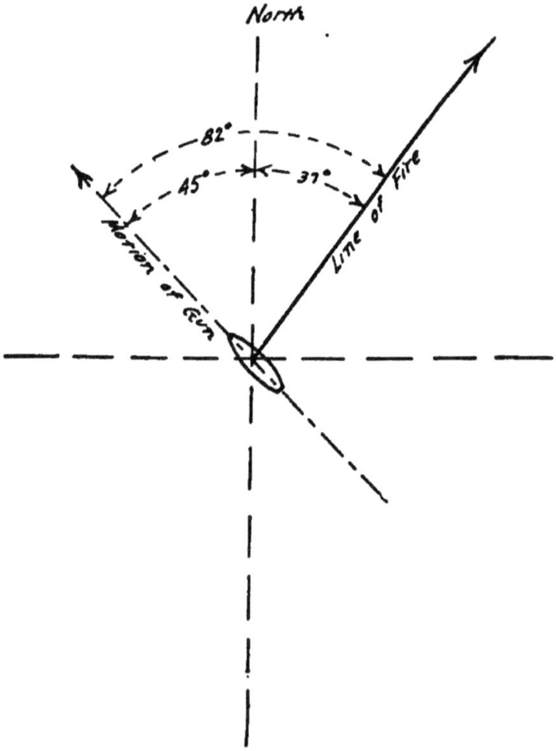

FIGURE 24.

moving in the opposite direction it would undershoot by the same amount. If the line of fire be 37° true, and the firing ship be steaming 315° true at 20 knots, the component speed in the line of fire would be 20 cos 82°, or (by the use of the traverse tables) 2.8 knots towards the target, and the gun would over-shoot $\frac{57 \times 2.8}{12} = 13.3$ yards.

Col. 15, target motion in range. **319. Column 15. Change of Range for Motion of Target in Plane of Fire of 12 Knots.**—This column is also constantly used. For our standard problem 12" gun at 10,000 yards, if the target be steaming directly towards the gun at 12 knots, the gun would overshoot the mark 84 yards unless the motion were allowed for in pointing; and if it were steaming at the same rate in the opposite direction it would undershoot by the same amount. If the line of fire were 37° true, and the target were steaming 175° true at 23 knots, the component of motion in the line of fire would be 23 cos 42°, or (by the use of the traverse tables) 17.1 knots toward the gun, and the gun would overshoot $\frac{84 \times 17.1}{12} = 143.6$ yards.

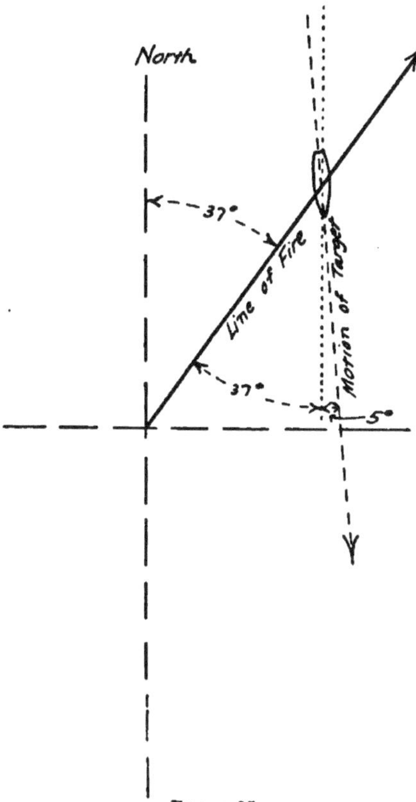

FIGURE 25.

320. Column 16. Deviation for Lateral Wind Component of 12 Knots.—This column is also constantly used. For our standard problem 12″ gun at 10,000 yards, if the wind were blowing perpendicular to the line of fire and across it from right to left, with a velocity of 12 knots, the shot would fall 14 yards to the left of the target **Col. 16, wind in deflection.**

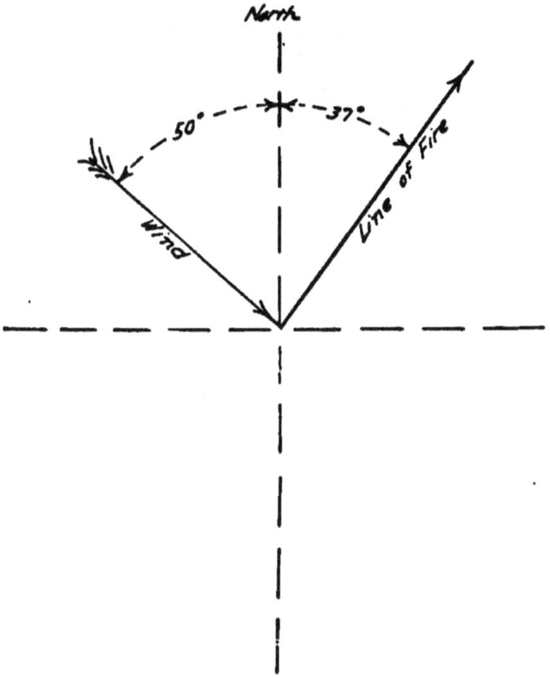

FIGURE 26.

unless the effect of the wind were allowed for in pointing. If the line of fire be 37° true, and the wind be blowing from 310° true at 23 knots, the wind component perpendicular to the line of fire would be 23 sin 87°, or (by the use of the traverse tables) 23 knots, and the shot would fall $\frac{14\times 23}{12}=27$ yards to the right of the target.

Col. 17, gun motion in deflection.

321. Column 17. Deviation for Lateral Motion of Gun Perpendicular to Line of Fire, Speed 12 Knots.—This column is also constantly used. For our standard problem 12" gun, at 10,000 yards, if the gun be moving at 12 knots perpendicular to the line of fire, and from right to left, the shot would fall 70 yards to the left of the

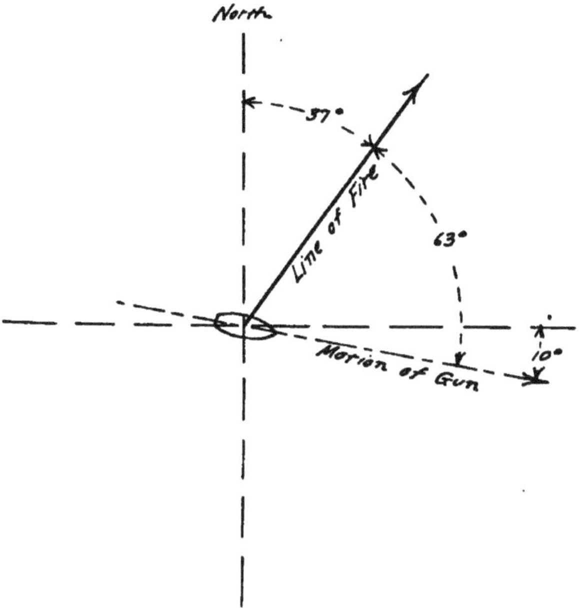

FIGURE 27.

target unless the motion were allowed for in pointing. If the line of fire be 37° true, and the firing ship be steaming 100° true at 21 knots, the component of this motion perpendicular to the line of fire would be 21 sin 63°, or (by use of the traverse tables) 18.7 knots to the right, and the shot would fall $\frac{18.7 \times 70}{12} = 109$ yards to the right.

322. Column 18. Deviation for Lateral Motion of Target Perpendicular to Line of Fire, Speed 12 Knots.—This column is also constantly used. Note that the change of range in yards for the given speed when the target is moving in the line of fire is always the same numerically as the deviation in yards for the same speed when the motion is perpendicular to the line of fire. This is manifestly correct, as the motion of the target, unlike any of the other motions considered, has no effect upon the actual motion of the projectile relative to the ground. This motion of the target simply removes the target from the point aimed at by an amount equal to the dis-

Col. 18, target motion in deflection.

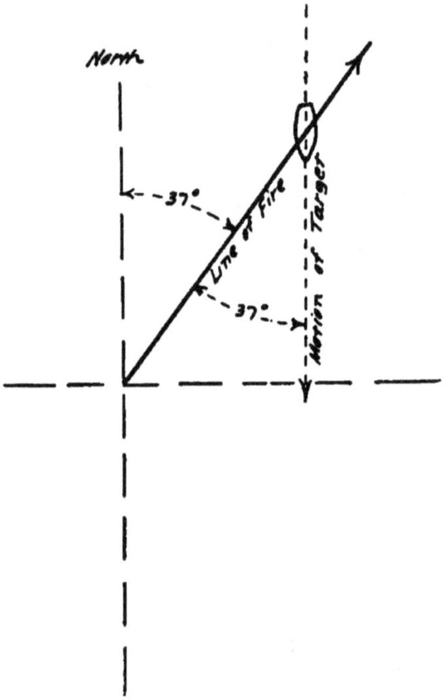

FIGURE 28.

tance traveled by it during the time of flight. For our standard problem 12" gun at 10,000 yards, if the target be moving at 12 knots perpendicular to the line of fire, from right to left, the shot would fall 84 yards astern of, that is, to the right of the target unless allowance were made for this motion in pointing. If the line of fire be 37° true, and the target be steaming 180° true at 20 knots, then the component of motion perpendicular to the line of fire would be 20 sin 37°, or (by the use of the traverse tables), 12 knots to the left, and the shot would fall $\frac{84 \times 12}{12} = 84$ yards to the left.

Relation between deflection in yards and in knots.

323. There is another most important use to which the data contained in this column is constantly put, and that is the determination of the point at which to set the deflection scale of the sight to compensate for any known deviation in yards. Deflection scales could just as properly be marked in any units, say parts of an inch motion of the sliding leaf either way from the central position, or simply in arbitrary divisions of convenient size; and some such method was formerly employed before the present more scientific and accurate methods of pointing were introduced. Whatever the system of marking the deflection scales, the essential point is that there must be some simple and convenient means of determining quickly how many divisions change in the set of the deflection scale is necessary to correct a deviation of a known number of yards at any given range. It has therefore been found most convenient to mark the deflection scale in "knots," meaning "knots speed of target," and to make the size of the divisions such that setting the scale over by 12 knots, that is, by 12 of the divisions, will produce at any given range the number of yards deviation shown in Column 18 for that range. Our telescopic sights have their deflection scales marked in this way. To avoid the confusion that was found to arise from the necessity for using the words "right" and "left" in giving orders for sight setting, the mark of zero deflection for the sight is now commonly marked as "50 knots," and to shift the point of fall of the shot to the left we lower the reading of the deflection scale ("left" and "lower" both begin with the letter *l*), and to shift the point of fall of the shot to the right we raise the reading of the deflection scale ("right" and "raise" both begin with the letter *r*). For our standard problem 12" gun, at 10,000 yards, if we wish to correct a deflection of 84 yards left, we wish to shift the point of fall of the shot that distance to the right, and we accordingly set the deflection scale at 62 knots. To correct a deflection of 84 yards right, we would similarly set the scale at 38 knots. If the deflection had been 25 yards, we would have set the deflection scale over $\frac{25\times 12}{84}=3.6$ knots, say 4 knots; and if we were correcting an error to the right (the original deflection setting having been 50), we would set the sight on 46 knots on the deflection scale; whereas had the original error been to the left the setting would be 54 knots.*

Col. 19, vertical position of point of impact.

324. Column 19. Change in Height of Impact for Variation of ±100 Yards in Sight Bar.—This column is also frequently used. For our standard problem 12" gun, at 10,000 yards, suppose the shot were striking at an estimated distance of 50 feet above the target, and we want to know how much to change the setting of the sight in range to hit. Manifestly, we would lower the sight in range by $\frac{50\times 100}{28}=172$ yards.

The above is of value in shooting at objects on shore, where it is in some cases easier to estimate the vertical distance of the point of impact from the target than it is the error in range; and also in direct flight spotting where the shot can be seen to pass over the screen.

325. We also see that, by the use of Column 19, a change, with our standard problem 12" gun of $\frac{20\times 100}{28}=72$ yards in range will change the vertical position of the point of impact 20 feet, at 10,000 yards range, that is, from the top to the bottom, or *vice versa*, of a target screen 20 feet high, which is the danger space at that range for such a target, and corresponds with the danger space as given in Column 7.

* See Appendix C for a description of the arbitrary deflection scale for sights, which has recently been adopted for service use.

326. If we were shooting at 10,000 yards on the sight bar, with the same gun, and gave a spot of "up 200," this would raise the position of the point of impact on the target screen, or rather in the vertical plane through it, a distance of $\frac{28\times 200}{100}=56$ feet.

327. In all wind and speed problems, draw roughly separate diagrams for gun, target and wind. Draw in each diagram a heavy line in the proper direction, to show the line of fire. For the gun and for the target, put the ship at the center, heading correctly, and draw a dotted line in the proper direction for the course of the gun or the target. For the wind draw a dotted line through the center with an arrow pointing in the direction towards which the wind is blowing. Find the angle, less than 90°, between course of gun or target or direction of wind, and line of fine. The cosine **Real wind and speed problem.**

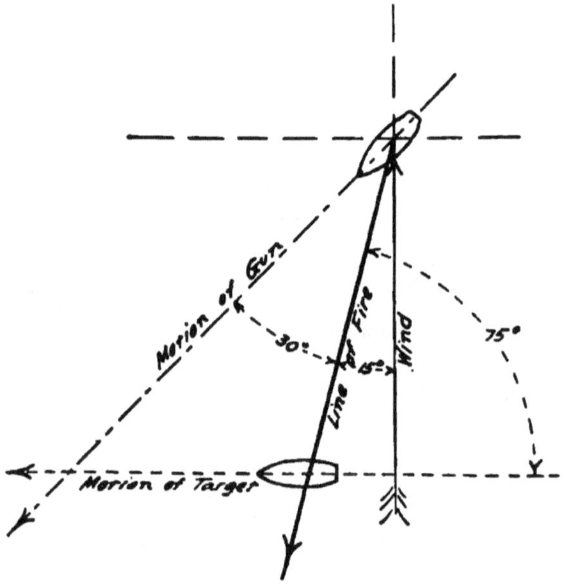

FIGURE 29

of that angle represents change in range, and the sine, change in deflection. We are now in a position to proceed to the solution of some every-day practical problems by the use of the range tables, and for the first one we will take a ship steaming southwest at 18 knots, which wishes to fire a 12″ gun ($V=2900$ f. s., $w=870$ pounds, $c=0.61$) at another ship that is 8000 yards distant and bears 30° off the port bow of the firing ship at the moment of firing. The target ship is steaming west at 22 knots, and the real wind is blowing from the south at 20 knots. The barometer is at 29.67″ and the thermometer at 20° F. The temperature of the powder is 70° F. Drying out of volatiles has raised the initial velocity of 25 f. s., and dampness of powder has reduced it 10 f. s. The shell weighs 875 pounds. How must the sights be set to hit? *

* See Appendix B for a description of the Farnsworth Gun Error Computer, by the use of which these problems may be solved mechanically.

For given atmospheric conditions $\delta = 1.089$, that is, the air is 8.9 per cent over standard density.

Use traverse tables for all resolutions of speeds.

Powder is 20° below standard, reducing V by $\frac{35}{10} \times 20$ . . . . -70 f. s.

Drying out of volatiles increases V by . . . . $+25$ f. s.

Dampness of powder reduces V by . . . . -10 f. s.

Total variation of initial velocity from standard . . . . -55 f. s.

Cause of variation. Speed of or variation in—	Affects.	Formulæ.	Range.		Deflection.	
			Short. Yds.	Over. Yds.	Right. Yds.	Left. Yds.
Gun	Range	$18 \cos 30 \times \frac{47}{12} = 15.6 \times \frac{47}{12}$	....	61.1	....	....
	Deflection	$18 \sin 30 \times \frac{56}{12} = 9 \times \frac{56}{12}$	....	....	42.0	....
Target	Range	$22 \cos 75 \times \frac{65}{12} = 5.7 \times \frac{65}{12}$	30.9	....	....	....
	Deflection	$22 \sin 75 \times \frac{65}{12} = 21.3 \times \frac{65}{12}$	....	....	....	115.4
Wind	Range	$20 \cos 15 \times \frac{17}{12} = 19.3 \times \frac{17}{12}$	27.3	....	....	....
	Deflection	$20 \sin 15 \times \frac{8}{12} = 5.2 \times \frac{8}{12}$	....	....	3.5	...
Initial velocity	Range	$55 \times \frac{229}{50}$	251.9	....	....	...
w	Range	$5 \times \frac{39}{10}$	19.5	....	....	...
δ	Range	$8.9 \times \frac{136}{10}$	121.0	....	....	...
			450.6 61.1	61.1	45.5	115.4 45.5
Point of fall of shot if uncorrected			389.5 yards short.			69.9 yards left.

To correct a deflection of 69.9 yards, set deflection scale to right $\frac{69.9 \times 12}{65} = 12.9$ knots of scale. Therefore to point correctly, set sights at

In range . . . . 8389.5 yards
In deflection . . . . 62.9 knots

or, to nearest graduations of sight scales, remembering to shoot short rather than over,

In range . . . . 8350 yards
In deflection . . . . 63 knots

Real wind and speed problem. **328.** A 12″ gun ($V = 2900$ f. s., $w = 870$ pounds, $c = 0.61$) mounted on board a ship steaming 45° (magnetic) at 18 knots, is to be fired at a target ship on the starboard bow of the firing ship and steaming 315° (magnetic) at 14 knots, at the moment when the firing ship is 9530 yards from the point of intersection of the two courses, and the target ship is 5500 yards from the same point. The barometer is at 28.25" and the thermometer at 80° F. The temperature of the powder is 105° F. Dampness of the powder has reduced the initial velocity, at standard temperature, to 2875 f. s. The shell is 7.5 pounds over weight. There is a real wind blowing from 260° by compass (Dev. 10° E.) at 20 knots. How should the sights be set to hit?

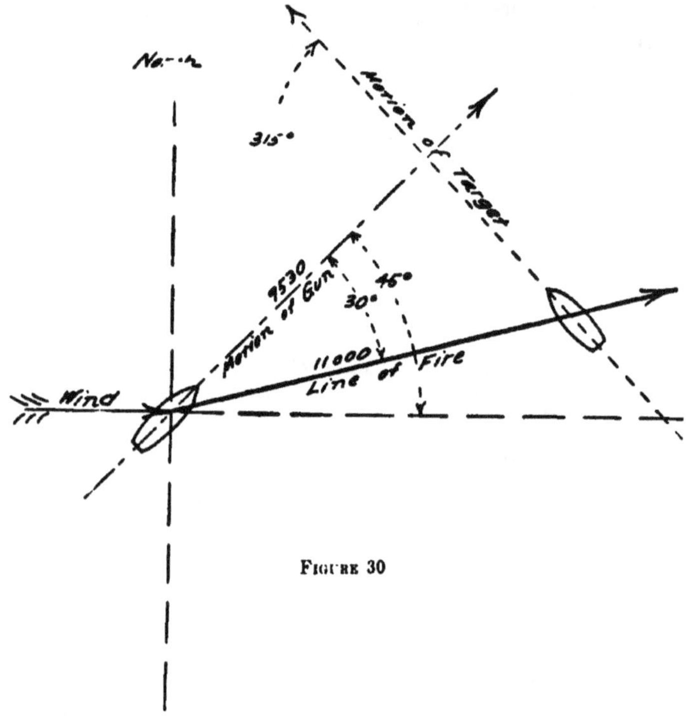

FIGURE 30

By use of the traverse tables, at the moment of firing, the target will be 30° on the starboard bow of the firing ship, distant 11,000 yards.

Temperature of powder $35 \times \frac{15}{10}$	+ 52.5 f. s.
Dampness	− 25.0 f. s.
Total variation in initial velocity	+ 27.5 f. s.

For the given atmospheric conditions, $\delta = 0.916$, and the air is therefore 8.4 per cent below standard density.

Use the traverse tables for all resolutions of speeds.

Cause of error. Variation in or speed of—	Affects.	Formulæ.	Range.		Deflection.	
			Short. Yds.	Over. Yds.	Right. Yds.	Left. Yds.
Gun	Range.....	$18 \cos 30 \times \frac{62}{12} = 93 \cos 30$	....	80.5	....	....
	Deflection..	$18 \sin 30 \times \frac{77}{12} = 115.5 \sin 30$	....	....	....	57.8
Target	Range.....	$14 \cos 60 \times \frac{94}{12} = 109.7 \cos 60$	....	54.8	....	....
	Deflection..	$14 \sin 60 \times \frac{94}{12} = 109.7 \sin 60$	....	....	95.0	....
Wind	Range.....	$20 \cos 15 \times \frac{32}{12} = 53.3 \cos 15$	....	51.5	....	....
	Deflection..	$20 \sin 15 \times \frac{17}{12} = 28.3 \sin 15$	....	....	7.3	....
Initial velocity....	Range.....	$27.5 \times \frac{297}{50}$	....	163.4	....	....
w................	Range.....	$7.5 \times \frac{42}{10}$	31.5	....	....	....
δ................	Range.....	$8.4 \times \frac{256}{10}$	....	215.0	....	....
			31.5	565.2 31.5	102.3 57.8	57.8
Point of fall of shot if uncorrected			......	533.7 yards over.	44.5 yards right.	

To correct for a deflection of 44.5 yards, set deflection scale to left by

$$\frac{12}{94} \times 44.5 = 5.7 \text{ knots}$$

Therefore to point correctly, set the sights

In range for................10466.3 yards
In deflection for............. 44.3 knots

or, to nearest graduations of scales, remembering to shoot short rather than over,

In range for..................10450 yards
In deflection .... 44 knots

329. In all the preceding discussions relative to the wind, both in Chapter 14 and in this chapter, we have dealt with the *real* wind, and it is now time to take up the discussion of the *apparent* wind. The difference between the two must always be clearly borne in mind. The *real wind* is the wind that is actually blowing; that is, as it would be recorded by a stationary observer; while the *apparent wind* is the wind that appears to be blowing to an observer on board a moving ship. Thus, in Figure 31, let W be the velocity of the *real* wind, blowing at an angle $a°$ with the direction of motion of the ship, and let G be the motion of the ship (in the same units as W).

320. Column 16. Deviation for Lateral Wind Component of 12 Knots.—This column is also constantly used. For our standard problem 12" gun at 10,000 yards, if the wind were blowing perpendicular to the line of fire and across it from right to left, with a velocity of 12 knots, the shot would fall 14 yards to the left of the target Col. 16, wind in deflection.

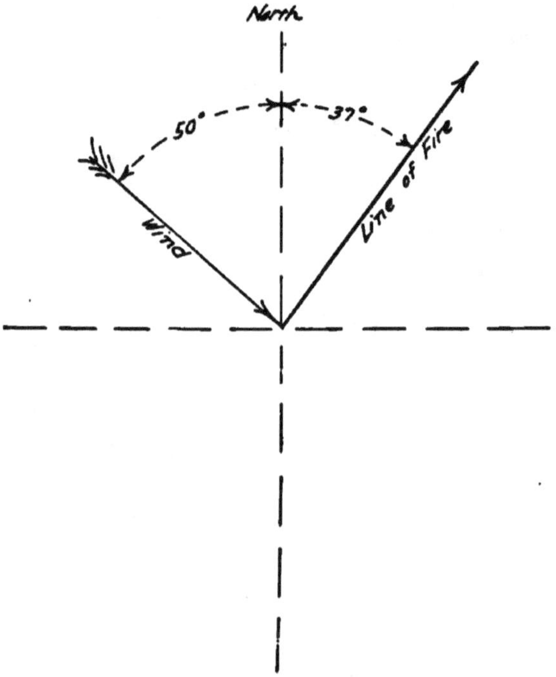

FIGURE 26.

unless the effect of the wind were allowed for in pointing. If the line of fire be 37° true, and the wind be blowing from 310° true at 23 knots, the wind component perpendicular to the line of fire would be 23 sin 87°, or (by the use of the traverse tables) 23 knots, and the shot would fall $\frac{14\times 23}{12}=27$ yards to the right of the target.

advance during its flight as far in the direction of the course of the ship as would the ship herself, because the initial sideways motion of the shell due to the motion of the gun in that direction would be retarded by the resistance of the air to such sideways motion of the shell after leaving the gun. In its sideways motion the shell has to overcome this air resistance. For example, for the above gun and conditions, the ship, during the time of flight, would travel 84 yards perpendicular to the line of fire (Column 18), but a wind effect equal to the speed of the ship, but in the opposite direction, would reduce the sideways motion of the shell in space by 14 yards (Column 16). Therefore the sideways motion of the shell in space due to the speed of the ship would be $84-14=70$ yards, which is the figure given in Column 17.

334. Again, if both ship and target were stationary, the other conditions being as given above, except that a real wind of 12 knots is blowing directly across the line of fire; we would then see, from Column 16, that the shell would be blown sideways during flight, or deflected, by 14 yards in the direction in which the wind is blowing, and this is the same amount as the difference between the travel of the ship and the travel of the shell in the direction of the course as given in the preceding paragraph. It will thus be seen that Column 17 in the range table allows for that portion of the apparent wind which is produced by the speed of the ship through still air. Hence to use Columns 13 and 16 for an apparent wind, which is the algebraic sum of the speed of the ship and of the velocity of the real wind, and Columns 14 and 17 for the motion of the gun, would be to correct twice for that portion of the apparent wind which is produced by the ship steaming in still air. The practical method of using the tables for apparent wind is further discussed in paragraph 338 of this chapter.

335. As an example of the above, an inspection of the range table for our standard problem 12" gun for 10,000 yards shows the following data:

	Error in Yards.
(a) Gun fired in vacuum as far as resistance of air is concerned, ship steaming at 12 knots towards or away from target (Col. 15)..	84 Over or Short
(b) Gun fired in vacuum as far as resistance of air is concerned, ship steaming at 12 knots perpendicular to line of fire (Col. 18)...	84 R. or L.
(c) Calm day, shot fired in air, ship steaming at 12 knots towards or away from target (Col. 14)................................	57 Over or Short
(d) Calm day, shot fired in air, ship steaming at 12 knots perpendicular to line of fire (Col. 17)............................	70 R. or L.
(e) Ship stationary, 12-knot breeze blowing from ship to target, or the reverse (Col. 13)	27 Over or Short
(f) Ship stationary, 12-knot breeze blowing perpendicular to the line of fire (Col. 16)..	14 R. or L.
(g) Ship steaming east at 12 knots, real wind from west of 12 knots, target abeam to starboard (Cols. 16 and 17 combined).......	84 Left
(h) Ship steaming east at 12 knots, real wind from east of 12 knots, target abeam to starboard (Cols. 16 and 17 combined).......	56 Left

336. In the above the target is considered as stationary in every case; if it be not stationary, then the errors introduced by its motion must be added algebraically from Columns 15 and 18. If motions be not in or perpendicular to the line of fire, then their resolved components in those two directions must be taken.

337. From what has already been said, the combined effects of the wind and of the motions of the firing and target ships may therefore be analyzed as follows:

Given a wind blowing, and both ship and target in motion, there are really four corrections that must be applied to correct for the combined errors produced by these three causes, although the columns of the range tables give separately corrections for only three causes. They are as follows:

322. Column 18. Deviation for Lateral Motion of Target Perpendicular to Line of Fire, Speed 12 Knots.—This column is also constantly used. Note that the change of range in yards for the given speed when the target is moving in the line of fire is always the same numerically as the deviation in yards for the same speed when the motion is perpendicular to the line of fire. This is manifestly correct, as the motion of the target, unlike any of the other motions considered, has no effect upon the actual motion of the projectile relative to the ground. This motion of the target simply removes the target from the point aimed at by an amount equal to the dis- **Col. 18, target motion in deflection.**

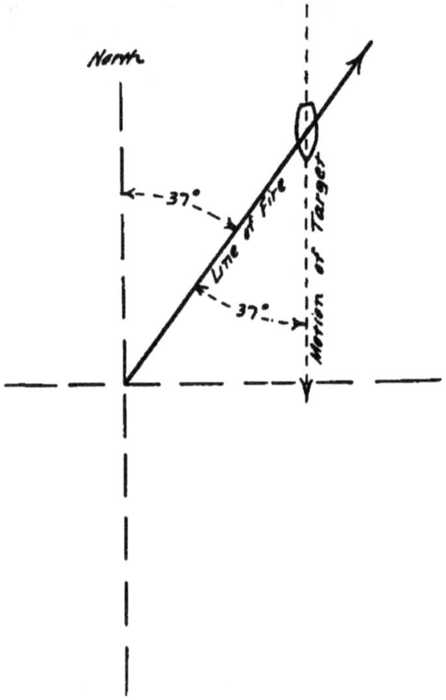

FIGURE 28.

tance traveled by it during the time of flight. For our standard problem 12" gun at 10,000 yards, if the target be moving at 12 knots perpendicular to the line of fire, from right to left, the shot would fall 84 yards astern of, that is, to the right of the target unless allowance were made for this motion in pointing. If the line of fire be 37° true, and the target be steaming 180° true at 20 knots, then the component of motion perpendicular to the line of fire would be 20 sin 37°, or (by the use of the traverse tables), 12 knots to the left, and the shot would fall $\frac{84 \times 12}{12} = 84$ yards to the left.

Cause of error.	Affects.	Formulæ.	Range.		Deflection.	
			Short. Yds.	Over. Yds.	Right. Yds.	Left. Yds.
Motion of gun. Cols. 15 and 18.	Range.....	$20 \cos 45 \times \frac{84}{12} = 14.1 \times \frac{84}{12}$	....	98.7	....	....
	Deflection..	$20 \sin 45 \times \frac{84}{12} = 14.1 \times \frac{84}{12}$	....	....	98.7	....
Apparent wind. Cols. 13 and 16.	Range.....	$32 \cos 17.5 \times \frac{27}{12} = 30.5 \times \frac{27}{12}$	68.625	....	....	....
	Deflection..	$32 \sin 17.5 \times \frac{14}{12} = 9.65 \times \frac{14}{12}$	....	....	....	11.258
			68.625	98.7	98.7	11.258
				68.625	11.258	
				30.075 yards over.	87.442 yards right.	

These are the combined errors caused by the motion of the gun and of the apparent wind.

341. If we plot the above speed of ship and apparent wind to scale, which is sufficiently accurate and much simpler and quicker than solving the oblique triangle mathematically, we will find that the corresponding real wind was blowing from 30° with a velocity of 17 knots an hour. Let us now compute the results by using the speed of the ship and the real wind by the methods originally explained, and compare them with the results obtained in the preceding paragraph by using the apparent wind. The work becomes:

Cause of error.	Affects.	Formulæ.	Range.		Deflection.	
			Short. Yds.	Over. Yds.	Right. Yds.	Left. Yds.
Motion of gun. Cols. 14 and 17.	Range.....	$20 \cos 45 \times \frac{57}{12} = 14.1 \times \frac{57}{12}$	....	66.975	....	....
	Deflection..	$20 \sin 45 \times \frac{70}{12} = 14.1 \times \frac{70}{12}$	....	....	82.25	....
Real wind. Cols. 13 and 16......	Range.....	$17 \cos 15 \times \frac{27}{12} = 16.4 \times \frac{27}{12}$	36.9	....	....	....
	Deflection..	$17 \sin 45 \times \frac{14}{12} = 4.4 \times \frac{14}{12}$	....	....	5.133	....
			36.9	66.975	87.383 yards right.	....
				36.9		
				30.075 yards over.		

The above are therefore the errors produced by the motion of the gun and real wind combined, and we see that the results are the same (within decimal limits) as those obtained in the preceding paragraph where we worked with the motion of the gun and the apparent instead of the real wind.

EXAMPLES.

1. Find the actual range for each gun given in the following table for the actual initial velocity given, by the use of Column 10 of the range table.

Problem.	DATA.						ANSWERS.
	Gun.			Initial velocity.		Range under standard conditions. Yds.	Range for actual initial velocity. Yds.
	Cal. In.	*w*. Lbs.	*c*.	Standard. f. s.	Actual. f. s.		
A	3	13	1.00	1150	1175	2467	2523.5
B	3	13	1.00	2700	2600	4050	3803.0
C	4	33	0.67	2900	2930	3250	3302.8
D	5	50	1.00	3150	3100	3675	3597.3
E	5	50	0.61	3150	3182	3130	3183.5
F	6	105	0.61	2600	2532	14525	14131.3
G	6	105	1.00	2800	2871	4250	4399.8
H	6	105	0.61	2800	2737	2950	2873.0
I	7	165	1.00	2700	2731	7350	7451.7
J	7	165	0.61	2700	2685	7450	7390.3
K	8	260	0.61	2750	2800	8450	8676.0
L	10	510	1.00	2700	2630	10430	10092.2
M	10	510	0.61	2700	2747	11425	11712.2
N	12	870	0.61	2900	2837	23975	23323.0
O	13	1130	1.00	2000	2100	10100	10764.0
P	13	1130	0.74	2000	1900	11500	10692.0
Q	14	1400	0.70	2000	1950	14400	13906.0
R	14	1400	0.70	2600	2683	14400	15057.4

2. Find the actual range of the guns given in the following table for the weights of projectile given, by the use of Column 11 of the range tables.

Problem.	DATA.						ANSWERS.
	Gun.			Standard initial velocity. f. s.	Standard range. Yds.	Actual weight of projectile. Lbs.	Actual range. Yds.
	Cal. In.	*w*. Lbs.	*c*.				
C	4	33	0.67	2900	3100	30	3199.0
D	5	50	1.00	3150	3600	54	3500.0
E	5	50	0.61	3150	4000	47	4099.0
F	6	105	0.61	2600	14600	110	14666.7
G	6	105	1.00	2800	4050	101	4114.3
H	6	105	0.61	2800	3600	107	3571.3
I	7	165	1.00	2700	7000	167	6981.4
J	7	165	0.61	2700	7000	160	7063.8
K	8	260	0.61	2750	8100	267	8041.2
L	10	510	1.00	2700	9600	515	9574.0
M	10	510	0.61	2700	11100	507	11116.2
N	12	870	0.61	2900	20800	875	20789.0
O	13	1130	1.00	2000	9000	1125	9015 9
P	13	1130	0.74	2000	11300	1135	11288.0
Q	14	1400	0.70	2000	13500	1413	13470.1
R	14	1400	0.70	2600	14200	1391	14220.7

3. Find the actual range of the guns given in the following table for the given atmospheric conditions by the use of Table IV of the Ballistic Tables and of Column 12 of the range tables.

Problem.	DATA.							ANSWERS.
	Gun			Standard initial velocity. f. s.	Standard range. Yds.	Atmosphere.		Actual range. Yds.
	Cal. In.	*w.* Lbs.	*c.*			Bar. In.	Ther. °F.	
A	3	13	1.00	1150	2000	28.10	5	1979.6
B	3	13	1.00	2700	3400	28.50	10	3296.5
C	4	33	0.67	2900	3500	29.00	15	3435.1
D	5	50	1.00	3150	4100	29.50	20	3973.0
E	5	50	0.61	3150	4500	30.00	25	4372.4
F	6	105	0.61	2600	13400	30.33	30	12844.7
G	6	105	1.00	2800	4300	30.75	35	4176.3
H	6	105	0.61	2800	3750	31.00	40	3690.7
I	7	165	1.00	2700	7300	30.50	50	7141.9
J	7	165	0.61	2700	7500	30.00	60	7470.0
K	8	260	0.61	2750	8200	29.50	70	8250.3
L	10	510	1.00	2700	10100	29.00	75	10295.0
M	10	510	0.61	2700	11200	28.50	80	11434.1
N	12	870	0.61	2900	19000	28.00	85	19684.8
O	13	1130	1.00	2000	9700	28.25	90	10000.8
P	13	1130	0.74	2000	11300	29.00	95	11564.0
Q	14	1400	0.70	2000	14000	30.00	100	14262.6
R	14	1400	0.70	2600	14500	31.00	97	14621.8

4. Find the errors in range and deflection caused by the *real* wind in the problems given below, using the traverse tables and Columns 13 and 16 of the range tables.

Problem.	DATA.								ANSWERS.	
	Gun.			Initial velocity. f. s.	Range. Yds.	Line of fire. °True.	Real wind.		Errors due to wind.	
	Cal. In.	*w.* Lbs.	*c.*				From. °True.	Velocity. Knots.	In range. Yds. Short or over.	In deflection. Yds. Right or left.
A	3	13	1.00	1150	2600	35	22	15	21.0 short	2.7 right
B	3	13	1.00	2700	4000	150	37	18	19.3 over	30.4 right
C	4	33	0.67	2900	3800	200	45	20	19.6 over	5.0 right
D	5	50	1.00	3150	4100	270	0	21	0.0	21.7 left
E	5	50	0.61	3150	3500	300	350	17	7.3 short	4.3 left
F	6	105	0.61	2600	13000	23	170	25	187.3 over	78.2 left
G	6	105	1.00	2800	3900	70	280	30	31.4 over	10.1 right
H	6	105	0.61	2800	4000	90	90	13	9.75 short	0.0
I	7	165	1.00	2700	7300	225	100	20	44.9 over	40.2 right
J	7	165	0.61	2700	6600	260	240	18	32.4 short	6.2 right
K	8	260	0.61	2750	8400	45	180	16	28.2 over	16.0 left
L	10	510	1.00	2700	10400	225	300	4	5.0 short	12.3 left
M	10	510	0.61	2700	11400	70	200	23	55.5 over	36.6 left
N	12	870	0.61	2900	24000	33	95	30	175.0 short	194.3 left
O	13	1130	1.00	2000	10000	330	115	20	87.1 over	33.6 left
P	13	1130	0.74	2000	11000	80	210	15	46.4 over	28.8 left
Q	14	1400	0.70	2000	14200	350	23	27	162.0 short	53.9 left
R	14	1400	0.70	2600	14000	37	105	19	34.9 short	47.0 left

7. Given the *apparent* wind, the motions of the gun and target, and the actual range and bearing of the target from the gun, as shown in the following table, compute the errors in range and in deflection resulting from those causes, and tell how to set the sights in range and in deflection in order to hit.

DATA.

Problem.	Gun.			Initial velocity. f. s.	Actual range Yds.	Bearing of target. °True.	Gun.		Target.		Apparent wind.	
	Cal. In.	w. Lbs.	c.				Course. °True.	Speed. Knots.	Course. °True.	Speed. Knots.	From. °True.	Velocity. Knots.
A .	3	13	1.00	1150	2300	15	45	6	80	10	180	10
B .	3	13	1.00	2700	3800	260	315	35	200	30	290	52
C..	4	33	0.67	2900	3400	45	220	22	260	25	48	15
D .	5	50	1.00	3130	4000	153	153	25	153	30	300	25
E .	5	50	0.61	3150	4100	75	67	25	80	32	10	42
F..	6	105	0.61	2600	11600	300	110	20	130	25	270	15
G .	6	105	1.00	2800	4000	45	180	20	90	20	315	18
H .	6	105	0.61	2800	3400	27	305	22	350	24	120	10
I..	7	165	1.00	2700	6600	265	37	18	190	19	15	37
J..	7	165	0.61	2700	6300	170	135	20	170	35	340	12
K .	8	260	0.61	2750	8100	200	220	21	315	30	300	30
L..	10	510	1.00	2700	9700	110	275	15	275	20	52	20
M .	10	510	0.61	2700	10700	270	330	18	330	25	190	35
N .	12	870	0.61	2000	20600	22	15	22	30	20	330	45
O..	13	1130	1.00	2000	10200	345	103	15	120	20	355	15
P..	13	1130	0.74	2000	10900	60	227	12	80	15	240	30
Q..	14	1400	0.70	2000	13800	320	340	21	165	19	300	25
R..	14	1400	0.70	2600	14200	125	17	21	23	17	325	20

ANSWERS.

Problem.	Combined errors		Set sights at—	
	Range. Yds. Short or over.	Deflection. Yds. Right or left.	Range. Yds.	Deflection. Knots.
A.	16.0 over	25.5 left	2284.0	56.5
B.	91.2 short	178.1 right	3891.2	6.0
C.	15.9 short	38.8 right	3415.9	34.0
D	19.6 over	13.3 left	3980.4	54.3
E.	37.2 short	1.8 right	4137.2	49.4
F.	32.8 short	130.0 right	11632.8	39.4
G.	88.2 short	12.9 right	4088.2	45.9
H	37.3 short	19.8 left	3437.3	58.5
I.	62.4 short	125.8 right	6662.4	29.3
J.	69.1 short	57.5 left	6369.1	61.9
K	62.5 short	262.3 left	8162.5	92.0
L.	4.8 short	34.6 right	9704.8	46.0
M.	50.1 short	11.3 right	10750.1	48.7
N	220.9 short	95.1 right	20820.9	44.6
O.	2.2 over	18.5 left	10197.8	51.6
P.	162.9 short	28.4 left	11062.9	52.4
Q.	413.4 over	265.7 right	13386.6	32.9
R.	59.4 over	22.4 left	14140.6	31.9

8. Given the data contained in the following table, find how the sights must be set in range and deflection in order to hit. Use traverse tables for all resolutions of forces.

	C.	E.	H.	J.	K.	M.	N.	P.	R.
Caliber of gun....	4	5	6	7	8	10	12	13	14
Standard initial velocity.........	2900	3150	2800	2700	2750	2700	2900	2000	2600
Standard weight of projectile....	33	50	105	165	260	510	870	1130	1400
Coefficient of form.	0.67	0.61	0.61	0.61	0.61	0.61	0.61	0.74	0.70
Course of firing ship, °true......	90	300	75	200	25	330	230	115	27
Speed of firing ship, knots...........	15	19	17	25	18	22	20	18	15
Course of enemy, °true...........	180	200	110	200	25	60	10	70	350
Speed of enemy, knots...........	28	21	19	20	30	20	15	22	18
Bearing of enemy at moment of firing, °true.......	135	260	165	20	25	330	90	80	70
Distance of enemy at moment of firing, yards.......	3400	4300	4000	7500	7000	10500	20000	11000	14500
Direction from which real wind is blowing, °true.	315	25	300	225	90	150	330	200	10
Velocity of real wind, knots.....	30	19	25	18	16	21	18	20	15
Barometer, inches.	30.70	30.00	30.50	30.25	30.00	29.50	29.00	29.33	30.15
Temperature of air, °F.........	50	25	75	80	30	15	80	90	40
Temperature of powder, °F......	80	65	95	97	75	70	95	100	60
Actual weight of projectile.......	30	52	107	160	267	500	877	1122	1415

ANSWERS.

Total error in range, yards....	10.0†	356.3§	6.6§	272.1†	496.0§	427.4§	487.1†	264.6†	1125.8§
Total error in deflection, yards...	69.1*	71.5‡	4.3*	10.1‡	13.3*	166.7*	483.6‡	100.2‡	160.8‡
Exact setting in range, yards....	3390.0	4656.3	4006.6	7227.9	7496.0	10927.4	19512.9	10735.4	15625.8
Exact setting in deflection, knots.	78.6	25.5	51.5	48.3	52.5	70.0	21.6	41.6	37.1
Actual setting in range, yards....	3350	4650	4000	7200	7450 or 7500	10900	19500	10700	15600
Actual setting in deflection, knots.	79	25 or 26	51 or 52	48	52 or 53	70	22	42	37

* = left, † = over, ‡ = right, § = short.

9. Given the data contained in the following tables, find how the sights should be set to hit. Use traverse tables for all resolutions of forces.

	C.	D.	F.	I.	K.	L.	N.	O.	Q.
Caliber of gun....	4	5	6	7	8	10	12	13	14
Standard initial velocity.........	2900	3150	2600	2700	2750	2700	2900	2000	2000
Standard weight of projectile....	33	50	105	165	260	510	870 *	1130	1400
Coefficient of form.	0.67	1.00	0.61	1.00	0.61	1.00	0.61	1.00	0.70
Course of firing ship, °true......	33	115	213	302	350	265	171	105	77
Speed of firing ship, knots......	35	27	25	20	20	19	16	18	23
Course of enemy, °true...........	357	307	245	45	135	0	180	81	349
Speed of enemy, knots...........	32	30	28	15	20	21	23	25	19
Bearing of enemy at moment of firing, °true.....	67	345	23	180	287	111	351	265	223
Distance of enemy at moment of firing, yards.....	3600	3400	13000	6800	7700	9300	16200	9700	14000
Direction from which apparent wind is blowing, °true...........	21	97	165	237	300	7	214	165	107
Apparent velocity of wind, knots..	52	43	38	28	27	5	25	22	30
Barometer, inches.	28.00	29.00	30.00	31.00	30.00	29.00	29.00	28.00	30.00
Temperature of air, °F.........	15	40	50	60	70	80	90	85	95
Temperature of powder, °F......	60	70	75	80	85	95	99	97	100
Actual weight of projectile.......	35	48	107	162	268	507	876	1123	1408

ANSWERS.

	C.	D.	F.	I.	K.	L.	N.	O.	Q.
Total error in range, yards....	204.1 §	159.2 §	265.5 §	261.3 §	30.1 §	219.8 †	829.6 †	582.9 †	366.7 †
Total error in deflection, yards...	45.9 ‡	71.2 ‡	73.0 ‡	126.5 ‡	151.6 ‡	242.3 ‡	101.2 ‡	28.0 *	351.3 *
Exact setting in range, yards....	3804.1	3559.2	13265.5	7061.3	7730.1	9080.2	15370.4	9117.1	13633.3
Exact setting in deflection, knots.	32.2	21.5	44.9	30.1	24.0	20.6	42.1	52.5	72.2
Actual setting in range, yards....	3800	3550	13250	7050	7700	9030	15350	9100	13600
Actual setting in deflection, knots.	32	21 or 22	45	30	24	21	42	52 or 53	72

* = left, † = over, ‡ = right, § = short.

PART V.

THE CALIBRATION OF SINGLE GUNS AND OF A SHIP'S BATTERY.

INTRODUCTION TO PART V.

The calibration of a ship's battery means, in brief, the process of adjusting the sights so that all the guns of the same caliber will shoot together when the sights are set alike, and so that the salvos will therefore be well bunched. Formerly it was considered necessary for every ship to calibrate her battery upon first going into commission, but now we find the work of manufacture and installation is ordinarily so well done that calibration practice is not considered necessary unless there are indications to the contrary. If the guns persistently scatter their salvos, and the reason for such a performance is not apparent, then it may become necessary to calibrate the battery; and, in any event, this form of test is so clearly illustrative of the principles involved in directing gun fire, that it should be thoroughly understood by every naval officer. Part V deals with this subject.

345. There are many causes which may operate to produce the condition in which one well-adjusted and well-pointed gun lands its shot at a point quite widely separated from the point of fall of the shot from another equally well-adjusted and well-pointed gun; as, for example, the fact that there is more give to the deck under one of the guns than under the other, etc.

Mean point of impact. **346.** If a great number of shot be fired from a gun, under as nearly as possible the same conditions, it will be found that the impacts are grouped closely together around one point, which point we will call the "mean point of impact." This point is in reality the mathematical center of gravity of all the impacts; and, with reference to the target (at the range for which the gun is pointed) this mean point of impact may be either on, short of, or over the target; and either on, to the right, or to the left of the target.

Mean dispersion. **347.** The point of fall of each individual shot is situated at a greater or less distance from the mean point of impact; and the arithmetical average of these distances from the mean point of impact for all the shots from the gun is called the "mean deviation from the mean point of impact" or the "mean dispersion" of the

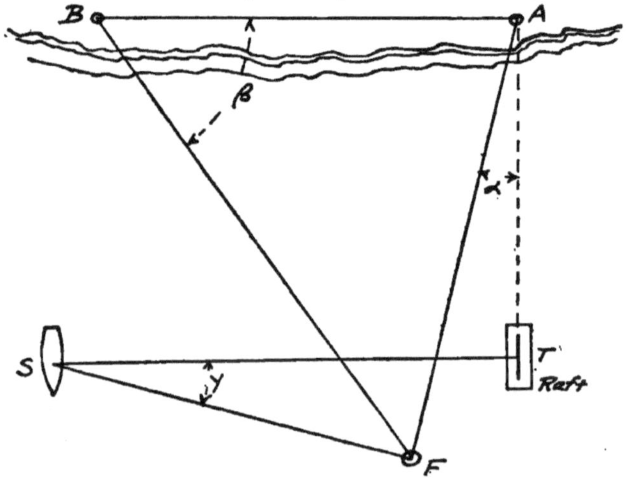

FIGURE 32.

gun. In dealing with these quantities it is customary to consider deviations or errors in range separately from those in deflection; so we would speak of the "mean deviation (or error) in range from the mean point of impact," and similarly for deflection. These quantities are also called the "mean errors" of the gun in range and in deflection.

Calibration range. **348.** The general plan of a calibration range is shown in Figure 32. A raft carrying a vertical target screen is moored in such a position that one or more observing stations, preferably two, may be established on shore, as shown at A and B. The ship is then moored at S, broadside to the target; and the screen of the latter should be as nearly as possible parallel to the keel of the ship. The angle STA should be as nearly a right angle as possible.

349. The base line AB must then be measured or determined by surveying methods; and then the positions of the ship, target, etc., must be accurately plotted, and their distance apart accurately determined.

(m) Weight of the shell.

(n) Any other information that may be desirable.

((i), (j) and (k) need only be recorded when a change occurs, but the record must be such that the conditions at the beginning and at the end of the practice, and at the moment when any individual shot is fired may be readily and accurately obtained from it.)

Necessity for care.

355. The members of the observing parties should realize the necessity for accurate observations and records. Nothing is more disastrous than carelessness in regard to details, as inaccuracy in any one of the apparently minor points may easily result in rendering the results of the whole practice entirely worthless. Such inaccuracies may readily be of such a nature that they cannot be detected, and might lead to confident entry into battle or target practice with a battery with which it is impossible to do good work owing to the undiscovered carelessness or inaccuracy of some person charged with some of the duties in regard to the observations taken during the calibration practice.

Plotting of observed points of fall.

356. Suppose we have four shots fired from a single gun, which fell as follows relative to the foot of the perpendicular from the center of the bull's eye upon the water:

No. 1..........a yards over..........a' yards to the right.
No. 2..........b yards short.........b' yards to the left.
No. 3..........c yards over..........c' yards to the right.
No. 4..........d yards short.........d' yards to the left.

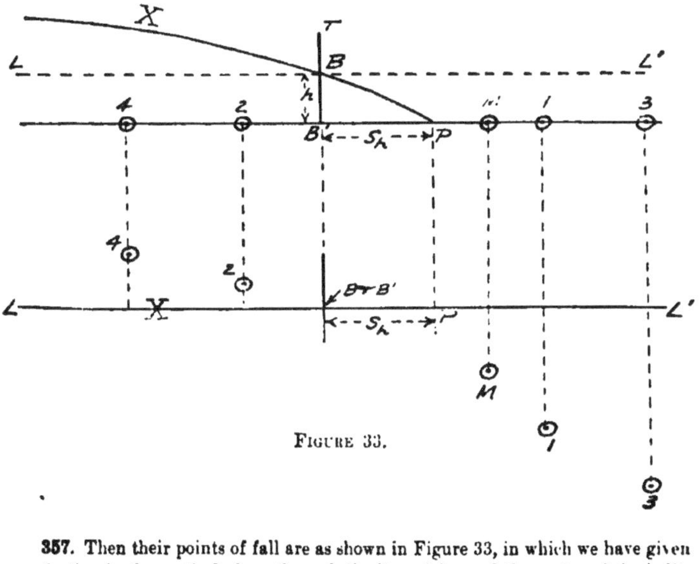

FIGURE 33.

357. Then their points of fall are as shown in Figure 33, in which we have given a projection in the vertical plane through the line of fire and the center of the bull's eye, and also the corresponding projection upon the horizontal plane of the water. T is the target, the center of the bull's eye being at B, which is h feet above the water. LL' is the line of sight such that the gun pointer looking along it sees the cross wires of the telescope on the center of the bull's eye. Now if the gun were in perfect

Calibration problem.

360. Let us suppose that six shots were fired on a calibration practice from a 12″ gun ($V=2900$ f. s., $w=870$ pounds, $c=0.61$) under the following conditions:

Actual distance of target from gun .... 8000 yards.
Sights set in range for .... 8000 yards.
Sights set in deflection at .... 38 knots.
Center of bull's eye above the water .... 12 feet.
Bearing of target from ship .... 45° true.
Wind blowing from .... 270° true.
Wind blowing with a velocity of .... 18 knots.
Barometer .... 30.00″.
Temperature of the air .... 75° F.
Temperature of the powder .... 94° F.
Weight of projectile .... 875 pounds.

Measured from the foot of the perpendicular upon the water through the center of the bull's eye, the shot fell.

No. 1..200 yards short; 90 yards left.
No. 2..150 yards short; 95 yards left.
No. 3..100 yards short; 95 yards left.
No. 4..150 yards short; 85 yards left.
No. 5..100 yards short; 75 yards left.
No. 6.. 50 yards short; 70 yards left.

Find the true mean errors in range and in deflection under standard conditions, and adjust the sight scales in range and in deflection in order to have the sights properly set; that is, under standard conditions, to have the mean point of impact at the point P when the sight is set for 8000 yards in range and for 50 knots on the deflection scale.

No. of shot.	Range. Short. Yds.	Deflection. Left. Yds.
1	200	90
2	150	95
3	100	95
4	150	85
5	100	75
6	50	70
Mean errors on foot of perpendicular through bull's eye.	6|750 125 yards short.	6|510 85 yards left.

The error in range due to the fact that the point of aim is at the bull's eye and not at the water line of the target is the correction that should be applied to the observed distance from the foot of the perpendicular on the water through the bull's eye in order to refer it to the point P as an origin. By Column 19 of the range tables, this would be $12 \times \frac{100}{20} = 60$ yards.

The error in deflection intentionally introduced in order to avoid wrecking the target, by setting the sight off in deflection, would be, by Column 18 of the range table, $(50-38) \times \frac{65}{12} = 65$ yards left.

Now to bring the observed errors to their true values under standard conditions, we proceed as follows:

Temperature of the powder is 4° above the standard, therefore the initial velocity is $4 \times \frac{35}{10} = 14$ f. s. above standard. From Table IV, the multiplier for Column 12 is +.18.

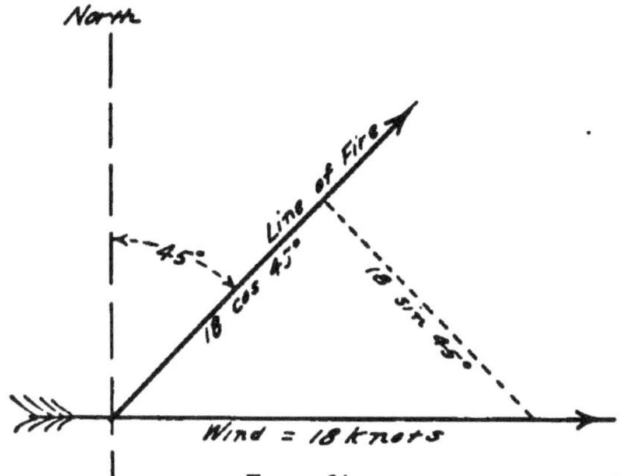

FIGURE 34.

Therefore we have, using the traverse tables to resolve the wind forces:

Cause of error.	Affects.	Formulæ.	Range. Short. Yds.	Range. Over. Yds.	Deflection. Right. Yds.	Deflection. Left. Yds.
Wind	Range.....	$18 \cos 45° \times \frac{17}{12} = \frac{12.7 \times 17}{12}$	....	18.0	....	....
	Deflection..	$18 \sin 45° \times \frac{8}{12} = \frac{12.7 \times 8}{12}$	....	....	8.5	....
re...............	Range.....	$5 \times \frac{39}{10}$	19.5	....	....	....
Atmosphere.......	Range.....	$.18 \times 136$	....	24.5	....	....
Velocity..........	Range.....	$14 \times \frac{229}{50}$	....	64.1	....	....
Height of bull's eye	Range.....	$12 \times \frac{100}{20}$	....	60.0	....	....
Intentional deflection.	Deflection..	$12 \times \frac{65}{12}$	....	....	....	65.0
			19.5	166.6	8.5	65.0
				19.5		8.5
Errors on point *P* as an origin for standard conditions........				147.1 over		56.5 left

Observed distance from target in range.......................125.0 yds. short
Error (where shot should have fallen)...........................147.1 yds. over

True mean error in range under standard conditions.............272.1 yds. short

Observed distance from line of fire through bull's eye in deflection.. 85.0 yds. left
Error (where shot should have fallen).......................... 56.5 yds. left

True mean error in deflection under standard conditions......... 28.5 yds. left

That is, under standard conditions, the mean point of impact of this gun is 272.1 yards short of and 28.5 yards to the left of the point of fall (P) of the perfect trajectory of the gun through the bull's eye. We want to so adjust the sight scales as to bring the mean actual trajectory of the gun into coincidence with the perfect trajectory of the gun; that is, to shift the mean point of impact of the gun to its proper theoretical position, that is, to the point P. To do this we:

1. Run up the sight in range until the pointer indicates 8272.1 yards. Then slide the scale under the pointer until the pointer is over 8000 yards on the scale. Then clamp the scale in this position.

2. From Column 18 of the range table, we see that 28.5 yards deflection at 8000 yards range corresponds to a movement of $28.5 \times \frac{12}{65} = 5.3$ knots on the deflection scale. Therefore set the sight in deflection at 55.3 knots. Then slide the deflection scale under the pointer until the pointer is over 50 knots on the scale. Then clamp the scale in that position.*

When the above process has been completed, the gun should shoot, under standard conditions, so that the mean point of impact will fall at P.

361. With the sights adjusted as described above, under standard conditions, the shot should fall at the range and with the deflection given by the sight setting; that is, the shot should all fall at the mean point of impact. And any variation from standard conditions should cause the errors indicated for such variations in the range tables; and such errors could be easily handled by the spotter. Of course this statement, if taken literally, means that all errors have been eliminated from the gun, and that all shots fired from it under the same conditions will strike in the same place, that place being the mean point of impact for those conditions. It is of course never possible to actually accomplish this, owing first to the inherent errors of the gun, and second to unavoidable inaccuracies in the work. If the work be well done, however, the result will be to come as near as is humanly possible to that most desirable perfect condition.

Mean dispersion. **362.** If the distance of the point of fall of each shot from the mean point of impact be found for every shot fired, and the arithmetical mean of these distances be found, we have a distance which is called the "mean dispersion from the mean point of impact." This information is desirable because it gives an idea of the accuracy and of the consistency of shooting of the gun. For example, one gun of a battery may have its mean point of impact with reference to a certain target at a distance, say, of 100 yards over and 25 yards to the right, but all of its shot may fall at, say, a mean distance of only 10 yards from the mean point of impact; that is, its shot will all be well bunched and closely grouped around the mean point of impact. Its mean dispersion from mean point of impact is small, and it is a good gun; for the spotter can readily bring its shot on the target, and when he has done this they will all fall there. If, on the contrary, with another gun, the mean point of impact be, say, only 10 yards over and 10 yards to the right of the target, but the mean dispersion from the mean point of impact be, say, 75 yards, the shot will fall scattered, the spotter will have difficulty in bringing the mean point of impact on the target and in keeping it there, and after he has done so the percentage of hits will be much smaller than

---

* For setting the sights preparatory to adjusting the scales, given the true mean errors, we may readily figure out the following rules:

Range . . . . { If the error be "short," add it to the standard range. If the error be "over," subtract it from the standard range.

Deflection . . . { If the error be "right," subtract its equivalent in knots from 50. If the error be "left," add its equivalent in knots to 50.

EXAMPLES.

1. For the following results of different calibration practices, compute the true mean errors under standard conditions and the mean dispersion from mean point of impact; and tell how to adjust the sight scales in each case in range and deflection to make the gun shoot as pointed when all conditions are standard.

14″ gun; $V=2600$ f. s.; $w=1400$ pounds; $c=0.70$.

	1.	2.	3.	4.	5.	6.	7.	8.
Actual distance of target from gun, yds.	13000	13500	14000	14500	13300	13700	14200	14400
Sights set in range for, yds.	13000	13500	14000	14500	13300	13700	14200	14400
Sights set in deflection for, knots	35	40	30	42	60	65	70	63
Center of bull's eye above water, feet	4	3	5	6	4	5	6	4
Bearing of target from ship, °true	45	180	80	315	270	250	345	0
Wind blowing from, °true	180	225	0	90	180	250	165	270
Wind blowing with a velocity of, knots.	12	15	18	20	25	15	18	22
Barometer, inches	28.50	29.00	29.50	30.00	30.50	31.00	30.25	29.75
Temperature of air, °F	60	65	70	75	80	85	90	83
Temperature of powder, °F	80	85	95	100	97	82	75	80
Weight of shell, pounds	1395	1390	1405	1410	1407	1393	1397	1404
Number of shots fired	4	4	4	4	4	4	4	4
Fall of—								
Shot No. 1	25	100	150	75	150	200	100	20
	S.	S.	Ov.	S.	S.	Ov.	S.	Ov.
	75	70	200	20	15	30	100	50
	L.	L.	L.	L.	R.	R.	R.	R.
Shot No. 2	50	75	200	90	100	250	75	25
	S.	S.	Ov.	S.	S.	Ov	S.	Ov.
	100	75	150	10	20	35	80	55
	L.	L.	L.	L.	R.	R.	R.	R.
Shot No. 3	100	50	175	20	125	275	50	30
	S.	S.	Ov.	Ov.	S.	Ov.	S.	Ov.
	150	50	175	15	30	50	110	60
	L.	L.	L	L.	R.	R.	R.	R.
Shot No. 4	75	25	150	10	110	225	0	22
	S.	Ov.	Ov.	Ov.	S.	Ov.		Ov.
	80	50	150	20	25	40	90	50
	L.	L.	L.	L.	R.	R.	R.	R.

ANSWERS.

	True mean errors.		Mean dispersion from M. P. of I.		Set sights for.		Clamp scales at.	
	Range. Yds.	Deflection. Yds.	Range. Yds.	Deflection. Yds.	Range. Yds.	Deflection. Knots.	Range. Yds.	Deflection. Knots.
1.	11.7 Ov.	79.0 R.	25.0	24.4	12988.3	42.6	13000	50
2.	8.4 S.	78.5 R.	37.5	11.3	13508.4	43.1	13500	50
3.	41.2 S.	20.7 R.	18.75	18.75	14041.2	48.5	14000	50
4.	449.4 S.	124.0 R.	48.75	3.75	14949.4	40.0	14500	50
5	332.9 S.	148.7 L.	16.25	5.00	13632.9	63.4	13300	50
6.	479.2 Ov.	133.7 L.	25.0	6.25	13220.8	61.6	13700	50
7.	89.2 Ov.	146,7 L.	31.25	10.0	14110.8	62.1	14200	50
8.	134.1 Ov.	168.8 L.	3.25	3.75	14265.9	63.7	14400	50

CHAPTER 19.

THE CALIBRATION OF A SHIP'S BATTERY.

Reasons for calibrating battery.

366. In the preceding chapter we have seen how a single gun is calibrated and the sights so adjusted that, so far as the inherent errors of the gun, etc., will permit, the gun will shoot, under standard conditions, as the sights indicate. It was stated that it is not possible to accomplish this result with absolute accuracy. If it were, we could adjust the sights of each gun of the battery separately, and then, if they were all mechanically just alike, we would have all the shot from each gun falling at its mean point of impact (within the limits of inherent errors), and the mean points of impact of all the guns would be the same. As a matter of fact, however, the mean points of impact of the several guns would not coincide, if this method were followed, and of course all the shot from any one gun would not all fall at its mean point of impact. Some remarks were made in the last chapter relative to the necessity for getting the guns so calibrated that the shot from all of them will fall together for the same sight setting, and, as a matter of fact, this is more important than it is to get them so that actual and sight-bar ranges coincide under standard conditions. Conditions are almost never standard during firing, and even if they were there are many other factors which prevent the actual and the sight-bar ranges from being the same. But if the mean points of impact of the several guns for the same sight setting can be brought very nearly into coincidence, then any variation of the resultant point from the target (that is of difference between actual and sight-bar ranges) can be readily handled by the spotter. This means that if the salvos are well bunched the spotter can control the fire successfully, but if the shots are scattered he cannot. We will now proceed with an entire battery to bring all guns to shoot together.

Standard gun.

367. Having calibrated each gun separately, as described in the preceding chapter, we now proceed to select a gun as the "standard gun," to the shooting of which we propose to make that of all the others conform, providing the performance of any one gun is good enough to justify selecting it for the purpose. From what we have seen in the preceding chapter we would naturally select one whose mean dispersion from mean point of impact is small, that is, one that bunches its shots; and, other things being equal, if we have one whose sights are very nearly in adjustment, we will use that one without changing the sight adjustment. Any gun may of course be selected as the standard, and the sights of the others brought to correspond to it, but the considerations set forth above would naturally govern, as a matter of common sense. If no gun be sufficiently accurate, or if none has its sights sufficiently well adjusted to justify its selection as a standard gun, then we must correct all guns to the mean point of impact. The practical method of bringing the sights of a number of guns to correspond is best shown by an actual problem.

short in range and the deflection scales for the 5 yards right in deflection of the standard gun, to be absolutely accurate; but, as the sight scales are graduated to 50-yard increments in range only, it is impracticable to go any closer in range. It would perhaps be well to adjust each deflection scale to 51 knots instead of 50, in order to allow for the 5 yards right deflection of the standard gun.

Different batteries.

369. When we wish to calibrate a ship's battery that is composed of separate batteries of different calibers, we calibrate each caliber by itself, as already described. The difference between the mean points of impact of the standard guns of the different calibers will be the difference between the centers of impact of the salvos from the several calibers, and this must be allowed for in firing all calibers together. To attempt to calibrate the sights of all calibers together by a readjustment of the sight scales would not be wise; for if they could be brought to shoot together at one range in this way, it would necessarily ensure dispersion of the several salvos at all other ranges. Therefore the only practical way of handling this proposition is to determine the error of each caliber at the range in use and apply it properly in sending the ranges to the guns; which means send different ranges to the guns of different calibers, so related that the results will bring the mean points of impact of the several calibers together at the range in use. As far as possible, these differences in ranges should be tabulated for different ranges. As the fire-control system is arranged, as a rule, to permit the control of each caliber battery independently of the others, this method presents no difficulties other than a little care on the part of the spotter group.

370. For instance, suppose that we have a ship with a mixed battery of 7", 8" and 12" guns; that each of these calibers has been calibrated at 8000 yards; and has had the mean point of impact of its salvos located with reference to the target as follows:

7" battery........100 yards over........3 knots right.
8" battery........ 50 yards short.......3 knots left.
12" battery........150 yards over........2 knots left.

Then if we wish to fire broadside salvos from this entire battery, the ranges and deflections should be sent to the guns as follows, for 8000 yards:

To the 7"........7900 yards........47 knots deflection.
To the 8"........8050 yards........53 knots.
To the 12"........7850 yards........52 knots.

If these errors have not been corrected by shifting scales on bore-sighting, they can only be overcome by the spotter's corrections.

EXAMPLES.

1. Having determined the true mean errors of guns under standard conditions, by calibration practice, to be as given in the following table; how should the sights of each caliber be adjusted to make all the guns of that caliber shoot together? (Six separate problems.)

Number of gun.	True mean errors of guns under standard conditions.											
	6"—G.		7"—J.		8"—K.		12"—N.		13"—P.		14"—R.	
	Errors at range of 4500 yards.		Errors at range of 6500 yards.		Errors at range of 8500 yards.		Errors at range of 10000 yards.		Errors at range of 11000 yards.		Errors at range of 13000 yards.	
	Range. Yds.	Defl. Yds.	Range. Yds.	Defl. Yds.	Range. Yds.	Defl. Yds.	Range. Yds.	Defl. Yds.	Range. Yds.	Defl. Yds.	Range. Yds.	Defl. Yds.
1..	25	20	50	30	100	5	100	15	125	25	75	15
	S.	R.	Ov.	L.	S.	R.	Ov.	L.	Ov.	L.	S.	L.
2..	50	30	75	40	120	15	75	10	100	30	100	15
	Ov.	R.	Ov.	L.	S.	L.	Ov.	L.	Ov.	L.	Ov.	R.
3..	75	35	100	25	90	20	50	20	75	25	75	20
	Ov.	L.	Ov.	R.	Ov.	L.	Ov.	R.	Ov.	R.	Ov.	R.
4..	5	5	75	15	75	25	0	5	100	30	50	20
	S.	L.	S.	L.	Ov.	R.		R.	S.	R.	S.	L.
5..	30	30	125	10	100	20	100	25	....	....	100	25
	Ov.	R.	S.	L.	Ov.	R.	S.	R.			S.	L.
6..	50	25	10	70	80	10	90	15	....	....	100	30
	S.	L.	S.	R.	S.	L.	S.	R.			Ov.	R.
7..	100	40	100	25	70	25	75	30	....	....	75	20
	S.	R.	Ov.	R.	S.	R.	Ov.	L.			Ov.	R.
8..	100	40	90	20	70	30	100	30	....	....	70	15
	Ov.	L.	S.	L.	Ov.	L.	S.	R.			S.	L.

ANSWERS.

Number of gun.	To bring all sights together for each caliber, set the sights for that caliber as given below, and then slide scales to standard readings and clamp.											
	6"—G.		7"—J.		8"—K.		12"—N.		13"—P.		14"—R.	
	Range. Yds.	Defl. Kts.	Range. Yds.	Defl. Kts.	Range. Yds.	Defl. Kts.	Range. Yds.	Defl. Kts.	Range. Yds.	Defl. Kts.	Range. Yds.	Defl. Kts.
1..	4520	43.0	6450	56.0	8600	49.25	9900	52.8	10875	52.0	13075	51.35
2..	4445	40.2	6425	38.0	8620	52.25	9925	52.1	10800	52.4	12900	48.65
3..	4420	58.4	6400	45.0	8410	53.00	9950	47.9	10825	48.0	12925	48.20
4..	Stan	dard.	6575	53.0	8425	46.25	Stan	dard.	11100	47.6	13050	51.80
5..	4465	40.2	6625	52.0	8400	47.00	10100	47.2	....	....	13100	52.25
6..	4545	55.6	6510	36.0	8580	51.50	10000	48.6	....	....	12900	47.30
7..	4595	37.4	6400	45.0	8570	46.25	9925	54.9	....	....	12925	48.20
8..	4395	59.8	6590	54.0	8430	54.50	10100	46.5	....	....	13070	51.35

PART VI.

THE ACCURACY AND PROBABILITY OF GUN FIRE AND THE MEAN ERRORS OF GUNS.

INTRODUCTION TO PART VI.

We have now learned all that mathematical theory can teach us with certainty about the flight of a projectile in air, about the errors that may be introduced into such flight by known causes, and about the methods of compensating for such errors. After all this has been done there must, in the nature of things, remain certain errors that cannot be either eliminated or covered by strict mathematical theories, and such errors are known as the inherent errors of the gun. It is the purpose of Part VI to discuss the general nature of these errors, their methods of manifesting themselves, and their probable effect upon the accuracy of fire.

successive points of impact more or less scattered about within a certain area. These causes are probably very numerous, it not even being certain that we have yet been able to recognize them all, and no satisfactory laws governing them have as yet been discovered, nor is it probable that such laws ever will be determined.

Summary. **373.** To summarize, it may be said that before entering on any theoretical investigation of the subject of gunnery we must first throw out all errors resulting from mistakes. We may then, by the study of exterior ballistics, learn certain principles governing the errors produced by certain known causes, and in consequence may learn how to eliminate such errors from our shooting. When all this has been done, however, we necessarily have left certain other causes of error which, although not great as compared with the others, are still sufficient to cause a scattering of the points of impact of successive shots from the same gun, even when fired under similar physical conditions. We manifestly cannot hope to eliminate these inherent errors, and therefore we must accept them as they are; all that we can do in regard to them is to investigate their probable effect upon the results of our shooting. It is this investigation that is to be undertaken in the last two chapters of this book, and it is to be noted that here we cannot speak of anything as a certainty, even in a theoretical and mathematical way, but can only say that, mathematically, it is probable or improbable that a certain thing will happen, and in addition attempt to measure the degree of probability or improbability which attaches to a certain effort.

Mean point of impact. **374. Mean Point of Impact.**—Let us suppose that all errors except the inherent errors of the gun have been eliminated, and that a large number of shots be fired, under as nearly the same physical conditions as possible, at a vertical target screen of sufficient size to receive all the shot under such conditions. Manifestly, if there were no errors of any kind whatsoever, all these shot would describe the same trajectory and strike the target at the same point. Of course this result can never be attained in practice, and the many causes of inherent error tend to scatter the several shot about the target, and only a certain percentage of absolute efficiency can be secured, no matter how skillfully the gun may be handled. The point which is at the geometrical center of all the points of impact on the screen is known as the "mean point of impact," and is of course the center of gravity of the group of points of impact. We may also speak of the mean point of impact in the horizontal plane as well as in the vertical plane as given above.

Mean trajectory. **375. Mean Trajectory.**—The mean trajectory of the gun for these conditions is the trajectory from the gun to the mean point of impact. It is manifestly the trajectory over which all the shot would travel were there no errors of any kind whatsoever.

Deviation or deflection. **376. Deviation or Deflection.**—Suppose Figure 35 to represent the vertical target screen, the point O at the center being the point aimed at. Suppose the shot struck at the point P. Then the deviation or deflection of the shot from the point aimed at is the distance OP in the direction shown. So considered, however, for manifest reasons, this information is not useful, so it is usual to speak of the horizontal deviation or deflection, which is a, and of the vertical deviation or deflection of the shot, which is b. And algebraic signs are assigned to these deviations or deflections, + being above or to the right and − below or to the left. Thus the deviations or deflections of the four points of impact shown in Figure 35 would be:

For P .... $+a$ and $+b$. For P'' .... $-a''$ and $-b''$.
For P' .... $-a'$ and $+b'$. For P'''.... $+a'''$ and $-b'''$.

In place of the signs we might speak of horizontal deviations as being to the right or to the left, and of vertical deviations as being above or below. In addition to the

Mean dispersion from mean point of impact.

379. Mean Dispersion from Mean Point of Impact.—Suppose we again consider our dispersions from the mean point of impact as an origin. Then it is evident that the "mean dispersion from mean point of impact," or "mean dispersion" as it is usually called, is the average distance or arithmetical mean of the distances of the points of impact of all the shot from the mean point of impact. Now as this latter point is the one at which every theoretically perfect shot should strike, it is evident that the mean dispersion from mean point of impact gives us a measure of the accuracy of the gun, that is, of the extent to which its shooting is affected by its inherent errors.

380. It must be said in regard to the above definitions, that the terms defined are often very loosely and more or less interchangeably used in service. The term "deflection" is ordinarily used only to represent lateral displacement, in either the vertical or the horizontal planes; and the term "deviation" is used for either vertical or lateral displacement or for displacement in range, in which case the terms "vertical deviation," "lateral deviation" or "deviation in range" are customarily used. There is also confusion in the use of the terms as to whether deviation or deflection from the point aimed at or from the mean point of impact is meant. The term "dispersion" is fairly regularly used as defined above, but even here the point as to whether dispersion from the point aimed at or from the mean point of impact is meant is often left obscure. The context of the conversation or written matter will usually show what is meant. In this book the terms will be used strictly as defined.

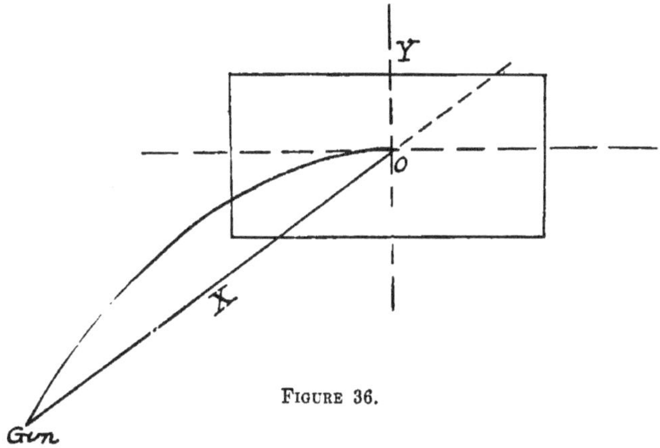

FIGURE 36.

System of coordinates.

381. For use in these last two chapters we will also introduce a special system of coordinates, as shown in Figure 36. This figure represents a perspective view of a vertical target screen of which O at the center is the mean point of impact in the vertical plane. The axis of X is the line from the muzzle of the gun to O, the mean trajectory being shown. Z is the horizontal axis and Y the vertical axis through the center of the target. It will be noted that in this system the axes of X and Z are interchanged from what they ordinarily are in geometry of three dimensions; and this is done in this particular subject to preserve the convention that has been consistently used throughout, that X and all functions thereof represent quantities pertaining to the range. In this system of coordinates it will be seen that, the mean

ing the lateral deviations from this mean point of impact, the following results were obtained:

Limits	Number of shot — To the right	Number of shot — To the left
Between 0 and 1 meter	14	13
Between 1 and 2 meters	8	8
Between 2 and 3 meters	2	5
	24	26

The mean lateral deviation was found to be 1.07 meter. Taking horizontal and vertical axes through the mean point of impact (assuming that the lateral deviations are the same in the horizontal and in the vertical plane, which is very nearly the case), laying off equal spaces to left and to right of the origin, each representing one meter, and constructing on each space a rectangle whose height represents, on any

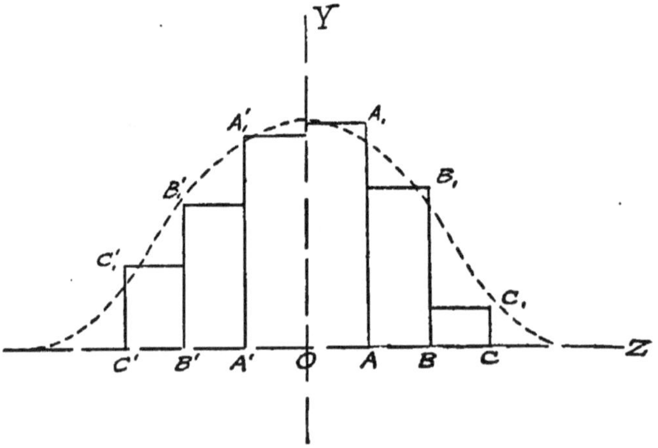

FIGURE 38.

convenient scale, the number of shots whose lateral deviations were within the limits corresponding to the space, we obtain Figure 38.

392. It will be seen that the distribution of the deviations is fairly symmetrical to the axis of Y, there being 26 to the left and 24 to the right; also that the maximum does not exceed three times the mean deviation; also that the area of each rectangle divided by the whole area of the figure is the measure of the probability (as defined) that any single deviation will fall within the limits represented by its base. Thus, the area $OAA_1=14$, divided by the total area, 50, is the probability, $\frac{14}{50}$, that any single deviation will lie between 0 and +1 meter, the area $OAA_1A_1'A'=27$, divided by the total area is the probability, $\frac{27}{50}$, that any single deviation will lie between +1 meter and −1 meter; and the total area divided by itself, $\frac{50}{50}=1=$certainty, is the probability that no deviation will exceed 3 meters.

impact, $\pi=3.1416$, and $\epsilon=2.7183$, and the factor $\frac{1}{\pi\gamma}$ has been introduced to make the whole area under the curve equal to unity

$$\left(\int_{-\infty}^{+\infty} \epsilon^{-\frac{z^2}{\pi\gamma^2}}\,dz=\pi\gamma\right)$$

thus obviating the necessity for dividing the partial area by the whole area whenever a probability is to be computed.

397. Figure 39 represents the probability curve for the Krupp 12-centimeter siege gun, taking its mean error to be 1.07 meter, as given by the 50 shots previously described. There is also shown in dotted lines, for comparison, the probability curve

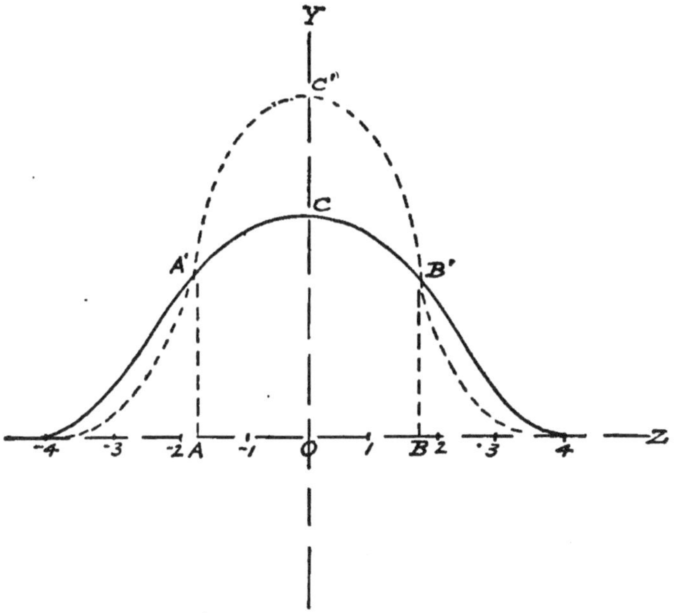

FIGURE 39.

for a gun whose mean error is three-quarters that of the 12-centimeter gun. In both cases the ordinates are exaggerated ten times as compared with the abscissæ.

398. The maximum ordinate being the value of y when $z=0$, is therefore inversely proportional to the mean deviation, that is, $y\Big]_{z=0}=\frac{1}{\pi\gamma}$; the probability that any one deviation will be less than $OB=OA$ is the numerical value of the area $AA'CB'B$ in the one case, and of the area $AA'C'B'B$ in the other; the probability that any one deviation will exceed $OB=OA$ is the area under that part of the curve which is to the left of AA' and to the right of BB'; the whole area under the curve has the numerical value of unity. It will be seen how very small is the probability that any deviation will exceed three times the mean deviation.

probability that the lateral deviation of any one shot will not exceed 2 meters. Therefore of 50 shots 43 should fall within 2 meters on either side of the mean point of impact, and actually 43 did so fall.

402. If P be the probability that the deviation of any single shot will not be greater than a, then evidently $100P$ will be the probable number of shots out of 100 which will fall within the limits $\pm a$; in other words, $100P$ is the percentage of hits to be expected upon a band $2a$ wide with its center at the mean point of impact. Thus we see from the table that the half width of the band which will probably receive 25 per cent of the shot is 0.4γ, while the half width of the band that will probably receive 50 per cent of the shot is 0.846γ. These facts are usually expressed by saying that the width of the 25 per cent rectangle is 0.80 and of the 50 per cent rectangle is 1.69 times the mean error.

403. The half width of the 50 per cent rectangle is known as the "probable error," or in our case the "probable deviation," since it is the error or deviation which is just as liable to be exceeded as it is not to be exceeded.

404. If we wish to find the probability of hitting an area whose width is $2b$ and whose height is $2h$, since the lateral and vertical deviations are independent of each other, the probability is the product of the two values of P taken from the table with the arguments $\frac{b}{\gamma_z}$ and $\frac{h}{\gamma_y}$, where γ_z and γ_y are the mean lateral and mean vertical deviations, respectively. Thus, supposing γ_z to be 4 feet and γ_y to be 5 feet, the probability of hitting with a single shot a 20-foot square with its center at the mean point of impact is $P_1P_2 = .954 \times .889 = .848$, $P_1 = .954$ being the value of P for $\frac{b}{\gamma_z} = \frac{10}{4} = 2.5$ and $P_2 = .889$ being the value of P for $\frac{h}{\gamma_y} = \frac{10}{5} = 2$.

EXAMPLES.

1. The coordinates (z, y) of 10 hits made by a 6-pounder gun on a vertical target at 2000 yards range, axes at center of target, were as follows, in feet:

$$(-10, +13)\quad(+11, +9)\quad(+4, -2)\quad(-1, +1)$$
$$(-4, +2)\quad(+2, +1)\quad(-1, -2)\quad(0, -4)$$
$$(-1, -3)\quad(-4, -4)$$

Find the mean point of impact and the mean vertical and lateral deviations.

Answers. $z_0 = -0.4$; $y_0 = +1.1$; $\gamma_y = 4.14$; $\gamma_z = 3.72$.

2. The coordinates of 8 hits made by a 28-centimeter gun on a vertical target at 4019 meters range, axes at center of target, were as follows, in centimeters:

$$(-80, -90)\quad(-10, +210)\quad(+30, -70)\quad(-70, +355)$$
$$(+30, +40)\quad(-220, -150)\quad(-40, +40)\quad(-65, +90)$$

Find the mean point of impact and the mean vertical and lateral deviations.

Answers. $z_0 = -53$; $y_0 = +53$; $\gamma_y = 123.9$; $\gamma_z = 53.7$

CHAPTER 21.

THE PROBABILITY OF HITTING WHEN THE MEAN POINT OF IMPACT IS NOT AT THE CENTER OF THE TARGET. THE MEAN ERRORS OF GUNS. THE EFFECT UPON THE TOTAL AMMUNITION SUPPLY OF EFFORTS TO SECURE A GIVEN NUMBER OF HITS UPON A GIVEN TARGET UNDER GIVEN CONDITIONS. SPOTTING SALVOS BY KEEPING A CERTAIN PROPORTIONATE NUMBER OF SHOTS AS "SHORTS."

Mean point of impact not at center of target.

405. In the preceding chapter we considered only the chance of hitting when the mean point of impact is at the center of the target, but this is far from being an attainable condition in the service use of guns, especially of naval guns. In fact to bring the mean point of impact upon the target is the main object to be attained in gunnery, for, from what has already been said, if the mean point of impact be brought into coincidence with the center of the target and kept there, we will get the maximum number of hits possible, and it is to the accomplishment of this that the spotter gives his efforts. Even with a stationary target, at a known range, however, it is difficult to so regulate the fire as to bring about and maintain this coincidence of center of target and mean point of impact; and when the target is moving with a speed and in a direction that are only approximately known; when the range is not accurately known; when there is a wind blowing which may vary in force and direction at different points between the gun and the target; when the density of the air may vary at different points between the gun and the target; and when the firing ship is also in motion, etc.; even the most expert regulation of the fire by the observation of successive points of fall can do no more than keep the mean point of impact in the neighborhood of the object attacked. All this applies to a single gun, and in salvo firing we have the additional trouble that the mean points of impact of the several guns cannot be brought into coincidence. This makes it necessary for the spotter to estimate the position of the mean point of impact of the whole salvo, that is, the mean position of the mean points of impact of all the guns, and it is this combined mean point of impact of all the guns that the spotter must determine in his own mind and endeavor to bring upon the target and keep there. The difficulties attending this process are manifest.

406. In Figure 40, let O be the mean point of impact of a single gun, and let $ABCD$ be the target at any moment, and let the coordinates of the center of $ABCD$, with reference to the horizontal and vertical axes through O be z_0 and y_0; also let the mean lateral and vertical deviations of the gun be γ_z and γ_y, respectively, and let the dimensions of the target be $2b$ and $2h$. Then the probability that a shot will fall between the vertical lines Cc and $C'c'$ is the tabular value of P for the argument $\frac{z_0+b}{\gamma_z}$, which we will call $P_z(z_0+b)$; and the probability that a shot will fall between Dd and $D'd'$ is the tabular value of P for the argument $\frac{z_0-b}{\gamma_z}$, which we will call $P_z(z_0-b)$. Therefore the probability that a shot will fall between Cc and Dd is one-half the difference of the two preceding probabilities, or

$$\tfrac{1}{2}[P_z(z_0+b)-P_z(z_0-b)] \qquad (224)$$

Similarly, the probability that a shot will fall between the horizontal lines $C'C$ and $B'B$ is

$$\tfrac{1}{2}[P_y(y_0+h)-P_y(y_0-h)] \qquad (225)$$

Hence the probability of hitting $ABCD$ is the product of the two expressions given in (224) and (225), or

$$\tfrac{1}{4}[P_z(z_0+b)-P_z(z_0-b)]\times[P_y(y_0+h)-P_y(y_0-h)] \qquad (226)$$

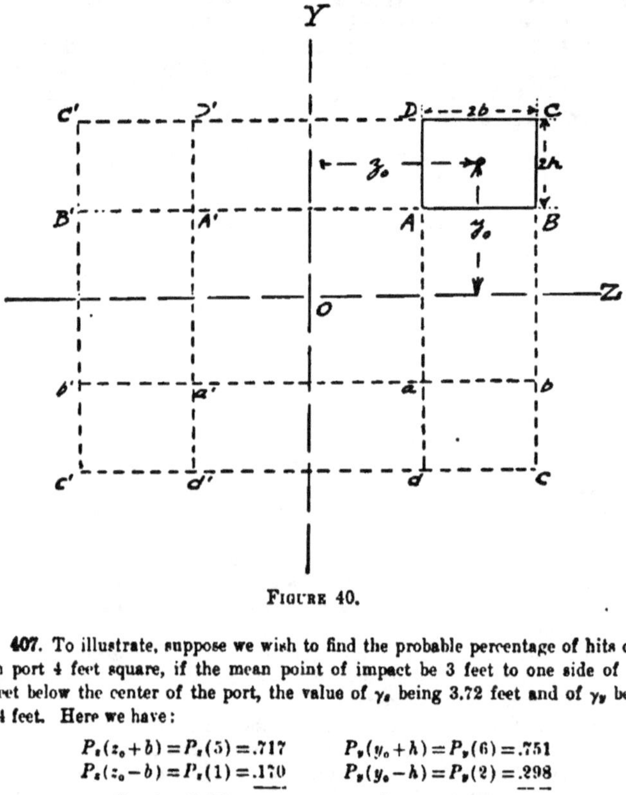

FIGURE 40.

407. To illustrate, suppose we wish to find the probable percentage of hits on a gun port 4 feet square, if the mean point of impact be 3 feet to one side of and 4 feet below the center of the port, the value of γ_z being 3.72 feet and of γ_y being 4.14 feet. Here we have:

$$P_z(z_0+b)=P_z(5)=.717 \qquad P_y(y_0+h)=P_y(6)=.751$$
$$P_z(z_0-b)=P_z(1)=.170 \qquad P_y(y_0-h)=P_y(2)=.298$$
$$P_z(5)-P_z(1)=.547 \qquad P_y(6)-P_y(2)=.453$$

From which we have $\qquad P=\tfrac{1}{4}\times.547\times.453=.062$

Therefore the percentage of hits under the given conditions would be 6.2 per cent. Under the same conditions, but with the mean point of impact at the center of the port, the percentage of hits would be 9.9 per cent.

Bearing of mean errors upon fire control.

408. From what has been said it is evident that the less the mean errors of the gun, the more important it becomes to accurately regulate the fire; for if the distance of the mean point of impact from the target be more than three times the mean error of the gun we would get practically no hits at all. Therefore a reduction in the mean error of the gun renders imperative a corresponding reduction in the distance within which the spotter must keep the mean point of impact from the target if hits are to be made. Therefore, unless good control of the fire be secured, a gun with a small mean error will make fewer hits than one with a larger mean error, and this has sometimes been used as an argument in favor of guns that do not shoot too closely. Conversely, however, if good control be secured—that is, if the spotter be competent and careful—the close-shooting gun will secure more hits than the other. Therefore the scientific method of securing hits is to have a competent spotter and a close-shooting gun; the other process is a discarding of science and knowledge and a falling back upon luck, which cannot but meet with disaster in the face of an enemy using proper and scientific methods.

409. To illustrate the statements contained in the preceding paragraph, we will take the case of a 6" gun firing at a turret 25 feet high by 32 feet in diameter, and 3000 yards distant. Suppose the mean vertical and lateral deviations each to be 10 feet; if the mean point of impact coincides with the center of the target, the probable percentage of hits will be 54.3 per cent; but if the sights be set for a range of 10 per cent more or less than the true distance the mean point of impact will be raised or lowered about 43 feet (this is one of the older 6" guns; not the one given in the accompanying range tables), and the percentage of hits will be reduced to 0.7 per cent. If, on the other hand, the mean errors of the gun were each 20 feet, or double the first assumption, while the percentage of hits with perfect regulation of fire (that is, with the mean point of impact at the center of the target) would be reduced to 18.2 per cent, that with sight setting for a range 10 per cent in error would be 4.7 per cent. Thus we see that if the fire be not accurately regulated a gun will be severely handicapped by its own accuracy if the range be not known within 10 per cent.

410. The work for the problem in the preceding paragraph is as follows:

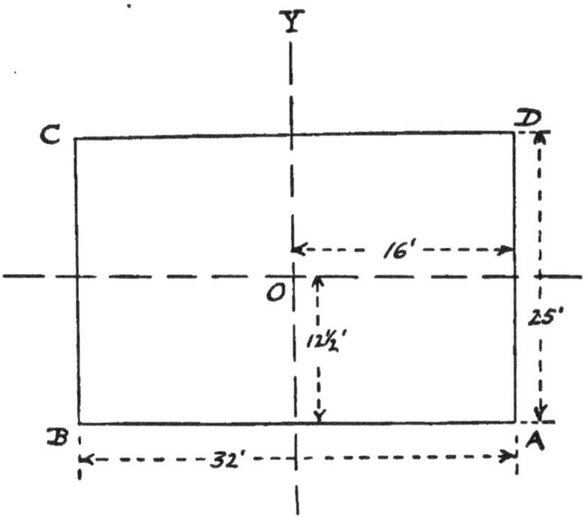

FIGURE 41.

Case 1. Mean deviation 10 feet. Mean point of impact at O (Figure 41).

$$\frac{a_1}{\gamma_z} = \frac{16}{10} = 1.6 \qquad P_z = .798$$

$$\frac{a_2}{\gamma_y} = \frac{12.5}{10} = 1.25 \qquad P_y = .681$$

$$P_z \times P_y = .543438$$

Therefore the percentage of hits is 54.3 per cent.

Case 2. Mean deviation 10 feet. Mean point of impact at O (Figure 42).
Chances of hitting between $A'D$ and $B'C$.

$$P_z(z_0+16)-P_z(z_0-16)=P_z(16)-P_z(-16) \qquad =1.596$$

$$z_0=0 \qquad \frac{a_1}{\gamma_z}=\frac{16}{10}=1.6 \qquad P_z(16)=.798$$

Chances of hitting between AB and CD.

$$P_y(y_0+12.5)-P_y(y_0-12.5)=P_y(55.5)-P_y(30.5) \qquad = .0168$$

$$y_0=43 \quad \frac{a_2}{\gamma_y}=\frac{55.5}{10}=5.55 \quad P_y(55.5)=1.0000 \qquad 4\,|\,.026208 \quad .0065$$

$$\frac{a_3}{\gamma_y}=\frac{30.5}{10}=3.05 \quad P_y(30.5)=\ .9832$$

$$.0168$$

Percentage of hits is 0.7 of 1 per cent.

Case 3. Mean deviation 20 feet. Mean point of impact at O (Figure 41).

$$\frac{a_1}{\gamma_z}=\frac{16}{20}=0.8 \qquad P_z=.477$$

$$\frac{a_2}{\gamma_y}=\frac{12.5}{20}=\ .625 \qquad P_y=.382$$

$$P_z\times P_y=.182214$$

Percentage of hits is 18.2 per cent.

Case 4. Mean deviation 20 feet. Mean point of impact at O (Figure 42).

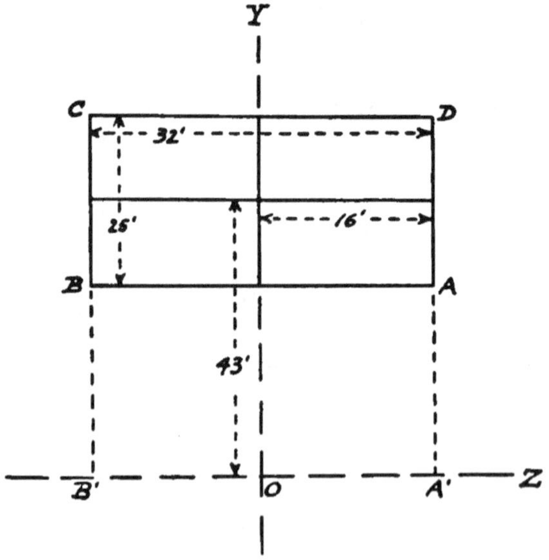

FIGURE 42.

Chances of hitting between $A'D$ and $B'C$.

$$P_z(z_0+16)-P_z(z_0-16)=P_z(16)-P_z(-16)= \qquad .954$$

$$\frac{a_1}{\gamma_z}=\frac{16}{20}=.8$$

Chances of hitting between *AB* and *CD*.

$$P_y(y_0+12.5)-P_y(y_0-12.5)=P_y(55.5)-P_y(30.5)=$$

$$\frac{a_2}{\gamma_y}=\frac{55.5}{20}=2.775 \quad P_y(55.5)=.97275$$

$$\frac{a_3}{\gamma_y}=\frac{30.5}{20}=1.525 \quad P_y(30.5)=.77550$$

$$P_y(55.5)-P_y(30.5)=.19725$$

$$\begin{array}{r} .19725 \\ 4\ \underline{|\ .1881765} \\ .047 \end{array}$$

Percentage of hits is 4.7 per cent.

411. If we know the percentage of hits at a given range on a target of given size, we can make a rough estimate of the mean errors of the gun by assuming that the mean point of impact was at the center of the target, and the greater the number of rounds fired the more nearly correct will this determination probably be. For example, on a certain occasion, the eighty 6″ gun of certain British ships, firing separately, made 295 hits out of 650 rounds fired; that is, 45.4 per cent of hits: on a target 15 feet high by 20 feet wide, at a mean range of 1500 yards. Here we have given that the product

$$P_z\left(\frac{10}{\gamma_z}\right)\times P_y\left(\frac{7.5}{\gamma_y}\right)=.454$$

Assuming that $\gamma_z=\gamma_y$, we may solve the above by a process of trial and error, that is, by assuming successive integral values of γ, and by this process we see that when $\gamma=7$ we have

$$P_z\left(\frac{10}{7}\right)\times P_y\left(\frac{7.5}{7}\right)=.745\times .581=.432$$

and as .432 is very nearly .454, we can say that the mean deviations are slightly less than 7 feet; and we could go on and determine the solution of the equation more accurately by trying 6.9 feet instead of 7 feet as the value of γ. This would probably not make the result any nearer the truth, however, as any correction resulting therefrom would probably be less than the error caused by the assumption that the mean point of impact was at the center of the target.

412. The number of rounds necessary to make at least one hit may be determined by the following method: Let p be the probability of hitting with a single shot; then $1-p$ is the probability that a single shot will miss; and $(1-p)^n$ is the probability that all of n shots will miss. Therefore the probability of hitting at least once with n shots is $P=1-(1-p)^n$. Solving this equation for n, we get

$$\log(1-P)=n\log(1-p)$$

$$n=\frac{\log(1-P)}{\log(1-p)} \qquad (227)$$

and by giving P a value near unity we can find the value of n which will make one hit as nearly certain as we wish.

413. As an example, taking a case in which 94 shots were fired from a mortar at a turret, and in which the calculated probability of a hit with a single shot was .011, let us see how many rounds would have to be fired to make the probability of at least one hit .95. In that case, $p=.011$, and so we have, from (227),

$$n=\frac{\log(1-.95)}{\log(1-.011)}=\frac{\log .05}{\log .989}=\frac{8.69897-10}{9.99520-10}=\frac{-1.30103}{-0.00480}=271$$

Therefore 271 shots must be fired to make the odds 19 to 1 that there will be at least one hit. The probability of at least one hit with the 94 shots fired was

$$P=1-(1-p)^{94}=1-.354=.646$$

419. Of course the only correct way of determining the mean errors of a given gun is by actually firing a large number of rounds at a target and measuring the deviations. That the errors are very small under favorable circumstances is illustrated in Figure 43, which represents a target made at Meppen on June 1, 1882, with a 28-centimeter gun, the distance of the target from the gun being 2026 meters (221 yards). The dotted cross is the mean point of impact, whose coordinates referred to the horizontal and vertical axes at the center of the target are $z = 32.4$ inches and $y = -11.6$ inches. The mean lateral deviation is 9.5 inches, and the mean vertical deviation is 11.6 inches. These actual deviations are considerably less than those encountered in service, which may be plausibly ascribed to the fact that in proving

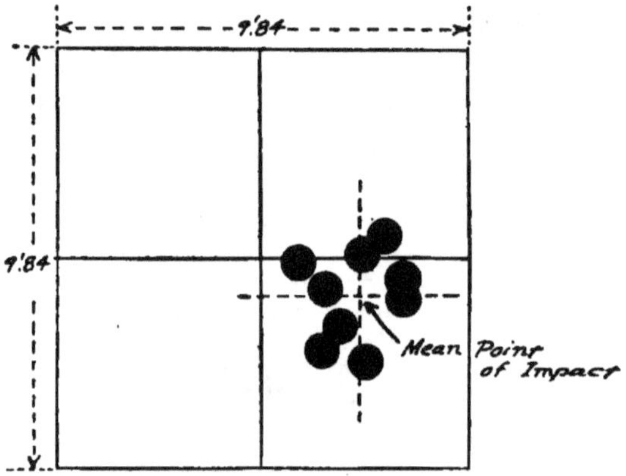

FIGURE 43.

ground firings greater care can be taken in pointing than is usually practicable under service conditions.

Effect of rolling, pitching and yawing.

420. The three angular motions of a ship's deck, caused by the rolling, pitching and yawing, greatly increase the actual mean errors of naval guns in service, but their effects depend so much upon the skill of the gun pointer, as well as upon the state of the sea and the characteristics of the particular ship and gun mounting, that only the roughest estimates of their values can be made. Many naval guns are mounted in broadside and only train from bow to quarter, and even those mounted on the midships line are likely to be most used in broadside; thus the roll, which is the greatest and most rapid of a ship's motions, has its largest component in the plane of fire, and acts principally to increase the vertical deviations. The principal effect of pitching, on the other hand, is to increase the lateral deviations by causing the plane of the sights to be more or less inclined, now to one side and now to the other of the plane of fire. Motion in azimuth, yawing, mostly due to unsteady steering, affects the lateral deviations only.

Motion of target.

421. If the target be in motion, the person controlling the fire of the gun must of course estimate its speed and direction in order to direct the fire at the point where the target will be when the projectile strikes, and his corrections must always vary in accuracy from round to round, thus increasing both the lateral and the vertical deviations. Furthermore, variations in the accuracy of the estimated corrections for the speed of the firing ship and for the effect of the wind must occur deviation in range only changes from 119 yards to 104 yards; and while in the case of smaller guns the mean deviation in range decreases more rapidly, still the change is always very much less proportionately than the change in range itself.

426. The principal use of knowledge of the mean deviation in range is in the regulation of gun fire by observation of the points of fall. Suppose the axis of Z, in Figure 44, represents the water-line of the target, the axis of X being the horizontal trace of the vertical plane of the mean trajectory, and let the distance from the axis of Z to the dotted lines aa, $a'a'$, bb, $b'b'$, cc, $c'c'$, dd, $d'd'$, etc., represent the mean deviation in range, γ_x, of the gun. Then if the point of impact be on the axis of Z, that is, on the water-line, half of all the shot will fall short; if it be on $a'a'$ the percent-

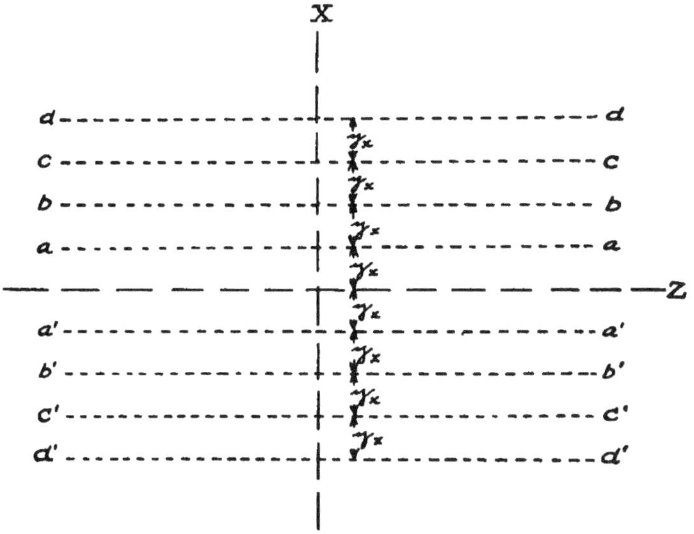

FIGURE 44.

age of shot that will fall short will be increased by the number which fall between the axis of Z and $a'a'$, or, from the table of probabilities, it will be $50 + \frac{57.5}{2} = 79$ per cent. If the mean range be still further short, so that the mean point of impact falls on $b'b'$, the percentage of shorts will be $50 + \frac{88.9}{2} = 94$ per cent; and, finally, if the mean point of impact be three or more times the mean deviation short, then practically all the shot will fall short. The same reasoning shows that if no shot strike short of the axis of Z, the mean point of impact is three or more times the mean deviation in range beyond the axis of Z; if about 6 per cent strike short, the mean point of impact is about twice the mean deviation in range beyond the axis of Z; and if about 21 per cent are short, it is about the mean deviation in range beyond the axis of Z. Thus, by observation of the percentage of shot which strike short it is possible to determine with some degree of accuracy how much the setting of the sight in range should be increased or decreased to bring the mean point of impact on the target.

427. Let us now suppose that we are going to fire salvos from a battery of 12″ guns, for which $V=2900$ f. s., $w=870$ pounds and $c=0.61$. Let us also assume that we have a vertical target 30 feet high and wide enough to eliminate the necessity for considering lateral deviations due to accidental errors. Let us take the mean errors of the gun in range, first as 40 yards, next as 60 yards, and then again as 80 yards; and also that they are approximately the same at all ranges. Let us also assume that the mean point of impact is at the center of the water-line of the target, in which case, as we have already seen, 50 per cent of the shot will fall short. Let us also assume that the three mean deviations correspond to total deviations of 150, 200 and 300 yards, respectively. Now let us see what percentage of the shot in each salvo will probably hit, at a range of 7000 yards, at which range the danger space for a target 30 feet high is, by the range table, 180 yards. **Method of "shorts."**

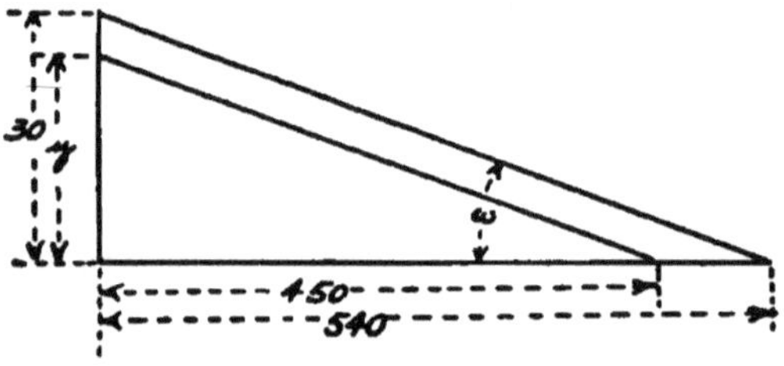

FIGURE 45.

1. Mean dispersion in range 40 yards; maximum dispersion in range 150 yards (Figure 45).

$$\tan \omega = \frac{30}{540} = \frac{1}{18}$$

$$\frac{y}{450} = \frac{1}{18} \qquad y=25 \text{ feet}$$

That is, for a maximum dispersion of 150 yards, or 450 feet, no shot would pass more than 25 feet above the water-line of the target, and all shots that do not fall short would hit. Therefore, by our assumption, we would have 50 per cent of shorts and 50 per cent of hits.

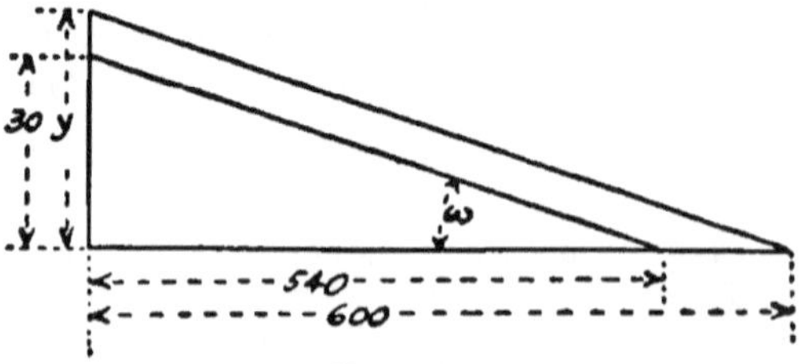

FIGURE 46.

2. Mean dispersion in range of 60 yards; maximum dispersion in range of 200 yards (Figure 46).

$$\frac{y}{600} = \frac{1}{18} \qquad y=33\tfrac{1}{3} \text{ feet}$$

Also the mean dispersion in range is 180 feet, therefore the mean vertical dispersion is

$$\gamma_v = 180 \tan \omega = \frac{180}{18} = 10 \text{ feet}$$

Our problem therefore becomes to find how many shot will pass between the top of the target and a line parallel to it and $3\frac{1}{3}$ feet above it, knowing that 50 per cent of the shot fired will fall short, and the other 50 per cent will pass between the water-line of the target and a horizontal line $33\frac{1}{3}$ feet above it. As we have already taken out the 50 per cent of the shot that fall short, the $\frac{1}{2}$ disappears from the formula, and we have

$$P_y(33) - P_y(30) = .009$$

$$\frac{a_1}{\gamma} = \frac{33}{10} = 3.3 \qquad P_y(33) = .992$$

$$\frac{a_2}{\gamma} = \frac{30}{10} = 3.0 \qquad P_y(30) = \underline{.983}$$

$$.009$$

That is, .9 of 1 per cent of the shot that do not fall short will pass over the top of the target, leaving 99.1 per cent of them as hits. Therefore, of the 100 per cent of shot fired, 50 per cent will fall short; 99.1 per cent of 50, or 49 per cent of them, will hit; and 1 per cent of them all will go over.

3. Mean dispersion in range 80 yards; maximum dispersion in range 300 yards.

$$\frac{y}{900} = \frac{1}{18} y = 50 \text{ feet} \qquad \gamma_v = 240 \times \frac{1}{18} = \frac{40}{3} \text{ feet}$$

and in the same manner as in 2, to find the number of shot that will pass between the top of the target and a horizontal line 50 feet above the water-line, we have

$$P_y(50) - P_y(30) = .035$$

$$\frac{a_1}{\gamma} = \frac{50 \times 3}{40} = 3.75 \qquad P_y(50) = .9975$$

$$\frac{a_2}{\gamma} = \frac{30 \times 3}{40} = 2.25 \qquad P_y(30) = \underline{.9275}$$

$$.07$$

Therefore 7 per cent will go over, and 93 per cent will hit out of the 50 per cent that do not fall short. Therefore we have that there will be 50 per cent of shorts, 46 per cent of hits and 4 per cent of overs. Proceeding similarly for other ranges, we can make up a table like the following:

Range. Yds.	Mean point of impact at water-line. Mean dispersion in range of— 40 yards. Percentage of— Shorts.	Hits.	Overs.	60 yards. Percentage of— Shorts.	Hits.	Overs.	80 yards. Percentage of— Shorts.	Hits.	Overs.	Danger space. Yds.
7000	50	50	0	50	49	1	50	46	4	180
10000	50	49	1	50	42	8	50	35	15	108
13000	50	42	8	50	32	18	50	25	25	70
15000	50	36	14	50	27	23	50	21	29	55
18000	50	28	22	50	20	30	50	15	35	39

The above mean dispersions are less than have been experienced at recent target practices.

The above chances of hitting are based only on vertical errors; if the target be short they will be materially reduced by the lateral errors.

428. For the above problem let us now suppose that the mean point of impact had been at the center of the danger space, instead of at the water-line, and we had desired to tabulate the same data as before. Let us start with the range of 7000 yards, for which the danger space is 180 yards, and compute the results for a mean dispersion in range of 40 yards, corresponding to a total dispersion of 150 yards.

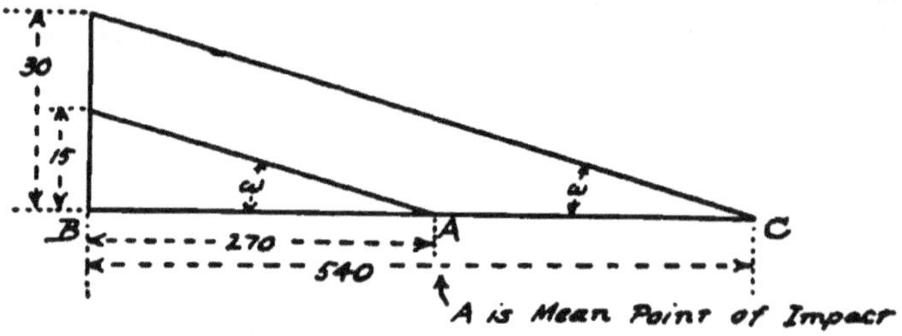

FIGURE 47.

All shot that fall less than 270 feet short of the mean point of impact are hits. For space between mean point of impact and target,

$$\frac{a}{\gamma} = \frac{270}{120} = \frac{9}{4} = 2.25 \qquad P = .9275$$

Therefore, for those short of the mean point of impact, 92.75 per cent will hit and 7.25 per cent will fall short. But only 50 per cent of the total number of shot fired fall shot of the mean point of impact, therefore the above percentages become, of the total,

Hits	46.375 per cent
Shorts	3.625 per cent

For the space between A and C, which is 270 feet, we know that any shot that falls between A and C hits, and any that falls beyond C is over. Therefore the work is the same as the above, and we have

Hits	46.375 per cent
Overs	3.625 per cent

Therefore the total is

Shorts	3.625 per cent
Hits	92.750 per cent
Overs	3.625 per cent

Working out similar data for the other ranges and dispersions gives us the following table:

Range. Yds.	Mean point of impact at center of danger space.									Danger space. Yds.
	Mean dispersion in range of—									
	40 yards.			60 yards.			80 yards.			
	Percentage of—			Percentage of—			Percentage of—			
	Shorts.	Hits.	Overs.	Shorts.	Hits.	Overs.	Shorts.	Hits.	Overs.	
7000	4	93	3	12	77	11	19	63	18	180
10000	14	72	14	24	53	23	30	40	30	106
13000	25	49	26	32	36	32	37	27	36	70
15000	29	42	29	36	29	35	40	21	39	55
18000	35	31	34	40	21	39	42	16	42	30

429. From the tables given in the two preceding paragraphs, if we assume the mean point of impact on the target, we see that, as the mean dispersion increases, the percentage of hits decreases very rapidly.

430. It will also be seen that, to get the greatest possible number of hits, a greater percentage of shorts is necessary at long ranges than at short ranges.

431. It will also be seen that, where the mean point of impact in range is at some distance from the target, an increase in dispersion gives an increase in the number of hits, which is in accord with the principles previously enunciated. It may be shown mathematically that the mean dispersion for maximum efficiency is equal to 80 per cent of the distance from the mean point of impact in range to the center of the danger space.

432. From what has been said, it will readily be seen that, in controlling the firing of salvos from a battery of similar guns, we desire to keep a certain proportion of the shot striking short of the target in order to get the maximum number of hits. There are also other good reasons for so keeping a number of the shot striking short. From what we have seen, we may determine certain general rules which will govern the spotter in thus controlling salvo firing. This question, however, is one that may more appropriately be considered at length in the study of another branch of gunnery, so there will be no further discussion of it in this book.

433. It will be interesting to compare the results of actual firing with the computed results in some one case, to see how closely the two agree, and to get some idea of the correctness for service purposes of percentages determined mathematically. Such results are given in the following table taken from Helie's well-known Traitė de Balistique. It represents the results of about 500 shots fired at Gavre from a 16.5-centimeter rifle at various angles of elevation:

	Probability that the lateral deviations will not exceed—				
	$\frac{\gamma_z}{4}$.	$\frac{\gamma_z}{2}$.	γ_z.	$2\gamma_z$.	$3\gamma_z$.
By table..........	0.158	0.310	0.575	0.889	0.983
By firing.........	0.176	0.300	0.592	0.885	0.988

10. Fire is opened with eight 3" guns on a torpedo-boat coming head on when she is at 1500 yards range. She covers 100 yards every 7.5 seconds, and each gun fires once every 7.5 seconds. The mean lateral and vertical deviations are each 6 feet. and the target offered is 6 feet high by 15 feet wide. If an error of 100 yards in the sight setting displaces the mean point of impact 3 feet vertically, and the sights are all set for 1000 yards range, what is the probable number of hits while the boat advances to 500 yards range? *Answer.* 10+.

11. The turrets of a monitor steaming obliquely to the line of fire present a vertical target consisting of two rectangles, each 24 feet wide by 12 feet high, and 36 feet from center to center. If the mean errors of a gun be 12 yards laterally and 8 yards vertically, would it be better to aim at a turret or half way between them? *Answers.* 1st case, $P=.057$; 2d case, $P=.061$.

12. A gun has 30 shell, one of which, if landed in a certain gun position, would silence the gun contained therein. The gun pit is 10 yards in diameter, and the probability of hitting it with the gun in question is .05. What would be the probability of silencing the gun, using all the ammunition? *Answer.* $P=.785$.

13. The 12" guns of a ship made 68 per cent of hits on a target 15 feet high by 20 feet wide at 1700 yards range. What was the probable value of the mean deviations, vertical and lateral? Supposing the mean deviation to be proportional to the range, what percentage of hits would the same guns make on the same target at 3400 and at 5100 yards? *Answers.* 5 feet; 25.9 per cent; 12.6 per cent.

14. If the probability of hitting a target with a single shot is .05, what will be the probability of making at least two hits with 50 shots? *Answer.* .721.

15. What is the greatest value of the mean deviation of a gun consistent with a probability equal to .90 of its making at least one hit in a hundred shots on a gun port 2 feet wide by 4 feet high? *Answer.* 5.95 feet.

16. Compute the data for 10,000 yards contained in paragraph 427.
17. Compute the data for 13,000 yards contained in paragraph 427.
18. Compute the data for 15,000 yards contained in paragraph 427.
19. Compute the data for 18,000 yards contained in paragraph 427.
20. Compute the data for 10,000 yards contained in paragraph 428.
21. Compute the data for 13,000 yards contained in paragraph 428.
22. Compute the data for 15,000 yards contained in paragraph 428.
23. Compute the data for 18,000 yards contained in paragraph 428.

APPENDIX A.

FORMS TO BE EMPLOYED IN THE SOLUTION OF THE PRINCIPAL EXAMPLES GIVEN IN THIS TEXT BOOK.

NOTES.

1. In preparing these forms the problem taken has been the 8" gun (gun K in the tables) for which $V = 2750$ f. s., $w = 260$ pounds, $c = 0.61$, generally for a range of 19,000 yards. More specific data is given at the head of each form.

2. In the problems under standard conditions, which should give the exact results contained in the range tables, it should be borne in mind that the latter are given, for the angle of departure to the nearest tenth of a minute, for the angle of fall to the nearest minute, for the time of flight to the nearest hundredth of a second, etc., only. Also that results given in the range tables are entered after the results of the computations have been plotted as a curve, and the faired results are those contained in the tables. Small discrepancies between the computed results and those given in the tables may therefore sometimes be expected.

3. Also, results obtained by direct computation are of course more accurate than those obtained by taking multiples of quantities given in the range tables, and small discrepancies may be expected in some such cases between computed results and those taken from the range tables.

INDEX TO FORMS IN APPENDIX A.

Form No.	Chapter No.	Example No.	Nature of Example.
1	8	7	Computing ϕ, etc., for a given range, by Ingalls' method of successive approximations.
2	8	8	Computing ϕ, etc., for a given range, by Ingalls' method, knowing f.
3	8	9	Computing ϕ, etc., for a given range, by Alger's method of successive approximations.
4	9	1	Computing the elements of the vertex for a given R and ϕ, by successive approximations.
5	9	2	Computing the elements of the vertex for a given R and ϕ, knowing f.
6	9	3	Deriving special formulæ for y and tan θ for a given trajectory
7	9	4	Computing values of y and θ for given abscissæ in a given trajectory.
8	10	1	Computing R, etc., for a given ϕ, by successive approximations.
9	10	2	Computing R, etc., for a given ϕ, knowing f.
10A 10B	11	1	Computing ϕ, ψ, θ, t and v for an elevated or depressed target.
11	12	2	Computing change in range resulting from a variation in initial velocity.
12	12	3	Computing change in range resulting from a variation in atmospheric density.
13	12	4	Computing change in range resulting from a variation in weight of projectile; method by direct computation.
14	12	5	Computing change in range resulting from a variation in weight of projectile; method by using Columns 10 and 12 of range table.
15	12	6	Computing change in position of point of impact in vertical plane through target resulting from a variation in the setting of the sight in range.
16	13	1	Computing the drift at a given range.
17	13	2	Computing sight-bar height and set of sliding leaf for a given range and deflection.
18	14	1	Computing the effect of wind.
19	14	2	Computing the effect of motion of the gun.
20	14	3	Computing the effect of motion of the target.
21	16	—	Computing the penetration of armor.
22	16	2	Range table computations, ϕ, etc.
23	16	3	Range table computations.
24	16	4	Range table computations.
25A 25B	17	8	Wind and speed problems. Real wind.
26	17	9	Wind and speed problems. Apparent wind.
27A	17	13	Reduced velocity by range tables.
27B	17	14	Reduced velocity by computation
28	18	1 and 2	The calibration of a single gun.
29	19	1	The calibration of a ship's battery.

Form No. 1.

CHAPTER 8—EXAMPLE 7.

FORM FOR THE COMPUTATION OF THE DATA CONTAINED IN COLUMNS 2, 3, 4 AND 5 OF THE RANGE TABLES; THAT IS, FOR THE VALUES OF THE ANGLE OF DEPARTURE (ϕ), ANGLE OF FALL (ω), TIME OF FLIGHT (T) AND STRIKING VELOCITY (v_ω) FOR A GIVEN RANGE, CORRECTING FOR ALTITUDE BY A SERIES OF SUCCESSIVE APPROXIMATIONS, THE ATMOSPHERE BEING CONSIDERED AS OF STANDARD DENSITY—INGALLS' METHOD.

FORMULÆ.

$C_1 = K = \frac{w}{cd^2}$; $Z = \frac{X}{C}$; $\sin 2\phi = AC$; $Y = A''C \tan\phi$; $\log\log f = \log Y + 5.01765 - 10$;

$\tan\omega = B' \tan\phi$; $T = CT' \sec\phi$; $v_\omega = u_\omega \cos\phi \sec\omega$

PROBLEM.

Cal. = 8″; $V = 2750$ f. s.; $w = 260$ pounds; $c = 0.61$; Range = 19,000 yds. = 57,000 ft.

$C_1 = K =$ (from Table VI) .... colog 9.17654 − 10

$X = 57000$ .... log 4.75587

$Z_1 = 8558.75$ .... log 3.93241

$A_1 = .08673 + \frac{.00198 \times 58.75}{100} - \frac{.00644 \times 50}{100} = .084673$ (from Table II)

$A_1 = .084673$ .... log 8.92775 − 10

$C_1 =$ .... log 0.82346

$2\phi_1 = 34°\ 19'\ 36''$ .... sin 9.75121 − 10

$\phi_1 = 17°\ 09'\ 48''$ (first approximation, disregarding f)

$A_1'' = 2948 - \frac{50}{100} \times \frac{(-.0064) \times 71}{.0031} + \frac{50 \times 0}{100} + \frac{.000273 \times 71}{.0031} = 3027.5$ (Table II)

$A_1'' = 3027.5$ .... log 3.48109

$C_1 =$ .... log 0.82346

$\phi_1 = 17°\ 09'\ 48''$ .... tan 9.48974 − 10

$Y_1 =$ .... log 3.79429

Constant .... log 5.01765 − 10

$f_1 =$ .... log 0.06485 .... loglog 8.81194 − 10

$C_1 =$ .... log 0.82346

$C_2 =$ .... log 0.88831 .... colog 9.11169 − 10

$X = 57000$ .... log 4.75587

$Z_2 = 7371.5$ .... log 3.86756

$A_2 = .06520 + \frac{.00164 \times 71.5}{100} - \frac{.00497 \times 50}{100} = .0638876$

$A_2 = .0638876$ .... log 8.80542 − 10

$C_2 =$ .... log 0.88831

$2\phi_2 = 29°\ 36'\ 14''$ .... sin 9.69373 − 10

$\phi_2 = 14°\ 48'\ 07''$ (second approximation)

$A_2'' = 2398 - \frac{50}{100} \times \frac{(-.0046) \times 67}{.0025} + \frac{50 \times 0}{100} + \frac{.001488 \times 67}{.0025} = 2499.5$

$A_2''=2499.5$		log	3.39786
$C_2=$		log	0.88831
$\phi_2=14°\ 48'\ 07''$		tan	9.42201−10
$Y_2=$		log	3.70818
Constant		log	5.01765−10
$f_2=$	log 0.05319	loglog	8.72583−10
$C_1=$	log 0.82346		
$C_3=$	log 0.87665	colog	9.12335−10
$X=57000$		log	4.75587
$Z_3=7572.15$		log	3.87922

$$A_3=.06851+\frac{.00170\times 72.15}{100}-\frac{.00520\times 50}{100}=.067137$$

$A_3=.067137$		log	8.82696−10
$C_3=$		log	0.87665
$2\phi_3=30°\ 21'\ 22''$		sin	9.70361−10
$\phi_3=15°\ 10'\ 41''$ (third approximation)			

$$A_3''=2465-\frac{50}{100}\times\frac{(-.0048)\times 68}{.0025}+\frac{50\times 0}{100}+\frac{.002237\times 68}{.0025}=2591.1$$

$A_3''=2591.1$		log	3.41349
$C_3=$		log	0.87665
$\phi_3=15°\ 10'\ 41''$		tan	9.43342−10
$Y_3=$		log	3.72356
Constant		log	5.01765−10
$f_3=$	log 0.05511	loglog	8.74121−10
$C_1=$	log 0.82346		
$C_4=$	log 0.87857	colog	9.12143−10
$X=57000$		log	4.75587
$Z_4=7538.75$		log	3.87730

$$A_4=.06851+\frac{.00170\times 38.75}{100}-\frac{.00520\times 50}{100}=.066569$$

$A_4=.066569$		log	8.82327−10
$C_4=$		log	0.87857
$2\phi_4=30°\ 13'\ 10''$		sin	9.70184−10
$\phi_4=15°\ 06'\ 35''$ (fourth approximation)			

$$A_4''=2465-\frac{50}{100}\times\frac{(-.0048)\times 68}{.0025}+\frac{50\times 0}{100}+\frac{.001669\times 68}{.0025}=2575.6768$$

$A_4''=2575.7$		log	3.41090
$C_4=$		log	0.87857
$\phi_4=15°\ 06'\ 35''$		tan	9.43137−10
$Y_4=$		log	3.72084
Constant		log	5.01765−10
$f_4=$	log 0.05476	loglog	8.73849−10
$C_1=$	log 0.82346		
$C_5=$	log 0.87822	colog	9.12178−10
$X=57000$		log	4.75587
$Z_5=7544.85$		log	3.87765

$$A_5=.06851+\frac{.00170\times 44.85}{100}-\frac{.00520\times 50}{100}=.06667245$$

$A_5 = .06667245$ .... log $8.82395 - 10$

$C_5 =$ .... log 0.87822

$2\phi_5 = 30° \ 14' \ 42''$ .... sin $9.70217 - 10$

$\phi_5 = 15° \ 07' \ 27''$ (fifth approximation)

$$A_5'' = 2465 - \frac{50}{100} \times \frac{(-.0048) \times 68}{.0025} + \frac{50 \times 0}{100} + \frac{.001773 \times 68}{.0025} = 2578.5$$

$A_5'' = 2578.5$ .... log 3.41137

$C_5 =$ .... log 0.87822

$\phi_5 = 15° \ 07' \ 27''$ .... tan $9.43175 - 10$

$Y_5 =$ .... log 3.72134

Constant .... log $5.01765 - 10$

$f_5 =$ .... log 0.05483 .... loglog $8.73899 - 10$

$C_1 =$ .... log 0.82346

$C_6 =$ .... log 0.87829 .... colog $9.12171 - 10$

$X = 57000$ .... log 4.75587

$Z_6 = 7543.65$ .... log 3.87758

$$A_6 = .06851 + \frac{.00170 \times 43.65}{100} - \frac{.00520 \times 50}{100} = .066652$$

$A_6 = .066652$ .... log $8.82381 - 10$

$C_6 =$ .... log 0.87829

$2\phi_6 = 30° \ 14' \ 21''$ .... sin $9.70210 - 10$

$\phi_6 = 15° \ 07' \ 10''$ (sixth approximation)

$$A_6'' = 2465 - \frac{50}{100} \times \frac{(-.0048) \times 68}{.0025} + \frac{50 \times 0}{100} + \frac{.001752 \times 68}{.0025} = 2577.9$$

$A_6'' = 2577.9$ .... log 3.41126

$C_6 =$ .... log 0.87829

$\phi_6 = 15° \ 07' \ 10''$ .... tan $9.43166 - 10$

$Y_6 =$ .... log 3.72121

Constant .... log $5.01765 - 10$

$f_6 =$ .... log 0.05481 .... loglog $8.73886 - 10$

$C_1 =$ .... log 0.82346

$C_7 =$ .... log 0.87827 .... colog $9.12173 - 10$

$X = 57000$ .... log 4.75587

$Z_7 = 7544.0$ .... log 3.87760

$$A_7 = .06851 + \frac{.00170 \times 44}{100} - \frac{.00520 \times 50}{100} = .066658$$

$A_7 = .066658$ .... log $8.82386 - 10$

$C_7 =$ .... log 0.87827

$2\phi_7 = 30° \ 14' \ 30''$ .... sin $9.70213 - 10$

$\phi_7 = 15° \ 07' \ 15''$ (seventh approximation)

$$A_7'' = 2465 - \frac{50}{100} \times \frac{(-.0048) \times 68}{.0025} + \frac{50 \times 0}{100} + \frac{.001758 \times 68}{.0025} = 2578.1$$

$A_7'' = 2578.1$ .... log 3.41130
$C_7 =$ .... log 0.87827
$\phi_7 = 15^\circ\ 07'\ 15''$ .... tan 9.43170−10

$Y_7 =$ .... log 3.72127
Constant .... log 5.01765−10

$f_7 =$ .... log 0.05481 .... loglog 8.73892−10
$C_1 =$ .... log 0.82346

$C_8 =$ .... log 0.87827

As $C_8 = C_7$, the limit of accuracy has been reached and the work of approximation can be carried no further.

By the preceding work we have derived the following data for the remainder of the problem:

$$\phi = 15^\circ\ 07'\ 15'' \qquad Z = 7544.0 \qquad \log C = 0.87827$$

From Table II, with the above value of Z,

$$\log B' = .2652 + \frac{.0023 \times 44}{100} + \frac{.0026 \times 50}{100} = .26751$$

$$T' = 4.600 + \frac{.092 \times 44}{100} - \frac{.173 \times 50}{100} = 4.5540$$

$$u_\omega = 1086 - \frac{9 \times 44}{100} + \frac{30 \times 50}{100} = 1097.0$$

$B' =$ .... log 0.26751
$C =$ .... log 0.87827
$\phi = 15^\circ\ 07'\ 15''$ .... tan 9.43170−10 .. sec 0.01530 ...... cos 9.98470−10
$T' = 4.554$ .... log 0.65839
$u_\omega = 1097$ .... log 3.04021

$\omega = 26^\circ\ 34'\ 40''$ .... tan 9.69921−10 .... sec 0.04850

$T = 35.642$ .... log 1.55196

$v_\omega = 1184.2$ .... log 3.07341

RESULTS.

	By above computations.	As given in range table.
ϕ	15° 07′ 15″	15° 07′ 00″
ω	26° 34′ 50″	26° 35′ 00″
T	35.642 seconds	35.64 seconds
v_ω	1184.2 foot-seconds	1184 foot-seconds

NOTE TO FORM No. 1.—The number of approximations necessary to secure correct results increases with the range, therefore problems for shorter ranges will not involve so much labor as the one worked out on this form.

Form No. 2.

CHAPTER 8—EXAMPLE 8.

FORM FOR THE COMPUTATION OF THE VALUES OF THE ANGLE OF DEPARTURE (ϕ), ANGLE OF FALL (ω), TIME OF FLIGHT (T) AND STRIKING VELOCITY (v_ω) FOR A GIVEN RANGE, MAXIMUM ORDINATE AND ATMOSPHERIC CONDITION.

FORMULÆ.

$C=\frac{f}{\delta}K$; $Z=\frac{X}{C}$; $\sin 2\phi = AC$; $\tan\omega = B'\tan\phi$; $T=CT'\sec\phi$; $v_\omega = u_\omega \cos\phi \sec\omega$

PROBLEM.

Cal. = 8″; $V=2750$ f. s.; $w=260$ pounds; $c=0.61$; Range = 19,000 yards = 57,000 feet; Barometer = 28.33″; Thermometer = 82.7° F.; Maximum ordinate = 5261 feet.

From Table III, $\delta=.91396$; $\frac{2}{3}Y=3507'$, hence $f=1.0962$ from Table V.

K = (from Table VI)		log 0.82346		
$f=1.0962$		log 0.03989		
$\delta=.91396$	log 9.96093 − 10	colog 0.03907		
$C=$		log 0.90242	colog 9.09758 − 10	
$X=57000$			log 4.75587	
$Z=7136.0$			log 3.85345	

From Table II.

$$A=.06201+\frac{.00138\times 36}{100}-\frac{.00475\times 50}{100}=.060204$$

$$\log B'=.2551+\frac{.0027\times 36}{100}+\frac{.0014\times 50}{100}=.25677$$

$$T'=4.238+\frac{.089\times 36}{100}-\frac{.163\times 50}{100}=4.1885$$

$$u_\omega=1124-\frac{10\times 36}{100}+\frac{34\times 50}{100}=1137.4$$

A = .060204 ....log 8.77963 − 10
B' = ...log 0.25677
T' = 4.1885 ....log 0.62206
u_ω = 1137.4 ....log 3.05591
C = ...log 0.90242......................log 0.90242

2ϕ = 28° 44′ 38″ ....sin 9.68205 − 10
ϕ = 14° 22′ 19″ ....tan 9.40864 − 10..sec 0.01381..cos 9.98619 −

ω = 24° 50′ 08″ ....tan 9.66541 − 10.............sec 0.04215

T = 34.537 ....log 1.53829

v_ω = 1214.1 ....log 3.08425

RESULTS.

ϕ.........14° 22′ 19″.
ω.........24° 50′ 08″.
T.........34.537 seconds.
v_ω.........1214.1 foot-seconds.

NOTE TO FORM No. 2.—To solve the above problem with strict accuracy the maximum ordinate should not be used, but the approximation method should be employed as in Form No. 1, starting with a value of $C_1 = \frac{K}{\delta}$, and proceeding as shown on Form No. 1. In order to get a series of shorter problems for section room work, an approximately correct value of the maximum ordinate is given in the above data, from which, by the use of the value of f obtained from Table V, an approximately correct value of C may be determined without employing the longer method of Form No. 1. The results are sufficiently accurate to enable the process to be used for the purpose of instruction in the use of the formulæ subsequently employed.

Form No. 2.

CHAPTER 8—EXAMPLE 9.

FORM FOR THE COMPUTATION OF THE VALUES OF THE ANGLE OF DEPARTURE (ϕ), ANGLE OF FALL (ω), TIME OF FLIGHT (T) AND STRIKING VELOCITY (v_ω) FOR A GIVEN RANGE, CORRECTING FOR ALTITUDE BY A SERIES OF SUCCESSIVE APPROXIMATIONS, FOR GIVEN ATMOSPHERIC CONDITIONS—ALGER'S METHOD; NOT USING TABLE II.

FORMULÆ.

$$C=\frac{fw}{\delta c d^2}\,;\quad S_{u_\omega}=S_V+\frac{X}{C}\,;\quad \sin 2\phi=C\left(\frac{A_{u_\omega}-A_V}{S_{u_\omega}-S_V}-I_V\right);\quad T=C\sec\phi\,(T_{u_\omega}-T_V)\,;$$

$$\tan\omega=\frac{C}{2\cos^2\phi}\left(I_{u_\omega}-\frac{A_{u_\omega}-A_V}{S_{u_\omega}-S_V}\right);\quad v_\omega=u_\omega\cos\phi\sec\omega\,;\quad Y=\frac{gT^2}{8}$$

PROBLEM.

Cal. = 8″; $V=2750$ f. s.; $w=260$ pounds; $c=0.61$; Range = 19,000 yards = 57,000 feet; Variation in V due to wind = −25 f. s.; Effective initial velocity = 2725 f. s.; Barometer = 30.50″; Thermometer = 10° F.

$w=260$ … log 2.41497
$\delta=1.144$ … log 0.05843 … colog 9.94157 − 10
$c=0.61$ … log 9.78533 − 10 .. colog 0.21467
$d^2=64$ … log 1.80618 … colog 8.19382 − 10

$C_1=$ … log 0.76503 … colog 9.23497 − 10
$X=57000$ … log 4.75587

$\frac{X}{C}=S_{u_\omega}-S_V=\Delta S_1=$ 9791.2 … log 3.99084

$S_V=$ 2565.2 — From Table I.

$S_{u_\omega}=12356.4$ — $A_{u_\omega}=1673.19$ — $T_{u_\omega}=7.650$

$u_\omega=939.8$ — $A_V=$ 100.23 — $T_V=0.819$ — $I_V=.04832$

$\Delta A_1=1572.96$ — $\Delta T_1=6.831$

$\Delta A_1=1573$ … log 3.19673
$\Delta S_1=9791.2$ … log 3.99084 } Subtractive.

$\frac{\Delta A_1}{\Delta S_1}=.16065$ … log 9.20589 − 10
$I_V=.04832$

$\frac{\Delta A_1}{\Delta S_1}-I_V=.11233$ … log 9.05050 − 10

$\Delta T_1=6.831$ … log 0.83448
$C_1=$ … log 0.76503 … log 0.76503

$2\phi_1=40°\ 50'\ 16''$ … sin 9.81553 − 10
$\phi_1=20°\ 25'\ 08''$ (first approximation) … sec 0.02819

$T_1=$ … log 1.62770

$T_1^2=$ … log 3.25540
$g=32.2$ … log 1.50786
8 … log 0.90309 … colog 9.09691 − 10

$Y_1=7247.1$ … log 3.86017
$\frac{2}{3}Y_1=4831.4$, hence $f_1=1.1359$, from Table V

10. Fire is opened with eight 3" guns on a torpedo-boat coming head on when she is at 1500 yards range. She covers 100 yards every 7.5 seconds, and each gun fires once every 7.5 seconds. The mean lateral and vertical deviations are each 6 feet, and the target offered is 6 feet high by 15 feet wide. If an error of 100 yards in the sight setting displaces the mean point of impact 3 feet vertically, and the sights are all set for 1000 yards range, what is the probable number of hits while the boat advances to 500 yards range? *Answer.* 10+.

11. The turrets of a monitor steaming obliquely to the line of fire present a vertical target consisting of two rectangles, each 24 feet wide by 12 feet high, and 36 feet from center to center. If the mean errors of a gun be 12 yards laterally and 8 yards vertically, would it be better to aim at a turret or half way between them? *Answers.* 1st case, $P=.057$; 2d case, $P=.061$.

12. A gun has 30 shell, one of which, if landed in a certain gun position, would silence the gun contained therein. The gun pit is 10 yards in diameter, and the probability of hitting it with the gun in question is .05. What would be the probability of silencing the gun, using all the ammunition? *Answer.* $P=.785$.

13. The 12" guns of a ship made 68 per cent of hits on a target 15 feet high by 20 feet wide at 1700 yards range. What was the probable value of the mean deviations, vertical and lateral? Supposing the mean deviation to be proportional to the range, what percentage of hits would the same guns make on the same target at 3400 and at 5100 yards? *Answers.* 5 feet; 25.9 per cent; 12.6 per cent.

14. If the probability of hitting a target with a single shot is .05, what will be the probability of making at least two hits with 50 shots? *Answer.* .721.

15. What is the greatest value of the mean deviation of a gun consistent with a probability equal to .90 of its making at least one hit in a hundred shots on a gun port 2 feet wide by 4 feet high? *Answer.* 5.95 feet.

16. Compute the data for 10,000 yards contained in paragraph 427.
17. Compute the data for 13,000 yards contained in paragraph 427.
18. Compute the data for 15,000 yards contained in paragraph 427.
19. Compute the data for 18,000 yards contained in paragraph 427.
20. Compute the data for 10,000 yards contained in paragraph 428.
21. Compute the data for 13,000 yards contained in paragraph 428.
22. Compute the data for 15,000 yards contained in paragraph 428.
23. Compute the data for 18,000 yards contained in paragraph 428.

APPENDIX A.

FORMS TO BE EMPLOYED IN THE SOLUTION OF THE PRINCIPAL EXAMPLES GIVEN IN THIS TEXT BOOK.

NOTES.

1. In preparing these forms the problem taken has been the 8" gun (gun *K* in the tables) for which $V=2750$ f. s., $w=260$ pounds, $c=0.61$, generally for a range of 19,000 yards. More specific data is given at the head of each form.

2. In the problems under standard conditions, which should give the exact results contained in the range tables, it should be borne in mind that the latter are given, for the angle of departure to the nearest tenth of a minute, for the angle of fall to the nearest minute, for the time of flight to the nearest hundredth of a second, etc., only. Also that results given in the range tables are entered after the results of the computations have been plotted as a curve, and the faired results are those contained in the tables. Small discrepancies between the computed results and those given in the tables may therefore sometimes be expected.

3. Also, results obtained by direct computation are of course more accurate than those obtained by taking multiples of quantities given in the range tables, and small discrepancies may be expected in some such cases between computed results and those taken from the range tables.

INDEX TO FORMS IN APPENDIX A.

Form No.	Chapter No.	Example No.	Nature of Example.
1	8	7	Computing ϕ, etc., for a given range, by Ingalls' method of successive approximations.
2	8	8	Computing ϕ, etc., for a given range, by Ingalls' method, knowing f.
3	8	9	Computing ϕ, etc., for a given range, by Alger's method of successive approximations.
4	9	1	Computing the elements of the vertex for a given R and ϕ, by successive approximations.
5	9	2	Computing the elements of the vertex for a given R and ϕ, knowing f.
6	9	3	Deriving special formulæ for y and tan θ for a given trajectory.
7	9	4	Computing values of y and θ for given abscissæ in a given trajectory.
8	10	1	Computing R, etc., for a given ϕ, by successive approximations.
9	10	2	Computing R, etc., for a given ϕ, knowing f.
10A, 10B	11	1	Computing ϕ, ψ, θ, t and v for an elevated or depressed target.
11	12	2	Computing change in range resulting from a variation in initial velocity.
12	12	3	Computing change in range resulting from a variation in atmospheric density.
13	12	4	Computing change in range resulting from a variation in weight of projectile; method by direct computation.
14	12	5	Computing change in range resulting from a variation in weight of projectile; method by using Columns 10 and 12 of range table.
15	12	6	Computing change in position of point of impact in vertical plane through target resulting from a variation in the setting of the sight in range.
16	13	1	Computing the drift at a given range.
17	13	2	Computing sight-bar height and set of sliding leaf for a given range and deflection.
18	14	1	Computing the effect of wind.
19	14	2	Computing the effect of motion of the gun.
20	14	3	Computing the effect of motion of the target.
21	16	—	Computing the penetration of armor.
22	16	2	Range table computations, ϕ, etc.
23	16	3	Range table computations.
24	16	4	Range table computations.
25A, 25B	17	8	Wind and speed problems. Real wind.
26	17	9	Wind and speed problems. Apparent wind.
27A	17	13	Reduced velocity by range tables.
27B	17	14	Reduced velocity by computation
28	18	1 and 2	The calibration of a single gun.
29	19	1	The calibration of a ship's battery.

$\Delta A_6 = 1216.7$ .... log 3.08518 } Subtractive.
$\Delta S_6 = 8769.5$ .... log 3.94302

$\frac{\Delta A_6}{\Delta S_6} = .13873$ .... log 9.14216 − 10

$I_7 = .04832$

$\frac{\Delta A_6}{\Delta S_6} - I_7 = .09041$ .... log 8.95622 − 10

$\Delta T_6 = 5.777$ .... log 0.76170

$C_6 =$ .... log 0.81285 ...... log 0.81285

$2\phi_6 = 35^\circ\ 59'\ 10''$ .... sin 9.76907 − 10

$\phi_6 = 17^\circ\ 59'\ 35''$ (sixth approximation) .... sec 0.02177

$T_6 =$ .... log 1.59632

$T_6^2 =$ .... log 3.19264

$g = 32.2$ .... log 1.50786

8 .... colog 9.09691 − 10

$Y_6 = 6272.0$ .... log 3.79741

$\frac{2}{3} Y_6 = 4181.3$, hence $f_6 = 1.1164$

$f_6 = 1.1164$ .... log 0.04782

$C_1 =$ .... log 0.76503

$C_7 =$ .... log 0.81285

We see that $C_7 = C_6$. Therefore further work will be simply a repetition of the last two approximations, and the limit of accuracy has been reached.

From the preceding work, therefore, we have the following data for the remainder of the problem:

$u_\omega = 997.4$ $\quad \frac{\Delta A}{\Delta S} = .13873$ $\quad \Delta T = 5.777$ $\quad \log C = 0.81285$

$\frac{\Delta A}{\Delta S} = .13873$ $\quad I_{u_\omega} = .31477$ From Table I.

$I_V = .04832$ $\quad \frac{\Delta A}{\Delta S} = .13873$

$\frac{\Delta A}{\Delta S} - I_V = .09041$ $\quad I_{u_\omega} - \frac{\Delta A}{\Delta S} = .17604$

$\frac{\Delta A}{\Delta S} - I_V = .09041$ ......log 8.95622 − 10

$I_{u_\omega} - \frac{\Delta A}{\Delta S} = .17604$ .... log 9.24561 − 10

$\Delta T = 5.777$ ....log 0.76170

$C =$ ....log 0.81285...... log 0.81285......log 0.81285

2 ....colog 9.69897 − 10

$u_\omega = 997.45$ ....log 2.9[illegible]

$2\phi = 35° 59' 10''$ ..sin 9.76907 − 10

$\phi = 17° 59' 35''$ ....2 sec 0.04354......sec 0.02177..cos 9.9[illegible]

$\omega = 32° 18' 28''$ .... tan 9.80097 − 10..............sec 0.0[illegible]

$T = 39.4745$ ....log 1.59632

$v_\omega = 1122.4$ ....log 3.05[illegible]

RESULTS.

ϕ.........17° 59′ 35″.
ω.........32° 18′ 28″.
T.........39.4745 seconds.
v_ω.........1122.4 foot-seconds.

Note to Form No. 3.—The number of approximations necessary to secure correct results increases with the range, therefore problems for shorter ranges will not involve as much labor as the one worked out on this form.

Form No. 4.

CHAPTER 9—EXAMPLE 1.

FORM FOR THE COMPUTATION OF THE ELEMENTS OF THE VERTEX FOR A GIVEN ANGLE OF DEPARTURE (ϕ) AND GIVEN ATMOSPHERIC DENSITY, CORRECTING FOR ALTITUDE BY A SERIES OF SUCCESSIVE APPROXIMATIONS.

FORMULÆ.

$$C=\frac{fw}{\delta c d^2}=\frac{f}{\delta}K;\quad a_0'=A=\frac{\sin 2\phi}{C};\quad Y=A''C\tan\phi;$$

$$\log\log f=\log Y+5.01765-10;\quad x_0=Cx_0;\quad t_0=Ct_0'\sec\phi;\quad v_0=u_0\cos\phi$$

PROBLEM.

Cal. = 8″; V = 2750 f. s.; w = 260 pounds; c = 0.61; Range = 19,000 yards; ϕ = 15° 07′ 00″; Barometer = 29.42″; Thermometer = 75° F.

K =		log 0.82346
δ = .96314	log 9.98383 − 10	colog 0.01617
C_1 =	log 0.83963	colog 9.16037 − 10
2ϕ = 30° 14′ 00″		sin 9.70202 − 10
a_{0_1}' = .0728435		log 8.86239 − 10
$A_1'' = 2670 - \frac{50}{100}\times\frac{(-.0053)\times 69}{.0028}+\frac{50\times 0}{100}+\frac{.0001435\times 69}{.0028}=2738.8$		
A_1'' = 2738.8		log 3.43756
C_1 =		log 0.83963
ϕ = 15° 07′ 00″		tan 9.43158 − 10
Y_1 =		log 3.70877
Constant		log 5.01765 − 10
f_1 =	log 0.05326	loglog 8.72642 − 10
C_1 =	log 0.83963	
C_2 =	log 0.89289	colog 9.10711 − 10
2ϕ = 30° 14′ 00″		sin 9.70202 − 10
a_{0_2}' = .0644355		log 8.80913 − 10
$A_2'' = 2398 - \frac{50}{100}\times\frac{(-.0016)\times 67}{.0025}+\frac{50\times 0}{100}+\frac{.0020355\times 67}{.0025}=2514.2$		
A_2'' = 2514.2		log 3.40040
C_2 =		log 0.89289
ϕ = 15° 07′ 00″		tan 9.43158 − 10
Y_2 =		log 3.72487
Constant		log 5.01765 − 10
f_2 =	log 0.05527	loglog 8.74252 − 10
C_1 =	log 0.83963	
C_3 =	log 0.89490	colog 9.10510 − 10
2ϕ = 30° 14′ 00″		sin 9.70202 − 10
a_{0_3}' = .0641385		log 8.80712 − 10
$A_3'' = 2398 - \frac{50}{100}\times\frac{(-.0016)\times 67}{.0025}+\frac{50\times 0}{100}+\frac{.0017385\times 67}{.0025}=2506.2$		

$A_3''=2506.2$ .... log 3.39901
$C_3=$ .... log 0.89490
$\phi=15^\circ\ 07'\ 00''$ .... tan 9.43158 − 10

$Y_3=$ .... log 3.72549
Constant .... log 5.01765 − 10

$f_3=$ .... log 0.05535 ...... loglog 8.74314 − 10
$C_1=$ .... log 0.83963

$C_4=$ .... log 0.89498 ...... colog 9.10502 − 10
$2\phi=30^\circ\ 14'\ 00''$ .... sin 9.70202 − 10

$a_{0_4}'=.06417$ .... log 8.80704 − 10

$$A_4''=2398-\frac{50}{100}\times\frac{(-.0046)\times 67}{.0025}+\frac{50\times 0}{100}+\frac{.001727\times 67}{.0025}=2505.9$$

$A_4''=2505.9$ .... log 3.39896
$C_4=$ .... log 0.89498
$\phi=15^\circ\ 07'\ 00''$ .... tan 9.43158 − 10

$Y_4=5315.25$ .... log 3.72552
Constant .... log 5.01765 − 10

$f_4=$ .... log 0.05536 ...... loglog 8.74317 − 10
$C_1=$ .... log 0.83963

$C_5=$ .... log 0.89499 ...... colog 9.10501 − 10
$2\phi=30^\circ\ 14'\ 00''$ .... sin 9.70202 − 10

$a_{0_5}'=.0641256$ .... log 8.80703 − 10

$$A_5''=2398-\frac{50}{100}\times\frac{(-.0046)\times 67}{.0025}+\frac{50\times 0}{100}+\frac{.0017256\times 67}{.0025}=2505.9$$

$A_5''=A_4''$, therefore the limit of accuracy has been reached, and we have for the data for the remainder of the problem:

$a_0'=.0641256$ $\qquad \log C=0.89499$

$$z_0=4100+\frac{100}{.0025}\left[.0017256-\frac{50\times(-.0046)}{100}\right]=4261.0$$

$$t_0'=2.036+\frac{.063\times 61}{100}-\frac{.079\times 50}{100}=2.0349$$

$$u_0=1595-\frac{21\times 61}{100}+\frac{66\times 50}{100}=1615.2$$

$C=$ .... log 0.89499 ...... log 0.89499
$\phi=15^\circ\ 07'\ 00''$ .... sec 0.01529 ...... cos 9.98471 − 10
$z_0=4261$ .... log 3.62951
$t_0'=2.0349$ .... log 0.30854
$u_0=1615.2$ .... log 3.20822

$x_0=33458$ .... log 4.52450

$t_0=16.551$ .... log 1.21882

$v_0=1559.3$ .... log 3.19293

RESULTS.

x_0 .... 11152.7 yards.
$y_0=Y$ .... 5315.25 feet.
t_0 .... 16.551 seconds.
v_0 .... 1559.3 foot-seconds.

NOTE TO FORM No. 4.—The number of approximations necessary to secure correct results increases with the range, therefore problems for shorter ranges will not involve as much labor as the one worked out on this form.

Form No. 6.

CHAPTER 9—EXAMPLE 3.

FORM FOR THE DERIVATION OF THE SPECIAL EQUATIONS FOR COMPUTING THE VALUES OF THE ORDINATE AND OF THE ANGLE OF INCLINATION OF THE CURVE TO THE HORIZONTAL AT ANY POINT OF THE TRAJECTORY WHOSE ABSCISSA IS KNOWN, WITH ATMOSPHERIC CONDITIONS STANDARD; CORRECTING FOR ALTITUDE.

FORMULÆ.

$$A=\frac{\sin 2\phi}{C}\ ;\ y=\frac{\tan\phi}{A}(A-a)x;\ \tan\theta=\frac{\tan\phi}{A}(A-a')$$

PROBLEM.

Cal.=8″; V=2750 f. s.; w=260 pounds; c=0.61; Range=19,000 yards; ϕ=15° 07′ 00″; log C=0.87827 (value corrected for f from work in example on Form No. 1).

C=	...........................colog	9.12173 − 10		
2ϕ=30° 14′ 00″	.... sin	9.70202 − 10		
A=.066643	.... log	8.82375 − 10	......colog	1.17625
ϕ=15° 07′ 00″	....		tan	9.43158 − 10
$\frac{\tan\phi}{A}$=4.0535	....		log	0.60783

RESULTS.

$$y=4.0535(.066643-a)x$$
$$\tan\theta=4.0535(.066643-a')$$

NOTE TO FORM No. 6.—To determine the above equations with accuracy for any given trajectory in air, the value of log C must be determined by the process of approximation given on Form No. 1, for the range for which the special equations are desired. This value of log C must then be used as was done in the above problem. An approximate result may be obtained by determining the value of f by means of the maximum ordinate given in the range table, from which the value of K may be approximately corrected for altitude.

Form No. 7.

CHAPTER 9—EXAMPLE 4.

FORM FOR THE COMPUTATION, FOR ANY GIVEN TRAJECTORY, OF THE ABSCISSA AND ORDINATE OF THE VERTEX AND OF THE ORDINATE AND OF THE ANGLE OF INCLINATION OF THE CURVE TO THE HORIZONTAL AT ANY POINT OF THE TRAJECTORY WHOSE ABSCISSA IS KNOWN, HAVING GIVEN THE SPECIAL EQUATIONS FOR y AND TAN θ FOR THE GIVEN TRAJECTORY.

FORMULÆ.

$$y_0 = Y = A''C \tan\phi;\quad x_0 = Cz_0;\quad y = \frac{\tan\phi}{A}(A-a)x;\quad \tan\theta = \frac{\tan\phi}{A}(A-a')$$

PROBLEM.

Cal. = 8″; $V = 2750$ f. s.; $w = 260$ pounds; $c = 0.61$; Range = 19,000 yards = 57,000 feet; $\log C = 0.87827$; $\phi = 15°\ 07'\ 00''$; $y = 4.0535(.066643 - a)x$; $\tan\theta = 4.0535(.066643 - a')$; $x_1 = 8000$ yards = 24,000 feet; $x_2 = 16,000$ yards = 42,000 feet.

For Vertex: From data, $A = .066643$, and for vertex $a_0' = A$, therefore, from Table II for $a_0' = .066643$.

$$A'' = 2465 - \frac{50}{100} \times \frac{(-.0048) \times 68}{.0025} + \frac{50 \times 0}{100} + \frac{.001743 \times 68}{.0025} = 2577.7$$

$$z_0 = 4200 + \frac{100}{.0025}\left[.001743 - \frac{(-.0048) \times 50}{100}\right] = 4365.7$$

$A'' = 2577.7$ .... log 3.41123
$C =$ .... log 0.87827 .... log 0.87827
$\phi = 15°\ 07'\ 00''$ .... tan 9.43158 − 10
$z_0 = 4365.7$ .... log 3.64005
$x_0 = 32,985$ feet = 10,995 yards .... log 4.51832
$y_0 = Y = 5261.1$ feet .... log 3.72108

For x_1 = 8000 yards = 24,000 feet:

$C =$ .... colog 9.12173 − 10
$x_1 = 24000$ .... log 4.38021
$z = 3176.4$ .... log 3.50194

$$a = .01781 + \frac{.00075 \times 76.4}{100} - \frac{.00131 \times 50}{100} = .017728$$

$$a' = .0408 + \frac{.0019 \times 76.4}{100} - \frac{.0031 \times 50}{100} = .040702$$

$A - .066643$ $\qquad$ $A = .066643$
$a = .017728$ $\qquad$ $a' = .040702$

$A - a = .048915$ .... log 8.68945 − 10
$A - a' = .025941$ .... log 8.41399 − 10
$\frac{\tan\phi}{A} = 4.0535$ .... log 0.60783 .... log 0.60783
$x_1 = 24000$ .... log 4.38021
$y_1 = 4758.7$ .... log 3.67749
$\theta = 6°\ 02'\ 10''$ .... tan 9.02182 − 10

For $x_2 = 16{,}000$ yards $= 48{,}000$ feet:

$C =$ .... colog 9.12173 − 10
$x_2 = 48000$ .... log 4.68124

$z = 6352.8$ .... log 3.80297

$$a = .05030 + \frac{.00137 \times 52.8}{100} - \frac{.00386 \times 50}{100} = .049093$$

$$a' = .1358 + \frac{.0044 \times 52.8}{100} - \frac{.0105 \times 50}{100} = .132873$$

$A = .066643$ $A = .066643$
$a = .049093$ $a' = .132873$

$A - a = .017550$ .... log 8.24428 − 10
$A - a' = (-).066230$ .... $(-)$log 8.82105 − 10

$\frac{\tan\phi}{A} = 4.0535$ .... log 0.60783 .... log 0.60783
$x_2 = 48000$ .... log 4.68124

$y_2 = 3414.7$ .... log 3.53335

$\theta_2 = (-)15°\ 01'\ 39''$ .... $(-)$tan 9.42888 − 10

For point of fall, $x = X = 19{,}000$ yards $= 57{,}000$ feet:

$C =$ .... colog 9.12173 − 10
$x = 57000$ .... log 4.75587

$z = 7544.0$ .... log 3.87760

$$a = .06851 + \frac{.00170 \times 44}{100} - \frac{.00520 \times 50}{100} = .066658$$

$$a' = .1946 + \frac{.0055 \times 44}{100} - \frac{.0140 \times 50}{100} = .190020$$

$A = .066643$ $A = .066643$
$a = .066658$ $a' = .190020$

$A - a = (-).000015$ .... $(-)$log 5.17609 − 10
$A - a' = (-).123377$ .... $(-)$log 9.09125 − 10

$\frac{\tan\phi}{A} = 4.0535$ .... log 0.60783 .... log 0.60783

$x = 57000$ .... log 4.75587

$y_\omega = (-)3.4657$ feet .... $(-)$log 0.53979

$\theta_\omega = (-)26°\ 34'\ 15''$ .... $(-)$tan 9.69908 − 10

RESULTS.

For vertex.	For $x_1 = 8000$ yards.	For $x_2 = 16{,}000$ yards.	For point of fall.
$x_0 = 10{,}995$ yards	$y_1 = 4758.7$ feet	$y_2 = 3414.7$ feet	$y_\omega = (-)3.4657$ feet
$y_0 = Y = 5261.1$ feet	$\theta_1 = 6°\ 02'\ 10''$	$\theta_2 = (-)15°\ 01'\ 39''$	$\theta_\omega = (-)26°\ 34'\ 15''$

Note to Form No. 7.—In the above problem of course the ordinate at the point of fall should be zero. The angle θ at the point of fall should equal $-\omega$; for which the work gives $\theta = (-)26°\ 34'\ 15''$, and the range table gives $\omega = 26°\ 35'\ 00''$. These comparisons give an idea of the degree of accuracy of the above method.

Form No. 8.

CHAPTER 10—EXAMPLE 1.

FORM FOR THE COMPUTATION OF THE VALUES OF THE RANGE (X), ANGLE OF FALL (ω), TIME OF FLIGHT (T) AND STRIKING VELOCITY (v_ω) FOR A GIVEN ANGLE OF DEPARTURE (ϕ) AND ATMOSPHERIC CONDITION, CORRECTING FOR ALTITUDE BY A SERIES OF SUCCESSIVE APPROXIMATIONS.

FORMULÆ.

$$C=\frac{f}{\delta}K;\ a_\phi'=A=\frac{\sin 2\phi}{C};\ X=CZ;\ Y=A''C\tan\phi;\ \text{loglog} f=\log Y+5.01765-10;$$

$$\tan\omega=B'\tan\phi;\ T=CT'\sec\phi;\ v_\omega=u_\omega\cos\phi\sec\omega$$

PROBLEM.

Cal.$=8''$; $V=2750$ f. s.; $w=260$ pounds; $c=0.61$; $\phi=15°\ 07'\ 00''$;
Barometer$=29.00''$; Thermometer$=82°$ F.

$K=$ .... log 0.82346
$\delta=.937$ ....log 9.97174−10..colog 0.02826

$C_1=$ .... log 0.85172......colog 9.14828−10
$2\phi=30°\ 14'\ 00''$ .... sin 9.70202−10

$a_{\phi_1}'=.0708435$ .... log 8.85030−10

$$A_1''=2601-\frac{50}{100}\times\frac{(-.0051)\times 69}{.0027}+\frac{50\times 0}{100}+\frac{.0008435\times 69}{.0027}=2687.7$$

$A_1''=2687.7$ ....log 3.42938
$C_1=$ ....log 0.85172
$\phi=15°\ 07'\ 00''$ ....tan 9.43158−10

$Y_1=$ ....log 3.71268
Constant ....log 5.01765−10

$f_1=$ ....log 0.05374......loglog 8.73033−10
$C'_1=$ ....log 0.85172

$C_2=$ ....log 0.90546...... colog 9.09454−10
$2\phi=30°\ 14'\ 00''$ .... sin 0.70202−10

$a_{\phi_2}'=.0625985$ .... log 8.79656−10

$$A_2''=2398-\frac{50}{100}\times\frac{(-.0046)\times 67}{.0025}+\frac{50\times 0}{100}+\frac{.0001985\times 67}{.0025}=2465.0$$

$A_2''=2465$ ....log 3.39182
$C_2=$ ....log 0.90546
$\phi=15°\ 07'\ 00''$ ....tan 9.43158−10

$Y_2=$ ....log 3.72886
Constant ....log 5.01765−10

$f_2=$ ....log 0.05378......loglog 8.74651−10
$C'_1=$ ....log 0.85172

$C_3=$ ....log 0.90750...... colog 9.09250−10
$2\phi=30°\ 14'\ 00''$ .... sin 9.70202−10

$a_{\phi_3}'=.062304$ .... log 8.79452−10

$$A_3''=2331-\frac{50}{100}\times\frac{(-.0045)\times 67}{.0024}+\frac{50\times 0}{100}+\frac{.002304\times 67}{.0024}=2458.1$$

$A_3'' = 2458.1$ .... log 3.39060
$C_3 =$ .... log 0.90750
$\phi = 15°\ 07'\ 00''$ .... tan 9.43158 − 10

$Y_3 =$ .... log 3.72968
Constant .... log 5.01765 − 10

$f_3 =$ .... log 0.05589 ...... loglog 8.74733 − 10
$C_1 =$ .... log 0.85172

$C_4 =$ .... log 0.90761 ...... colog 9.09239 − 10
$2\phi = 30°\ 14'\ 00''$ .... sin 9.70202 − 10

$a_{0_4}' = .0622885$ .... log 8.79441 − 10

$$A_4'' = 2331 - \frac{50}{100} \times \frac{(-.0045)\times 67}{.0024} + \frac{50\times 0}{100} + \frac{.0022885 \times 67}{.0024} = 2457.7$$

$A_4'' = 2457.7$ .... log 3.39053
$C_4 =$ .... log 0.90761
$\phi = 15°\ 07'\ 00''$ .... tan 9.43158 − 10

$Y_4 =$ .... log 3.72972
Constant .... log 5.01765 − 10

$f_4 =$ .... log 0.05589 ...... loglog 8.74737 − 10
$C_1 =$ .... log 0.85172

$C_5 =$ .... log 0.90761

which equals log C_4; therefore the limit of approximation has been reached, and we have the following data:

$A = .0622885 \qquad \log C = 0.90761 \qquad \phi = 15°\ 07'\ 00''$

$$Z = 7100 + \frac{100}{.00158}\left[.002785 - \frac{50 \times (-.00475)}{100}\right] = 7267.9$$

$$\log B' = .2578 + \frac{.0025 \times 67.9}{100} + \frac{.0017 \times 50}{100} = .26035$$

$$T' = 4.327 + \frac{.090 \times 67.9}{100} - \frac{.165 \times 50}{100} = 4.3056$$

$$u_\omega = 1114 - \frac{10 \times 67.9}{100} + \frac{33 \times 50}{100} = 1123.7$$

$C =$ .... log 0.90761 .... log 0.90761
$Z = 7267.9$ ...... log 3.86141
$\phi = 15°\ 07'\ 00''$ .... tan 9.43158 − 10 .. sec 0.01529 .. cos 9.98471 − 10
$B' =$ .... log 0.26035
$T' = 4.3056$ .... log 0.63403
$u_\omega = 1123.7$ .... log 3.05065

$X = 58752$ ...... log 4.76902

$\omega = 26°\ 11'\ 44''$ .... tan 9.69193 − 10 .... sec 0.04707

$T = 36.052$ .... log 1.55693

$v_\omega = 1208.9$ .... log 3.08243

RESULTS.

R .... 19,584 yards.	T .... 36.052 seconds.
ω .... 26° 11′ 44″.	v_ω .... 1208.9 foot-seconds.

Note to Form No. 8.—The number of approximations necessary to secure correct results increases with the angle of departure, therefore problems for a smaller angle of departure will not involve so much labor as the one worked out on the form.

Form No. 9.

CHAPTER 10—EXAMPLE 2.

FORM FOR THE COMPUTATION OF THE VALUES OF THE HORIZONTAL RANGE (R), ANGLE OF FALL (ω), TIME OF FLIGHT (T) AND STRIKING VELOCITY (v_ω) FOR A GIVEN ANGLE OF DEPARTURE (ϕ), ATMOSPHERIC CONDITION AND MAXIMUM ORDINATE.

FORMULÆ.

$$C=\frac{f}{\delta}K;\ A=\frac{\sin 2\phi}{C};\ X=CZ;\ \tan\omega=B'\tan\phi;\ T=CT'\sec\phi;$$

$$v_\omega=u_\omega\cos\phi\sec\omega$$

PROBLEM.

Cal. = 8″; V = 2750 f. s.; w = 260 pounds; c = 0.61; ϕ = 15° 07′ 00″; Barometer = 29.00″; Thermometer = 82° F.; Maximum ordinate = 5400 feet; $\frac{2}{3}Y$ = 3600 feet.

K = ... log 0.82346
f = 1.099 .... log 0.04100
δ = .937 ....log 9.97174 − 10..colog 0.02826
C = ... log 0.89272......colog 9.10728 − 10
2ϕ = 30° 14′ 00″ .... sin 9.70202 − 10
A = .064461 .... log 8.80930 − 10

$$Z=7200+\frac{100}{.00161}\left[.000871-\frac{50\times(-.00486)}{100}\right]=7405.0$$

$$\log B'=.2620+\frac{.0024\times5}{100}+\frac{.0023\times50}{100}=.26407$$

$$T'=4.508+\frac{.092\times5}{100}-\frac{.170\times50}{100}=4.4276$$

$$u_\omega=1095-\frac{9\times5}{100}+\frac{31\times50}{100}=1110.1$$

C = ...log 0.89272..................log 0.89272
Z = 7405 ....log 3.86953
ϕ = 15° 07′ 00″ ....tan 9.43158 − 10..sec 0.01529..cos 9.98471 − 10
B' = ...log 0.26407
T' = 4.4276 ....log 0.64617
u_ω = 1110.1 ....log 3.04536
X = 57843 ......log 4.76225
ω = 26° 23′ 24″ ....tan 9.69565 − 10..............sec 0.04780
T = 35.824 ....log 1.55418
v_ω = 1196.4 ....log 3.07787

RESULTS.

	From above work.	From work with same data on Form No. 8.
R	19,281 yards	19,584 yards
ω	26° 23′ 24″	26° 11′ 41″
T	35.824 seconds	36.052 seconds
v_ω	1196.4 foot-seconds	1208.9 foot-seconds

NOTE TO FORM No. 9.—To solve the above problem with strict accuracy it must be done as shown on Form No. 8. In order to get a series of shorter problems for section room work, an approximately correct value of the maximum ordinate is given and employed as above. The comparison of results by the two methods given at the bottom of the above work gives an idea of the degree of inaccuracy resulting from the employment of the method given on this form.

Form No. 10A.

CHAPTER 11—EXAMPLE 1 (WHEN y IS POSITIVE).

FORM FOR THE COMPUTATION OF THE VALUES OF THE ANGLE OF ELEVATION (ψ) (THE JUMP BEING CONSIDERED AS ZERO), ANGLE OF INCLINATION TO THE HORIZONTAL AT THE POINT OF IMPACT (θ), AND TIME OF FLIGHT TO (t) AND REMAINING VELOCITY AT (v) THE POINT OF IMPACT WHEN FIRING AT A TARGET AT A KNOWN HORIZONTAL DISTANCE FROM THE GUN AND AT A KNOWN VERTICAL DISTANCE ABOVE THE HORIZONTAL PLANE OF THE GUN, FOR GIVEN ATMOSPHERIC CONDITIONS.

FORMULÆ.

$$C=\frac{f}{\delta}K;\ \tan p=\frac{y}{x};\ z=\frac{X}{C};\ \sin 2\phi_a=aC;\ \sin(2\phi-p)=\sin p(1+\cot p\sin 2\phi_a);$$

$$A=\frac{\sin 2\phi}{C};\ \tan\theta=\frac{\tan\phi}{A}(A-a');\ t=Ct'\sec\phi;\ v=u\cos\phi\sec\theta;\ \psi=\phi-p$$

PROBLEM.

Cal.=8″; V=2750 f. s.; w=260 pounds; c=0.61; Gun below target 900 feet; Horizontal distance=18,000 yards=54,000 feet; Maximum ordinate=4470 feet; Barometer=29.00″; Thermometer=40° F.; $\frac{2}{3}Y$=2980 feet.

K= .... log 0.82346
f=1.0804 .... log 0.03358
δ=1.021 ....log 0.00903......colog 9.99097−10

C= .... log 0.84801......colog 9.15199−10
y=900.............log 2.95424......Subtractive.
x=54000...........log 4.73239 .... log 4.73239

p=0° 57′ 18″ ......tan 8.22185−10

z=7662.6 .... log 3.88438

$$a=.07021+\frac{.00172\times 62.6}{100}-\frac{.00532\times 50}{100}=.068627$$

$$a'=.2001+\frac{.0056\times 62.6}{100}-\frac{.0143\times 50}{100}=.19646$$

$$u=1077-\frac{8\times 62.6}{100}+\frac{29\times 50}{100}=1086.5$$

$$t'=4.692+\frac{.093\times 62.6}{100}-\frac{.175\times 50}{100}=4.6627$$

$C=$ .... log 0.84801
$a=.068627$ .... log 8.83649 − 10

$2\phi_\omega=$ .... sin 9.68450 − 10
$p=0°\ 57'\ 18''$ .... cot 1.77815

$\cot p \sin 2\phi_\omega=29.016$ .... log 1.46265
$\cot p \sin 2\phi_\omega=30.016$ .... log 1.47735
$p=\ 0°\ 57'\ 18''$ .... sin 8.22185 − 10

$2\phi-p=30°\ 01'\ 02''$ .... sin 9.69920 − 10
$p=\ 0°\ 57'\ 18''$

$2\phi=30°\ 58'\ 20''$ .... sin 9.71149 − 10
$\phi=15°\ 29'\ 10''$
$p=\ 0°\ 57'\ 18''$

$\psi=14°\ 31'\ 52''$
$C=$ .... colog 9.15199 − 10

$A=.07303$ .... log 8.86348 − 10

$A=$ .07303
$a'=$ .19646

$-a'=(-).12343$ .... (−)log 9.09143 − 10
$\phi=15°\ 29'\ 10''$ .... tan 9.44258 − 10 .. sec 0.01606 .. cos 9.98394 − 10
$A=.07303$ .... log 8.86348 − 10 .. colog 1.13652
$t'=4.6627$ .... log 0.66864
$u=1086.5$ .... log 3.03603
$C=$ .... log 0.84801

$\theta=(-)25°\ 05'\ 38''$ .... (−)tan 9.67053 − 10 .... sec 0.04306

$t=34.097$ .... log 1.53271

$v=1156.2$ .... log 3.06303

The range table gives for $R=18{,}500$ yards ...... $\phi=14°\ 26.9'$
for $R=18{,}600$ yards ...... $\phi=14°\ 34.9'$

Therefore, for an angle of elevation of $\psi=14°\ 31.9'$, the sight setting in range would be $R=18500+\frac{5\times 100}{8}=18562.5$ yards.

RESULTS.

ψ .... 14° 31′ 52″.
θ .... (−)25° 05′ 38″.
t .... 34.097 seconds.
v .... 1156.2 foot-seconds.
Setting of sight in range .... 18,550 yards.

NOTE TO FORM No. 10A.—Note that the work on this form, for a target higher than the gun, is the same as that on Form No. 10B for the same problem with the gun higher than the target, down to and including the determination of the value of $\cot p \sin 2\phi_\omega$, except that the sign of that quantity and of the position angle (p) is positive in Form No. 10A, and negative in Form No. 10B. Compare the results obtained on these two forms, having in mind the remarks made in paragraphs 191, 192 and 193 of Chapter 11 of the text.

Form No. 10B.

CHAPTER 11—EXAMPLE 1 (WHEN y IS NEGATIVE).

FORM FOR THE COMPUTATION OF THE VALUES OF THE ANGLE OF ELEVATION (ψ) (THE JUMP BEING CONSIDERED AS ZERO), ANGLE OF INCLINATION TO THE HORIZONTAL AT THE POINT OF IMPACT (θ), AND THE TIME OF FLIGHT TO (t) AND REMAINING VELOCITY AT (v) THE POINT OF IMPACT WHEN FIRING AT A TARGET AT A KNOWN HORIZONTAL DISTANCE FROM THE GUN AND AT A KNOWN VERTICAL DISTANCE BELOW THE HORIZONTAL PLANE OF THE GUN, FOR GIVEN ATMOSPHERIC CONDITIONS.

FORMULÆ.

$$C=\frac{f}{\delta}K;\ \tan p=\frac{y}{x};\ z=\frac{X}{C};\ \sin 2\phi_z=aC;\ \sin(2\phi-p)=\sin p(1+\cot p\sin 2\phi_z);$$

$$A=\frac{\sin 2\phi}{C};\ \tan\theta=\frac{\tan\phi}{A}(A-a');\ t=Ct'\sec\phi;\ v=u\cos\phi\sec\theta;\ \psi=\phi-p$$

PROBLEM.

Cal.=8″; V=2750 f. s.; w=260 pounds; c=0.61; Gun above target 900 feet: Horizontal distance=18,000 yards=54,000 feet; Maximum ordinate=4470 feet; Barometer=29.00″; Thermometer=40° F.; $\frac{2}{3}Y$=2980 feet.

K= .... log 0.82346
f=1.0804 .... log 0.03358
δ=1.021 ....log 0.00903..colog 9.99097−10

C= .... log 0.84801......colog 9.15199−10
y=(−)900.........(−)log 2.95424 } Subtractive.
x=54000 ....log 4.73239 } .... log 4.73239

p=(−)0° 57′ 18″...(−)tan 8.22185−10

z=7662.6 .... log 3.38438

$$a=.07021+\frac{.00172\times 62.6}{100}-\frac{.00532\times 50}{100}=.068627$$

$$a'=.2001+\frac{.0056\times 62.6}{100}-\frac{.0143\times 50}{100}=.19646$$

$$u=1077-\frac{8\times 62.6}{100}+\frac{29\times 50}{100}=1086.5$$

$$t'=4.692+\frac{.093\times 62.6}{100}-\frac{.175\times 50}{100}=4.6627$$

$C=$ .... log 0.84801

$a=.068627$ .... log 8.83649 − 10

$2\phi_s=$ .... sin 9.68450 − 10

$p=(-)0°\ 57'\ 18''$ .... (−) cot 1.77815

$\cot p \sin 2\phi_s=(-)29.016$ .... (−) log 1.46265

$1+\cot p \sin 2\phi_s=(-)28.016$ .... (−) log 1.44741

$p=(-)0°\ 57'\ 18''$ .... (−) sin 8.22185 − 10

$2\phi-p=\ \ 27°\ 50'\ 10''$ .... (+) sin 9.66926 − 10

$p=(-)\ \ 0°\ 57'\ 18''$

$2\phi=\ \ 26°\ 52'\ 52''$ .... sin 9.65528 − 10

$\phi=\ \ 13°\ 26'\ 26''$

$p=(-)\ \ 0°\ 57'\ 18''$

$\psi=\ \ 14°\ 23'\ 44''$

$C=$ .... colog 9.15199 − 10

$A=.06416$ .... log 8.80727 − 10

$A=\ \ .06416$

$a'=\ \ .19646$

$1-a'=(-).13230$ .... (−) log 9.12156 − 10

$\phi=13°\ 26'\ 26''$ .... tan 9.37836 − 10 .. sec 0.01206 .. cos 9.98794 − 10

$A=.06416$ .... log 8.80726 − 10 .. colog 1.19273

$t'=4.6627$ .... log 0.66864

$u=1086.5$ .... log 3.03603

$C=$ .... log 0.84801

$\theta=(-)26°\ 13'\ 58''$ .... (−) tan 9.69265 − 10 .... sec 0.04720

$t=33.784$ .... log 1.52871

$v=1178.0$ .... log 3.07117

The range table gives for $R=18{,}400$ yards...... $\phi=14°\ 19.0'$
for $R=18{,}500$ yards...... $\phi=14°\ 26.9'$

Therefore, for an angle of elevation of $\psi=14°\ 23.7'$, the sight setting in range would be $R=18400+\dfrac{4.7\times 100}{7.9}=18459.5$ yards.

RESULTS.

ψ .... 14° 23′ 44″.

θ .... (−) 26° 13′ 58″.

t .... 33.784 seconds.

v .... 1178.0 foot-seconds.

Setting of sight in range .... 18,450 yards.

NOTE TO FORM No. 10B.—Note that the work on this form, for a target lower than the gun, is the same as that on Form No. 10A for the same problem with the target higher than the gun, down to and including the determination of the value of $\cot p \sin 2\phi_s$, except that the sign of that quantity and of the angle of position (p) is minus in Form No 10B and plus in Form No 10A. Compare the results obtained in the two cases, having in mind the remarks made in paragraphs 191, 192 and 193 of Chapter 11 of the text.

Form No. 11.

CHAPTER 12—EXAMPLE 2.

FORM FOR THE COMPUTATION OF THE CHANGE IN RANGE RESULTING FROM A VARIATION FROM STANDARD IN THE INITIAL VELOCITY, OTHER CONDITIONS BEING STANDARD.

FORMULÆ.

$$C=\frac{fw}{cd^2}=fK;\ Z=\frac{X}{C};\ \Delta R_V=\frac{\Delta_{VA}}{B}\times\frac{\delta V}{\Delta V}\times R$$

PROBLEM.

Case 1.—Correcting for Altitude by Table V.

Cal.=8"; $V=2750$; $w=260$ pounds; $c=0.61$; Range=19,000 yards=57,000 feet; Maximum ordinate=5261 feet; Variation from standard of $V=+75$ f. s.; $\frac{2}{3}Y=3507$ feet.

$K=$ ....log 0.82346
$f=1.0962$ ....log 0.03989
$C=$ ....log 0.86335......colog 9.13665−10
$X=57000$ .... log 4.75587
$Z=7807.6$ .... log 3.89252

$$\Delta_{VA}=.00556+\frac{.00012\times7.6}{100}-\frac{.00049\times50}{100}=.0053241$$

$$B=.1377+\frac{.0040\times7.6}{100}-\frac{.0093\times50}{100}=.13335$$

$\Delta_{VA}=.0053241$ .... log 7.72625−10
$R=19000$ .... log 4.27875
$B=.13335$ ....log 9.12500−10......colog 0.87500
$\delta V=(+)75$ .... log 1.87506
$\Delta V=100$ ....log 2.00000..........colog 8.00000−10
$\Delta R_V=(+)568.93$ yards .... log 2.75506

PROBLEM.

Case 2.—Using Corrected Value of C Obtained by Successive Approximations on Form No. 1.

Cal.=8"; $V=2750$ f. s.; $w=260$ pounds; $c=0.61$; Range=19,000 yards=57,000 feet; log $C=0.87827$; Variation from standard of $V=+75$ f. s.

$C=$ ....colog 9.12173−10
$X=57000$ .... log 4.75587
$Z=7544.0$ .... log 3.87760

$$\Delta_{VA}=.00520+\frac{.00012\times44}{100}-\frac{.00046\times50}{100}=.0050228$$

$$B=.1261+\frac{.0038\times44}{100}-\frac{.0038\times50}{100}=.12337$$

$\Delta_{V_A}=.0050228$		log 7.70094 − 10
$R=19000$		log 4.27875
$B=.12337$	log 9.09121 − 10	colog 0.90879
$\delta V=(+)75$		log 1.87506
$\Delta V=100$	log 2.00000	colog 8.00000 − 10
$\Delta R_V=(+)580.15$		log 2.76354

Note to Form No. 11.—The method of Case 2 is of course the more accurate, and gives the range table result. The method shown in Case 1 is introduced to give practice in the use of this formula without the necessity of taking up the successive approximation method in order to determine the value of *C* accurately.

Form No. 12.

CHAPTER 12—EXAMPLE 3.

FORM FOR THE COMPUTATION OF THE CHANGE IN RANGE RESULTING FROM A VARIATION FROM STANDARD IN THE DENSITY OF THE ATMOSPHERE, OTHER CONDITIONS BEING STANDARD.

FORMULÆ.

$$C=\frac{fw}{cd^2}\ ;\ Z=\frac{X}{C}\ ;\ \Delta R_\delta=-\frac{(B-A)R}{B}\times\frac{\Delta C}{C}$$

PROBLEM.

Case 1.—Correcting for Altitude by Table V.

Cal.=8″; $V=2750$ f. s.; $w=260$ pounds; $c=0.61$; Range=19,000 yards=57,000 feet; Maximum ordinate=5261 feet; Variation in density=+15 per cent; $\frac{2}{3}Y=3507$ feet.

$K=$ .... log 0.82346
$f=1.0962$ .... log 0.03989

$C=$ .... log 0.86335 ...... colog 9.13665 − 10
$X=57000$ .... log 4.75587

$Z=7807.6$ .... log 3.89252

$A=.07368+\frac{.00178\times 7.6}{100}-\frac{.00556\times 50}{100}=.071035$

$B=.1377+\frac{.0040\times 7.6}{100}-\frac{.0093\times 50}{100}=.133354$

$B=.133354$
$A=.071035$

$B-A=.062319$ .... log 8.79462 − 10
$R=19000$ .... log 4.27875
$B=.13335$ .... log 9.12500 − 10 ...... colog 0.87500
$\frac{\Delta C}{C}=.15$ .... log 9.17609 − 10
$\Delta R_\delta=(-)1331.9$ .... log 3.12446

PROBLEM.

Case 2.—Using Corrected Value of C Obtained by Successive Approximations on Form No. 1.

Cal.=8″; $V=2750$ f. s.; $w=260$ pounds; $c=0.61$; Range=19,000 yards=57,000 feet; log $C=0.87827$; Variation in density =+15 per cent.

$C=$ .... colog 9.12173 − 10
$X=57000$ .... log 4.75587

$Z=7544.0$ .... log 3.87760

$A=.06851+\frac{.00170\times 44}{100}-\frac{.00520\times 50}{100}=.066658$

$B=.1261+\frac{.0038\times 44}{100}-\frac{.0088\times 50}{100}=.123372$

$B = .123372$

$A = .066658$

$B - A = .056714$ .... log 8.75369 − 10

$R = 19000$ .... log 4.27875

$B = .12337$ .... log 9.09121 − 10 ...... colog 0.90879

$\frac{\Delta C}{C} = .15$ .... log 9.17609 − 10

$\Delta R_s = (-)\,1310.1$ .... log 3.11732

Note to Form No. 12.—The method of Case 2 is of course the more accurate, and gives the range table result. The method shown in Case 1 is introduced to give practice in the use of this formula without the necessity for taking up the successive approximation method in order to determine the value of *C* accurately.

Form No. 13.

CHAPTER 12—EXAMPLE 4.

FORM FOR THE COMPUTATION OF THE CHANGE IN RANGE RESULTING FROM A VARIATION FROM STANDARD IN THE WEIGHT OF THE PROJECTILE, OTHER CONDITIONS BEING STANDARD. DIRECT METHOD WITHOUT USING COLUMNS 10 AND 12 OF THE RANGE TABLES.

FORMULÆ.

$$C=\frac{fw}{cd^2};\quad \delta V=-0.36\frac{\Delta w}{w}V;$$

$$\Delta R_W=\Delta R_W'+\Delta R_W''=\frac{\Delta_{VA}}{B}\times\frac{\delta V}{\Delta V}\times R+\frac{(B-A)R}{B}\times\frac{\Delta w}{w}$$

PROBLEM.

Case 1.—Correcting for Altitude by Table V.

Cal. = 8″; $V=2750$ f. s.; $w=260$ pounds; $c=0.61$; Range = 19,000 yards = 57,000 feet; Maximum ordinate = 5261 feet; Variation in weight = +10 pounds; $\frac{2}{3}Y=3507$ feet.

$K=$	log 0.82346	
$f=1.0962$	log 0.03989	
$C=$	log 0.86335	colog 9.13665 − 10
$X=57000$		log 4.75587
$Z=7807.6$		log 3.89252

$$\Delta_{VA}=.00556+\frac{.00012\times 7.6}{100}-\frac{.00049\times 50}{100}=.00532412$$

$$A=.07368+\frac{.00178\times 7.6}{100}-\frac{.00556\times 50}{100}=.071035$$

$$B=.1377+\frac{.0040\times 7.6}{100}-\frac{.0093\times 50}{100}=.133354$$

$\Delta w=+10$		log 1.00000
$w=260$		colog 7.58503 − 10
$V=2750$		log 3.43933
.36		log 9.55630 − 10
$\delta V=(-)$		log 1.58066
$\Delta_{VA}=.0053241$		log 7.72625 − 10
$R=19000$		log 4.27875
$B=.13335$	log 9.12500 − 10	colog 0.87500
$\delta V=(-)$		(−) log 1.58066
$\Delta V'=100$	log 2.00000	colog 8.00000 − 10
$\Delta R_w'=(-)288.84$		log 2.46066
$B=.133354$		
$A=.071035$		
$B-A=.062319$		log 8.79462 − 10
$R=19000$		log 4.27875
$B=.13335$		colog 0.87500
$\Delta w=+10$		log 1.00000
$w=260$		colog 7.58503 − 10
$\Delta R_w''=(+)341.51$		log 2.53340
$\Delta R_w=+\ \ 52.67$ yards,		

hence an increase in weight gives an increase in range for this gun at this range, therefore this quantity would carry a negative sign in Column 11 of the range table for this range.

PROBLEM.

Case 2.—Using Corrected Value of C Obtained by Successive Approximations on Form No. 1.

Cal.=8"; $V=2750$ f. s.; $w=260$ pounds; $c=0.61$; Range=19,000 yards=57,000 feet; $\log C=0.87827$; Variation in weight=+10 pounds.

$C=$	colog	9.12173−10
$X=57000$	log	4.75587
$Z=7544.0$	log	3.87760

$$\Delta_{VA}=.00520+\frac{.00012\times 44}{100}-\frac{.00046\times 50}{100}=.0050228$$

$$A=.06851+\frac{.00170\times 44}{100}-\frac{.00520\times 50}{100}=.066658$$

$$B=.1261+\frac{.0038\times 44}{100}-\frac{.0088\times 50}{100}=.123372$$

$\Delta w=+10$	log	1.00000
$w=260$	colog	7.58503−10
$V=2750$	log	3.43933
.36	log	9.55630−10
$\delta V=(-)$	log	1.58066
$\Delta_{VA}=.0050228$	log	7.70094−10
$R=19000$	log	4.27875
$B=.12337$ ....log 9.09121−10	colog	0.90879
$\delta V=(-)$	log	1.58066
$\Delta V=100$ ....log 2.00000	colog	8.00000−10
$\Delta R_w'=(-)294.53$	log	2.46914

$B=.123372$
$A=.066658$

$B-A=.056714$	log	8.75369−10
$R=19000$	log	4.27875
$B=.12337$	colog	0.90879
$\Delta_w=+10$	log	1.00000
$w=260$	colog	7.58503−10
$\Delta R_w''=(+)335.94$	log	2.52626

$\Delta R_w=(+)\ 41.44$

hence an increase in weight gives an increase in range for this gun at this range, and this quantity would carry a negative sign in Column 11 of the range table for this range.

NOTE TO FORM No. 13.—The method of Case 2 is of course the more accurate, and gives practically the range table results. The method shown in Case 1 is introduced to give practice in the use of these formulæ without the necessity for taking up the successive approximation method in order to determine the value of C accurately.

Form No. 14.

CHAPTER 12—EXAMPLE 5.

FORM FOR THE COMPUTATION OF THE CHANGE IN RANGE RESULTING FROM A VARIATION FROM STANDARD IN THE WEIGHT OF THE PROJECTILE, OTHER CONDITIONS BEING STANDARD. SHORT METHOD. USING DATA CONTAINED IN COLUMNS 10 AND 12 OF THE RANGE TABLES.

FORMULÆ.

$$\delta V = 0.36\,\frac{\Delta w}{w}\,V;\ \Delta R_w = \Delta R_w' + \Delta R_w'' = \Delta R_V \times \frac{\delta V}{\delta V'} + \frac{\Delta w}{w} \times \Delta R_C \times \Delta\delta$$

PROBLEM.

Cal. = 8″; $V = 2750$ f. s.; $w = 260$ pounds; $c = 0.61$; Range = 19,000 yards; From Column 10 of range table, $\Delta R_{50V} = 387$ yards; From Column 12 of range table, $\Delta R_{10C} = 874$ yards; Variation in weight = +10 pounds.

$\Delta w = +10$	log	1.00000
$w = 260$	colog	7.58503 − 10
$V = 2750$	log	3.43933
.36	log	9.55630 − 10
$\delta V = (-)$	log	1.58066
$\Delta R_{50V} = 387$	log	2.58771
$\delta V = (-)$	(−)log	1.58066
$\delta V' = 50$	colog	8.30103 − 10
$\Delta R_w' = (-)294.71$	(−)log	2.46940
$\Delta R_{10C} = 874$	log	2.94151
$\Delta w = +10$	log	1.00000
$w = 260$	colog	7.58503 − 10
$\Delta\delta = 10$	log	1.00000
$\Delta R_w'' = (+)336.15$	log	2.52654

$\Delta R_w = (+)\ 41.44$ yards,

hence an increase in weight gives an increase in range for this gun at this range. therefore this quantity would carry a negative sign in Column 11 of the range table at this range.

Note to Form No. 14.—The method gives practically the range table result.

Form No. 15.

CHAPTER 12—EXAMPLE 6.

FORM FOR THE COMPUTATION OF THE CHANGE IN THE VERTICAL POSITION OF THE POINT OF IMPACT IN THE VERTICAL PLANE THROUGH THE TARGET RESULTING FROM A VARIATION IN THE SETTING OF THE SIGHT IN RANGE, ALL OTHER CONDITIONS BEING STANDARD.

FORMULA.

$$H = \Delta X \tan \omega$$

PROBLEM.

Cal. = 8″; V = 2750 f. s.; w = 260 pounds; c = 0.61; Range = 19,000 yards; ω = 26° 35′ 00″ (from range table); Variation in setting of sight = +150 yards.

ΔX = 450	........................log	2.65321
ω = 26° 35′ 00″	........................tan	9.69932 − 10
H = +225.18 feet	........................log	2.35253

Form No. 16.

CHAPTER 13—EXAMPLE 1.

FORM FOR COMPUTATION OF THE DRIFT.

FORMULA.

$$D=\frac{\mu}{n}\times\frac{\lambda}{h}\times\frac{C^2D'}{\cos^2\phi}\times\text{Multiplier}$$

PROBLEM.

Case 1.—Correcting for Altitude by Table V.

Cal.=8"; V=2750 f. s.; w=260 pounds; c=0.61; Range=19,000 yards=57,000 feet; ϕ=15° 07′ 00″ (from range table); Maximum ordinate=5261 feet (from range table); $\frac{2}{3}Y$=3507 feet.

K=	log	0.82346		
f=1.0962	log	0.03989		
C=	log	0.86335	colog	9.13665−10
X=57000			log	4.75587
Z=7807.6			log	3.89252

$$D'=484+\frac{22\times7.6}{100}-\frac{38\times50}{100}=466.67$$

D'=466.67			log	2.66901
Multiplier=1.5			log	0.17609
μ=.53			log	9.72428−10
n=25	log	1.39794	colog	8.60206−10
$\frac{\lambda}{h}$=.32			log	9.50515−10
C=	log	0.86335	2 log	1.72670
ϕ=15° 07′ 00″	sec	0.01529	3 sec	0.04587
D=281.29 yards			log	2.44916

PROBLEM.

Case 2.—Using Corrected Value of C and ϕ Obtained by Successive Approximations on Form No. 1.

Cal.=8"; V=2750 f. s.; w=260 pounds; c=0.61; Range=19,000 yards=57,000 feet; log C=0.87827; ϕ=15° 07′ 15″ (from Form No. 1).

C=	colog	9.12173−10
X=57000	log	4.75587
Z=7544.0	log	3.87760

$$D'=422+\frac{20\times44}{100}-\frac{33\times50}{100}=414.3$$

$D' = 414.3$		log 2.61731
Multiplier $= 1.5$		log 0.17609
$\mu = .53$		log 9.72428 − 10
$n = 25$	log 1.39794	colog 8.60206 − 10
$\frac{\lambda}{\lambda} = .32$		log 9.50515 − 10
$C =$	log 0.87827	2 log 1.75654
$\phi = 15°\ 07'\ 15''$	sec 0.01530	3 sec 0.04590
$D = 267.50$ yards		log 2.42733

NOTE TO FORM No. 16.—The method of Case 2 is of course the more accurate, and gives practically the range table result. The method shown in Case 1 is introduced to give practice in the use of this formula without the necessity for taking up the successive approximation method in order to determine the exact values of C and ϕ.

Form No. 17.

CHAPTER 13—EXAMPLE 2.

FORM FOR COMPUTATION OF SIGHT BAR HEIGHTS AND SETTING OF SLIDING LEAF.

(Permanent Angle $= 0°$.)

FORMULÆ.

$$h = l \tan \phi \qquad d = \frac{l \sec \phi}{R} D$$

PROBLEM.

Cal. $= 8''$; $V = 2750$ f. s.; $w = 260$ pounds; $c = 0.61$; Range $= 19{,}000$ yards; $\phi = 15°\ 07'\ 00''$; Sight radius $= 41.125''$; Deflection $= 266$ yards right.

$\phi = 15°\ 07'\ 00''$		tan 9.43158 − 10	sec 0.01529
$l = 41.125$		log 1.61411	log 1.61411
$R = 19000$	log 4.27875		colog 5.72125 − 10
$D = 266$			log 2.42488
$h = 11.110''$		log 1.04569	
$d = 0.59639''$ left			log 9.77553 − 10

Form No. 18.

CHAPTER 14—EXAMPLE 1.

FORM FOR THE COMPUTATION OF THE EFFECT OF WIND.

FORMULÆ.

$$W_x = \frac{W \times 6080}{60 \times 60 \times 3}\,;\quad n = \frac{V^2 \sin 2\phi}{gX}\,;$$

$$\Delta R_W = W_x\left(T - \frac{n}{2n-1} \times \frac{X \cos\phi}{V}\right);\quad D_W = W_z\left(T - \frac{X}{V \cos\phi}\right)$$

PROBLEM.

Cal.=8″; V=2750 f. s.; w=260 pounds; c=0.61; Range=19,000 yards=57,000 feet; ϕ=15° 07′ 00″; T=35.6 seconds (ϕ and T from range table); Wind component along line of fire=15 knots an hour with the flight; Wind component perpendicular to the line of fire=10 knots an hour to the right.

15	log 1.17609	
10		log 1.00000
6080	log 3.78390	log 3.78390
60×60×3=10800	colog 5.96658−10	colog 5.96658−10
W_x=	log 0.92657	
W_z=		log 0.75048
V=2750		2 log 6.87866
2ϕ=30° 14′ 00″		sin 9.70202−10
X=57000	log 4.75587	colog 5.24413−10
g=32.2		colog 8.49214−10
n=2.0746		log 0.31695
$2n$=4.1492		
$2n-1$=3.1492	log 0.49820	colog 9.50180−10
n=2.0746		log 0.31695
ϕ=15° 07′ 00		cos 9.98471−10
X=57000		log 4.75587
V=2750		colog 6.56067−10
13.182		log 1.12000
T=35.640		
22.458		log 1.35137
W_x=		log 0.92657
ΔR_W=189.64 yards over		log 2.27794
X=57000		log 4.75587
V=2750		colog 6.56067−10
ϕ=15° 07′ 00″		sec 0.01529
21.47		log 1.33183
T=35.64		
14.17		log 1.15137
W_z=		log 0.75048
D_W=79.771 yards right		log 1.90185

Form No. 19.

CHAPTER 14—EXAMPLE 2.

FORM FOR THE COMPUTATION OF THE EFFECT OF THE MOTION OF THE GUN.

FORMULÆ.

$$G_s = \frac{G \times 6080}{60 \times 60 \times 3}\,;\quad n = \frac{V^2 \sin 2\phi}{gX}\,;$$

$$\Delta R_G = \frac{n}{2n-1} \times \frac{X \cos\phi}{V} G_s\,;\quad D_G = \frac{X}{V \cos\phi} G_s$$

PROBLEM.

Cal. = 8"; V = 2750 f. s.; w = 260 pounds; c = 0.61; Range = 19,000 yards = 57,000 feet; ϕ = 15° 07′ 00″ (from range table); Speed component in line of fire = 9 knots an hour against the flight; Speed component perpendicular to the line of fire = 18 knots an hour to the left.

9	log 0.95424	
18		log 1.25527
6080	log 3.78390	log 3.78390
60 × 60 × 3 = 10800	colog 5.96658 – 10	colog 5.96658 – 10
G_s = ...	log 0.70472	
G_s = ...		log 1.00575
V = 2750		2 log 6.87866
2ϕ = 30° 14′ 00″		sin 9.70202 – 10
g = 32.2		colog 8.49214 – 10
X = 57000	log 4.75587	colog 5.24413 – 10
n = 2.0746		log 0.31695
$2n$ = 4.1492		
$2n - 1$ = 3.1492	log 0.49820	colog 9.50180 – 10
n = 2.0746		log 0.31695
X = 57000		log 4.75587
ϕ = 15° 07′ 00″		cos 9.98471 – 10
V = 2750		colog 6.56067 – 10
G_s = ...		log 0.70472
ΔR_G = 66.791 yards short		log 1.82472
X = 57000		log 4.75587
V = 2750		colog 6.56067 – 10
ϕ = 15° 07′ 00″		sec 0.01529
G_s = ...		log 1.00575
D_G = 217.56 yards left		log 2.33758

Form No. 20.

CHAPTER 14—EXAMPLE 3.

FORM FOR THE COMPUTATION OF THE EFFECT OF MOTION OF THE TARGET.

FORMULÆ.

$$T_s = \frac{T \times 6080}{60 \times 60 \times 3}\ ;\ \Delta R_T = T_s T;\ D_T = T_s T$$

PROBLEM.

Cal.=8″; $V=2750$ f. s.; $w=260$ pounds; $c=0.61$; Range=19,000 yards; Time of flight=35.64 seconds (from range table); S_s=Speed component in line of fire in knots per hour=17 knots with flight; S_s=Speed component perpendicular to line of fire in knots per hour=19 knots to left.

$T=35.64$	log 1.55194......	log 1.55194
$S_s=17$	log 1.23045	
$S_s=19$		log 1.27875
6080	log 3.78390......	log 3.78390
$60\times60\times3=10800$	colog 5.96658−10..	colog 5.96658−10
$\Delta R_T=341.09$ yards over.................	log 2.53287	
$D_T=381.22$ yards right..................................		log 2.58117

NOTE TO FORM No. 20.—Note that this example is simply the arithmetical problem of determining how far the target will move in the given direction at the given speed during the time of flight; the speeds being given in knots per hour, and the results required in yards for the time of flight.

Form No. 21.

CHAPTER 16—EXAMPLE 1.

FORM FOR THE COMPUTATION OF THE PENETRATION OF HARVEYIZED (E_1) AND OF FACE-HARDENED (E_2) ARMOR BY CAPPED PROJECTILES.

FORMULÆ.

Harveyized Armor (Davis).

$$E_1^{0.8}=\frac{vw^{0.5}}{K'd^{0.5}}$$

$\log K'=3.25312$

Face-Hardened Armor (De Marre).

$$E_2^{0.7}=\frac{vw^{0.5}}{Kd^{0.75}}\times\frac{1}{\text{De Marre's Coefficient}}$$

$\log K=3.00945$

PROBLEM.

Cal. = 8″; $V=2750$ f. s.; $w=260$ pounds; $c=0.61$; Range = 19,000 yards; $v_\omega=1184$ f. s. (from range table); De Marre's coefficient = 1.5.

$w=260$	log 2.41497	0.5 log 1.20748
$v_\omega=1184$		log 3.07335
$v_\omega w^{0.5}=$	log 4.28083	log 4.28083
$K'=$	colog 6.74688 − 10	
$K=$		colog 8.99055 − 10
$d=8$ … log 0.90309	0.5 colog 9.54846 − 10	0.75 colog 9.32268 − 10
$E_1^{0.8}=$	log 0.57617	
	10	
	8 ⌊ log 5.76170	
$E_1=5.2506''$	log 0.72021	
		log 0.59406
		10
		7 ⌊ log 5.94060
		log 0.84866
De Marre's coefficient = 1.5		colog 9.82391 − 10
$E_2=4.7051''$		log 0.67257

Form No. 22.

CHAPTER 16—EXAMPLE 2.

FORM FOR THE COMPUTATION OF ϕ, ω, T, v_ω, D, Y, AND THE PENETRATION, GIVEN R AND f; ATMOSPHERIC CONDITIONS STANDARD.*

FORMULÆ.

$$C=\frac{fw}{cd^2}=fK;\ Z=\frac{X}{C};\ \sin 2\phi=AC;\ \tan\omega=B'\tan\phi;\ v_\omega=u_\omega\cos\phi\sec\omega$$

$$D=\frac{\mu\lambda}{nh}\times\frac{C^2D'}{\cos^2\phi};\ E_1^{0.8}=\frac{v_\omega w^{0.5}}{K'd^{0.5}}\ \text{(Harveyized—Davis)}$$

$$Y=A''C\tan\phi;\ (E_2\times1.5)^{0.7}=\frac{v_\omega w^{0.5}}{Kd^{0.75}}\ \text{(Face hardened—De Marre)}$$

PROBLEM.

Cal. = 8″; $V=2750$ f. s.; $w=260$ pounds; $c=0.61$; Range = 19,000 yards = 57,000 feet; $f=1.1345$.

log K 0.82346
log f 0.05481
log C 0.87827
colog C .... 9.12173 — 10
log X 4.75587
log Z 3.87760
$Z = 7544.0$

(2) $\phi = 15° 07' 15''$
log C 0.87827
log A .... 8.82386 — 10
log sin 2ϕ .... 9.70213 — 10
$2\phi = 30° 14' 30''$

(3) $\omega = 26° 34' 40''$
log B' 0.26751
log tan ϕ .... 9.43170 — 10
log tan ω .... 9.69921 — 10

(4) $T = 35.642$ seconds
log C 0.87827
log T' 0.65839
log sec ϕ 0.01530
log T 1.55196

(5) $v_\omega = 1184.2$
log u_ω 3.04021
log cos ϕ .... 9.98470 — 10
log sec ω 0.04850
log v_ω 3.07341

(6) $D = 267.50$
log μ (.53) .... 9.72428 — 10
colog n (25) .... 8.60206 — 10
log $\frac{\lambda}{h}$ (.32) .... 9.50515 — 10
log constant .... 7.83149 — 10
log C^2 .... 1.75654
log $\sec^2\phi$ 0.04590
log D' 2.61731
2.25124
log 1.5 (if used) 0.17609
log D 2.42733

$$A = .06851+\frac{.00170\times44}{100}-\frac{.00520\times50}{100}=.066658$$

$$A'' = 2465-\frac{50}{100}\times\frac{(-.0048)\times68}{.0025}+\frac{50\times0}{100}+\frac{.001758\times68}{.0025}=2578.1$$

$$\log B' = .2652+\frac{.0023\times44}{100}-\frac{.0026\times50}{100}=.267512$$

$$T' = 4.600+\frac{.092\times44}{100}-\frac{.173\times50}{100}=4.55398$$

$$u_\omega = 1086-\frac{9\times44}{100}+\frac{30\times50}{100}=1097.04$$

$$D' = 422+\frac{20\times44}{100}-\frac{33\times50}{100}=414.30$$

(8) $Y = 5263.4$ feet
log A'' 3.41130
log C 0.87827
log tan ϕ .... 9.43170 — 10
log Y 3.72127

(9) Harveyized armor. $E_1 = 5.2515$ in.
log $w^{0.5}$ 1.20748
colog K' .... 6.74688 — 10
colog $d^{0.5}$ .... 9.54846 — 10
log v_ω 3.07341
log $E_1^{0.8}$ 0.57623
log E_1 .... 0.72028

(9) Face hardened. $E_2 = 4.706$ in.
log $w^{0.5}$ 1.20748
colog K .... 6.99055 — 10
colog $d^{0.75}$ .... 9.32268 — 10
log v_ω 3.07341
log $(E_2\times1.5)^{0.7}$ 0.59412
log $(E_2\times1.5)$ 0.84874
colog 1.5 .... 9.82391 — 10
log E_2 .... 0.67265

RESULTS.

$\phi = 15° 07' 15''$	$D = 267.50$ yards.
$\omega = 26° 34' 40''$.	$Y = 5263.4$ feet.
$T = 35.642$ seconds.	$E_1 = 5.252$ inches.
$v_\omega = 1184.2$ f. s.	$E_2 = 4.706$ inches.

* If we have a problem in which f is not known, then we must first determine the value of ϕ for the given range by the use of Form No. 1 in paragraph 273, Chapter 16.

Form No. 23.

CHAPTER 16—EXAMPLE 3.

FORM FOR THE COMPUTATION OF S, ΔR_V, ΔR_C, ΔR_w FOR A GIVEN R AND f.

FORMULÆ.

$$C=\frac{fw}{cd^2}=fK;\; Z=\frac{X}{C};\; S=\frac{h}{3}\cot\omega\left(\frac{1+\frac{h}{3}\cot\omega}{R}\right);\; \Delta R_V=\frac{\Delta_{VA}}{B}\times\frac{\delta V}{\Delta V}\times R;$$

$$\Delta R_\delta=\frac{(B-A)R}{B}\times\frac{\Delta\delta}{\delta};\; \delta V=0.36\,\frac{\Delta w}{w}V;$$

$$\Delta R_w=\Delta R_w'+\Delta R_w''=\Delta R_V\times\frac{\delta V}{\delta V'}+\frac{\Delta w}{w}\times\Delta R_\delta\times\Delta\delta$$

PROBLEM.

Cal. = 8"; $V=2750$ f. s.; $w=260$ pounds; $c=0.61$; Range = 19,000 yards = 57,000 feet; $\phi=15°\ 07'\ 15''$; $\omega=26°\ 34'\ 40''$; $f=1.1345$; $h=20$ feet; $\Delta w=\pm 5$ pounds.

log K 0.82346
log f 0.05481
log C 0.87827
colog C .... 9.12173 — 10
log X 4.75587
log Z 3.87760
$Z = 7544.0$

(7) $S = 13.335$ yards

log $\frac{h}{3}$ (6.6667) 0.82391
log cot ω 0.30079
log (6.6667 cot ω) 1.12470
colog R .... 5.72125 — 10
log $\frac{6.6667}{R}$ cot ω .... 6.84595 — 10
$\frac{6.6667}{R}$ cot ω = .00070
$1+\frac{6.6667}{R}$ cot ω
= 1.0007 .... log 0.00030
6.6667 cot ω .... log 1.12470
log S 1.12500

(10) $\Delta R_V = 386.77$ yards

log Δ_{VA} .... 7.70094 — 10
colog B 0.90879
log δV (50) 1.69897
colog ΔV (100) .... 8.00000 — 10
log R 4.27875
log ΔR_{wV} 2.58745

RESULTS.

S = 13.335 yards.
ΔR_{wV} = 386.77 yards.
ΔR_δ = 873.43 yards.
ΔR_w = ± 20.70 yards.

$\Delta_{VA} = .00520 + \frac{.00012\times 44}{100} - \frac{.00046\times 50}{100} = .0050228$

$A = .06851 + \frac{.00170\times 44}{100} - \frac{.00520\times 50}{100} = .066658$

$B = .1261 + \frac{.0038\times 44}{100} - \frac{.0088\times 50}{100}$
$= .123372$

(12) $\Delta R_\delta = 873.43$ yards

log ($B - A$) .... 8.75369 — 10
log R 4.27875
colog B 0.90879
log (0.1) .... 9.00000 — 10
log ΔR_δ 2.94123

(11) $\Delta R_w = \pm 20.70$ yards

log Δw 0.69897
colog w .... 7.58503 — 10
log V 3.43933
log 0.36 .... 9.55630 — 10
log δV 1.27963

log ΔR_{wV} 2.58745
log δV 1.27963
colog $\delta V'$ (50) .... 8.30103 — 10
log $\Delta R_w'$ 2.16811

log $\Delta R_{w\delta}$ 2.94123
log Δw 0.69897
colog w .... 7.58503 — 10
log $\Delta\delta$ (10) 1.00000
log $\Delta R_w''$ 2.22523
$\Delta R_w' = \mp 147.27$
$\Delta R_w'' = \pm 167.97$
$\Delta R_w = \pm\ 20.70$

An increase in weight gives an increase in range for this gun at this range, therefore this quantity would carry a negative sign in Column 11 of the range table for this range.

Form No. 24.

CHAPTER 16—EXAMPLE 4.

FORM FOR THE COMPUTATION OF EFFECTS OF WIND AND OF MOTION OF GUN AND TARGET; ALSO CHANGE IN HEIGHT OF POINT OF IMPACT FOR VARIATION IN SETTING OF SIGHT IN RANGE FOR A GIVEN θ AND f.

FORMULÆ.

$$n=\frac{V^2 \sin 2\phi}{gX};\quad \Delta R_W=W_s\left(T-\frac{n}{2n-1}\times\frac{X\cos\phi}{V}\right);\quad D_W=W_s\left(T-\frac{X}{V\cos\phi}\right);$$

$$\Delta R_G=\left(\frac{n}{2n-1}\times\frac{X\cos\phi}{V}\right)G_s;\quad D_G=\frac{X}{V\cos\phi}G_s;\quad \Delta R_T=T_sT;$$

$$D_T=T_sT;\quad W_s=\text{Etc.}=\frac{W\times 6080}{3\times 60\times 60}$$

PROBLEM.

Cal. = 8″; V = 2750 f. s.; w = 260 pounds; c = 0.61; Range = 19,000 yards = 57,000 feet; ϕ = 15° 07′ 15″; T = 35.642 seconds; ω = 26° 34′ 40″.

Value of n

log V^2	6.87866
log sin 2ϕ	9.70213 — 10
colog g (32.2)	8.49214 — 10
colog X	5.24413 — 10
log n	0.31706

n = 2.0752
$2n$ = 4.1504
$2n - 1$ = 3.1504

(13) ΔR_W = 151.74 yards

log n	0.31706
log X	4.75587
log cos ϕ	9.98470 — 10
colog $(2n-1)$	9.50163 — 10
colog V	6.56067 — 10
log $\frac{nX\cos\phi}{(2n-1)V}$	1.11993

$\frac{nX\cos\phi}{(2n-1)V}$ = 13.180
T = 35.642

log	22.462	1.35145
log W_s		0.82966
log ΔR_W.		2.18111

(16) D_W = 95.740 yards

log X	4.75587
colog V	6.56067 — 10
log sec ϕ	0.01530
log $\frac{X}{V\cos\phi}$	1.33184

$\frac{X}{V\cos\phi}$ = 21.470
T = 35.642

log	14.172	1.1[illegible]143
log W_s		0.82966
log D_W		1.98109

Value of W_s, W_s, G_s, G_s, T_s, T_s for a component of 12 knots.

log 12	1.07918
log 6080	3.78390
colog 3	9.52288 — 10
colog $(60)^2$	6.44370 — 10
log W_s, etc.	0.82966

(14) ΔR_G = 89.040 yards

log $\frac{nX\cos\phi}{(2n-1)V}$	1.11993
log G_s	0.82966
log ΔR_G	1.94959

(17) D_G = 145.04 yards

log $\frac{X}{V\cos\phi}$	1.33184
log G_s	0.82966
log D_G	2.16150

(15) $\Delta R_T = D_T$ = 240.78 yards

log $T_s = T_s$	0.82966
log T	1.55196
log $\Delta R_T = D_T$.	2.38162

(19) H = 150.08 feet

log X = 300	2.47712
log tan ω	9.69921 — 10
log H_{300}	2.17633

RESULTS.

n = 2.0752.
ΔR_W = 151.74 yards.
D_W = 95.740 yards.
ΔR_G = 89.040 yards.
D_G = 145.04 yards.
$\Delta R_T = D_T$ = 240.78 yards.
H = 150.08 feet.

Form No. 25A.

CHAPTER 17—EXAMPLE 8.

FORM FOR THE SOLUTION OF REAL WIND AND SPEED PROBLEMS.

PROBLEM.

Cal. = 8″; V = 2750 f. s.; w = 260 pounds; c = 0.61; Range = 7500 yards; Real wind, direction from, 225° true; velocity, 15 knots an hour; Motion of gun, course, 355° true; speed, 20 knots an hour; Motion of target, course, 320° true; speed, 25 knots an hour; Target at moment of firing, 75° true; distant, 7500 yards; Barometer = 30.00″; Thermometer = 10° F.; Temperature of powder = 75° F.; Weight of projectile = 263 pounds.

Temperature of powder, $\frac{-35}{10} \times 15 = -52.5$ foot-seconds.

Use Table IV to correct for density. Use traverse tables for resolution of wind and speeds.

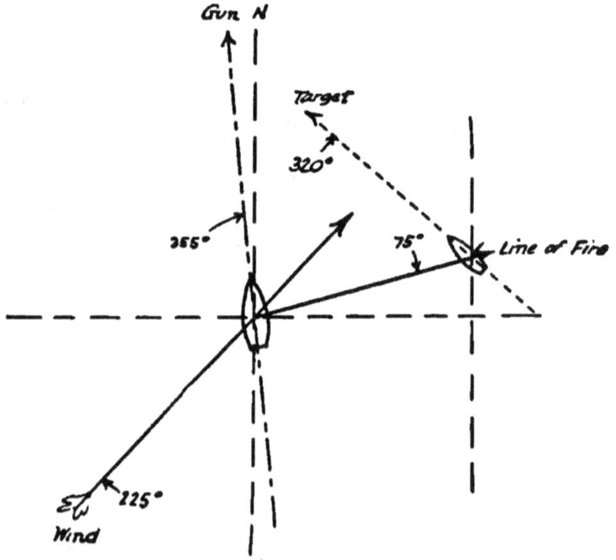

Cause of error. Speed of or variation in.	Affects.	Formulæ.	Errors in— Range. Short. Yds.	Over. Yds.	Deflection. Right. Yds.	Left. Yds.
Gun	Range.....	$20 \cos 80 \times \frac{44}{12} = \frac{3.5 \times 44}{12}$	....	12.8	....	....
	Deflection..	$20 \sin 80 \times \frac{55}{12} = \frac{19.7 \times 55}{12}$	....	....	....	90.3
Target	Range.....	$25 \cos 65 \times \frac{68}{12} = \frac{10.6 \times 68}{12}$	....	60.1	....	....
	Deflection..	$25 \sin 65 \times \frac{68}{12} = \frac{22.7 \times 68}{12}$	....	....	128.6	....
Wind	Range.....	$15 \cos 30 \times \frac{24}{12} = \frac{13 \times 24}{12}$	....	26.0	....	....
	Deflection..	$15 \sin 30 \times \frac{13}{12} = \frac{7.5 \times 13}{12}$	....	....	....	8.1
Initial velocity...	Range.....	$52.5 \times \frac{207}{50}$	217.4	....	....	....
w................	Range.....	$3 \times \frac{43}{5}$	25.8	....	....	....
Density...........	Range.....	1.25×180	225.0	....	....	....
			468.2	98.9	128.6	98.4
$30.2 \text{ yards} \times \frac{12}{68} = 5.3$ knots on deflection scale.			98.9		98.4	
			369.3		30.2	

Set sights at:

Exactly..........in range, 7869.3 yards; in deflection, 44.7 knots.

Actually.........in range, 7850.0 yards; in deflection, 45.0 knots.

Remember to shoot short rather than over.

Form No. 25B.

CHAPTER 17—EXAMPLE 8.

FORM FOR THE SOLUTION OF REAL WIND AND SPEED PROBLEMS.

PROBLEM.

Cal. = 8"; $V = 2750$ f. s.; $w = 260$ pounds; $c = 0.61$; Range = 7000 yards; Real wind, direction from, 160° true; velocity, 20 knots an hour; Motion of gun, course, 260° true; speed, 18 knots an hour; Motion of target, course, 170° true; speed, 23 knots an hour; Target at moment of firing bearing, 115° true; distant, 7000 yards; Barometer = 29.00"; Thermometer = 85° F.; Temperature of powder = 95° F.; Weight of projectile = 258 pounds.

Temperature of powder, $\frac{+35}{10} \times 5 = +17.5$ foot-seconds.

Use Table IV for correction for density. Use traverse tables for resolving speeds.

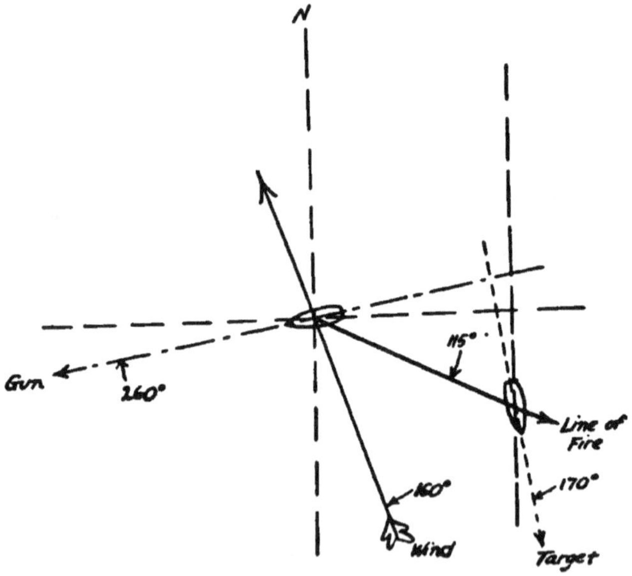

Cause of error. Speed of or variation in.	Affects.	Formulæ.	Errors in — Range. Short. Yds.	Errors in — Range. Over. Yds.	Errors in — Deflection. Right. Yds.	Errors in — Deflection. Left. Yds.
Gun	Range	$18 \cos 35 \times \frac{42}{12} = \frac{14.7 \times 42}{12}$	51.5	....	....	....
	Deflection	$18 \sin 35 \times \frac{52}{12} = \frac{10.3 \times 52}{12}$	....	....	44.6	....
Target	Range	$23 \cos 55 \times \frac{63}{12} = \frac{13.2 \times 63}{12}$	69.3	....	....	....
	Deflection	$23 \sin 55 \times \frac{63}{12} = \frac{18.8 \times 63}{12}$	....	....	....	98.7
Wind	Range	$20 \cos 45 \times \frac{21}{12} = \frac{14.1 \times 21}{12}$	24.7	....	....	....
	Deflection	$20 \sin 45 \times \frac{11}{12} = \frac{14.1 \times 11}{12}$	....	....	....	12.9
Initial velocity	Range	$17.5 \times \frac{197}{50}$	....	69.0	....	....
w	Range	$2 \times \frac{43}{5}$	....	17.2	....	....
Density	Range	$.69 \times 157$	....	108.3	....	....
			145.5	194.5	44.6	111.6
				145.5		44.6
		$67 \text{ yards} \times \frac{12}{63} = 12.8$ knots on deflection scale.		49.0		67.0

Set sights at:

Exactly..........in range, 6951 yards; in deflection, 62.8 knots.

Actually.........in range, 6950 yards; in deflection, 62.0 knots.

Remember to shoot short rather than over.

Form No. 26.

CHAPTER 17—EXAMPLE 9.

FORM FOR THE SOLUTION OF APPARENT WIND AND SPEED PROBLEMS.

PROBLEM.

Cal. = 8″; V = 2750 f. s.; w = 260 pounds; c = 0.61; Range = 7300 yards; Apparent wind, direction from, 45° true; velocity, 30 knots an hour; Motion of gun, course, 80° true; speed, 21 knots an hour; Motion of target, course, 100° true; speed, 28 knots an hour; Target at moment of firing bearing 300° true; distant, 7300 yards; Barometer = 28.50″; Thermometer = 10° F.; Temperature of powder = 60° F.; Weight of projectile = 255 pounds.

Temperature of powder, $\frac{-35}{10} \times 30 = -105$ foot-seconds.

Use Table IV for correction for density. Use traverse tables for resolution of speeds.

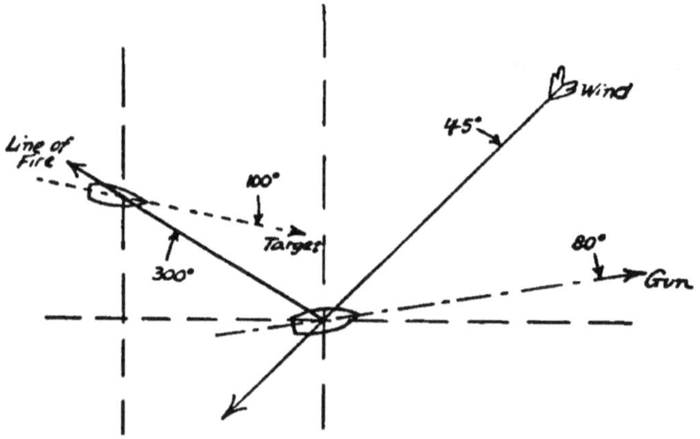

Cause of error. Speed of or variation in.	Affects.	Formulæ.	Errors in—			
			Range.		Deflection.	
			Short. Yds.	Over. Yds.	Right. Yds.	Left. Yds.
Gun............	Range.....	$21 \cos 40 \times \frac{66}{12} = \frac{16.1 \times 66}{12}$	88.6	....	....	....
	Deflection..	$21 \sin 40 \times \frac{66}{12} = \frac{13.5 \times 66}{12}$	....	....	74.3	....
Target..........	Range.....	$28 \cos 20 \times \frac{66}{12} = \frac{26.3 \times 66}{12}$	....	144.7	....	....
	Deflection..	$28 \sin 20 \times \frac{66}{12} = \frac{9.6 \times 66}{12}$	....	....	....	52.8
Wind...........	Range.....	$30 \cos 75 \times \frac{23}{12} = \frac{7.8 \times 23}{12}$	....	14.9	....	....
	Deflection..	$30 \sin 75 \times \frac{12}{12} = \frac{29 \times 12}{12}$	....	....	....	29.0
Initial velocity....	Range.....	$105 \times \frac{203}{50}$	420.3	....	....	....
w................	Range.....	$43 \times \frac{5}{5}$	....	43.0	....	....
Density...........	Range.....	$.69 \times 171$	118.0	....	....	....
			632.9	202.6	74.3	81.8
			202.6			74.3
7.5 yards deflection $\times \frac{12}{66} = 1.4$ knots on deflection scale.			430.3			7.5

Set sights at:

Exactly..........in range, 7730.3 yards; in deflection, 51.4 knots.

Actually.........in range, 7700.0 yards; in deflection, 51.0 knots.

Remember to shoot short rather than over.

Form No. 27A.

CHAPTER 18—EXAMPLE 13.

FORM FOR THE COMPUTATION OF THE CORRECT SIGHT-SETTING IN RANGE USING REDUCED VELOCITY, WITHOUT THE USE OF REDUCED VELOCITY RANGE TABLE.

FORMULÆ.

$$C = fK;\quad Z = \frac{X}{C};\quad \sin 2\phi = AC$$

PROBLEM.

Cal. = 6", V_1 = 2800 f. s.; V_2 = 2600 f. s.; w = 105 pounds; c = .61; Range = 3000 yards = 9000 feet; maximum ordinate = 53 feet; $\frac{2}{3}Y$ = 35 feet, hence f = 1.0011 from Table V.

K = (from Table VI) .... log 0.67956
f = 1.0011 .... log 0.00047

C = ... log 0.68003......colog 9.31997 − 10
X = 9000 .... log 3.95424

Z = 1880.2 .... log 3.27421

From Table II

$$A = .00994 + \frac{.00065 \times 80.2}{100} = .010461$$

A = .010461 .... log 8.01957 − 10
C = ... log 0.68003

$2\phi = 2°\ 52'\ 13''$ .... sin 8.69960 − 10
$\phi = 1°\ 26.1'$

From Range Table "H" this ϕ corresponds to

$$R = 3100 + 13 = 3113 \text{ yards}$$

Form No. 27B.

CHAPTER 18—EXAMPLE 14.

FORM FOR THE COMPUTATION OF THE CORRECT SIGHT-SETTING IN RANGE USING REDUCED VELOCITY, WITH THE USE OF REDUCED VELOCITY RANGE TABLE.

PROBLEM.

Cal. = 6″; $V_1 = 2800$ f. s.; $V_2 = 2600$ f. s.; $w = 105$ pounds; $c = .61$; Range = 3000 yards. From Range Table " F " for Range = 3000 yards, we have

$$\phi = 1° \ 26.1'$$

This angle of departure in Range Table " H " gives

$$R = 3400 + 13 = 3413 \text{ yards}$$

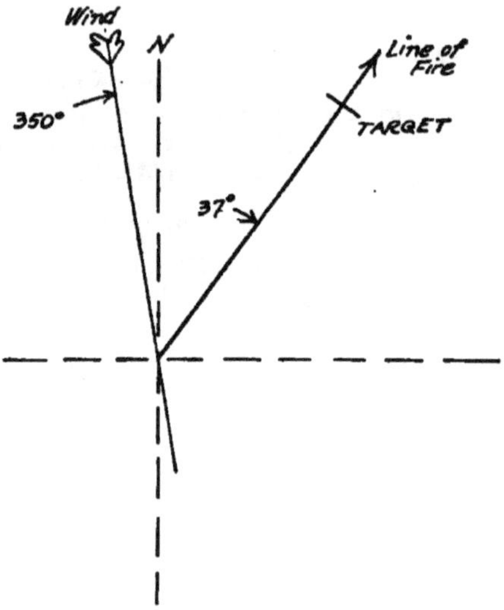

			Short. Yds.	Over. Yds.	Right. Yds.	Left. Yds.
Wind............	Range.....	$8 \cos 47 \times \frac{31}{12} = \frac{5.5 \times 31}{12}$	14.2	....	....	....
	Deflection..	$8 \sin 47 \times \frac{17}{12} = \frac{5.9 \times 17}{12}$	....	....	8.4	....
w..............	Range.....	$8 \times \frac{41}{5}$	65.6	....	....	....
Density...........	Range.....	$.318 \times 229$	....	72.8	....	....
Initial velocity ...	Range.....	$35 \times \frac{227}{50}$	....	158.0	....	....
Height of bull's eye............	Range.....	$12 \times \frac{100}{31}$	....	38.7	....	....
Intentional deflection............	Deflection..	$10 \times \frac{80}{12}$	....	....	....	66.7
			79.8	270.4 79.8	8.4	66.7 8.4
Errors on point P as an origin for standard conditions........				190.6		58.3

Observed distance from target in range................. 100.0 yards short.
Error (where shot should have fallen)................. 190.6 yards over.

True mean error in range under standard conditions...... 290.6 yards short.
Observed distance from target in deflection.............. 70.7 yards left.
Error (where shot should have fallen)................... 58.3 yards left.

True mean error in deflection under standard conditions.. 11.7 yards left.

That is, under standard conditions the mean point of impact of the gun is 290.6 yards short of and 11.7 yards to the left of the point *P*. We wish to adjust the sight scales so that the actual mean point of impact of the gun shall be at *P*. To do this we:

1. Run up the sight until the pointer indicates 8790.6 yards in range, then slide the scale under the pointer until the latter is over the 8500-yard mark on the former, and then clamp the scale.

2. 11.7 yards in deflection equals $\frac{12}{80} \times 11.7 = 1.8$ knots on the deflection scale at the given range. Set the sight for a deflection of 51.8 knots, then slide the scale until the 50-knot mark is under the pointer, and then clamp the scale.

MEAN DISPERSION FROM MEAN POINT OF IMPACT.

Number of shot.	In range.			In deflection.		
	Fall relative to target. Short or over. Yds.	Position of mean point of impact relative to target. Short or over. Yds.	Variation of each shot from mean point of impact. Short or over. Yds.	Fall relative to target. Right or left. Yds.	Position of mean point of impact relative to target. Right or left. Yds.	Variation of each shot from mean point of impact. Right or left. Yds.
1..............	100 short	100 short	0	85 left	70 left	15
2..............	125 short	100 short	25	80 left	70 left	10
3..............	85 short	100 short	15	60 left	70 left	10
4..............	90 short	100 short	10	55 left	70 left	15
			4)50			4)50
			12.5			12.5

Mean dispersion from mean point of impact:

In range.................................. 12.5 yards.

In deflection.............................. 12.5 yards.

Form No. 29.

CHAPTER 19—EXAMPLE 1.

FORM FOR THE COMPUTATIONS FOR THE CALIBRATION OF A SHIP'S BATTERY.

PROBLEM.

Cal. = 8″; $V = 2750$; $w = 260$ pounds; $c = 0.61$; Range = 8500 yards.

For a battery of eight of the above guns, having determined the true mean errors to be as given below (by previous calibration practice), how should the sights of the guns be adjusted to make all the guns shoot together?

Note that no one of the guns shoots closely enough to be taken as a standard gun. At 8500 yards, one yard in deflection equals $\frac{12}{80} = .15$ knot on deflection scale.

Number of gun.	Errors.		With reference to point *P*, each gun shot.			To bring all sights together set them for each gun as follows:	
	Range. Yds.	Deflection. Yds.	In range. Yds.	In deflection. Yards.	In deflection. Knots.	In range. Yds.	In deflection. Kts.
1..........	25 short	25 left	25 short	25 left	3.75 left	8525	53.75
2..........	100 over	50 left	100 over	50 left	7.5 left	8400	57.50
3..........	100 short	75 right	100 short	75 right	11.25 right	8600	38.75
4........	75 short	50 right	75 short	50 right	7.5 right	8575	42.50
5..........	150 over	100 left	150 over	100 left	15.0 left	8350	65.00
6..........	75 short	75 left	75 short	75 left	11.25 left	8575	61.25
7..........	80 short	80 right	80 short	80 right	12.0 right	8580	38.00
8..........	90 over	25 right	90 over	25 right	3.75 right	8410	46.25

After the sights have been set as indicated above, move the sight scales under the pointers until the latter are over the 8500-yard marks in range and over the 50-knot marks in deflection, and then clamp the scales.

APPENDIX B.

THE FARNSWORTH GUN ERROR COMPUTER.

PURPOSE AND USE.

1. This instrument was devised by Midshipman J. S. Farnsworth, U. S. N., class of 1915, during his first class year at the Naval Academy.

2. It is intended for the purpose of determining quickly and accurately, by mechanical means and without computations, the errors in range and in deflection introduced into gun fire by: *

(a) Wind.

(b) Motion of firing ship.

(c) Motion of target ship.

(d) Variation from standard in the temperature of the powder.

(e) Variation from standard in the density of the atmosphere.

Plate I shows the device on an enlarged scale, so that the graduations can be clearly seen. The radial arm shown at the right of the drawing is secured to the same axis as the discs.

3. The uses and advantages of the instrument are readily apparent. It can be used by both spotting and plotting groups if desired, but presumably it would be used in the plotting room. Its use will enable the initial errors to be allowed for in firing ranging shots to be accurately and quickly determined, so that with it a spotter has a vastly greater chance of having the ranging shot strike within good spotting distance of the target than by any "judgment" or "rule of thumb" methods. This should enable a ship to begin to place her salvos properly in a shorter time and with less waste of ammunition than could be done without the device.

4. Errors due to changes in courses, speeds, wind, or other conditions during firing can be similarly quickly obtained by the use of the computer.

5. The accompanying drawing (Plate I) shows the device arranged for working with apparent wind, and for determining deflection errors directly in knots of the deflection scale of the sight, and not in yards. The device could be equally well arranged for real wind, for deflections in yards, or for any other desired system, by simply drawing the proper spiral curves on the smaller disc; but the arrangement shown here is believed to be the most useful one for service conditions. The drawing

---

* Throughout this description the "errors" have been considered and not the "corrections." In the practical use of the computer it must be remembered that, having determined an "error" the "correction" to compensate for it is numerically equal but of opposite sign. Thus, an "error" of 100 short calls for a correction of "up 100," etc.

A very clear and concise statement of the purpose and principle of the gun error computer is contained in the following extract from a report thereon submitted to the commander-in-chief of the United States Atlantic fleet by Ensign H. L. Abbott, U. S. N.:

"The gun error computer is a combination of a set of curves showing the correction to be applied at various ranges to range and deflection for unit variation from normal of the conditions considered, such as wind; and of a specially graduated numerical or circular slide rule for modifying the correction for unit variation to give the correction for the actual variation. This instrument can be made to take the place of the range tables, and with its aid the corrections for any particular set of conditions can be picked out with much greater ease and facility than with the present cumbrous range tables and accompanying necessary calculations."

does not show the three curves in colors, as they should be drawn on a working device, each curve being of a radically different color from the others; and the powder temperature error and density error curves are not shown on the drawing. In the following descriptions it is assumed that the several curves would be drawn as follows:

Wind range curve in red.

Wind deflection curve in green.

Target and gun range curve in black.

Powder temperature error curve in blue.

Density error curve in yellow.

METHOD OF CONSTRUCTION.

6. In external appearance and in some principles of construction, the device is similar to an omnimeter. It consists, as shown on the plate, of two circular discs, an outer or larger, and an inner or smaller one, concentrically secured on the same axis and capable of independent rotary motion around that axis; and, in addition, of a radial arm secured on the same axis and capable of free rotary motion around that axis. These parts should be so arranged that the radial arm can be clamped to the inner disc without clamping the two discs together, and so that the two discs can be clamped together without clamping the radial arm to the inner disc. The radial arm should be made of some transparent material, with the range scale line scribed radially from the center of the axis down the middle of the arm.

7. The salient features of the device are:

(a) **The Range Circle.**—The graduations on the outside of the larger circle on the larger disc.

(b) **The Deflection Circle.**—The graduations on the inside of the larger circle on the larger disc.

(c) **The Speed Circle.**—The graduations on the outside of the smaller circle on the larger disc. This circle is in coincidence with the periphery of the smaller or inner disc.

(d) **The Correction Circle.**—The graduations on the periphery of the smaller disc.

(e) **The Range and Deflection Curves.**—Drawn on the face of the smaller disc, spirally, from the center of the disc outward. They are the:

(1) *Wind range curve.*

(2) *Wind deflection curve.*

(3) *Target and gun range curve.*

(4) *Powder temperature curve.*

(5) *Density curve.*

(f) **The Radial Arm.**—Bearing the range scale.

Of the above, *a*, *b* and *c* are all on the larger disc, and their positions relative to one another are therefore fixed. Also *d* and *e* are both on the smaller disc, and their positions relative to each other are therefore fixed. However, *a*, *b* and *c* can be rotated relative to *d* and *e*. The range scale, being on *f*, can be rotated relative to either or to both of the discs.

8. Of the above, only the curves vary for different guns. It would therefore be necessary to construct the apparatus and then have the curves scribed on it for the particular type of gun with which the individual instrument is to be used. Thus, there would be one computer for each caliber of gun on board. Plate I shows the device as arranged for the 12″ gun for which $V=2900$ f. s., $w=870$ pounds and $c=0.61$; the necessary data for its construction having been obtained from the range table for that gun.

9. The mathematical principles involved in the construction of the several elements of the device are described herein (the description being based on the assumption that the reader is not familiar with the omnimeter).

(a) **Range Circle.**—The entire circumference is divided into parts representing logarithmic increments in the secant of the angle, from zero degrees to the angle whose logarithmic secant is unity (84°+). These increments are laid down on the circle in a counter-clockwise direction according to the logarithmic secants, and the scale is marked with the angles corresponding to the given logarithmic secants. For example, the point marked 23° lies in a counter-clockwise direction from the zero of the scale, and at a distance from it equal to .03597 of the circumference (log sec 23° = 0.03597).

(b) **Deflection Circle.**—The entire circumference is divided into parts representing logarithmic increments in the sine of the angle, from the angle whose logarithmic sine is 9.00000 − 10(5°+) to 90°. These increments are laid down on the circle in a clockwise direction according to the logarithmic sines, and the scale is marked with the angles corresponding to the given logarithmic sines. For example, the point marked 23° lies in a clockwise direction from the zero of the scale, and at a distance from it equal to .59188 of the circumference (log sine 23° = 9.59188 − 10). The zero of the scale coincides with the zero of the scale of the range circle.

(c) **Speed Circle.**—The entire circumference is divided into parts representing logarithmic increments in the natural numbers from 1.0 to 10 (the decimal point may be placed wherever necessary, and the point marked "10" may be considered as the "zero" of this scale, and will hereafter be referred to as such in this description). The increments are laid down on the circle in a counter-clockwise direction from zero, and the divisions of the scale are marked with the numbers corresponding to the given logarithms. For example, the number 2.3 lies in a counter-clockwise direction from the zero, and at a distance from it equal to .36173 of the circumference (log 2.3 = 0.36173). The zero of this scale coincides with the zeros of the range and deflection circles.

(d) **Correction Circle.**—The construction of the correction circle is exactly the same as that of the speed circle, except that the scale is laid down in a clockwise direction from the zero.*

(e) **Range and Deflection Curves.**—Each of these is based on the data in the appropriate column of the range table for the given gun, and these curves are therefore different for different guns. The method of plotting them is described below.

(f) **Range Scale.**—A radius of appropriate length to fit the discs is subdivided as a range scale. These divisions are purely arbitrary, and Plate I shows the increments in range as decreasing in relative magnitude on the scale as the range increases; so that the divisions are larger and more easily and accurately read at the ranges that will most likely be used; becoming smaller as the range becomes very great. The size of these divisions, either actual or relative to one another, does not affect the work of the instrument, provided this range scale be prepared first and then used in plotting the error curves in the manner described below.†

---

* Those familiar with the omnimeter will perceive that up to this point the principles of that instrument have been followed; but that the scales of the range circle (logarithmic secants) and speed circle (logarithms of numbers) have been laid down in the opposite direction from those on the omnimeter.

† If the device be made of a good working size, these divisions may all be made of the same size and still be clearly read, and this is the best way to construct it.

10. To plot the range and deflection curves for wind and for motion of firing or target ship, the data is obtained from the proper column in the range table for the error and gun under consideration (Columns 13, 14, 15, 16, 17 and 18). Thus, for instance, to locate the point of the **wind range curve** for a range of 10,000 yards for the given 12" gun, Column 13 of the range table (Bureau Ordnance Pamphlet No. 298) shows that the error in range caused by a 12-knot wind blowing along the line of fire is 27 yards, and it would therefore be 2.25 yards for a 1-knot wind. Therefore the desired point of the curve is plotted on the inner disc on a radius passing through the 2.25 mark on the correction circle, and at a distance from the center corresponding to 10,000 yards on the range scale. Enough points are plotted in this manner to enable an accurate curve to be scribed through them. The other curves are plotted in a similar manner, but instead of plotting deflection curves in "yards error," they are plotted in "knots error of the deflection scale of the sight," thus enabling the deflection error to be determined directly in knots for application to the sight drums. For example, for the wind deflection curve, the data for plotting would be found by dividing the data in Column 16 of the range table for the given range by the corresponding data in Column 18. Approximate values of the correction scale reading are marked at intervals along the curves to aid the operator in placing the decimal point correctly and in getting the result in correct units.

11. To plot the **powder temperature curve**, it will be seen from Column 10 of the range table that, for a range of 15,000 yards, 50 f. s. variation from standard in the initial velocity causes 379.65 yards error in range, therefore 1 foot-second variation in initial velocity would cause 7.593 yards error in range. From the notes to the range table, it will be seen that, for this gun, 10° variation from standard in the temperature of the powder (90° being the standard) causes a change of 35 f. s. in initial velocity, but recent experiments show that this value is too high, and that for each 10° variation in temperature, the change in initial velocity is only 20 f. s. Consequently, a variation of one degree from standard in the temperature of the powder would cause an error of $2.0 \times 7.593 = 15.186$ yards in range. Therefore, to locate the point on the curve corresponding to 15,000 yards range, place the desired point on the face of the smaller disc on a radius passing through the 15.186 mark on the correction circle, and at a distance from the center corresponding to 15,000 yards on the range scale.

12. Before proceeding to a description of the method of plotting the **density curve**, a brief preliminary discussion of another point is necessary. As the density of the air depends upon two different variables, one being the barometric reading and the other the temperature of the air (assuming, as is done in present methods, that the air is always half saturated), it is not practicable from a point of view of easy operation to lay down a single curve for use in determining the density corresponding to given readings of barometer and thermometer. Therefore a sheet of auxiliary curves is necessary for this purpose, for use in connection with the computer. Such a set of curves is shown on Plate II, and is good for any gun. It is really a graphic representation of Table IV of the Ballistic Tables (the table of multipliers for Column 12), and values of the multiplier can be taken from these curves much more quickly than they can be obtained from the table by interpolation. These curves have been designated **atmospheric condition curves**, and on Plate II show as straight lines, giving values for the multipliers ten times as great as those given in the table. This has been done in order to have the computer retain the principle on which it is constructed for all other errors; namely, that the first reading taken from the correction circle by bringing the range mark on the range scale into coincidence with the proper curve shall show the error due to unit variation in the quantity under consideration. (The same thing could be done in this case by plotting the curve for

scale was brought to cut the wind range curve, and the reading was noted where the range scale line cut the correction circle, that reading was 5 yards, or the error due to a 1-knot wind blowing along the line of fire. Now had the zeros of the correction and speed circles been in coincidence when this was done, when the inner disc was moved around in a counter-clockwise direction until the five of the correction circle coincided with the zero of the speed circle, the zero of the correction circle moved a distance equal to log 5. Now when the motion of the inner disc was continued in the same direction until the 5 of the correction circle coincided with the 45 of the speed circle, the zero of the correction circle moved a further distance in the same direction equal to log 45. The total travel of the zero of the correction circle must therefore have been $\log 5 + \log 45 = \log 225$; and the reading on the speed circle now coincident with the zero of the correction circle (the measure of the total travel of that zero) must be 225 yards, which is the error in range due to a 45-knot wind in the line of fire. The decimal point has moved one digit to the right because of the fact that the zero of the correction circle traveled between one and two complete circumferences during the operation. Now clamp the two discs together as they stand. If the range scale on the radial arm be first placed at the zero of the speed circle (where we read 225 on the correction circle), which is also the zero of the range or log secant circle; and then be moved in a counter-clockwise direction until the range scale line is coincident with the 50° mark on the range circle, the range scale line will have traveled a distance from the 225 mark on the correction circle equal to log sec 50°, and if the range scale line be then followed across from the 50° mark on the range circle to the correction circle, the reading on the latter will be $\log 225 - \log \sec 50°$, or $\log 225 + \log \cos 50°$; that is, the logarithm of $225 \times \cos 50°$, which is the desired result; and reading off the anti-logarithm on the correction circle corresponding to the above result, the reading will be 144 yards, which is the desired error; that is, the error in range caused by an apparent wind of 45 knots blowing at an angle of 50° with the line of fire. The sign of the error, that is, whether it is a "short" or an "over," will at once be apparent from a glance at the plotting board, on which the direction of the apparent wind should be indicated relative to the line of fire.

18. To determine the deflection due to the wind, proceed in a similar manner, using the wind deflection curve (green), and taking the angle from the deflection circle. Setting the radial arm with the 15,000-yard mark of the range scale in coincidence with the wind deflection curve gives, from the correction circle, that a 1-knot wind perpendicular to the line of fire causes an error of 0.245 knots (on the deflection scale of the sight) in deflection. Moving the .245 mark of the correction circle around to coincide with the 45-knot mark on the speed circle and reading the zero of the correction (or speed) circle will give 11.0 knots as the error due to a 45-knot wind perpendicular to the line of fire (this would not be noted in actual practice unless the wind were actually blowing perpendicularly to the line of fire, in which case it would be the desired result); and reading across from the 50° mark on the deflection circle to the correction circle would give 8.5 knots as the amount of error in deflection. As before, the sign of the error must be determined from the plotting board. What was really done here, after determining the value 0.245, was to perform the addition $\log 0.245 + \log 45 = \log 11$, and then the addition $\log 11 + \log \sin 50° = \log 8.5$. That is, the value 0.245 was first found mechanically, and then the compound operation $0.245 \times 45 \times \sin 50° = 8.5$ was mechanically performed.

19. As the apparent wind was used in the preceding operations, the errors for the motion of the gun would be taken from the same curve as those for the motion of the target. For the error in range the method is exactly the same for both gun motion and target motion as for the wind error in range, using the target and gun

23. Having shown how to manipulate the computer in detail, it will be seen that the process of use in the plotting room would be about as follows:

FORM FOR USE IN CONNECTION WITH FARNSWORTH ERROR COMPUTER.

Range, yards.	Errors in.			
	Range. Yds.		Deflection. Knots.	
	Short.	Over.	Right.	Left.
Temperature of powder: Standard, 90°; actual, —°.				
Atmospheric conditions: Barometer, —"; ther., —°.				
Motion of gun: Speed, — knots; angle, —°.				
Apparent wind: Velocity, — knots; angle, —°.				
Sums.				
Preliminary errors.				
Motion of target: Speed, — knots; angle, —°.				
Final errors (signs to be changed to give "corrections").				

(a) By "angle" is meant that angle *less than* 90° which the course of the firing ship, direction of the apparent wind, or course of the target ship makes with the line of fire.

(b) The **preliminary errors** include all those that will presumably be known long enough in advance to afford reasonable time for their determination.

(c) The temperature of the powder and the readings of the barometer and thermometer will be known before starting the approach. The first two lines of the above form may therefore be filled out when work begins, and will presumably remain constant throughout the action.

(d) As soon as plotting begins and the proposed line of fire and range are determined with sufficient accuracy, the plotter determines the angles made by the course of the firing ship and by the apparent wind (the information relative to the latter being sent down by the spotter) with the proposed line of fire, and the errors for gun motion and wind are determined and entered in their proper columns. The algebraic additions necessary to give the preliminary errors are then made and entered. This leaves only target motion to be accounted for, and as soon as the plotter has the necessary information he gives the "angle" and speed of the target ship, the errors caused thereby are taken from the computer and entered in their columns, and then two simple algebraic additions give the total errors required. The necessary corrections for application to the sights for the ranging shot can then be sent to the guns.

24. The computer is readily available for the solution of any right triangle, in addition to the purpose for which it was devised. In the case of angle from 81° to 90°, the sines are practically equal to unity and the cosines are negligible, and

(3) Turn the smaller disc and radial arm together until the range scale line cuts the speed circle at the T° mark. Read the desired error on the correction circle coincident with the zero of the speed circle.

(4) A powder temperature higher than the standard always gives an increase in range, and the reverse.

(b) To Determine the Error in Range Resulting from a Variation from Standard in the Density of the Atmosphere.

Error in Range.—(Use yellow curve, Column 12.)

(1) Bring the given range on the range scale into coincidence with the density curve, and clamp the radial arm and smaller disc together.

(2) Determine the value of the multiplier from the atmospheric condition curves for the given readings of barometer and thermometer.

(3) Turn the smaller disc and radial arm together until the range scale line cuts the speed circle at the mark indicating the value of the multiplier determined from the atmospheric condition curves. Read the desired error on the correction circle coincident with the zero of the speed circle.

(4) A negative sign on the multiplier always means a "short," and a positive sign an "over."

(c) To Determine Errors Due to an Apparent Wind of Known Velocity and at a Known Angle to the Line of Fire.

Error in Range.—(Use red curve, Column 13.)

(1) Rotate radial arm until wind range curve intersects range scale on runner at given range, and clamp radial arm to upper disc.

(2) Rotate lower disc until range scale line on radial arm intersects speed circle at apparent wind velocity in knots. Clamp discs together; unclamp radial arm.

(3) Rotate radial arm until range scale line intersects range circle at angle to line of fire at which wind is blowing.

(4) Read across by range scale line to correction circle, and note result; the desired range error in yards.

(5) Determine sign of error by glance at plotting board.

Error in Deflection. (Use green curve, Column 16.)

(1) Rotate radial arm until wind deflection curve intersects range scale on radial arm at given range, and clamp radial arm to inner disc.

(2) Rotate lower disc until range scale line on radial arm intersects speed circle at apparent wind velocity in knots. Clamp discs together; unclamp radial arm.

(3) Rotate radial arm until range scale line intersects deflection circle at angle to line of fire at which wind is blowing.

(4) Read across by range scale line to correction circle, and note result; the desired error in knots.

(5) Determine sign of error by glance at plotting board.

(d) To Determine Errors Due to Motion of Gun (or Target) at Given Speed and Angle with Line of Fire.

Error in Range.—(Use black curve, Column 15.)

(1) Rotate radial arm until target and gun range curve intersects range scale on radial arm at given range, and clamp radial arm to upper disc.

(2) Rotate lower disc until range scale line on radial arm intersects speed circle at speed of gun (or target) in knots. Clamp discs together and unclamp radial arm.

(3) Rotate radial arm until range scale line intersects range circle at angle to line of fire made by course of gun (or target).

(4) Read across by range scale line to correction circle, and note result; the desired range error in yards due to motion of gun (or target).

fo1
anc
therefore applies to the values of the multipliers given in the table.

Read across by range scale line to correction circle, and note result; the range error in yards due to motion of gun (or target).

APPENDIX C.

ARBITRARY DEFLECTION SCALES FOR GUN SIGHTS.

INTRODUCTORY.

1. In many cases, notably in turret sights, the system of marking the deflection scales of sights in "knots," as described in this text book, is no longer carried out; these scales being marked in arbitrary divisions instead, the manner of constructing and using which scales will now be explained.

2. The method of controlling deflection by means of "deflection boards" and "arbitrary scales" was devised for the purpose of relieving the sight setters of the responsibility of keeping the deflection pointer on a designated deflection curve. The principle upon which the method is based is in no way different from the standard method of controlling deflection by means of knot curves. It differs in the method of application, in that one curve sheet upon which the knot curves are drawn performs the functions of the curve drums formerly fitted upon each individual sight. Many of the sights still in service are adapted for the use of either method of deflection control, and it will be seen by trying both methods that they give the same results, regardless of which one is used.

3. The method of bringing the point of impact on the target in deflection in no way differs from that of bringing the point of impact on the target in range, except that deflection correction controls the angle of the sight with respect to the axis of the gun in the horizontal plane, while range correction controls it in the vertical plane. If the point of impact be short of the target, or, in other words, too low, the sight is raised; if the point of impact is to the left in deflection, the rear end of the telescopic sight is moved to the right, and *vice versa*. In either case it is the angle between the axis of the telescope and the axis of the gun that is changed, for range in the vertical plane, and for deflection in the horizontal plane.

4. To arrive at a clear understanding of the principle of deflection, it should be comprehended that all deflection measurements can be reduced to angular measurements. If the horizontal angle between the axis of the gun and the line of sight be the same for all the guns of the same caliber firing, then the corresponding deflection, whether measured in knots or in yards, will also be the same for all those guns. It is thus seen that the sights for all types can be so constructed that the unit of measurement for deflection is an angle.

PRINCIPLE OF ARBITRARY SCALES.

5. In the method of controlling deflection by the use of "deflection boards" and "arbitrary scales," the unit of measurement, that is, the angle corresponding to one division of the scale, is the angle that is subtended by one-half of a chord of 0.2 of an inch at 100" radius; that is, it is the angle whose tangent is .001. By using this unit of measurement, the divisions on the arbitrary scale (*G*, Plate III), are all equal to 0.1 of an inch on all deflection boards for all sights for all guns, and all deflection boards are therefore uniform in construction. The arbitrary scale fitted to each sight is graduated so that one division of the sight scale corresponds to this

METHOD OF USE.

9. The deflection board is designed primarily for use in the plotting room, but it can be used at any other point that may be desired, such as the spotter's top or in the turrets.

10. When about to open fire, the knot curve to be used should be determined by computation (or by the use of the gun error computer) in the same manner as has been explained for the deflection sight scale marked in knots; but this would no longer be sent out to the guns as the setting of the sights in deflection. Instead, the pointer *E* is placed at the top to indicate the curve to be used (the 45-knot curve on Plate III). The scale *G* is then run down the board to correspond to the range to be used (14,000 yards on the plate). The pointer *H* is then run along the scale *G* until it is over the proper curve on the sheet (45 knots), and the reading under the same pointer on the scale *G* will then be the number of divisions of the arbitrary sight scale at which the sights should be set to give the desired deflection (40 divisions on the plate). As the curves on the sheet are the drift curves for the gun, the sight setting in arbitrary divisions of the scale thus found will of course include the drift correction.

11. As the range varies during the firing, the scale *G* is moved up and down to follow it, and the pointer *H* is moved to the right or left to keep it over the proper curve on the sheet (45 on the plate). The pointer *H* will then always indicate on the scale *G* the proper sight setting in deflection in the markings of the arbitrary scale.

12. In case the spotter's corrections indicate the use of a new curve at any time, the pointer *E* is shifted to that curve, and the new readings for the arbitrary scale are read off from the scale *G* by the pointer *H* (which is now following the new curve) and sent to the sight setters.

13. By this process the sight setters are relieved of all responsibility in regard to the deflection setting other than that of setting the sight for the scale readings which they receive from time to time from the deflection operator, and it is no longer necessary for them to be continually following a drift curve on the sight drum as the range increases or decreases.

CONTROL OF DEFLECTION WITHOUT THE USE OF KNOT CURVES.

14. If preferred, or if no deflection board be at hand, a table may be made up showing the value in knots of one or more divisions of the arbitrary deflection scale at different ranges, from which the spotter can estimate first his initial sight setting in deflection, and afterwards any changes that he may desire to make. So far as the deflection in yards is concerned, all that is necessary is a knowledge of the fact that for all guns, at all ranges, with all arbitrary deflection scale sights, one division of the arbitrary scale causes or corrects a deflection in yards equal to one one-thousandth of the range; while for the transformation from "knots" to "arbitrary divisions" and the reverse, a table can be used similar to:

Range in Yards.	Deflection in—	
	Knots.	Divisions of Arbitrary Scale.
5000	5	3.5
10000	5	4.0
15000	5	4+
20000	5	4.5

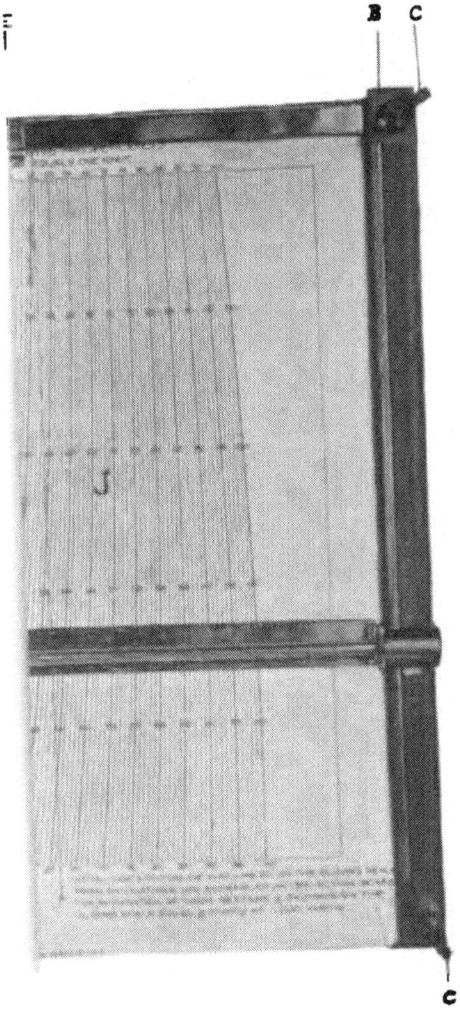

LECTION BOARD.

the
; to
ods
les.
les,

un,
ion

ATMOSPHERIC DENSITY TABLES,

BEING REPRINTS OF

TABLE III AND TABLE IV,

FROM THE

RANGE AND BALLISTIC TABLES, 1914,

PRINTED TO ACCOMPANY THIS

TEXT BOOK OF EXTERIOR BALLISTICS.

NOTES.

1. By the use of these two tables, especially of Table IV, in conjunction with the range table for any particular gun, may be solved all practical problems relating to the use of the range table in controlling the fire of that particular gun, by the methods explained in Chapter 17 of this text book, on the practical use of the range tables. These two tables are all that is necessary, also, in conjunction with the range tables, for the solution of calibration problems, as given in Chapters 18 and 19.

2. If it be desired to solve general ballistic problems for any particular gun, however, it will be necessary to have at hand the other tables contained in the edition of Range and Ballistic Tables printed to accompany this text book.

CPSIA information can be obtained
at www.ICGtesting.com
Printed in the USA
LVHW081006050520
655038LV00011B/230

9 780342 167401